THE AMERICAN
CIVIL WAR AND
THE ORIGINS OF
MODERN WARFARE

Edward Hagerman

THE AMERICAN CIVIL WAR AND THE ORIGINS OF MODERN WARFARE

Ideas, Organization, and Field Command

INDIANA UNIVERSITY PRESS

Bloomington & Indianapolis

MANUFACTURED IN THE UNITED STATES OF AMERICA

Library of Congress Cataloging-in-Publication Data

Hagerman, Edward.
   The American Civil War and the origins of modern
warfare.

   Bibliography: p.
   Includes index.
   1. United States.   Army—History—Civil War,
1861–1865.   2. Confederate States of America.
Army—History.   3. United States—History—Civil War,
1861–1865—Campaigns.   4. Military art and science—
History—19th century.   I. Title.
E491.H16   1988   973.7   87-46015
ISBN 0-253-30546-2

E
491
. H16
1988

FOR BEVERLEY

CONTENTS

ORGANIZATIONAL IRONY

NEW THRESHOLDS OF MODERN WARFARE

Acknowledgments

My debts extend through the many years during which this study came to fruition. Theodore Ropp and Irving Holley were there at the beginning and bear part of the responsibility for what has come to pass. Long ago, discussions with John Kirkland about intellectual and institutional culture helped shape my thoughts about military ideas and organization and their relationships. William Skelton, while a colleague at Ohio State University, broadened my understanding of the antebellum army. I owe a special debt to David Gaddy, who generously shared his knowledge of Confederate signals organization. Michael Musick was especially helpful in locating obscure sources on field transportation and supply in the National Archives. Marc Egnal made valuable suggestions on my early writings about George McClellan, and Joseph Ernst read the entire manuscript and tightened the conceptual presentation. The manuscript owes much to Beverley Fingerhut's insistence upon organizational and stylistic common sense. I am grateful to Florence Judt and Krys Galvin, who shared the agony of typing the many drafts of the manuscript. And finally, this book is for my parents and my children, who have attempted to understand the social deviance of a historian in the family.

Portions of this book first appeared in articles, and are used with the kind permission of the publishers: "From Jomini to Dennis Hart Mahan: The Evolution of Trench Warfare and the American Civil War," *Civil War History* (1967); "The Professionalization of George B. McClellan and Early Civil War Field Command: An Institutional Perspective," *Civil War History* (1975); "The Tactical Thought of R. E. Lee and the Origins of Trench Warfare in the American Civil War," *The Historian* (1975); "The Reorganization of Field Supply and Field Transportation in the Army of the Potomac, 1863: The Flying Column and Strategic Mobility," *Military Affairs* (1980); "Field Transportation and Strategic Mobility in the Union Armies," *Civil War History* (1988).

Introduction

The American Civil War ushered in a new era in land warfare. In this war, mass armies first experienced the widespread impact of industrial technology, while American armies first encountered both the consequences of this new technology and the belated development of the mass army in America. In addition, the American armies had to adapt industrial technology and mass armies to the particular ideological, social, and geographical realities of mid-nineteenth-century America. In their parts and their interaction, these challenges were frequently new to warfare, and generally new to American armies. The response of Civil War soldiers and field commanders shaped tactical and strategic organization into new forms; and these forms made the Civil War arguably the first modern war.

The American soldier was not ready for the challenges that would push him over what might be called the critical threshold of modern land warfare. In theory and doctrine, the United States followed the lead of France, and there was no reason before the Civil War to question the prestige of the Napoleonic tradition. The Americans filtered this legacy through the conservative French Empire and Restoration generation of military thinkers, who bypassed the romantic world view of the Revolutionary reformers, led by Jacques Antoine Guibert and Pierre Joseph Bourcet, and reverted back to the eighteenth-century quest for universal principles. Following the French lead, American tactical and strategic thought, except for an antebellum undercurrent in tactics that allowed for historical and peculiarly American factors, crossed the threshold of change peering backward into the eighteenth century.

Early modern warfare was transformed most conspicuously by the technology of the Industrial Revolution. The rifled musket, the weapon that first challenged traditional tactical forms, made its full impact felt for the first time during the Civil War. This devastating increase in firepower doomed the open frontal assault and ushered in the entrenched battlefield. The recently invented machine gun was not yet a factor; rifled artillery and ordnance were still in their technological youth and had an erratic and limited impact; and the new breechloading rifle was rarely used as an infantry weapon. The infantryman's muzzle-loading rifled musket, combined on defense with traditional smoothbore artillery, drove infantry, artillery, and cavalry alike from the open field of battle. The new firepower reduced artillery to the defense and forced cavalry to fight dismounted beside the infantry, while cavalry, as a mobile force with the superior firepower of the repeating carbine, sought new roles in the attack and defense of communications, as well as in reconnaissance.

Offensive infantry tactics, largely in response to the rifled musket, developed in two directions: on the one hand, the extension of the skirmish order was reminiscent of the extended skirmish order of Guibert and the French Revolutionary armies; and on the other hand, there was the novel development of assaults by rushes, with the spade accompanying the rifle. The classical line and column of Empire and Restoration doctrine faded. As the rifled musket forced the Civil War soldier to dig in on the offense as well as on the defense, scenes of trench warfare anticipated World War I.

Industrial technology also affected the command and control of mass armies. Allowing for British experiments in the Crimea, the electric telegraph established its presence in battle, as did an advanced system of visual signals that used the telegraphic alphabet. Though there were limited precedents, the first significant technological development and application of gas-filled observation balloons in warfare—and hence of military aeronautics—took place during the Civil War. The war also saw the first appointment of an army signal officer in military history, as well as the origins of the Signal Corps as a branch of military service.

Civil War armies were the first to use the railroad to move and supply troops in the field; the industrial technology of railroads and steam-powered water transportation, combined with the technological anomaly of animal-drawn field transportation and supply, shaped the logistics of land maneuver through World War II. It is true, of course, that not until the development of motorized field transport and, to some extent, the airplane were modern logistical possibilities complete. But the realization of these possibilities was more gradual than even historians sometimes acknowledge. For example, during its World War II blitzkrieg campaigns, the German army, except for its panzer and other elite motorized units, was still foot-bound and dependent on animals for its conveyance and supply. Viewed from this historical perspective, the horse, mule, and wagon played a modern transitional role, tying together technological developments in railroad and water transportation, while keeping modern armies moving in the field away from their railheads and water supply bases.

The Civil War reorganization of animal-drawn field transport and supply brought into play American geographical factors that gave new form to an old logistical mode. As modern warfare with mass armies spread from western Europe to the more thinly populated territories and greater expanses of America, the traditional transportation and supply standards of western European armies collapsed. Napoleon had experienced this in Russia, but French doctrine did not take heed, even though Antoine Henri Jomini, the most influential interpreter of the Napoleonic Wars, saw and warned of the problem.

The geographical scope of warfare in the nineteenth and twentieth centuries was increasingly universal; and static logistical models that accepted a fixed milieu based on western Europe had to give way to changing geographical as well as to historical factors. Civil War armies learned this lesson. Beginning the war with inadequate French logistical models, they quickly improvised a realistic standard for mid-nineteenth-century America—the Union armies ended the war, for example, with a wagon standard three and one-half times that of Napoleon's armies.

The development of a transportation and supply system responsive to the demands of American geography was the answer to the threat of positional trench warfare. It was the maturing organization of animal-drawn field transport, and the mobile railroad of the Military Railroad Construction Corps of the Quartermaster Department accompanying him, that enabled William T. Sherman to make his slow, methodical advance from Chattanooga to Atlanta. And the strategy of Sherman's prolonged raids to Savannah and through the Carolinas was built primarily upon a restructured system of animal-drawn conveyance and supply that made it possible to live off the land during rapid extended maneuvers.

Ideological factors new to combat also played a role in Sherman's 1864–65 campaign. His strategy of total war against the will of the enemy's population, and against the territory, resources, and communications needed to support the enemy's armies, was not new. But war waged against the enemy's will fought by citizen armies in the ideological context of mid-nineteenth-century nationalism was new both to American armies and to warfare. By contrast, Napoleon's armies had sought where possible to avoid war against the enemy's population. But this was feasible only when that population avoided war with the invading army.

By the mid-nineteenth century, nationalism and civil war bred new rules for warfare. Sherman's concept and practice of total war first fulfilled the prognosis of the German theorist Karl von Clausewitz, who, prior to his death in 1831, had predicted that the growing emotional nature of war, fought with nationalistic citizen armies, increasingly would intensify conflict with civilian populations. Though Clausewitz's ideas did not shape military thought beyond the Prussian army until the late nineteenth century, Sherman's 1864–65 campaigns were a forerunner of intensifying nationalistic warfare in the nineteenth and twentieth centuries.

Also new was the way in which Sherman waged total war: on the one hand, by attacking the enemy's will, territory, resources, and communications, and on the other hand, by maneuvers dependent upon the traditional principles of diversion, dispersion, and surprise. More novel still was the fact that the former provided the means to achieve the latter: the captured resources enabled Sherman to live off the land, while he destroyed or sent behind Union lines what resources he did not use, thus depriving the enemy's army of the supplies it needed to stay in the field. Sherman further supported maneuver with a strategy of terror, starving the enemy's population if it supported partisans or cavalry. These strategic combinations in the context of total war were new to the development of modern warfare; and the reorganization of animal-drawn field transportation, combined at various times with rail and steam-powered water transportation, made them possible.

Although the Civil War had limited influence on European—and, arguably, American—military thought, that does not alter its place in the continuum of modern warfare. An interesting example of belated influence was the impact of Sherman's 1864–65 campaigns on the British military theorist B. H. Liddell Hart, Sherman's biographer and the most influential theorist of strategic maneuver between the two world wars. The British and German field commanders who restored maneuver during World War II were in Liddell Hart's debt. And though Liddell Hart was not a student of logistics, his strategy of the "indirect approach" rested ultimately on transportation and supply. Sherman's logistics were of particular historical relevance—if not an influence—for the World War II German Wehrmacht, which did not make the relatively early transition of the American and British armies to motorized field transport. Nowhere was the logistical and strategic continuum between Liddell Hart and Sherman, and between World War II and the Civil War, more conspicuous than in the German army's foot-bound mass with its horse-drawn trains spread across western and central Europe, and then across Russia during its early blitzkrieg campaigns.

The Civil War introduced other social and ideological factors that influenced tactical and strategic ideas and organization. The social phenomenon of the mass army itself was not a creation of modern warfare, though the Civil War first introduced mass organization to American armies. The French Revolutionary and Napoleonic eras added the citizen armies of modern nationalism. And, with deference due the historical place of the Engish Civil War, the American Civil War brought to modern armies the expanding individualistic ethos of liberal democracy and capitalism in its distinct mid-nineteenth-century American form.

The American democrat as soldier, for instance, expected reasonable tactical conditions if he was to risk his life with modern weapons. Even before the appearance of the rifled musket, Dennis Hart Mahan, the most influential American tactical theorist of the mid-nineteenth century, deemphasized the frontal assault in favor of the entrenched "active defense." Part of his reasoning was the ideological argument that the frontal assaults of the Napoleonic tradition wasted citizen soldiers who were valuable members of civilian society. With the impact of the rifled musket on the Civil War battlefield, both the citizen soldiers and their field commanders increasingly came to share this wisdom. Another social and ideological factor affecting tactical organization was the relative effectiveness of the short-term citizen soldier fighting on the defense over the offense, especially with the rifled musket shifting tactical dominance to the defense.

Social and material considerations accompanied geography as factors influencing the reorganization of the supply, and consequently the transportation, standards of Civil War armies. The material expectations and individualistic ethos of the American democrat and capitalist as soldier significantly affected logistics during and after the war. For example, the well-fed Union army had a ration standard double that of Napoleon's armies. It also abandoned one successful method of reducing Civil War supply and transportation, and did not implement an arguably successful experiment to reduce the bulk of the ration standard. In both cases, Ulysses S. Grant, general in chief and de facto field commander of the Army of the Potomac, seems to have accepted the material expectations of the Union citizen soldier. Modern ideological motives thus played their part in the friction of factors influencing logistical organization and strategic mobility.

The greatest organizational challenge to mobility, however, may have been organization itself. The Napoleonic armies contributed to greater maneuverability the small-unit structure from company to corps that subsequently characterized modern armies. Civil War field commanders experimented somewhat with this arrangement, but their major contribution to command and control through restructuring the army was in the reorganization of cavalry and artillery. These commanders were also confronted with the development of an adequate staff system. The traditional forms of command and control, which focused on the personal direction of the army commander, had served mass armies in the past. But this system depended upon relatively contracted lines of operation, relatively easy, familiar, and mapped terrain, densely populated (hence contracted) foraging area, and stability in technology and other factors affecting tactical and strategic mobility. Fighting for the first time with mass armies in American terrain, with change affecting all aspects of mobility, required new staff procedures. There was need for a comprehensive doctrine to coordinate strategic planning, bureau organization, and the operational command and control of armies in the field.

Here the Civil War armies made a hesitant beginning. High command in the Union army worked out a modern, if somewhat informal, staff system coordinating grand strategic planning and bureaucratic organization. It resembled the French staff system, though there is no evidence of French influence during the war. Confederate high command also had some semblance of modern staff organization. But only in Union logistics, and then only in the East, did the Civil War produce a modern staff organization that coordinated planning between high command, bureaus, and operational command and control in the field. In addition, isolated developments in particular areas of tactical and strategic organization anticipated, if they did not fully achieve, modern staff procedures. There is no evidence that Civil War staff development, any more than antebellum military thought, paid heed to the Prussian general staff, the existing system best designed to cope with the turbulence of the change to modern forms of warfare.

One hindrance to the development of a modern idea of staff was the prevailing mechanistic world view in military culture. The crisis created by new conditions demanding new structures forced practical if not theoretical change. But practical responses needed the support of a systematic world view, with logic that emphasized the historical development of ideas and institutions.

The origins of this historical world view, of course, preceded the Civil War. In military thought, Jomini's German contemporary and critic Clausewitz initiated the reaction against the mechanistic cast of mind that would most influence nineteenth- and twentieth-century thinking. Clausewitz, variously interpreted as a follower of Kant and Hegel and a precursor of Marx, anticipated the form that tactics and strategy increasingly would assume. His influence on military professionalism through the German general staff would make him the most influential philosopher of war from the late nineteenth century through World War II. But though Clausewitz's writings were known, they were not digested by the Civil War generation of American officers; his international star would rise only after Prussia's victory over the French army in the Franco-Prussian War, 1870–71.

Yet the Civil War soldier was the first to face the challenges that Clausewitz had anticipated—and eventually would inform. He was the first to feel the full range of technological, social, ideological, geographical, and organizational factors that increasingly would force tactical and strategic organization into modern forms of warfare. The Civil War professional officer, aided and abetted by the citizen soldier, did respond. He did so, as could be expected, with some deference to tradition, and with more than a little ambivalence and contradiction in the changes he wrought. His actions were as often the practical responses to immediate conditions as they were the product of critical reflections on the nature of warfare. He nevertheless developed tactical and strategic ideas and organization that occupy a crucial place in the transition to modern warfare and in the emergence of the modern American army.

In sum, this book attempts to make two basic contributions to the understanding of the Civil War and modern military culture. There is an attempt to break new ground in the analysis of the theory, doctrine, and practice of field fortification in the tactical evolution of trench warfare. There is also a new analysis of the development of field transportation and supply to move and maneuver Civil War armies in the field. My original contributions to the remaining areas of organizational change build upon the work of others. I also attempt to synthesize developments in tactics and strategy around the dominant problem of mid-nineteenth-century field command: the threat of positional trench warfare, and efforts to sustain the mobility of armies in the field. While pursuing these themes, this work shows that the history of tactical and strategic ideas and organization shared a dominant theme of mid-nineteenth-century America, namely, the emergence of intellectual and institutional forms for mass industrial society, shaped by American history, culture, and geography.

One might anticipate criticism of this organizational perspective from students of strategy and tactics who are pursuing other themes and exploring other motives, ranging from politics, to personality, to culture, to seeking the interaction of men and leadership in the "fog" or "friction" of factors explaining why and how men fight. And though the focus of this study is the dialogue between field command and the development of tactical and strategic ideas and organization, the analysis sometimes speculates on these other themes as part of the reason why ideas and organization took the course that they did. It is perhaps important, therefore, to emphasize what the study does and does not claim to do.

This work does not claim any special status for its perspective in any complete explanation of tactical and strategic decision making in Civil War field command. My analysis acknowledges that a balanced weighting of factors is necessary for such a history; while it argues that any such weighting must include this development of tactical and strategic ideas and organization. Where ideas and organization seem to weigh especially heavy as motives in the fog or friction of war, I sometimes risk saying so. But I pass to others any systematic synthesis of ideas and organizational development with other perspectives for a complete explanation of motives, soldiers, and the Civil War. While this work will contribute to any such synthesis, it is my hope that it will be seen primarily as a study of how tactical and strategic ideas and organization evolved in response to mid-nineteenth-century American industrial technology, society, ideology, and geography, as well as to the tactical and strategic objectives of Civil War armies.

IDEAS AND EDUCATION

1

Theory, Doctrine, and the Tactical Maze

From Jomini to Dennis Hart Mahan

THE FRENCH CONNECTION

The transition from fluid strategic and tactical movement in the early campaigns of Napoleon to the trench warfare of the American Civil War began in the period of the French Empire and the Restoration. While France's military thinkers interpreted the Napoleonic legacy, the generation of American military writers that began to emerge by the 1830s modified the French influence in response to peculiarly American circumstances, technological change, and the lessons of a number of indecisive wars.

Reflecting the milieu in which it arose, the military synthesis of the post-Napoleonic generation was cautious and conservative, more concerned with codification than with change. Rejected was the innovational outlook of the French Revolutionary reformers, led by Bourcet and Guibert, as was Napoleon's application of their theories in his early campaigns. The Revolutionary reformers had been preoccupied with mobility, pursuing victory through flexibility in strategic and tactical movement. The new orthodoxy favored a concentrated and direct strategic approach on the decisive point in the enemy's line.

Primarily responsible for this transformation was Antoine Henri Jomini. His writings between 1804 and 1839 set the dominant trend in Continental and American strategic thought until German victories in 1870 pushed Karl von Clausewitz's interpreters to the center of the Continental stage. Born in 1779, Jomini missed the fervor of the Revolutionary generation and the romantic world view that inspired its greatest theorist, Jacques Antoine Guibert. He came to intellectual maturity during a period of codification and a quest for stability in all spheres of social activity, including the waging of war.

Jomini's first exposure to war came as a staff officer in Napoleon's armies during the Empire, by which time the Revolutionary tradition of mobility, diversion, dispersion, and surprise had largely given way to the direct strategic approach, with ultimate dependence upon mass and the frontal assault. Jomini's quest for a valid tactical and strategic system reflected an acknowledged debt to Frederick the Great and an unacknowledged debt to Frederick's eighteenth-century English interpreter, Henry Lloyd. The concepts Jomini set forth in his first work, *Treatise on Great Military Operations* (1804–1816), for example, were plagiarisms, sometimes word for word, from Lloyd's *The History of the Late War in Germany: Between the King of Prussia and the Empress of Germany and Her Allies*, written between 1766 and 1790. Throughout his writings, Jomini tended to evaluate Napoleon by Frederick's standards.[1]

Like the Revolutionary reformers, Jomini considered the cutting of an opponent's lines of communication by maneuver the preferred way to wage war. He also praised battlefield envelopment movements that turned an enemy's flank. But while he praised maneuver, he also had a cautious reservation about its use. He considered strategic maneuver, and particularly battlefield flanking operations, so difficult to execute that they were not dependable except under particularly advantageous conditions. Napoleon possessed the genius to make the strategic concepts of the reformers work. But Napoleons, as Jomini knew, were rare. And even Napoleon, he observed, had confronted problems that made mass and direct tactical confrontation generally more attractive than maneuver. Under normal circumstances, Jomini advocated what he considered the less desirable but more dependable recourse to a direct and concentrated strategic approach on interior lines, a strategy that rested ultimately on the massed frontal assault to exploit vulnerable points in the enemy's line.[2]

Dependence upon an offensive tactical solution involved the risk of positional stalemate and the specter of trench warfare, should technological or other developments shift the balance to the defense, and should strategic maneuver subsequently not be restored. Military thought and doctrine traditionally had given the tactical defense its due. And Jomini treated the entrenched defense with respect almost equal to that accorded the offense. But the spirit of the Revolutionary and Napoleonic periods emphasized the superiority of the frontal assault in most situations. The traditional debate on the relative strength of the tactical offense and defense leaned toward the offense. The changing nature of warfare did not completely undermine the primacy of the frontal assault until the American Civil War, but the transition began much earlier.

The undercurrent of respect for the entrenched defense combined with the cautious temperament of the Restoration generation of French military thinkers helped prepare American tactical thought for the changing conditions of warfare in the Civil War. American tactical and strategic thinking in the early and mid-nineteenth century largely followed the French lead; and alongside the prevailing emphasis on the frontal assault, there existed in the military thought of both countries a systematic qualification on its use.

While Jomini built an offensive strategic system that rested on the continued supremacy of the frontal assault, his deference to both defensive positional strategy and the tactical defense is an indication of the caution of his generation of military thinkers. This caution is readily apparent from an analysis of his most influential work, *Summary of the Art of War* (first published in English in 1854, though an excerpted summary of maxims from his *Treatise on Great Military Operations* was translated and added to Francois Gay de Vernon's *A Treatise on the Science of War and Fortification*, which was a West Point text from 1817 to 1830). Jomini's ideas on the relative merits of the tactical defense versus the tactical offense again show the influence of Frederick the Great. The author, as noted, tended to interpret Napoleon through Frederick's standards, which he in turn saw to be based on the principle of maximum result with minimum risk, a sentiment in the spirit of the Empire and Restoration period.[3]

The distinction of according the tactical defense a formal place in French (and subsequently American) military doctrine in the post-Revolutionary generation, and of predicating formal doctrine on the role that field fortification was to play in both the defense and the offense, fell primarily not to Jomini, but to Francois Gay de Vernon. Gay de Vernon was professor of fortification and the art of war at the École Polytechnique, the military school Napoleon established to train the elite of the French army. Napoleon enhanced the influence he was exerting from his professorship when, in 1805, he ordered Gay de Vernon's *Treatise on the Science of War and Fortification* published for use as a text at the École Polytechnique, as well as at all other French military schools.

In the tactical debate over the offense versus the defense, Gay de Vernon expressed the same views as Jomini. Although the publication of his *Treatise on the Science of War and Fortification* followed Jomini's first publication by a year, the manuscript, based on lectures at the École Polytechnique, was probably conceived before Jomini wrote. Though Gay de Vernon gave due credit to his sources, there is no reference to Jomini. The similarity in outlook between the two theorists no doubt followed from their common debt to Frederick the Great and to Henry Lloyd, to whom Gay de Vernon frequently referred.

In the story of the transition to trench warfare, the role assigned to field fortification was the most important feature of doctrine on the tactical defense. It was not the principles and details of fortification construction, however, that were of primary significance. Both were already developed and did not undergo notable change in the early and mid-nineteenth century. The only major adjustment was the accommodation of construction to the increased range and firepower of the new weapons. Gay de Vernon is significant to this story for setting forth when and to what extent field fortifications should be used. He called for an army in the field, when fighting from a tactical defense, to secure its front, flanks, and rear with field fortifications. If pursuing the tactical offense, it was to entrench only its flanks and rear. He further advocated the practice of the Roman armies in fortifying their camps. On the grounds that armies are always susceptible to surprise, he believed that their "habitual attitude" should at all times be defensive.[4] American tactical doctrine followed the French lead and similarly digested Gay de Vernon. His *Treatise on the Science of War and Fortification*, translated for use as a textbook at the United States Military Academy in 1817, remained in use there until 1830 and was used as the basis for field manuals.

CONTINUITY, CHANGE, AND CONTRADICTION IN AMERICAN TACTICAL THOUGHT

In the 1830s, rumblings of discontent against the priority given to the open frontal assault began to be heard from West Point. A new generation of U.S. military thinkers began to raise the role of entrenchment to a more prominent place. The Americans were sensitive to local circumstances and only loosely tied to the post-Revolutionary era. At first they modified current doctrine to develop a tactical system suitable to an American army. Although the new outlook did not displace orthodox emphasis on the open frontal assault, it did provide an alternative.

The most significant figure among the American theorists was Dennis Hart Mahan. After graduating first in his West Point class of 1824, Mahan was assigned to the Corps of Engineers and immediately appointed to the faculty of the Military Academy. Before assuming his teaching duties, however, he spent four years in France as a student and observer, including one year at the School of Engineering and Artillery at Metz. In 1830 he returned to his faculty post at West Point.

Mahan's years of study left him dissatisfied. Prevailing doctrine, he thought, was acceptable for a professional army on the European model, organized and fighting under European conditions. But for the United States, which in case of war would have to depend upon a civilian army held together by a small professional nucleus, the French tactical system was unrealistic. He set out to remedy this defect immediately upon returning to take up his teaching appointment. In 1832, Mahan was appointed professor of military and civil engineering and of the science of war, a position he held until his death in 1870. His senior position, a pragmatic technologically oriented society, and the elite status of the engineering corps in the U.S. Army assured him a wide and knowledgeable hearing.

West Point was assigned to the Corps of Engineers, and from the beginning of the nineteenth century until after the Civil War, the corps dominated both the Academy and the United States Army. The superintendents of West Point were appointed from the Corps of Engineers; from 1816 to 1866, the inspector of West Point was always the chief of the corps. In peacetime, providing engineers for civilian projects was one of the Military Academy's primary functions.

In 1832, Mahan introduced field fortification into the curriculum at the senior level in his course on military and civil engineering and the science of war. The best students were likely to give this course considerable attention owing to the emphasis upon technical engineering knowledge in an officer corps dominated by the Corps of Engineers. The top 10 to 20 percent of each graduating class, depending upon demand, would be commissioned into the Corps of Engineers, and this group would contribute a disproportionate share of Civil War field commanders above the divisional level.[5]

Mahan helped compensate for the lack of space in the curriculum for the study of the principles of war by infusing his military engineering courses with tactical principles. Practical instruction in military engineering at West Point was particularly strong in fortification, partially compensating for the lack of classroom time.[6] For the brief period of the short-lived five-year course at West Point, 1858–61, Mahan had time to teach a subcourse on the science of war. But owing to its late date of introduction and brief life, the five-year course had negligible influence on Civil War field commanders.[7]

Mahan also kept his ideas before a small elite group through a postgraduate course in theoretical engineering for his subordinate faculty. Standardized in content about 1845, the two-year course met biweekly. The focus was on the problem of attack and defense. Mahan also presided over the Napoleon Club, a military round table designed to engage the West Point faculty in a critical study of Napoleon's campaigns.[8]

By force of personality and intellect, Mahan exploited to full advantage his unique opportunity to influence the Civil War generation of regular officers.

> The cadet who came before Mahan with merely a superficial knowledge of the subject inevitably found himself in a pitiable plight. There never was a quicker eye or sharper tongue for shams of any kind. . . . No cadet, from the head of the class down to the foot, was safe from his sarcasm or proof against his prodding. They feared him as they admired him. They gloried in his teaching as one does in a desperate battle . . . after it is over. There was just one quality in a pupil which he apostrophized again and again as indispensable to the would-be commander of fighting men. Without it, brilliancy, knowledge, book-learning, study, strategy and tactics, all combined were of little worth. "Common sense," said Mahan, "was worth them all, and was that one quality without which no man could hope to win."[9]

Mahan's son, who was also his student, further commented that his father held that "the only really practical man is one who is thoroughly grounded in theory."[10]

Mahan further influenced tactical doctrine by writing treatises that were adopted as official textbooks, and by expounding their contents in the classroom. Also, regular army and militia manuals were taken directly from his textbooks, assuring that the farthest corner of American military organization was exposed to his ideas.[11] Mahan's most important works were *A Complete Treatise on Field Fortification* (1836) and *An Elementary Treatise on Advanced-Guard, Out-Post, and Detachment Service of Troops* (1847). *Field Fortification* contained the essential elements of his modifications of the French-derived tactical system; although it was first published in 1836 to replace Gay de Vernon's text, Mahan had abandoned Gay de Vernon to lecture from his own manuscript when he returned from France in 1830. Further editions of this work appeared without revision (despite claims of the publishers to the contrary) in 1846, 1852, and 1860. A wartime edition appeared in 1862, and still others after the war.

Steeped in French thought, but acutely sensitive to American conditions, Mahan modified the current orthodoxy by rejecting one of its central tenets—primary reliance on offensive assault tactics. He was aware that the United States was dependent for its defense upon its small, hence not to be indiscriminately wasted, professional officer corps in command of militia troops. These citizen soldiers were inadequately trained, disciplined, and experienced to fight by the standards of regulars. Mahan noted that American soldiers were also valuable members of the community, and, not to be overlooked by any military man in an egalitarian ideology, they were voters. With these considerations in mind, he rebelled against the callous disregard for life that he saw to be implicit in the use of the massed frontal assault.[12]

> To [Napoleon] we owe those grand features of the art [of war], by which any enemy is broken and utterly dispersed by one and the same blow. . . . But . . . for the attainment of his ends on the battlefield he has shown a culpable disregard of the soldier's blood, and has often pursued to excess his attack by masses. To do the *greatest damage to our enemy with the least possible exposure to ourselves*, is a military axiom lost sight of only by ignorance of the true ends of victory.[13]

Guided by this principle, Mahan constructed a tactical system in which he advocated the primacy of active defense. "The chief object of entrenchments is to enable the assailed to meet the enemy with success, by first compelling him to approach under every disadvantage of position, and then, when he has been cut up, to assume the offensive, and drive him back at the point of a bayonet."[14] Mahan did not, however, maintain the superiority of the entrenched defense. Like all military writers at this time, he believed frontal assaults, if properly executed, could carry entrenched positions; where circumstances recommended them, such as in turning a flank or where surprise was possible, he advocated their use. Prior to the publication of *Out-Post* in 1847, he made important contributions to conventional assault tactics.

The principal theoretical debate was over the use of lines in two-rank formation and the use of large and small columns. Close order was accepted except for the loose or extended order of the skirmish line that preceded the line of battle and, at the point of attack, retired to aid the flanks.[15] Mahan's major contribution to this debate was his advocacy of an offensive tactical organization similar to that of Jomini.

It mixed the predominance of the close-order line with small columns as dictated by the particular circumstances of battle. Prior to the adoption of the rifled musket, the smoothbore musket made close order essential to concentrate firepower. Loose order made the tactical command and control of extended lines extremely difficult prior to the development of advanced visual and telegraphic signals for tactical communication. And loose order was generally detrimental to tactical discipline. Without the devastating impact of rifled musket fire, there was little incentive to revise close-order assault tactics.

But even while contributing to conventional assault tactics, Mahan as early as *Field Fortification* opposed them for American troops under normal circumstances. In the same book, he anticipated the impact of the rifled musket, which was not developed as a practical infantry weapon until the 1840s. Especially revealing in his close examination of a table by a German authority on rifled muskets which indicated that troops with rifles were over three and a half times more effective at approximately 170 yards than with smoothbores, and almost equal to the deliberate fire of skirmishers at 85 yards.[16]

In *Out-Post*, published in 1847 concurrent with the development of a practical muzzleloading rifled musket made possible by Colonel Claude Etienne Minié's invention of the "Minié ball," Mahan revised his view of open assault tactics. When it was necessary to launch a frontal assault against entrenched positions, he advocated that the close-order line and small columns be replaced by the regular infantry advancing in the loose order of skirmishers. The line would take advantage of available cover and close by rushing within about 200 yards. He also gave unqualified support to artillery preparation for assault on entrenchments.[17] Mahan thus anticipated the development of Civil War offensive as well as defensive tactics.[18]

The details Mahan laid down in *Field Fortification* for the form of construction under various circumstances—including the role of so-called hasty entrenchments—illustrate the sophistication of thought on field fortification and dispel any illusion that the Civil War soldier had to improvise everything he knew. Mahan's study on field fortification varied in no significant way from Gay de Vernon's, either in details of construction or in specifications as to who should entrench and under what circumstances. Mahan's innovation was in his adaptation of basic principles to the character of the American army.[19]

The basic principle of all fortified positions was that of the "flanked disposition," that is, a disposition "susceptible of such a configuration that the ground over which the enemy's columns must pass should be swept by flank, cross and reverse fires. All the parts of a fortified line should reciprocally protect and flank each other within good musket range."[20] Working from this principle, field fortifications fall into two general categories: lines, or complex entrenchments, and hasty entrenchments.

Lines, or complex entrenchments, are of two classifications: continuous lines and lines with intervals. Continuous lines consist of works, such as redoubts, lunettes, redans, or bastions, connected with "curtains" of entrenchments. There are no openings in the curtains except for ordinary outlets. The curtains can be either straight or indented. The latter provide superior flanking and are used principally "in place of a straight curtain between two advanced works which are too far apart to protect each other and the space between them." They serve "to convert the direct fire of a right line into a flank and cross fire."[21] Lines with intervals consist of detached works, [22] which are "enclosed partly or throughout their perimeters, arranged in defensive relation with each other, and presenting wide intervals between them defended only by fire."[23] Redans are placed in the intervals, behind and between the works. About 200 yards to the rear and opposite the works, cavalry are placed behind epaulments, from where they venture out to attack the flanks of the enemy.[24]

In adjusting the principles and details of lines to derive the greatest benefit from a militia-oriented army and from his active defense, Mahan had reservations about both continuous lines and lines with intervals. Although continuous lines provided "an admirable defense for militia troops owing to the confidence which they inspire," they were, Mahan stated, "not suited to an active defense." Troops took too long to extricate themselves from the entrenchments, enabling a repulsed assailant to retreat in good order, Mahan thought. Furthermore, in defiling through the narrow outlets provided to resume the offensive, the assailed were extremely vulnerable to a renewed assault. Lines with intervals, on the other hand, were ideal for the renewal of the offense.[25] Mahan was unwilling, however, to entrust them to other than well-disciplined troops. An American army, in his eyes, needed an arrangement that would combine the virtues of both continuous lines and lines with intervals.

Mahan believed that the system proposed by the chief of the French army's Corps of Engineers, General Rogniat, in his *Considérations sur l'art de la guerre*, fulfilled this need. Rogniat's system combined the bastion line, with double flank arrangement for continuous lines, and the line with intervals. The French engineer surmounted the chief objection to closed lines—that of hindering an active defense—by advocating minimum-size profiles for lunettes and curtains. This enabled the infantry to march from their entrenchments in order of battle. As Mahan noted, one of the advantages claimed for this system was "the short time required to form the works, by which an army may entrench its field of battle in one night."[26]

Mahan's rejection of the static defense, accompanied by his insistence on the active defense, led him to repudiate "all advanced works up in front of the principal entrenchments; and . . . all dispositions of works in several lines, where the object is to retreat, successively from one to the other."

> A retreat carries with it all the moral effect of a defeat; it inspirits the assailant; renders the retreating corps timid; and impairs the confidence of the troops of the second line in the strength of their own positions when they see the first line carried with such ease. Add to this the confusion that must ensue among the best disciplined troops, under such circumstances, and the importance attached to the principle will be fully justified.[27]

Mahan further objected to the construction of several lines of detached works, because a retreat to successive lines weakened the order of battle by too great a dissemination of troops. Such works also were too great in extent to permit proper direction of the battle. Reserves would be too far in the rear to be brought up in time to act offensively against a repulsed enemy, while maneuver would be difficult with the ground cut up with such a multiplication of works. As a final objection, Mahan commented that "the time and labour required to throw up so many works are altogether beyond what can be disposed of in the ordinary circumstances of an army."[28]

Entrenchment was not restricted to the main line of battle. Also provided for was the entrenchment of reserves,[29] cavalry,[30] skirmishers,[31] and even pickets.[32] Mahan further called for the entrenchment of outposts, detachments,[33] and the advanced-guard,[34] which brings us into the realm of the second classification of field works: hasty entrenchments.

Mahan's general dictum relating to hasty entrenchment was that troops were to take advantage of natural cover should it be available, and to construct artificial entrenchments when natural obstacles were absent. He was quite explicit, however, that "the line of skirmishers, besides availing themselves of the natural covers of the position . . . will form abatis in front of the more accessible points."[35] Instructions for the construction of an abatis were that large limbs of trees should be felled to point in the direction of the enemy, while a ditch should be dug behind the abatis. An abatis was to be strengthened by a slight parapet "made of the trunks of trees laid on each other with a shallow ... trench behind them; the earth from which is thrown against the trunks."[36] Convoys, or supply trains, were to be entrenched when stopped for the night or when threatened with attack.[37] Encampments were also to be entrenched "on the same rules and general principles [that] apply ... to other positions."[38] Mahan devoted a chapter of his *Treatise on Field Fortification* to "combining artificial and natural obstacles, so as to draw the greatest resources from both" in strengthening the strong and weak points of a position. He provided instructions for the adaptation of artificial fortifications to forests, mountain sites, precipices, river crossings, villages, etc., and covered such details as the artificial strengthening of hedges, walls, and houses.[39]

Thus, side by side with the tactical outlook of the post-Revolutionary generation of French thinkers, there grew up in the 1830s and 1840s this systematic formalization of an American tactical organization championing the "active" entrenched defense.[40] Mahan's work was widely circulated by his teaching, textbooks, and manuals, and most Civil War officers, whether volunteer or regular, probably knew of it. On the other hand, there was not an officer of the Civil War generation who did not know the orthodox tactical views of the post-Revolutionary generation, as well. Military orthodoxies—like others—having a tendency to linger, Mahan's decrees failed to win universal applause. His intrusion on military thought and doctrine was unusually abrupt for the inbred conservatism of institutional thought to assimilate.

One obstacle to the general ascendancy of Mahan's tactical system was the need to come to terms with Jomini. If one accepted the conservative emphasis in Jomini's strategic thought, there was no alternative but to accept the frontal assault upon which this strategy ultimately depended. So long as victory by the frontal assault was considered feasible, the difficulties and risk of maneuver could be avoided.

Mahan's scepticism about the frontal assault was accompanied by an appropriate strategic response. He avoided the conservative disposition that recommended mass and the direct approach on interior lines, a strategy oriented around victory by frontal assaults concentrated against weak points in the enemy's line. Mahan emphasized victory by maneuver. But whereas Jomini—in that part of his thinking that recognized maneuver as the best, if the most risky, strategy—saw the purpose of maneuver to be the defeat of the enemy's army, Mahan emphasized maneuver to occupy the enemy's territory or strategic points. One can presume a logical connection in so logical a mind between this strategy and Mahan's scepticism about a conventional tactical victory. At the same time, Mahan may have been influenced by the ideas of the Archduke Charles, expressed in his prestigious *Principes de la stratégie, developpés par la relation de la campagne de* 1796 *en Allemagne* (1818). Or he may have appreciated what Jomini at times seemed to ignore. With the reorganization of mass armies into smaller units with the Revolutionary and Napoleonic reforms, it was difficult to destroy an army with a tactical victory unless the enemy was incompetent. Armies were no longer burdened by the heavy organizational weight of the traditional mass army. Reorganized into companies, regiments, brigades, divisions, and corps, the modern army had the mobility to escape on interior lines. In retreat it could maintain the necessary order to defend itself against attack from behind entrenchments—the role of which the Archduke Charles emphasized.

Mahan's favorite student, Henry Halleck, in his *Elements of Military Art and Science* (1846), also emphasized the same strategic ideas as the Archduke Charles.[41] Halleck, like Mahan, recognized that the defense was outpacing the attack. He considered Mahan the most advanced theorist on field fortification. And, like Mahan, he considered the American militiaman from behind breastworks to be equal to the best European troops. But Halleck's study was, by his own admission, a compendium of contemporary ideas, with no attempt at originality. And the eclectic nature of the compendium contributed to existing ambiguities. For while on the one hand he appears to give more weight to the strategic ideas of the Archduke Charles, on the other, he at times appears to lean toward Jomini's conservative tendency favoring the concentrated and direct approach by interior lines against the enemy's army. Though Halleck's study was never a text at West Point, it was probably the most widely read book among contemporary officers. Experience in the Mexican War contributed to the muddy waters of antebellum military thought.[42]

The Mexican War (1846–1848) was the only American war to inform the generation of officers who fought the Civil War. It was fought with a small, relatively well-trained army armed for the most part with smoothbore weapons.[43] Rifled muskets usually were restricted in accordance with prevailing doctrine to two companies or fewer per regiment deployed as skirmishers. Contemporary tendencies in tactical and strategic thought fought out some of their controversies on the Mexican War battlefields and carried ambiguous lessons into the theoretical debate leading to the Civil War.

General Winfield Scott, the American commander in Mexico, and General Zachary Taylor, the other hero to emerge from the Mexican War battlefields, presented conflicting examples for the generation they influenced. Taylor aggressively pursued the frontal assault, while Scott avoided it. Scott, though not a West Point graduate, was a serious student of warfare. He had assimilated the strategic ideas of Jomini devoid of Jomini's caution about turning maneuvers. Familiar with and respectful of the ideas of Mahan, Scott was influenced in his field command decisions by the young engineering officers on his staff, who had been educated by Mahan. His preference for the holding siege operation in combination with turning movements perhaps reflected the direct influence of his young staff officers.

The early Mexican War failure of frontal assaults by green volunteer regiments in the Battle of Cerro Gordo and the slaughter of a frontal assault at the Battle of Molino del Rey reinforced the pro-Mahan sentiment of McClellan, and probably other young officers who were disposed favorably to Mahan. Even Ulysses Grant had ambivalent reactions to the frontal assault. While generally praising its results, Grant is also on record as being supportive of entrenched holding-turning movements, wary of frontal assaults, and full of admiration for the ability of the engineers to provide cover in holding-turning operations, notably at the Battle of Contreras.

But the American army did resort to the frontal assault with sufficient results to bolster the alternate current of thought. Even McClellan conceded that the volunteers were so ordered and disciplined by the end of the war that there was little difference between their performance and that of regulars. In one strategic falling-out with his staff during the Battle of Chapultapec, Scott, arguing against a turning movement in opposition to the engineering officers on his staff, launched a successful frontal assault with experienced troops. The professional officers present, including Grant, again were nearly unanimous in considering the costly offensive (25 percent killed or missing) a mistake. But success stood on the record as a victory for assault tactics against fortified positions—and for the direct strategic approach over maneuver. And this costly episode in the tactical history of the Mexican War was an exception when compared to the relatively light losses for the American army in frontal assaults. On the other side of lessons to be learned, Henry Halleck—like McClellan a promising young engineering officer and military intellectual influenced by Mahan—warned that the successful frontal assaults in the Mexican War had benefited greatly from the poor construction and defense of the Mexican works.

The lessons of the war were ambiguous. Civil War field commanders no doubt shaded their Mexican War memories toward their basic dispositions and military world views, whether grounded in experience, theory, personality, or culture. Most Mexican War veterans, including

Grant, Bragg, Albert S. Johnston, Jackson, Beauregard, Lee, and Jefferson Davis, went into the Civil War as orthodox advocates of the frontal assault. Mexican War lessons applied early in the Civil War by exponents of offensive tactics were within prevailing doctrine. The role of the bayonet, particularly in the crucial Battle of Churubusco, probably had an exaggerated influence on those inclined to the orthodox point of view. They, in turn, ignored the extensive use of skirmish tactics beyond conventional norms. From the other side of the debate, Mexican War veterans such as McClellan and Halleck no doubt carried memories slanted toward their antebellum predisposition to seek an alternative to conventional assault tactics. The strategic lessons similarly could weigh on both sides of the tactical debate. Was the strategic objective victory by maneuver as an alternative to a frontal assault; or was the objective a direct strategic approach leading ultimately to a tactical confrontation?[44]

By the 1850s, advances in weaponry were increasingly difficult to ignore. The percussion cap was invented in 1814, and by 1820 it had come into general use, replacing the flintlock.[45] By itself, the percussion cap made little impact. The chain of invention that brought about the increase in firepower necessary to influence tactics began in 1832, when a Captain Norton of the British army invented a cylindroconoidal bullet. When fired, its hollow base automatically expanded to engage the rifling of the barrel, thus giving the bullet a horizontal spin. In 1843, a French army captain, Claude Etienne Minié, perfected Norton's principle and produced the "Minié ball." Previously too slow to load, the rifle became a practical weapon on the battlefield. The Minié ball could be dropped down the muzzle of a rifle almost as easily as if it were round. This provided the horizontal spin unobtainable with the smoothbore. The net result was additional range, velocity, and accuracy.[46]

The increased firepower was somewhat slow to be felt. Technical problems and normal resistance to a major innovation hindered a rapid transition to rifled weapons. Amid experiment and controversy, armies sought the best weapons and the appropriate tactics. Although all European armies adopted some variety of rifled shoulder weapon relatively early, standardization was uncommon.[47] The rifled musket was introduced for the British infantry in 1851. In 1854, the Enfield came into service. The Tige rifle was adopted for general use in the French infantry in 1857, although the light infantry was so armed much earlier. The Russians and Austrians relatively early adopted the practice of arming a few sharpshooters in each company with rifles. The Prussian army began to introduce the Dreyse breechloading needle gun in 1840. By the late 1850s the breechloader was standard in guard regiments, and at least one battalion in each line regiment, and by 1865 the entire infantry, was so armed. Tactical revision to exploit the increased fire-power of the breechloader began in 1847, leading to smaller, more maneuverable company columns and making it theoretically possible for all infantry to fight as skirmishers. Orthodoxy tended to prevail, but younger officers experimented with the possibilities of the 1847 regu-lations that would play such an important part in the Austro-Prussian War in 1866. Owing to its complicated structure, the breechloading rifle, and consequently the tactical development that accompanied it, were unfavorably received outside Prussia. The United States Army converted to the rifled musket in the 1840s but rejected both the re-peating rifle and the breechloader for infantry because of mechanical problems. There was even an undercurrent of tactical opinion in the U.S. Army that continued to champion the smoothbore over the rifled musket for all foot soldiers but skirmishers.[48]

While the short War of Italian Independence in 1859 was the first to see large numbers of infantry on both sides armed with rifled shoulder weapons, the Crimean War marked their first significant use in any numbers. The impact of the increased firepower was particularly evi-dent: while the Russians had the advantage in artillery and cavalry, their infantry, with the exception of sharpshooters, was armed with smooth-bore muskets. By contrast, practically all British infantrymen as well as the French light infantry were armed with rifled weapons.

The obsolescence of traditional weapons was clearly apparent at the Battle of Alma, September 20, 1854; at the time of the unsuccessful Russian assaults on the entrenched British positions on the Inkerman Plateau on November 5 of the same year; and during the Russian assaults on the entrenched French and Sardinian positions on the Tchernaya, August 16, 1855. The combined role of the rifled musket and defensive field fortification was particularly evident in the latter two battles.[49] Neither European nor American military thinkers appear to have di-gested the lessons of these telling incidents, though George McClellan made passing reference to the futility of the Russian assaults on the Inkerman Plateau while a member of an American military commission to Europe.

Most attention fell on the siege of Sebastopol, and rifled weapons were not responsible for the trench warfare that developed around that city. The campaign of entrenchment and counterentrenchment around Sebastopol was largely the outcome of a numerically inferior Russian army taking up defensive positions as their only sensible alternative. With no way to turn these positions, the British, French, and Turks had no choice but to undertake a siege campaign of counterentrenchment.

Rifled weapons contributed to the intensity of the trench war after it became a fact, but owing to their general scarcity, their impact was limited. Rifled artillery was not sufficiently developed at this time to be significant. Sharpshooters with rifled weapons, abundant in both armies, played the most striking role. The Russian engineer Todleben's highly effective use of sharpshooters in rifle pits—which were extended into trenches of counterapproach between siege lines—was a further portent of the tactical impact of well-aimed rifle fire from entrenched positions. More obvious, however, was the effectiveness of the rather crude Russian field fortifications, a further indication that the tactical defense was outpacing assault tactics.

But in the immediate aftermath of the Crimean War, Jomini saw fit to defend the continued validity of the orthodoxy he was instrumental in establishing.[50] Replying directly to the question of what impact the new rifled weapons would have on war in the future, he forecast no significant change. Regarding developments at the siege of Sebastopol, he wrote: "This . . . contest between two vast entrenched camps, occupied by entire armies . . . is an event without precedent, which will have no equal in the future; for the circumstances which produced it cannot occur again. Moreover, this contest cannot influence in any respect the great combinations of war, nor even the tactics of battles."

Jomini believed that the new weapons "would probably have an influence on the details of tactics, but that, in great strategic operations and the grand combinations of battles, victory would now as ever, result from the application of the principles which had led to the success of great generals in all ages." He rejected the notion that "battles will become mere duels with the rifle, where the parties will fire upon each other, without maneuvering, until one or the other shall retreat or be destroyed." He rejected as well the notion that "whole armies will be deployed as skirmishers," and that "formations of lines deployed in two or three ranks, or lines of battalions in columns" would become obsolete.

Jomini's only concession to the impact of the new weapons was a modification of assaults in columns to allow for greater maneuverability and to exploit the greater firepower. He sought to make columns more maneuverable by substituting columns by company for columns by battalion. But he did not recommend the complete abandonment of battalion columns. Second, he recommended increasing the firepower of the infantry by an increased number and wider distribution of sharpshooters in the regular formations, a plan that called for the regiments of light infantry to be distributed among troops of the line. Jomini's tactical response to the weapons revolution derived from his belief that the increase in firepower gave as much advantage to the tactical offense as to the tactical defense.[51]

Many rallied to his side. Napoleon III backed up Jomini's post-Crimean pronouncements on the field of battle. Before he launched his campaign against the Austrians in the War of Italian Independence, he exclaimed that the new firearms would have no effect upon the continued preeminence of the massed frontal assault and the bayonet.[52] Successful frontal assaults by the French at Magenta and Solferino strengthened orthodox tactics while obscuring the real lesson, namely, the potential of the increased firepower of rifled infantry weapons in the hands of veteran troops. More than one-third of Napoleon's army had more than seven years' experience. Although the French army was in the process of arming its infantry of the line with rifles, the light infantry was entirely so armed. And, although the French infantry of the line attacked in battalion columns, the sharpshooters of the veteran skirmish line, fed at times by whole battalions, executed successful frontal assaults on the Austrian columns. Hailed as victories for shock action, French successes were in fact victories for firepower.[53]

Hostilities ended before the elements of change had the opportunity to register an impact. Napoleon's successful use of frontal assaults obscured the more significant lesson to be learned. Committed to the prevailing trends in military thought, Europe accepted the surface results and ignored the deeper lessons. American military observers were on hand, but if they saw the signs, they did not compile their reports in time to have any influence on the Civil War generation.

At West Point, Mahan's understudy as assistant professor of civil and military engineering and the science of war, Captain W. P. Craighill, was among those doing their best to perpetuate resistance to change in American military circles. As cotranslator (with Captain G. H. Mendell of the Corps of Topographical Engineers) of the 1862 English edition of Jomini's *Summary of the Art of War*, he included an appendix of Jomini's previously discussed post-Crimean treatise in which the author denied that the increased firepower of the new infantry weapons would have any significant impact on the waging of war. Craighill also translated the 1864 English edition of the French General G. H. Dufour's *Strategy and Tactics*, which was essentially a paraphrase of Jomini's *Summary of the Act of War*.

There was considerable support for the continuing domination of élan and open assault tactics in immediate antebellum and early Civil War military writing. Brigadier General Daniel Butterfield's *Camp and Outpost Duty for Infantry*, published as late as 1862 as a camp and pocket manual, was an example from a prominent Union officer of the extreme attitude that élan and shock were the essential ingredients of infantry assault tactics.[54]

Other American tactical writers who anticipated the increased firepower tended to follow the lead of Jomini rather than Mahan, seeing the new weapons as aiding the offense as much as the defense. For example, Cadmus M. Wilcox, in his *Rifles and Rifle Practice* (1859), didn't see the rifled musket strengthening the entrenched defense. It merely rendered the defense less complicated by allowing simple works defended by the rifle to replace more elaborate works. He anticipated that the greater range of the rifle would provoke battle more easily and that command and control would be more difficult. But he believed that intensified discipline plus keeping troops covered as long as possible was the only adjustment necessary to preserve the primacy of offensive assault tactics. John Gibbon, in *The Artillerist's Manual* (1860), saw that the rifle would make the bayonet obsolete in infantry tactics, but he believed that the loss of fire discipline would dissipate the rifle's tactical impact. The fact that the infantry had training adapted both to the increased range of the rifled musket and to the bayonet reflects the contradictions of tactical thought and doctrine in coming to terms with technological change by the outbreak of the Civil War.[55]

The principal theoretical adjustment to the increased firepower of the rifled musket in assault tactics was to increase the speed and mobility of tactical movement. First introduced by the French and adapted to the U.S. Army in 1855 by William J. Hardee in his *Rifle and Light Infantry Tactics*, the new drill introduced double-quick time (165 steps per minute) and the run and allowed changes in the order of march to be made in motion rather than after coming to a halt. Hardee also altered the order of precedence of the companies in regimental organization and went to the two-rank organization of the line. He further substituted bugle for drum signals to improve tactical command and control.

Both Winfield Scott's *Infantry Tactics* (1852)[56] and Silas Casey's *Infantry Tactics*, which replaced Scott as official doctrine in 1862, emphasized Hardee's work and were acknowledged to be based on the *French Ordinances* of 1831 and 1845. Casey also contributed tactical doctrine for brigade and larger-unit tactics and made revisions that improved deployment from column to line. He gave more emphasis to the division column than had Hardee. Otherwise Casey was a composite of Hardee's first two volumes and Scott's third. The Confederate army followed the Union army in adopting his revisions.[57]

The lack of an integrated tactical system for infantry, artillery, and cavalry doctrine compounded the ambivalence of thinking on the merits of the offense versus the defense in infantry tactics. Cavalry and artillery tactics both continued to emphasize the offensive assault. Cavalry tactics complemented conventional infantry assault tactics, emphasizing shock and the role of the saber. But the tactical arms developed independently.

The major debate in cavalry tactics was over the single- versus the two-rank formation. The U.S. Army in 1861 authorized Philip St. George Cooke's *Cavalry Tactics*, which called for a single-rank formation with some provision for the use of the double rank. The Confederates adopted the same system in the form of Joseph Wheeler's *A Revised System of Cavalry Tactics*. The purpose of the single-rank preference was to reduce the confusion of command and control when two ranks merged in line of battle, and re-formed after the charge. There were other reasons, such as believing the single-rank system was easier to teach to volunteers. But most significant, the single line was recommended because its advocates believed it provided greater initial shock. Advocates of the single line were predisposed, therefore, to support the continuing predominance of the offense over the defense, of shock over firepower. In another case of tactical ambiguity in Civil War thought and doctrine, Cooke's authorized tactical system coexisted with the War Department's two-line system, which dated from 1841 and was not revised until after the war.[58]

Artillery theory emphasized both the offensive and defensive role of field artillery, with the emphasis again on the offensive role in support of infantry assault tactics. A dawning awareness that the rifled musket had made obsolete the Napoleonic-era tactics of wheeling field artillery batteries in front of infantry advances to blow a hole in the defensive line existed uneasily with an admittedly cautious deference to the continuing role of the offensive rush of field artillery. Evan Mahan admired the offensive rush in *Out-Post*. There was some interpretation of the Mexican War experience to favor the offensive rush of artillery.

Yet the prevailing emphasis in American artillery doctrine firmly subordinated the artillery to the infantry. Mahan's recommendation, despite his cautious admiration of the offensive rush, was that field artillery advance in battery formation on the flanks of the infantry line or, in the case of columns, near their head. Jomini's offensive standard was for about one-third of the guns to occupy the enemy's artillery and two-thirds to fire on infantry and cavalry. Jomini liked the concentrated offensive cannonade where a breach of the line was to be attempted. Defensively, American doctrine followed Jomini's emphasis on battery organization with the equal distribution of batteries along the line, with a warning that they were not to be too scattered, and that defensive organization should be adaptable to circumstances. Mahan advocated

600-yard intervals between batteries. The artillery manual adopted in 1859, *Instruction for Field Artillery*, retained much of the 1845 manual that it had replaced from the Mexican War era. There was some discussion in American thought of the Napoleonic concentration of artillery at the division and corps level with a reserve. But the discussion had no impact on American doctrine, where artillery continued to be organized at the regiment and brigade level with no reserve.

Technology continued to favor the smoothbore Napoleon as the principal field artillery piece. Rifled cannon, though prevalent in American artillery organization, were in their technological infancy. They were generally unpopular with artillery officers and field commanders. In 1860, the ordnance board recommended that half the bronze cannon in service be rifled; but the technology of the smoothbore could not tolerate the strain of rifled fire, and results were poor. There was a variety of rifled artillery, the most common being the Parrot ten-pounder and the three-inch ordnance rifle. But technological problems persisted. The British Armstrong and Whitworth guns were sound weapons, but they were not introduced in sufficient numbers or early enough in the war to have any significant effect. Even with good rifled weapons, there remained the problem of inadequate devices for indirect ranging and firing. Improvisation in this respect would go so far during the Civil War as to have signal officers and even balloonists sometimes perform this function. Training artillerists in rifled weapons was also more difficult and time-consuming than with the traditional smoothbore.

There was an accompanying awareness on the part of some officers, such as McClellan, that American terrain would blunt the greater range of rifled artillery. The decision to favor the Napoleon, combined with the technological failings of rifled artillery, weighed for the greater effectiveness of artillery as a defensive weapon once the rifled musket made its impact felt on offensive tactics. Jefferson Davis, while secretary of war, contributed to the ambiguity of artillery doctrine. Davis de-emphasized the role of artillery in tactical organization when he drew from the Crimean War the lesson that the rifled musket blunted its offensive role. At the same time, memories of the effective role of artillery in the Mexican War sustained its prestige among veterans who would exercise Civil War field command.[59]

Antebellum American military organization was without a modern staff concept or a modern system of signals to command and control the extended lines of mass armies. American military thought, including the Delafield Commission to Europe in 1855–59, showed no interest in the general staff concepts being developed by the Prussian army. The U.S. armies entered the Civil War with the traditional model of a field commander exercising direct control using staff officers as couriers. Adequate for small armies or the traditionally concentrated lines of mass armies, this system was inadequate for the extended lines of the large, Civil War armies in American terrain.

The technological state of antebellum signals development combined with staff procedures to further hinder tactical mobility and favor the defense over the offense. The technology of a modern semaphore system was in an embryonic state at the outbreak of war. Limited European experimentation with telegraphic communications, both tactical and strategic, was largely ignored in antebellum military thought. Telegraphic communication would be developed in response to the demands of the Civil War battlefield.[60]

In the aftermath of the indecisive wars on the Continent, and on the eve of the American Civil War, Mahan's infantry tactics received vocal support from some of his former students. James St. Clair Morton, a young captain of engineers and a former student of Mahan—second in the West Point class of 1851—expressed the sentiments of the American military reformers when, in 1859, he wrote:

> The grand principles of waging war indeed remain the same, but the rules which have in some sort expressed their application have virtually sustained a revolution. To continue to rely upon such rules until new ones have been issued by some modern Vauban, Bulow, or Jomini, is unwise. . . . I admit that the stamp of European authority is pretty good evidence of the sterling value of a military dogma; but in the absence of new rules from such quarters, let us rather do without any than follow the old ones which will . . . lead us astray.[61]

In addition to appreciating the need to accommodate tactical thought to American conditions, American reform thought in the 1850s recognized the ascendancy of the entrenched defense as a result of the introduction of rifled infantry weapons. Furthermore, it saw this development as indicative of a trend toward positional warfare which would be marked by endless entrenchment. George B. McClellan, another of Mahan's outstanding students—second in the class of 1846—destined to play a major role in the Civil War transition to trench warfare, observed military developments in the Crimean War at first hand. McClellan, while a member of the American Military Commission to Europe in 1855–56, noted the ascendancy of the defense in his observations on the Crimean War. He observed that the Russian performance at Sebastopol behind "simple temporary fortification of rather greater dimension than usual . . . proved that temporary works in the hands of a skillful garrison are susceptible of a longer defense than was generally supposed."[62] Mahan, like McClellan, noted approvingly that the Russian chief engineer Todleben's field fortifications at Sebastopol had proved adequate. The Russian army's defense of Sebastopol supported Mahan in making the entrenched defense the basis of his tactical system. And McClellan, who was the only member of the commission to comment on the earlier battles, further supported the direction of Mahan's thinking when he berated the Russian General Menshikov for his disastrous frontal assault against the entrenched British positions on the Inkerman Plateau.[63]

In 1858, James St. Clair Morton made his first impact on formal doctrine. Having caught the ear of the secretary of war, John B. Floyd, who encouraged young officers to present their opinions to him, Morton began to propagandize for an adjustment of military thought to the new conditions of war and to American circumstances. He especially impressed Floyd with his *Letter to the Hon. John B. Floyd, Secretary of War, presenting for his consideration a new plan for the seacoast of the United States*. Floyd ordered this brief treatise published, and to give Morton time to develop his ideas, he had him assigned to a tour of duty as a lighthouse keeper. The results were Morton's *Memoir on the Dangers and Defenses of New York City* (1858) and *Memoir on American Fortification* (1859). Floyd ordered both officially adopted.

In these works, Morton, like Mahan, stressed the principle that a military system must be adapted to available resources. In the case of the United States, the system should be adapted to the militia and to the country's limited financial assets.[64] Morton specifically applied this principle to coastal defense, although he intended the implications to be much wider. Morton, like Mahan, believed that militia should fight always from behind entrenchments. And, if the United States could not afford to build and maintain permanent fortifications, he perceived that the impact of increased firepower on the principles of fortification would allow fewer troops to man more extended temporary works. He had the example of the Crimean War to support his confidence in temporary fortifications.[65] Morton thus constructed a case for the combination of militia and temporary field works as the most intelligent way to defend the United States with the resources at hand.

In the Civil War, Morton was to obtain the opportunity to wield influence in a more practical manner. He alternately served as chief engineer, Army of the Ohio (June 9, 1861–October, 1862); chief engineer, Army of the Cumberland (October 27, 1862–August, 1863, and September 17–November 14, 1863); and commander of the pioneer brigade in the Army of the Cumberland at Stones River and Chickamauga.

He fortified Chattanooga, Nashville, Murfreesboro, Clarksville, and Fort Donelson. From January to May 16, 1864, he was assistant to the chief engineer of the U.S. Army. He then served as chief engineer in Burnside's corps in the Army of the Potomac until June 17, 1864, when he was killed while laying out a line for Burnside's troops to entrench prior to the first attack on the outer works of Petersburg. In his *Permanent Fortification*, published in 1863 but probably written in 1860, Mahan repeated the arguments Morton had presented as he extended his tactical system to the defense of American cities.

It is only appropriate that Mahan should have made the most striking prognosis of the evolution of trench warfare. On the eve of the Civil War, he wrote:

> The art of fortification, in its progress, has kept pace with the measures of the attack; its successive changes having been brought about by changes either in the arms used by the assailant or by some new mode of assault. The same causes must continue to produce the same effects. At no past period has mechanical invention, in its bearing on the military art, been more active than at the present day. . . . The great destruction of life, in open assaults, by columns exposed within so long a range, must give additional value to entrenched fields of battle; and we may again see fieldworks play the part they did in the defense of Sebastopol; and positions so chosen and fortified that not only will the assailant be forced to entrench himself to assail them, but will find the varying phases of his attack met by corresponding changes in the defensive dispositions.[66]

TACTICS, STRATEGY, AND ORGANIZATION

Although Mahan and a few others envisioned what was coming, their ideas, even if generally acknowledged, would not have been enough. More important was the need to acknowledge the spirit of Mahan's inquiry, namely, his departure from a mechanistic application of maxims to an analysis of tactics in the context of changing historical circumstances, relating not only to technology but also to social and ideological factors affecting war. Only from such a revision in world view could American military professionalism develop a modern view of tactics and strategy within the context of organizational demands shaped by historically grounded factors of change. Should the breakdown of offensive tactics challenge the concentrated strategic approach on interior lines, with an emphasis on mass over maneuver, American strategic thought would need to either reach into that part of its heritage that emphasized maneuver, or accept a positional trench war of attrition. And a strategy of maneuver, including battlefield flanking maneuvers, would place even greater stress on the need for innovation in strategic and tactical reorganization to move mass citizen armies in North American terrain.

Jomini, and the mechanistic tradition that he symbolized, did emphasize the need for military preparedness, as well as the efficient exploitation of a nation's human and material resources to maintain an efficient military establishment. Jomini even called for a general staff capable of applying these elements, and for an organization calculated to advance the theoretical and practical education of its officers.[67] In elaboration, he dealt specifically with such staff functions as logistics, topographical surveys, and tactical communications. But Jomini followed the mechanistic pattern of the eighteenth-century military world view in separating these elements from the formal considerations of tactics and strategy. He dealt with tactics and strategy strictly in geometric terms.

Only in the Prussian general staff was there the development of a structure to coordinate tactical and strategic theory and doctrine, grand strategic planning, bureau organization, and operational command and control. Elsewhere, field command was centered on the personalized tradition of the army commander assisted by a specialized staff that reflected his view of organizational needs. A general staff doctrine with field staffs to implement it was absent. Prussian military culture, grounded in the historically oriented world view that was revolutionizing German thought, began to view military theory, doctrine, and organization as a product of changing historical factors. French military thought and the world it dominated remained locked in pursuit of the absolute mechanistic principles demanded by eighteenth-century empiricism. Not until the Prussian defeat of the French army in the Franco-Prussian War of 1870 would French military culture surrender its dominance to that of Prussia and Germany.

American military thought, not having experienced cause to innovate, followed the French lead. Such examples of the mechanistic separation of strategy and planning as the separation of bureau organization from strategic planning met generally perceived military needs and prevailing cultural imperatives prior to the Civil War.[68] The elements Jomini emphasized as essential to military preparedness, and which would be placed under a modern definition of strategy, were ignored by a people with a social and political ideology hostile to both the peacetime and centralized military organization entailed in Jomini's recommendations. In responding to the realities of modern warfare, the generation of American military theorists who modified post-Revolutionary thought broke the mold only in tactical thought. Military thinking, and even more strategic organization, remained essentially within the Napoleonic tradition filtered through an eighteenth-century world view. A broader vision was necessary to pose an alternative to the mechanistic paradigm.

EARLY CHANGE
AND CONTINUITY
IN THE EAST

2

Tactical and Strategic Reorganization

McClellan and the Origins of Professionalism

EDUCATION FOR FIELD COMMAND

General George B. McClellan's command of the Army of the Potomac provided an arena for early Civil War problems in tactical and strategic organization; and McClellan's background presents a case study in how U.S. army officers prepared for mid-nineteenth-century field command. By the 1820s, as society increasingly organized around science, technology and industrial development, the burgeoning professional subcultures in America, including the officer corps of the U.S. Army, began to exchange the interdependent social roles of the preindustrial community for functional definitions of their place in society. McClellan encountered the emerging professional world view from his youth. His West Point education followed his upbringing in a professional household; his father was a famous surgeon and teacher who also served as the physician at West Point. And like other young officers, particularly from the Corps of Engineers, McClellan became an industrial manager (a senior railroad executive).

Born in 1826 and graduated from the Academy in 1846, McClellan matured within the growing professionalism that had produced the army reforms of 1821. Designed to prevent a repetition of the unpreparedness exposed in the War of 1812, the reforms created a permanent professional core for an army still dominated by the militia system. West Point was the training ground for the new officers. McClellan's education and his early experience as a professional officer reflected contradictions between inherited traditional forms and mid-nineteenth-century requirements that he would carry into the Civil War. His pioneering role in the development of the American army and modern warfare abruptly presented him with a need that antebellum American military organization could not provide: a structure that would develop and integrate theory, doctrine, organization, and operational planning to sustain the tactical and strategic mobility of an army in the field.

McClellan's education contained the embryo of a modern form of military thinking. But the orthodox world view defined tactics and strategy largely as static applications of Napoleonic maxims, filtered through the mechanistic eighteenth century world view resurrected by the Restoration generation of French military thinkers. The dominance of the Corps of Engineers as the elite of the new professional officers accentuated this tendency. The ideas of Sylvanius Thayer, West Point's superintendent from 1817 to 1833, had a lasting influence; Thayer equated military professionalism with a mastery of applied scientific and mathematical principles to implement given principles of warfare. There was little allowance for a continuing evaluation of strategy and tactics as a complex of historically based factors. Only in Mahan's tactical ideas and their codification in doctrine was there anticipation of a modern historically and socially grounded military world view.

McClellan also had to cope with the decentralized militia-based organization that was part of the preindustrial tradition of American social and political thought. He inherited the Anglo-American suspicion of a professional, permanent, and centralized military establishment that dated at least from the English Civil War. Though the value of a professional officer corps had its public defenders, some influential public and congressional opinion, especially in the North, tended to justify the Military Academy primarily as a source of civil engineers for internal improvements. This mood was a deterrent to any attempt to define war as a complex problem of theory, organization, and administration in industrial society. It was a mood that would not change until forced to by circumstances.

Many professional officers reflected the cultural ambiguity of preindustrial versus modern institutional traditions. For example, some of these officers, especially from the elite Corps of Engineers, identified more with the civilian vocation of civil engineering than with their roles as military professionals. And there was an active debate among West Point graduates before, during, and after McClellan's Academy experience, over whether or not a professional soldier had the right, even duty, to simultaneously perform alternate roles in society. Without making exaggerated claims with respect to cause and effect, the debate among his contemporaries—and subsequently among historians—over McClellan's motives with respect to his professional military role in relation to his social, political, and ideological involvements might benefit from being placed in the context of the general transition from the preindustrial community to organized industrial society.[1]

McClellan graduated second in his West Point class of 1846, where he was a protégé of Mahan. Assigned to the Corps of Engineers, he went directly to the staff of the American commander in the Mexican War, General Winfield Scott. As noted, McClellan's experience in Mexico reinforced his predisposition to Mahan's preference for field fortification and turning maneuvers as an alternative to the frontal assault. The improved performance of Mexican War volunteers with training and experience did mollify his initial scepticism about the tactical discipline and order of other than regular soldiers.

McClellan stayed in the army after the war and was one of the few officers to contrast their experience with first-hand observation of military developments abroad. He was a member of the 1855–56 military commission to Europe and, as noted, observed from the Crimea that the first significant use of rifled infantry weapons shifted the tactical balance from the open frontal assault to entrenched tactical deployment. His remaining observations from Europe generally adhered to existing maxims. He missed the Prussian officer corps' general staff concept to organize mass warfare in industrial society; also their pioneering efforts in military education that would enable the staff system to function. The only indication that McClellan was at all reflecting on modern staff organization came in a letter to Jefferson Davis, then secretary of war, dated July 1, 1857. McClellan recommended to Davis a volume of Russian cavalry regulations and instructions. He praised it for setting out "the general principles of war, with—enough—detail to indicate the means of applying them in a few general cases." McClellan proposed that this volume be published for all branches of the U.S. Army. Then, in a recommendation that anticipated modern staff procedure at this technical level, at least, he advocated that commanding officers and inspectors periodically ensure that every officer "has a copy and is fully acquainted with its contents."

McClellan's failure to notice and reflect further on staff developments was not for lack of opportunity. During his tour of duty with a company of engineers stationed at West Point following the Mexican War, he was the most active member of the Academy's Napoleon Club. In its analysis of warfare through Napoleon's campaigns, the club studied the large-scale disposition of troops.[2] Was staff organization a theoretical blind spot in McClellan's military world view? Was he caught in an American ideological aversion to the centralized and permanent military organization necessary to make the staff system work? Did he share the specter of Prussian authoritarianism? Was he confident that what had worked in the past would work in the future? Did he not change his mind until Prussian victories broke the prestige of the Napoleonic tradition? Or did he reflect a West Point education so mechanistic as to ignore Jomini's observations on staff, and to preclude theory beyond the narrowly defined limits of technology, tactics, and a geometric view of strategy?

The staff problems were more than those incident to a new organization compounded by the normal frictions and dislocation of the early stages of a war. And they stemmed from more than just the unanticipated size of the armies needed to wage the Civil War. Large armies on the scale of McClellan's Army of the Potomac had existed in Europe for almost 200 years. The staff precedents adopted from the French would perhaps have sufficed had the forms of tactical and strategic organization, and the historical conditions that shaped them, remained constant. But they didn't. Field command would have benefited from the Prussian staff concept: comprehensive organization in the field that coordinated strategic planning, bureau organization, and operational planning. While anticipation of modern warfare in this respect did develop at the level of high command and bureau organization, it generally did not extend to field operations, with the one exception of Union logistics. Personalized and special staffs remained the rule, as they did for European armies except in Prussia.

McClellan's modification of this system indicated that he sensed the problem. But, like other Civil War field commanders, he did not make the transition to any semblance of the German staff organization. McClellan had a historical sense of change with respect to conditions affecting command and control. But though he made some innovations in the right direction, like his American contemporaries he failed to develop an adequate general staff concept.

McClellan did live in a military culture that appreciated how railroads had revolutionized strategic mobility by allowing massed concentration over great distance. The former railroad chief engineer and manager would express this awareness at the beginning of the Civil War, even while early war conditions limited the value of rail transportation to his campaigns.[3] An early appreciation of the strategic potential of railroads was a subsidiary benefit from the efforts of industry interests to convince the public to support their development. A lengthy discussion on railroads and strategy appeared in the military literature of the antebellum period. The debate indicated a dawning awareness that in this one area, war was total, an integration of broader technological, social, and economic realities in mass industrial society. But this awareness failed to integrate railroads into a broader strategic and organizational view of warfare.[4]

The involvement of army engineers in transportation development no doubt contributed to consciousness of the strategic capacity of railroads at the outbreak of war. At the same time, early models of railroad organization had a narrow technical definition of professionalism. Historical links consequently may have resulted in the army and railroads mutually reinforcing outlooks antagonistic to a modern general staff concept. Between 1821 and 1826, the U.S. Army established lines of authority and accountability. But the emphasis was on efficiency in moving information and orders rather than on a modern integrated structure for analysis and decision making. It was a case of bureaucratic form becoming the content.

There is controversy over the extent to which the young army officers who played a role in early railroad management brought military organization to the industry. Whether they brought their army experience or merely an analytical mode of reasoning from their military education is difficult to determine. But between 1827 and 1861, these managers, who would return to play a military role in the Civil War, did develop railroad organization with military antecedents.

The railroads came to run on a hierarchical bureaucratic model. Senior and middle managers coordinated and evaluated the work of line officers. Railroad management also developed new internal administrative procedures, including new accounting methods, and new ways to move information and instructions through the operational chain of command, including between managers and line officers. But the bureaucracy tended to become the end rather than the means. Efficiency and economy became the central issues. A cult of accountability came to dominate as the system bogged down in a limited technical ethos. If any broader vision was present, it existed in an unreceptive organizational environment.[5] The link between army and railroad development was not conducive to the development of a modern general staff concept.

FROM WESTERN VIRGINIA
TO THE PENINSULA

Such was the milieu in which George McClellan matured as a professional soldier. Such was the progression of his thought when, with the outbreak of the Civil War, he took a commission first as a general of Ohio volunteers, then as major general in the regular army in command of the Department of Ohio. In his first campaign, McClellan advocated battlefield turning maneuvers in combination with a tactical outlook that was consistent both with the teachings of his mentor Mahan and with his own Crimean War observations.

Assigned to drive a Confederate force of some 10,000 from strategic positions in the Kanawha Valley in Virginia, McClellan found General Robert Garnett—a former West Point commandant who had been a tactics instructor at the Academy—entrenched in well-chosen defensive positions. McClellan pronounced that "no prospect of a brilliant victory shall induce me to depart from my intention of gaining success by maneuvering rather than by fighting. I will not throw these raw men of mine into the teeth of artillery and entrenchments if it is possible to avoid it. A direct assault would result in a heavy and unnecessary loss of life." McClellan entrenched a holding force in front of Garnett's main position and, with a little luck and the efforts of a fellow officer from the Corps of Engineers, General W. S. Rosecrans, in command of the turning maneuver, turned the Confederates out of their positions.[6]

General Irvin McDowell, in command of Union troops at the First Battle of Manassas less than two weeks later, similarly entrenched his troops in a holding-turning maneuver, the engineering and pioneering troops doing the entrenching. McDowell's general order for the movement or return of troops indicated the extent of his commitment to tactical entrenchment:

> Each column is provided with entrenching tools and axes, and if the country affords facilities for obstructing our march, it also gives equal facilities for sustaining ourselves in any position we obtain. Troops will march without tents, and wagons will only be taken with them for ammunition, the medical department, and for *entrenching tools*.

McDowell's advocacy of the use of field fortification that extended even to the open field of battle was an early indication of the direction of tactical and related strategic thought in the eastern armies of the Union.[7]

The use of telegraph in the field for strategic communication during the western Virginia campaign was another significant precursor of later developments. McClellan was the first commander to use it in this way.

He notes resistance to this innovation from "old and experienced" officers, another anticipation of things to come. The use of Anson Stager's Telegraph Corps (later Military Telegraph), under the command of Captain Thomas David in the Department of Western Virginia, enabled McClellan to change the plan of battle three times in three days, probably an unprecedented event in military history.[8]

But McClellan was commanding a small, more easily maneuverable army. When he took command of the Union troops before Washington six days after the defeat at Manassas, he faced the task of dealing with a force that would grow to more than 100,000 men. McClellan's plan to transport this enormous army by sea around the Confederate positions reinforced his commitment to victory by strategic maneuver. To build, move, and support his army both at the supply base and in the field, he would have to overcome the early lack of coordination in the American military establishment, attributable both to the early "fog of war" and to basic organizational deficiencies. He also would have to cope with attitudes that supported the prevailing view of warfare, a problem enhanced by the public nature of a war fought not only on home soil but practically on the doorstep of the government. McClellan had to balance political pressure to protect Washington and political and public expectations of a quick victory against strictly military considerations of an organizational nature. His development of an army capable of strategic maneuver in the face of these obstacles would test his preparation as a professional soldier against the emerging realities of warfare, while political and public pressure would test his ability to cope with the friction of strategic decision making.

McClellan shared the general apprehension of the professional officer about his militia inheritance. The individualistic, localized, preindustrial community ideals of the militia tradition enhanced a wariness among citizen soldiers of centralized and regularized mass organization. Yet this tradition was a reality of institutional life that McClellan could not ignore. Problems of tactical discipline with nonregular officers and troops were particularly acute in the early stages of the war.[9] McClellan escaped the more extreme problems of mobilization within the militia system. As commander of the Army of the Potomac, he had the advantage of centralized organization in Federal training camps under the command of regular army personnel. He benefited from the Union decision to concentrate the permanent army.

McClellan sided with the general in chief, Winfield Scott, in his support of a tactical organization that kept the regular army separate. It had been argued that the regular army should be split up to train the volunteer brigades, which were suffering in training camp from a day-to-day shuffle of different officers using different drills and training techniques. The availability of 728 Academy graduates was sufficient, if so distributed, to train an army of half a million men. But Scott prevailed in keeping the regulars intact as a nucleus of an expandable army. McClellan supported Scott's view, except to provide regulars as general officers in command of new brigades.

By the spring of 1862, the Army of the Potomac had regular officers with Mexican War experience in command down through divisional level, including reserve divisions and some reserve brigades. But McClellan still depended heavily upon nonregulars in all areas of tactical and strategic organization. He showed ingenuity in improvised organization with citizen soldiers. But there is a question about how these nonregulars affected McClellan's confidence in his army and his consequent tactical and strategic decisions. His intermittent condemnation and praise of the citizen soldier reflected a continuing ambivalence about nonprofessionals; and his early tenure cost him the advantage of the citizen soldier maturing and adapting to the realities of modern warfare through experience.

McClellan altered the basic coordinating staff structure in a manner that reflected the ambiguity of the mesh of modern and traditional military culture that was his experience. He modified prevailing procedures with the appointment of a chief of staff for the Army of the Potomac. This was a concession to Continental staff theory not included in his prewar writings. Whether European precedent or common sense influenced his decision is open to question. But McClellan did not complete the Prussian general staff model. He failed to appoint staff officers to the lower command echelons, where the adjutant or adjutant general remained the principal staff officer.

In his memoirs, McClellan praised the Prussian system and attributed his failure to adopt it to a lack of trained officers.[10] But his memoirs were published in 1887, after the Prussian general staff had proved itself on the battlefield. His reports and correspondence during the preparation for the Peninsula campaign, as well as his private papers for his time in command, failed to express these retrospective insights. It is true that McClellan lacked officers with staff training. But he had the freedom to use some of the regular officers with staff ability with selected civilian soldiers with administrative and organizational experience to improvise a system on the Prussian model. There are no indications that his thoughts on staff went beyond his actions.

The task of staff organization was the framework for a complex of interacting problems that McClellan had to resolve to establish tactical and strategic mobility under the changed conditions of warfare. His commitment to strategic maneuver in combination with entrenched tactical dispositions presented numerous difficulties, which were compounded by inertia and resistance to change. The shortage of engineering officers and troops, for instance, hindered McClellan's attempts to organize the construction of field works. He kept up his pleas for engineering personnel, but a high proportion of the Corps of Engineers remained assigned to civilian work or to military tasks not connected to field operations, and connected only peripherally to the general conduct of the war.[11] When his attempts to persuade Lincoln and Congress to place higher official priority on the mobilization of engineering troops met with apathy and limited success, McClellan unofficially improvised an engineering organization from the ranks. Not until July, 1863, did Congress pass an act that accepted his precedent. Union field commanders in the western theater did not follow his lead until late in 1864.[12]

McClellan radically reorganized his artillery, as well. He implemented the plan of his chief of artillery, Major William F. Berry, to replace the battery organization with a Napoleonic form of concentration at the divisional level. McClellan also followed Napoleon in adopting a concentrated reserve. In the Army of the Potomac, this reserve originally numbered almost 40 percent of the total. The western armies of the Union did not reorganize in a divisional concentration with a general reserve until autumn, 1863. McClellan further bent doctrine with his emphasis on the defensive over the offensive role of artillery. McClellan sided with most artillery officers in preferring the smoothbore Napoleon to rifled artillery. Noting in particular that the wooded terrain of Virginia would nullify the effect of long-range rifled guns, he requested that two-thirds of his field guns be smoothbores, a request that could not be accommodated until the Maryland campaign that led to the Battle of Antietam.[13]

In his artillery organization, McClellan had the advantage of drawing heavily from the regular army, and he received, as requested, half the total artillery of the regular army equipped as field batteries. Just under half his total of 299 pieces at the time of the Peninsula campaign were manned by regular officers.[14]

In addition to reorganizing for the tactical defense, McClellan confronted organizational problems that were pertinent both to tactical movement and maneuver, and to the broader problem of strategic mobility. Maneuvering the extended lines of mass armies required a high level of discipline and coordination. Tactical doctrine emphasized a primary deployment in line from a column of march. The new firepower of the rifled musket would extend deployment in line. This, in turn, would spread out the order of march, as the columns of the tactical units had to march far enough apart to allow for the extended deployment in line of battle. With the increasingly extended front in large armies with large supply trains, and with the greater area of exposed flank that had to be covered in tactical deployment, the field commander could no longer personally control the order of movement and battle. He could lay out the plan, but then he had to depend upon his communications and command procedures, his personnel and technical resources. Densely wooded terrain and an inadequate road system exacerbated these organizational problems.

Staff theory and organization constituted the major procedural problem. There was not an adequate concept or structure to coordinate the tactical components of a large mid-nineteenth-century army in undulating and wooded terrain. McClellan inherited staff procedures so distended they did not even include topographical surveying and intelligence as staff functions. For example, he prepared for the Peninsula campaign without accurate topographical information and with a civilian detective agency for his intelligence organization.

Organizational problems combined with the technical problems affecting the mobility of armies. Chief of these was the underdeveloped and experimental state of military signals so essential to tactical mobility.[15] The application of telegraphic technology would dominate Civil War and particularly Union signals organization. Signals development was motivated in part by the natural momentum of new technology carried from civilian to military organization. But the primary motive was recognition of the benefits of this technology to tactical and strategic coordination. The increasingly extended lines of large American armies, especially their tactical extension with the rifled musket, as well as the rough terrain, challenged existing technology based on wigwag signals supplemented by couriers. The previous organization of signals as merely a special staff function was also challenged. At the same time, innovation brought all the psychological and organizational problems of change for army officers asked to abandon familiar technology and doctrine.

McClellan was an innovator in signals development. He was also a victim of the usual transitional problems, which were accentuated by the lack of an adequate staff system to implement change in command and control procedures. Both as commander of the Army of the Potomac and as general in chief, McClellan reinforced his early sensitivity to the use of telegraphic signals during his campaign in western Virginia. Upon assuming command of the Army of the Potomac, McClellan, on August 20, 1861, appointed Alfred J. Myer, who had developed a system of semaphores with a telegraphic alphabet, signal officer of the Army of the Potomac. When McClellan succeeded Winfield Scott as general in chief, he additionally appointed Myer signal officer of the U.S. Army. It was the first such appointment in military history. McClellan can be credited with originating the process that would institutionalize the Signal Corps as a branch of military service.

Electrical telegraphic communication adapted to military needs had received a stormy introduction to Union signals organization. Experiments with telegraphy in European armies began with the British in the Crimean War, but only the Prussian army had an electrical system of military telegraph as a permanent part of army organization prior to the Civil War. Civilian telegraphic communication, on the other hand, was well established in the United States by the Civil War. Three companies had connected all of the cities and many towns, except in the West. And Western Union had spread a line to San Francisco during the winter of 1861–62. Shortly after Fort Sumter, Secretary of War Simon Cameron, in April, 1861, had Thomas Scott, president of the Pennsylvania Railroad, set up the Military Telegraph primarily to provide administrative lines. Although the Military Telegraph was successful in maintaining strategic communications as early as the western Virginia campaign and Bull Run, Lincoln did not give legitimacy to its role within army organization until October, 1861. Thereafter it performed well and was accepted as the source of communications, though its independence of military authority remained an annoyance to field commanders. The attempt by the Military Telegraph also to take over telegraphic tactical communications from the Signal Corps created a jurisdictional dispute that lasted most of the war.

Much of this conflict was attributable to Anson Stager, the Western Union official who was head of the Military Telegraph. Ambitious and aggressive, Stager had a mature organization and militarily adaptable telegraphic technology developed through civilian experience. Armed with the money and the free-enterprise zeal of his backers, he lobbied hard against Myer's Signal Corps for control of military telegraph. At the same time, he lobbied successfully, with the enthusiastic support of Secretary of War Stanton, for independence from the military hierarchy in the operation of the system. Although personnel of the Military Telegraph were commissioned in the Quartermaster Department, and for administrative convenience were technically under the command of the quartermaster general, in practice, Secretary of War Stanton directly controlled its operation.

Stager and Myer came into immediate jurisdictional dispute as ideological, professional, and personal considerations clouded a common-sense division of authority in which the Military Telegraph would be responsible for strategic communications and the Signal Corps for tactical communications. With telegraphic signals not a formal part of Myer's authority, Stager aggressively pushed the case for the Military Telegraph's organizational and technological advantages. Myer and his Signal Corps were vulnerable. Myer seems initially to have preferred visual over telegraphic signals. There is no evidence that he appreciated European military experiments with telegraphy, including tactical communications, even though he had been familiar with them from student days.[16] He didn't pursue telegraphic experiments until Stager challenged the authority of the Signal Corps. Myer's ad hoc improvisation with a portable electric telegraph had potential, but his Signal Corps was at a technological and organizational disadvantage against the Military Telegraph.

The jurisdictional conflict was secondary to McClellan's basic problem of improvising a modern signals organization, whatever the source. Originally, Myer had set up a central camp of instruction in Georgetown, just outside Washington. But organizational experimentation in the field by General Ambrose Burnside during the "Burnside Expedition" set the pattern for training that would thereafter prevail in the Union army. Burnside received the second detachment from Myer's camp in late December, 1861, and assigned it to run a training camp which instructed twenty-two officers and a proportionate number of men for his army. McClellan followed Burnside's example. When the signal demands of the Army of the Potomac grew so great that they claimed Myer himself and emptied the signal camp at Georgetown, McClellan transferred the training of the Signal Corps to field camps.

Signals organization in the field was a further problem. With his enormous army's appetite for trained personnel, McClellan could not afford to assign trained signal officers from the field to staff a permanent camp. He also encountered the not-unexpected resistance to signals duty by both officers and men. Beyond the normal aversion to innovation in military or other organizational structures, there was resentment of the practice of temporary assignment to the Signal Corps accompanied by random recall to the original unit. This practice interrupted career stability and affected promotional opportunities. The situation would not be alleviated until June, 1862, when a general order forbade recall without the permission of the adjutant general of the U.S. Army.

A related problem was the reluctance of divisional commanders in an army short of trained officers to commit valuable men to what they conservatively considered the lower priority of signals. When discretionary details provided unsatisfactory results, McClellan gave strict orders for assignment that gathered about 80 officers and 160 enlisted men. But continuing resistance from an officer corps that did not wish to legitimize a new branch of service stalled legislation for an independent Signal Corps until March 3, 1863. This reluctance would be reflected in the difficulties of establishing signals instruction at West Point, which was not introduced as part of the regular curriculum until July, 1863. It was casually discontinued late the same year, as the acting signal officer of the U.S. Army, William Nicodemus, would wryly note, for "some cause unknown," despite the existence of a War Department order to the contrary. Signaling would not return to West Point until 1867.[17]

The technical problems of early signals development compounded organizational dilemmas. Telegraphic signals worked well in strategic communications, where Stager's Morse equipment adapted to military usage proved its worth from the beginning. Remembering his experience in western Virginia, McClellan gave Stager a vote of confidence. He issued an order on November 25, 1861, to give Stager all assistance,[18] anticipating the general order of April 8, 1862, to give all aid to the Military Telegraph.[19] The Military Telegraph functioned well during the Peninsula campaign, sustaining strategic communications between headquarters and the army during the movement to the Peninsula, connecting all the headquarters on the Peninsula, and keeping McClellan advised on all operations along his front. It also maintained strategic communication for Union troops fighting Jackson in the Shenandoah Valley. The major technical problem involved tactical communication.

The Signal Corps struggled with extended lines in American terrain which offered limited visibility for visual signals. Myer's neglect of telegraphic signals resulted in his hasty improvisation of a portable telegraph field train to fend off Stager's attempt to take over all military telegraph. Myer had hoped to have more advanced experimental equipment ready for the Peninsula. But it was not ready, owing to technical problems and the lack of authorization to continue development. Myer consequently sent his alternate choice, a field train equipped with the experimental Beardslee electromagnetic telegraph. The shortage of adequately trained personnel and technical deficiencies limited its usefulness. Though a feasible experiment, the Beardslee suffered from short range, often got out of synchronization between sending and receiving, was slow, and was limited in its portability.

The Signal Corps, however, was to play out its role with visual signals based upon Myer's development of a modern system of semaphores with a telegraphic alphabet. Myer also developed a cipher disk early in the war that enabled the Union Signal Corps to change the code hourly if need be. This nearly eliminated the problem of interception. But even with visual signals, there were early technical and personnel problems that required time and experience to resolve.

Problems of tactical mobility were part of the larger issue of strategic mobility. McClellan faced unprecedented difficulties in moving his large army to the Peninsula, sustaining it once there, and moving the troops in the field. His greatest task was to find sufficient field transportation. His principal organizational problems in this regard were to work out an adequate standard for baggage, field supply, and field transportation, and to develop a system to meet those standards in the field away from the base of supply.

The baggage problem was difficult. Officers and men alike insisted on an unrealistic standard of living in the field. The quartermaster general, Montgomery Meigs, began early to strive toward the Napoleonic standard of baggage. But he admitted that through the initial stages of the war, there was no established wagon allowance in the baggage train. Generals commanding troops in the field made requests of Meigs ranging from fifteen wagons per regiment to six.

Nor was there a set of transportation standards for the supply train for subsistence and forage. To complicate matters more, the Civil War feed allowance for animals was probably inadequate for an army in the field. By contemporary standards of animal nutrition, the provision for horses was sufficient only in the Union camps, where it was excessive.[20] For a good day's march, regulation forage would give a 1,600-pound horse about 70 to 75 percent of its requirements. Under extreme conditions, horses received less than 60 percent of needs. The standard for mules was better, providing 80 to 90 percent of the requirements of a normal day's march. The unanticipated consequences of this hidden nutritional factor would contribute to an abnormal attrition of horses. This would be particularly disruptive because the immature supply system of the early fighting was not a trustworthy source of replacement.

A statistical analysis of Civil War field supply and transportation also suggests what experience would verify: that the early Napoleonic mode of logistical thinking placed too much emphasis on foraging for American conditions. The supply train carried twelve pounds grain per horse and nine to ten pounds per mule.[21] This left the remaining fourteen pounds of hay or fodder in the horses' standard of twenty-six pounds and the mules' standard of twenty-three to twenty-four pounds to be foraged. According to John Moore's statistical projections for Civil War logistics, even the most populous of Civil War campaigning areas would have difficulty meeting that requirement under ideal conditions. The expectations were completely unrealistic in a country that had been foraged during the previous passage of armies. Even Jomini noted that the Napoleonic system, designed for the populous area and mature road systems of western Europe, broke down in thinly populated country.

Meigs's advocacy of the Napoleonic standard of twelve wagons per 1,000 men for all the needs of an army in the field was far too restrictive by Moore's statistical calculations for the army's basic needs.[22] It also failed to recognize that the ration standard, and the corresponding transportation burden, of the American soldier was double that of the Napoleonic soldier. All of these factors were burdens to McClellan's strategic mobility should he attempt to move any distance for any length of time away from his base of supply. But formal standards of baggage, supply, and transportation at the time of the Peninsula campaign were merely distant objectives amid a scramble to meet immediate practical needs. Supplying a mass army was a new American experience. Inadequately trained, understaffed, and poorly organized, the supply departments were as raw as the troops in the field. McClellan complained after the war that the heads of some supply departments had a difficult transition from their Mexican War outlook to a realistic appreciation of the problems of supplying mass armies.[23]

Montgomery Meigs admitted to much waste and some fumbling in the Quartermaster Department. Considering the deficiencies of staff organization, the department performed well to prepare and move the Army of the Potomac. It was able to save time when the government bypassed contract competition and requisitioned crucial materials.

The Army of the Potomac began the Peninsula campaign with a standard of 45 wagons per 1,000 men. It had 21,000–25,000 horses and mules for the trains and approximately 5,000 wagons for approximately 110,000 men present for duty. Advocates of the Napoleonic standard of 12 wagons per 1,000 men, such as Meigs, would understandably look askance at McClellan's transportation standard. Yet, John Moore's statistical analysis of Civil War transportation needs suggests that it was realistic, especially considering early organizational problems that frustrated the attempt to cut down on excessive baggage and unauthorized additions to the supply trains.[24]

The regulation load of a four-horse team on good roads was 2,800 pounds. For a six-mule team on a macadamized road, it was 4,000–4,500 pounds; on a solid dirt road, 3,000–3,500 pounds; and on a dirt track in rough country, 1,800–2,500 pounds, plus, in all cases, five to ten days' grain for themselves. On good roads the regulation speed was two and one-half miles per hour.[25] Normal campaigning conditions were dirt tracks, emphasizing another factor in any calculation of Civil War wagon standards.

Union control of the sea enabled McClellan to move out of the Washington entrenchments and bypass the Confederate land defenses that blocked the overland route to Richmond. On the Peninsula, the supply bureaus again performed quite well under the circumstances. They established depots and resupplied them by sea. Their failure to ship horses for the supply trains when they shipped the wagons slowed the campaign. It also demonstrated the inadequacies of staff procedures, as well as the inexperience of both field officers and quartermaster personnel. But the Quartermaster Department learned from its errors, and the Army of the Potomac, except for periodic shortages of wagons, had sufficient supplies.

Yet there was an accompanying awareness of the limitations of movement away from supply depots.[26] Considering the lack of experience, the limited personnel, and the built-in deficiencies in the system, the performance of the supply bureaus was quite impressive. At the outset, Meigs had appropriately noted that "a few days or weeks only have been allowed for the outfit of expeditions which other nations would spend months in preparing."[27] Once the Army of the Potomac was on the Peninsula, the supply bureaus managed to supply what for the time was equivalent to the population of a large American city. They carried this mass army through a protracted offensive campaign and then supplied it during a lengthy withdrawal. The greatest weakness was in the distribution of goods, a problem again attributable to the combination of inexperience and an inadequate staff system.

Once in the field, McClellan's army hung from this immature structure for tactical and strategic mobility. McClellan's maneuver by sea to the Virginia Peninsula below Yorktown did not interfere with Confederate communications, nor did it solve the problem of getting past the entrenched defenses behind which the Confederates blocked his route up the Peninsula to Richmond. At Yorktown, McClellan found his way barred by three bastioned lines. This was the most formidable of field work systems, in which bastioned forts which afford mutual flanking are connected by rifle trenches with parapets. McClellan immediately felt the shortcomings of his staff procedures. He bemoaned "the want of precise topographical information." Worse still, available information was generally so inaccurate as to lead troops astray. Surveying as he went, McClellan did have his topographical engineers prepare maps, which were to be useful in later campaigns in the area.[28] McClellan was encountering, as he aptly put it, "causes . . . which frustrated . . . expectations." And he suffered the frictions and frustrations of being first.

Existing command procedures prevented the coordination of McClellan's troop movements in the forests of the Peninsula. Tactical communication was a particular problem. The ground was usually too flat and wooded for the use of Myer's new and relatively untried semaphore system of visual signals. The experimental telegraph train with the Beardslee equipment was late to arrive, then broke down because of technical failures and a shortage of skilled operators.[29] Inaccurate intelligence reports from the Pinkerton detective agency exaggerated Confederate numbers, though there is reason to question McClellan's military judgment about probable numbers. And nature compounded problems when rain turned already poor roads to muddy mires. All of the problems no doubt reinforced political and perhaps personality, cultural, and ideological motives that weighed on the side of McClellan's caution.

The presence of a Confederate ironclad prevented the Union navy from getting up the James to assist in a flanking operation. McClellan abandoned all hope of turning the Confederate positions when Lincoln, in response to Jackson's diversionary movement into the Shenandoah Valley, ordered McDowell's troops en route to turn the Yorktown positions back to protect Washington. "It was now out of my power to turn Yorktown," McClellan wrote. "I had . . . no choice left but to attack it directly in front, as I best could with the force at my command."[30] Allowing for political and other motives contributing to the "fog" or "friction" of early Civil War field command, McClellan, as a student of strategy, was no doubt appreciating the reservations of Jomini about circumstances conducive to maneuver.

But McClellan did not equate direct frontal attack with open frontal assaults. In accordance with formal tactical doctrine for the assault of a bastioned system of field works, he laid siege to one section of the line. Although his use of offensive entrenchments for siege operations was orthodox doctrine, his actions emphasized his commitment to the undercurrent in American tactical thought that opposed quick resort to the open frontal assault.

With politicians, the press, and most military men expecting McClellan to carry the enemy works by open assault tactics, his refusal to be stampeded perhaps suggested, among other motives, his commitment to his tactical outlook. It also reinforced his consistent refusal to use the open assault against an entrenched enemy. Because of its limited presence in the Confederate army at this early stage of the war, the rifled musket could not have been a significant motive. The unexpected need to arm mass armies had caught the American arsenals so short as to leave both the Union and Confederate forces armed largely with smoothbore weapons until late 1862. McClellan's commitment to the tactical defense early in the war would have to be based on motives similar to Mahan's earlier nontechnological arguments.[31] His improvisation of an engineering organization to conduct the siege further reflected his attempts to reorganize for the tactical realities of modern warfare.[32]

Johnston, fearing a turning movement by land or water, withdrew from the Yorktown defenses. When McClellan, in pursuit, moved into an unoccupied section of the previously prepared Williamsburg fortification, Johnston withdrew to the Richmond defenses, all the while drawing McClellan directly up the Peninsula with no chance for maneuver. McClellan stopped his pursuing wing at the Chickahominy River, nine miles from Richmond, to await the remainder of his army before advancing on Richmond. While waiting, he dug in, committing himself again to entrenched positions in offensive operations. Although there was an underlying trend in even orthodox doctrine that allowed fortification in the field when positions were even momentarily defensive, as these were, it was reluctantly acknowledged by most military men and politicians in the early stages of the Civil War.

But Johnston, unwilling to sit and wait for McClellan to unite his forces, attacked McClellan's entrenched positions. The attack displayed the advantages of the entrenched defense and the difficulties of assault tactics. Johnston encountered his own problems of command procedure and tactical communications with green troops in difficult terrain. Uncoordinated Confederate divisions went in piecemeal. Union troops repulsed the first Confederate attack at their entrenchments and abatis. The battle deteriorated into a large-scale firefight, with both sides improvising shelter wherever and whenever they could find it. Indicative of the changing tactical realities, frontal assaults, coordinated movements, all the niceties of organized warfare, gave way to the hastily entrenched battlefield.[33] After two days of this firefight, the Confederates withdrew.

Because of muddy roads, the other wing of the Union army was unable, in McClellan's opinion, to get to Fair Oaks to "unite the two wings of the army in time to make a vigorous pursuit of the enemy, with the prospect of overtaking him before he reached Richmond." McClellan refused, in the best Jominian tradition, to undertake "an advance involving the separation of the two wings by the impassable (flood swollen) Chickahominy, which would have exposed each to defeat in detail." Consequently, while waiting for the other wing to join him, he ordered his troops at Fair Oaks "to strengthen their positions by a strong line of entrenchments, which protected them while the bridges were being built, gave security to the trains, liberated a larger fighting force; and offered a safer retreat in the event of disaster."[34] The consistency of his tactical commitment grew. That was June 1. On June 25, "our bridges and entrenchments being at last completed," McClellan ordered "an advance of his picket line preparatory to a general forward movement." The entrenched enemy strongly resisted. Then on June 26, "the day upon which I had decided as the time for our final advance, the enemy attacked our right in strong force, and turned my attention to the protection of our communications and depots of supplies."

It was with good reason that McClellan worried about his supply lines. With poor communications and intelligence, he had no accurate information on Stonewall Jackson's location or numbers. He knew only that Jackson had turned his right and threatened his communications on the north bank of the Chickahominy. Also, the inaccurate intelligence reports of Pinkerton's civilian agency led him to overestimate the enemy's numbers in the Richmond fortifications as being greater than his own, although there are grounds for the charge that McClellan believed the less than believable. More realistic and less cautious military estimates were in order. But again, real organizational problems, though no doubt combined with other motives, encouraged McClellan's cautious behavior.

McClellan argued that he could not concentrate on the north bank because the enemy held the roads leading to his supply depot. In his estimate, it would have been impossible to send forward supply trains in advance of the army in that direction, and the guarding of those trains would have "seriously embarrassed our operations in the battle." Also, McClellan noted that the forces on the Richmond side of the river could have fallen on his rear if he had moved his south bank forces from in front of the Richmond defenses.

Tactically consistent, McClellan refused to storm the strong Richmond defenses. He maintained that he did not have adequate rations— owing largely to the shortage of supply wagons—to undertake the lengthy siege he considered necessary to overcome the extensive system of bastioned works. He predicted, if again perhaps overcautiously, that if defeated at Richmond he would lose his supply train before he could retreat to the flotilla waiting on the James River fifteen miles below Richmond. Unable to move offensively, McClellan chose to transfer his army to this base of supplies on the James.[35] The enemies' withdrawal from Yorktown, coupled with Union destruction of the *Merrimac*, now opened the river to Union gun boats, made it secure as a supply route, and left McClellan's flanks protected.

The pervading tone of the Federal battle reports during the offensive operations around Richmond was uncertainty and confusion as commanders and field officers struggled with coordination in dense forests with roads turned to mud by heavy rains. Insufficient topographical information, problems of coordinating field operations with the extended lines of a mass army with an inferior staff and communications system, an inadequate system of supply, and inaccurate intelligence with the fate of an army and possibly a nation in the balance gave McClellan legitimate cause for caution as he coped with the fog of early Civil War field command.

McClellan's command problems deriving from his lack of a modern concept of staff were compounded by a further failing in staff outlook, personality, or both. He did not delegate authority.[36] In his predisposition to run the show himself, he was still very much an eighteenth-century field commander. This tendency revealed itself most visibly in movements after the Confederate evacuation of Yorktown. McClellan's staff headquarters broke down completely under the combined weight of inexperience and inadequate procedures. Not a single division in the Army of the Potomac had the rations or transportation for immediate movement. McClellan reacted to this crisis by increasingly assuming personal authority for decisions deep into his command structure. He supervised logistics; he posted troops; he inspected postings and directed sundry other details.

The dilemma that his staff system was inadequate to coordinate his army must have come abruptly home to McClellan when officers with staff responsibility frequently failed or refused to follow orders; at the same time, they refused to take the initiative to lead. Inexperienced, short in numbers, and without a system that clearly defined their responsibilities and coordinated their activities, they floundered. McClellan lost faith in his staff without seeing the problem in terms of organization. In fairness to McClellan, there is evidence that the inefficiencies and negligence of the chief quartermaster, General Stewart Van Vliet, and some of his subordinates, went beyond mere problems of organization.

But McClellan's casual change of plan in his movements from Yorktown to the Chickahominy, as well as his neglect to properly coordinate his plan with the Navy, showed a striking failure to comprehend both the logistical problems he created and the inability of his staff to handle them. Perhaps his success while changing plans three times in three days in his western Virginia campaign had bred false confidence. If so, it is remarkable that so meticulous a military thinker did not see that the lessons of fighting with the small army of the western Virginia campaign could not be applied to an army in excess of 100,000 men. The blind spot of staff organization seemed to reflect McClellan's professional education in a view of warfare more oriented to tactics and technological technique than to strategic organization.

McClellan was not without an eye for organizational talent. He saw Colonel Rufus Ingalls in the quartermaster department of his army and began to rely on him to hold together his provisional supply system. Yet McClellan's continued practice of giving orders for difficult logistical assignments without consultation or warning, and not having quartermaster or ordnance personnel accompany supplies, continued to create confusion.

McClellan's greatest logistical disaster occurred during the retreat to the James. Inadequate staff procedures to move the trains were largely responsible for a loss of almost half his 5,000 wagons, reducing the army to 2,578 wagons for just under 100,000 men present for duty. This was a standard of only 26 wagons per 1,000 men. Yet the army coped reasonably well during the retreat, in part no doubt because of Ingalls's efforts to hold together the ad hoc organization to move the trains. In the aftermath of the Peninsula campaign, Ingalls, promoted by McClellan to chief quartermaster of the Army of the Potomac, would be the first to establish an order of march for the wagon trains, with an accompanying staff system to make it work.

In another failure to improvise a staff system, McClellan failed to use his cavalry as guides. In one resulting incident, General Fitz John Porter, with only one cavalry guide, got lost en route to Malvern Hill. An example of staff breakdown on the retreat to the James perhaps best reflected McClellan's reluctance to delegate authority. The retreat was delayed for a day and a half when General John Barnard, a distinguished professional soldier in command of the engineers in the Army of the Potomac, was slow to respond to McClellan's order to send out engineers to reconnoiter and select new positions for the retreating army. Barnard's failure to follow orders may have been a highly unprofessional object lesson, on his part, to emphasize his complaint about McClellan's excessive interference without due consultation in his engineering command. In the case of Barnard, the Union army's most distinguished engineer, McClellan had no basis for complaining that lack of professional competence was grounds for interference.

It is consistent with McClellan's theoretical predisposition that his one movement toward modern staff development was in siege operations. He attempted to resolve the early chaos of such operations on the Peninsula by appointing a "director of the siege"; a subordinate "general of the trenches," usually a brigade commander on a twenty-four-hour tour of duty, reported to the director and implemented his orders of the day. Even this specialized and limited breakthrough to a modern staff concept should not be minimized. In a professional world view disposed to technical and tactical concerns, staff theory was the great void. Even McClellan's limited vision in one area was unusual for this stage of the war or later.

McClellan's experience with the experimental state of signals during the Peninsula campaign reflected his commitment to technological invention. While Stager's Military Telegraph would prove its value in strategic communications from the beginning, Myer's Signal Corps encountered nothing but problems in tactical communications. The dense woods of the Peninsula made visual signaling extremely difficult. The construction of observation towers gave the Signal Corps limited success, but only at Malvern Hill were signals reasonably effective. More typical was Seven Pines, where terrain rendered visual signals impossible. The extension of the Beardslee telegraph line from McClellan's headquarters to General Stoneman's at Mechanicsville on May 24 was the first use of the portable field telegraph by an American army. Some success was mixed with failure, mostly as a result of equipment limitations or breakdown, or inadequately trained personnel. As might be expected at this early stage of signals development, the ground lines were carelessly cut, not only by wagons running over them, but also by curious and poorly disciplined soldiers casually cutting the wire. But McClellan, in his reports on the campaign, kept the vision he had displayed in his early support of signals innovation. He continued his practical efforts to secure a place for the Signal Corps in formal military organization, applauded the performance of its experimental telegraph train, and praised its performance in battle.

McClellan's support of technological innovation extended even to giving Professor T. S. C. Lowe's gas-filled balloons a place in his tactical organization. He early encouraged Lowe in the military use of his balloons to make observations from the defenses of Washington. A pioneer in antebellum balloon development, Lowe successfully lobbied the Union army to make use of his balloons through the mediation of Professor Joseph Henry, secretary of the Smithsonian Institute, Secretary of War Simon Cameron, and the Corps of Topographical Engineers.

The balloon was invented in 1783, but was little improved until the mid-nineteenth century. Lowe led the way in developing balloons durable enough for long-range place-to-place transportation and, crucial to military use, for frequent and extended periods of observation. He also advanced the technology of getting balloons inflated fast enough to be used with some frequency—a minimum of three hours fifteen minutes, according to Lowe, and after spring, 1863, two hours thirty minutes. The only prior use of balloons for military observation had been by the French, who made limited use of them for reconnaissance during the Revolutionary Wars and at the Battle of Solferino in 1859. But Lowe's balloons were the first to be used regularly for military purposes, giving the Union Aeronautic Department—later the Aeronautic Corps—a special place in the origins of military aeronautics.

McClellan ensured that Lowe had his chance in early field operations. After making useful observations from the Washington defenses, he took Lowe's balloons to the Peninsula, where they proved a valuable vehicle for observations on troop movements, the location of the enemy's entrenchments, and mapping. Lowe's balloons made the first civilian telegraph communications from a balloon on June 18, 1861, and the first military telegraph communications from a balloon during the Peninsula campaign. Admiral Foote made a significant use of one of Lowe's balloons to telegraph indirect ranging and firing instructions that enabled his fleet to concentrate its fire during its successful attack on Island No. 10. After the Peninsula, the balloons returned to Washington; they arrived too late for the Battle of Antietam, owing largely, it appears, to a foul-up in staff procedures. But they again provided useful observations at Fredericksburg and Chancellorsville. General Joseph Hooker, who assumed command of the Army of the Potomac for the Chancellorsville campaign, was less appreciative of Lowe than McClellan and Ambrose Burnside. Uncomfortable with Lowe's independence and disrespect for formal lines of military authority, Burnside placed his balloons under the command of the chief engineer of the Army of the Potomac, who effectively pushed Lowe out of the service. The balloon service was terminated shortly thereafter, and the equipment was handed over to Alfred Myer in his capacity as signal officer in the Army of the Potomac. Myer, no doubt distracted by other problems and priorities, showed little interest in finding the money and men to continue the service. He sent the balloon train to Washington, where it was disbanded. As Russell J. Parkinson, the historian of early American aeronautics, observes, the balloon service proved too novel a technical service to find a place in service doctrine. It seems to have been the one change too many in the rapidly changing milieu of old service doctrine adapting its ideas and organization to new technology. Parkinson further notes that the rejection of free-flight ballooning in favor of the more conservative fixed observation balloons anchored by ropes made the balloon "in essence a portable observation tower," properly belonging to the Signal Corps, but as such, it "contributed nothing to the art of war." Perhaps Myer shared these sentiments when, after attachment to the Topographical Engineers, the Quartermaster Department, and the Corps of Engineers, the balloons finally landed in his lap. Balloons successfully established their limited place largely as specialized technical services on the personal staffs of field commanders. While giving McClellan high marks in this respect for encouraging Lowe, McClellan rejected Lowe's more revolutionary competitor, John La Mountain, who had success on the staffs of Major General Benjamin Butler at Fortress Monroe, and Brigadier General William B. Franklin's division in the Army of the Potomac between September 27, 1861, and February 19, 1862. La Mountain advocated free ballooning over enemy lines on favorable surface winds from the east, rising with the discard of ballast to return on favorable west winds. As Parkinson notes, free ballooning had revolutionary and unrealized potential for long-range and strategic observation. McClellan's support of Lowe brought military aeronautics through a significant historical development, but its time had not yet come.[37]

At the same time that McClellan encouraged technological innovation, he did not assume the necessary organizational initiative in the conflict between Stager and Myer. A common-sense division of authority would, as noted, have placed Stager's Military Telegraph in charge of strategic communications and Myer's Signal Corps in charge of tactical communications. To divide authority along technological lines, as Stager wished, rather than along functional lines, was poor organization. Although this technological division, with the Military Telegraph gaining control over all telegraph, was not a practical problem for McClellan, the jurisdictional dispute went on nevertheless. And McClellan remained silent when he should have played the key role in resolving the controversy.

McClellan would not be around to be party to Lincoln's decision of November, 1863, that would place field telegraph under the control of Stager's Military Telegraph, or for Stager's subsequent replacement of the Beardslee equipment with conventional telegraph lines. But he could have made early decisions that would have prevented the division of authority in tactical communications. Not until 1865, when it was too late to have effect, would the Military Telegraph and Signal Corps, on Myer's initiative, begin to discuss formal procedures for the coordination of the two signals organizations.

Reflecting McClellan's theoretical and organizational strength, his withdrawal to the James was a skilled display of entrenched defensive tactics.[38] Fighting also revealed the conflicting currents of contemporary tactical thought. Lee planned to defeat McClellan with battlefield flanking maneuvers, but failed for the increasingly familiar complex of organizational reasons. Left with no alternative but a tactical solution, he committed himself to frontal assaults against McClellan's entrenched positions. In the Battle of Mechanicsville and the series of actions known as the Seven Days' Battles, McClellan repeatedly repulsed Lee's attacks.[39] Lee found that the rough terrain made it as difficult for him to approach McClellan's well-chosen position as it had been for McClellan during his offensive. Lee's tactical coordination frequently broke down as the lines of volunteers made their way through forest and swamps and up rugged hillsides. McClellan proved the effectiveness of his controversial concentration of artillery for the tactical defense. Lee was unable to bring his artillery into play because of the terrain. In the one instance where he did, at Malvern Hill, he failed to concentrate his batteries. McClellan's concentrated artillery drove them to cover the moment they appeared. The infantry had to carry the attack alone. In perhaps the most spectacular artillery display of the war, McClellan's concentrated artillery accounted for over half of the Confederate losses.[40]

At the Battle of Mechanicsville, the Confederate attackers suffered approximately 2,000 casualties, six times those of the entrenched Federals; at Gaines Mill, 8,000 compared to 4,000—and one Confederate division lost over 1,000 men in a single charge.[41] These statistics and Confederate tactical failure seemed to justify McClellan's pronouncement after the Peninsula campaign that "new levies—cannot be expected to advance without cover under—the fire from defenses and carry them by assault."[42] Events were supporting Mahan's and McClellan's reservations about the cost of the open frontal assault. In areas other than tactics, McClellan failed to transcend the theoretical models and organizational structures of American military culture.

THE MARYLAND CAMPAIGN, ANTIETAM AND AFTER

When McClellan took command of the Army of the Potomac to check Lee's raid into Maryland, he returned to the problems he had left. The tactical development of the Battle of Antietam generally reinforced the lessons of the Peninsula, though there were some anomalous developments to confuse tactical issues. McClellan's most conspicuous departure from past form was his failure to entrench at Antietam. Was he intimidated by the criticism that had surrounded his conduct of the Peninsula campaign, particularly criticism of his entrenching activity as a symbol of his "defensive cast of mind"? Was the intimidation intensified by Lee's failure to entrench at Antietam? Did McClellan believe that circumstances dictated he be offensive in appearance as well as in action? One can only speculate.

The lessons of Antietam were certainly against the continuing use of open infantry assault tactics. The battle produced the worst single day's slaughter of the Civil War. McClellan again displayed the effectiveness of his defensive artillery tactics against attacking infantry. And in his own offensive actions, he confirmed the problem of conventional assault tactics in two lines. The 2nd Division, one of the most experienced and best-led of the Army of the Potomac, had its lines intermingle, with loss of order and tactical control, when it attacked with close lines in an attempt to reduce the impact of rifle fire.[43]

McClellan did achieve at Antietam an anomaly in Civil War tactics: the effective use of rifled artillery fire in offensive support of infantry assaults. Although McClellan was critical of the value of rifled artillery, he made the best of his opportunities. When circumstances offered the chance to concentrate his artillery on the heights of the east bank of Antietam Creek, he was quick to make the most of it. To add to the tactical potpourri, the orthodox advocates of assault tactics were even accorded another Federal bayonet attack to accompany the two that had occurred during the Peninsula campaign.

McClellan did not adjust as creatively to the changing tactical nature of warfare in handling his cavalry arm as in handling infantry and artillery. He reduced his cavalry, as on the Peninsula, to subsidiary tactical roles. He had conventionally divided his already limited cavalry on the Peninsula for distribution among divisions and corps rather than concentrating them for long-range reconnaissance, for raiding, and for coping with the concentrated cavalry of the enemy under Jeb Stuart. One result of this failure was Stuart's embarrassing raid and unobstructed ride around McClellan's army. McClellan did note the crucial role of cavalry in reconnaissance during the Peninsula campaign, while he complained of insufficient mounts for the purpose.[44] After a bad start, he made better use of cavalry for reconnaissance during the retreat from the Chickahominy to Harrison's Landing. But the improvement was the result of increasing experience rather than the needed reorganization to free more troops for strategic roles.

Within the tactical organization of cavalry, McClellan failed to anticipate such developments as their use as mobile mounted infantry. The Union cavalry had played a peripheral tactical role in the fighting on the Peninsula. They had been used in one instance to decoy the Confederate infantry by sounding artillery bugle calls and deploying as a battery. McClellan had made one attempt to concentrate 250 troopers of the 5th Cavalry, the largest concentration in the army, to throw back the Confederate breakthrough of the Union lines at Gaines Mill. The fact that even the disorganized and battered Confederate infantry quickly dispersed the attack, killing 150 of the 250 troopers, was further indication of the obsolescence of orthodox cavalry tactics. The most practical use McClellan found for his cavalry was a novel deployment in close-order skirmish line to his rear to prevent straggling during the Battle of Malvern Hill.

At Antietam, McClellan repeated his conventional tactical organization of cavalry. This time, though, he concentrated his entire cavalry force behind the center of his line to serve as follow-up support for an infantry breakthrough. It is surprising that a commander so sensitive to the effect of rifled fire on infantry tactics would ignore the lesson to be learned from the success of the Confederate infantry at Gaines Mill against the Union's mounted counterattack.

McClellan concentrated his cavalry at the cost of using it to protect his flanks, a decision that drew criticism. Again at Antietam, McClellan acknowledged the role of cavalry to cover the flanks, but complained, as he had with regard to the reconnaissance role, that he lacked sufficient horses[45]—which he did, unless he reorganized his cavalry and reduced their traditional tactical role. He also repeated his auxiliary use of cavalry at Malvern Hill as a skirmish line to prevent straggling.

McClellan's conservative use of cavalry, contrasted to his imaginative use of infantry and artillery, must be viewed against his stature as an expert on the subject. McClellan was the author of a cavalry manual, *Regulations and Instructions for the Field Service of the U.S. Cavalry in Times of War* (1861), which espoused conventional two-rank tactics. He also conventionally emphasized the role of the saber. As the cavalry expert on the Delafield Commission to Europe, McClellan accepted single-line tactics while recommending that the two-rank system be retained. The section of his report on cavalry was very technical in nature, without the sense of change to parallel his radical observations on infantry tactics. His lack of reflection on a modern staff and strategic role for cavalry was consistent with the technical and tactical emphasis of the Delafield Commission. One can hardly fail to speculate on whether the otherwise forward-looking McClellan was not the victim of his vested interests in the one area where he was an established expert.[46]

With respect to the strategic aspects of mobility, McClellan's plight in moving his army suggested why an army fighting from a positional defense was unlikely to have its communications endangered by a major strategic maneuver to its rear, at least not by the Army of the Potomac.

McClellan's only guide to Lee's numbers remained Pinkerton's intelligence service, which continued to report the Confederate forces to be greater in number than his own.[47] Even with conflicting evidence, McClellan, with the Union potentially at stake, was understandably cautious. In addition, as on the Peninsula, he had no precise topographical information.[48] His communications and intelligence were inadequate to eliminate the dangers of surprise, and he complained of a lack of cavalry to conduct reconnaissance.[49] Concern with these organizational problems dominated the correspondence of the Maryland campaign, and the concern was shared by all.

The Military Telegraph was effective in strategic communication, while the Signal Corps, growing in efficiency and self-confidence, established fifty-one stations during the Maryland campaign. The precariousness of visual signals was emphasized again when a dense fog prevented their operation during the Battle of Antietam itself. There is some evidence that McClellan may have developed reservations about the role of the Military Telegraph in field operations. He indicated concern about its independence from complete military control, and about Stager's lack of interest and imagination in tactical communications. In the aftermath of Antietam, McClellan told Myer: "When I start from this camp, I want to break loose from the regular telegraph lines and depend upon those under my command."[50]

McClellan's greatest organizational barrier to strategic mobility was field supply and transportation, although considerable progress was made in procurement. Except for the mentioned ordnance shortages, the supply of material was good. The Subsistence and Quartermaster departments, after initial fumblings owing largely to inexperience, were learning to exploit available resources and improvise with inadequate organizational structures. They made up shortages and coordinated activity between Washington and supply officers in the field. McClellan complimented the quartermaster and commissary organization of the Army of the Potomac for their high degree of competence and imagination.[51] But the Maryland campaign was particularly arduous for the transportation and supply system for so large an army so early in the war. The Army of the Potomac, with between 120,000 and 130,000 men, lived on what it carried and foraged for ten days, a long period of detached movement for any stage of the war. It moved on a standard of approximately thirty wagons per 1,000 men.

Reorganization of the wagon trains during the Maryland campaign increased their mobility and speed and eliminated the traffic jams that had occurred on the Peninsula. Meigs, McClellan, and Ingalls together worked on reforms that replaced the ad hoc organization where each quartermaster, without an order of march or knowledge of the roads, acted on his own judgment. In its place emerged some semblance of a modern staff doctrine in which brigade and regimental quartermasters distributed through the train implemented explicit and detailed orders of march from the chief quartermaster. In the aftermath of the Maryland campaign, McClellan nevertheless argued that he had needed a minimum standard of forty wagons per thousand to adequately supply his army with subsistence and half-rations of forage alone. He argued, and Meigs implicitly agreed, that the army was able to make do only because it had met with no serious opposition or delays, and because the roads were in excellent condition. Had they been delayed, the army would have consumed its supplies before they could have been renewed.[52]

Excessive baggage trains were part of the problem. McClellan and Ingalls continued efforts to bring order out of the early chaos. In a general order for the Army of the Potomac issued August 10, 1862, McClellan had set strict standards in the baggage train: for a full regiment, six wagons; for headquarters of an army corps, four; for headquarters of a division or brigade, three. These limits were not to be exceeded, and were to be reduced to correspond as practicable with the numbers of officers and men present. McClellan also set strict guidelines for tent supply and baggage. Meigs's establishment of baggage standards for the Union army over the next two months essentially followed the interpretation of the experience of the Army of the Potomac by McClellan and Ingalls.[53]

While the Army of the Potomac refurbished to resume the offensive after Antietam, Meigs, in a general order September 14, 1862, restricted officers' baggage in the field to "the ordinary mess-chest and a valise or carpet bag. No trunks or boxes will be permitted in the baggage trains." He also stopped the privates from carrying carpet bags and boxes in the regimental wagons; and he forbade the practice of "carrying sutlers' goods in regimental or quartermaster wagons under the guise of quartermaster and commissary stores." To impress the seriousness of the general orders, Meigs called for close inspection and the dismissal from service of officers who permitted any abuse of them.[54]

In the general order of October 18, 1862, Meigs extended McClellan's baggage standard for the Army of the Potomac to the Union army. He additionally provided a standard of three wagons for a light artillery battery or squadron of cavalry. The contents of regimental, battery, and squadron wagons were restricted to forage for the teams, cooking utensils and rations for the troops, hospital stores, and officers' baggage, each category strictly proportioned. In active campaigning, the allowance of tents was strictly limited: "Officers' baggage will be limited to blankets, one small valise, or carpet bag, and a moderate mess kit. The men will carry their own blankets and shelter tents, and reduce the contents of their knapsacks as much as possible."[55]

As McClellan, Ingalls, and Meigs struggled in the aftermath of Antietam with the logistical problem of moving the army away from its base of supply, the most difficult problem was to establish a standard and develop an organization to meet its needs for subsistence, forage, and transportation. In the debate over McClellan's failure to take the offensive after the Battle of Antietam, McClellan maintained and Meigs agreed that the country in which the Army of the Potomac was campaigning was destitute of supplies, having been "ravaged by the repeated passage of armies." McClellan had insufficient means of transportation to enable him "to advance more than twenty to twenty-five miles beyond a railway or canal terminus." And only two railway lines supplied the Army of the Potomac.[56] McClellan was in no position, it was mutually agreed, to pursue a retreating enemy.

Meigs nevertheless was still thinking in terms of the Napoleonic standard of supply. In his report of October 9, 1862, he quoted Napoleon in support of his recommendation of 480 wagons to 40,000 men, or 12 wagons per 1,000 men.[57] On November 18, 1862, Meigs reiterated that "Napoleon asserts, and there is no higher authority, that an army of 40,000 men with a train of four hundred eighty wagons can carry with it a month's provision. He [Napoleon] considered that the men and the extra or lead horses could carry ten days' and the four hundred eighty wagons twenty days' rations. That is at the rate of twelve wagons to one thousand men."

> This applies only to an army in motion. When the army remains in one place for a length of time, it consumes the forage of the vicinity and the trains are increased in order to supply the horses of the cavalry, artillery, and of the trains themselves with forage. A horse requires nearly twenty-six pounds per day of food, while a soldier's ration weighs but three pounds.[58]

Within Meigs's comments was the germ of an idea that would eventually bring results: that the men could carry a substantial proportion of their rations. The idea of using supplementary animals as pack animals to carry subsistence and grain also had possibilities that would eventually be explored, especially with the persistent shortage of wagons and the problem of moving wagons through countryside with primitive roads. But McClellan was too early to benefit from ideas that were not yet even working doctrine.

McClellan and Ingalls responded to the experience of the Maryland campaign, rather than to Napoleonic models. They requested enough transportation to carry subsistence and forage to undertake an offensive campaign, detached from either railroad or water transportation, in country destitute of foraging possibilities.[59] John Moore's statistical analysis of the progression in wagon needs with the increasing radius of foraging area, in ratio to the population and to the increasing size of an army, supports McClellan's experience. Moore's comparison of wagon requirements with the population density of Napoleonic France and the campaigning area of the Civil War suggests the folly of precedent against common sense and experience.

McClellan's expedition free from his base of supply could be achieved in one of two ways: a supply train in a continuous circuit from the railhead or supply depot to the field, or a self-contained supply train that accompanied the army, sending back wagons as they were emptied. Moore's statistical analysis of field transportation and supply shows that the former choice was impracticable for a movement of any distance.[60]

WAGONS REQUIRED TO DELIVER 500 TONS/DAY

Distance in daily marches (D/M)*	2	3	4	5	6	7	8
Number of wagons required	1,440	2,260	3,140	4,105	5,150	6,280	7,500

D = total distance of the march by road
M = daily march of the wagons

The second alternative was more promising. Existing practice called for full rations of three pounds per day, horses and mules to be provided with twelve and nine to ten[61] pounds per day respectively, to be supplemented by foraging. By this standard, the requirements of a self-contained army of 100,000 men returning supply wagons to base when emptied were:[62]

DAYS WITH 10.5 POUNDS GRAIN AND FULL RATIONS	WAGONS REQUIRED Remaining	Detached
4.5	1,300	1,255
9.5	2,920	2,500
14.3	4,980	4,080
19.0	7,780	5,740
23.8	11,670	7,570

This and the above table assume the following constants: wagon load, 3,000 pounds; daily march of wagons, fifteen miles; six animals per wagon; practical nutritional standards per animal, 20 pounds.

To undertake his ten-day expedition on about half the animals' needs, which appears to have been his intention in recognition of the limited foraging possibilities, McClellan, by this second alternative, needed over 6,500 wagons for his army of 120,000 men, or a standard of about 55 wagons per 1,000 men.

Foraging in the thinly populated countryside of Civil War campaign areas stretched logistical resources to the limits. The amount of forage available in a given area is proportionate to the population density. An army of 100,000 men would need access to approximately 10 percent of the yearly production of an area. This does not allow for specialization of crops or for thinly populated grasslands, both of which would be negative factors. But the steady state in this mathematical model is in accord with most Civil War foraging conditions; so the assumed state is generally the reality. These figures emphasize the extent to which foraging required a dispersion of foraging parties and an enormous number of wagons. Armies of 50,000 men or more dependent upon foraging were extremely limited in their movement away from a supply base, while armies of 20,000 to 30,000 men could survive in rich areas.

The steady state in this model is merely an arithmetical guess that must be adjusted to particular situations and to the fact that wartime conditions required armies to improvise short of ideal states. Such factors as the standards of horse supply in ratio to troops, the weight hauled by wagons with different road conditions, and the average distance traveled per day varied. The steady state of 3,000 pounds per wagon was high, the average being between 2,000 and 2,500 pounds in actual campaigning. Wagons and animals could be requisitioned with varying success from local areas and abandoned when depleted. Some subsistence could be driven on the hoof. Conceding these and other limiting factors, this model is an informative reference, when used with the experience of the Maryland campaign, for how reasonable McClellan's and Ingalls's transportation demands were in relation to perceived and real needs.

Although an epidemic of hoof-and-mouth disease took a severe toll on McClellan's horse supply just after the Battle of Antietam, by the beginning of October, Ingalls had managed to collect 3,219 baggage and supply wagons and 32,885 animals (6,471 team horses, 10,392 mules). He noted that "many additional supplies were absolutely necessary to move the army."[63] The statistics for October indicate the growing displacement of the horse by the less vulnerable mule. By the end of the month, Ingalls had collected 3,911 baggage and supply wagons and 37,897 animals (8,893 team horses; 12,483 mules). And with the complete integration of the III, XI, and XII Corps with the army in the field, he wrote McClellan that "subsequently, our trains were increased to near six thousand wagons and sixty thousand animals of all kinds—we could then haul ten days' supply."[64] Ingalls allotted half the wagons for subsistence and grain.[65] He had, by both the modern statistical model and the experience of the Maryland campaign, come up with a realistic standard for his mass army in American terrain.

The inadequate standard of animal nutrition, combined with lack of foraging opportunities in depleted countryside, posed a problem. Since animals could obtain only a small portion of the fourteen pounds a day army regulation called to be foraged, the attrition would be heavy, especially in horses. With experience in making ends meet derived from the Maryland campaign and the Peninsula; with some diversion of wagons for subsistence and forage made possible as baggage reform took effect; with the transportation system delivering a reduced subsistence ration to armies in the field until February, 1863; and with a growing acceptance of the huge attrition of horses accompanied by their gradual replacement by the more durable mule, Ingalls and McClellan had reason for cautious optimism that the Army of the Potomac could make a ten-day march free of its base of supply.

Although the supply system worked with increasing efficiency within its ad hoc and improvised organization, the inadequate staff system to coordinate bureaus internally as well as to link them with field armies continued to play some havoc. Inexperience characteristic of any early wartime transition compounded structural problems. Personnel were insufficient to do the job. There was a breakdown in keeping track of supplies, as well as in unloading them at the railroad sidings. The Army of the Potomac received provisions in fits and starts. Some units would get supplies, while others would be so short of some crucial commodity as to be completely incapacitated.[66] In one representative instance, after McClellan complained that a shipment had failed to arrive, Meigs sent messengers to trace it. The supplies were found to have been shipped but not received. When they could not be located in transit, Meigs concluded that they were in some of the many unloaded cars congesting the sidings, though he did not know where.

Meigs noted that the Quartermaster Department and the railroads were doing everything within their powers. With limited personnel and only two rail lines, he pointed out, they did not have adequate facilities to distribute supplies to an army whose numbers rivaled those of a large city. They were particularly lacking in the personnel to unload shipments at their destination. Meigs also complained of some problems of coordination arising from civilian control of the railroads.[67]

The quartermaster reports of this period do indicate improvement in supply and transportation performance. Large-scale railroad repairs and construction had been going forward for several months. There was an accompanying increase in rolling stock. Coordination and efficiency gained through experience began to replace what a short time before had been confusion and consternation, although not all was perfect by any means. Not until February, 1863, for instance, could the transportation system furnish troops with full rations.[68] But the supply system was rapidly overcoming early confusion. By the end of October, McClellan and Ingalls agreed that the Army of the Potomac was ready to move.

When it moved, it could do so with new efficiency. Organizational reforms instituted by McClellan, Ingalls, and Meigs in the movement of the army's train during the Maryland campaign overcame, as noted, the traffic problems of the Peninsula campaign. And Ingalls was a pioneer in working out a systematic ordering of the movement of the army's train. Each army developed its own system, the systems varying with time and place. But to put these achievements in the Army of the Potomac in perspective, other Civil War armies generally failed to organize a satisfactory plan to manage their trains until the war was more than half over.[69]

McClellan, ironically, was dismissed for inactivity on November 8 while leading over 100,000 men in one of the most impressive strategic movements of the war. His army moved detached from his base of supply at Berlin, a few miles below Harper's Ferry, to new supply bases at Salem and Rectortown on the Manassas Gap Railroad. The huge expedition left Berlin between October 26 and November 1 and arrived at Salem and Rectortown between November 4 and November 7, the day McClellan received the order from Lincoln removing him from command. Ingalls's report records a successful, well-disciplined march. His report for the period September 2 to November 9 presents a picture of the increasing effectiveness of the quartermaster organization of the Army of the Potomac, including improved coordination with the Quartermaster Department. By the time the army made its march, it had, in Ingalls's words, "become well instructed, experienced, zealous and practical."[70]

Whether the Army of the Potomac would have been successful under McClellan where it failed under his successor, Ambrose Burnside, must remain conjecture. A step-by-step study of McClellan's attempts to achieve both tactical and strategic mobility during his command indicates his entanglement in all of the ambiguities and contradictions of a military world view and organization poorly prepared as yet for modern war. And McClellan was the first Union field commander of a mass army to filter this heritage of organizational theory and doctrine through the "fog" of the mid-nineteenth-century transition from traditional to modern warfare. He was the first to feel the friction of mass armies, industrial technology, and the restructuring of American institutional and intellectual culture complicated by political and geographical factors.

Prior to assuming field command, McClellan accepted the two innovations in a basically eighteenth-century view of warfare that responded to the realities of the mid-nineteenth century: Mahan's rejection of the open frontal assault for an offensive tactical organization that emphasized the primary role of field fortification; and the general awareness of the strategic potential of railroads. He made a further tactical innovation when he reorganized his field artillery for defensive tactical concentration. He made a gesture to the beginnings of a modern staff system. Beyond this, he improvised within the existing organizational structures. In some areas, such as field transportation and supply, common sense and experience began to modify inadequate inherited structures to meet the needs of modern war. In others, such as tactical communication, technical developments necessary to coordinate mass modern armies were too experimental to be of much use. Terrain and weather placed severe limitations on visual signals regardless of efficiency. McClellan's early tenure as field commander prevented his deriving the full benefits of citizen armies maturing through experience.

McClellan's well-known conservative political ideology, perhaps a genuine aversion to the brutality and cost of offensive tactics, his political disagreements with Lincoln's administration, his tendency to get involved in social and political roles and debates outside his military career, and perhaps an exaggerated respect for Southern military prowess must be considered among the motives that affected his behavior. Yet one must also take into account the internal consistency of his military logic. McClellan's military actions are consistent with the arguments he presented in his conscientious official correspondence and reports, even allowing for other motives weighing on the side of caution. His one inconsistent act was his failure to entrench at Antietam, a lapse probably motivated by public, political, and military pressure following his fall from favor after the Peninsula campaign for what politicians considered an overcautious defensive outlook.

The failure of others in similar or more favorable circumstances tends to support McClellan's military if not his political judgment. The conventional military criticism centers around his performance in strategic maneuver when faced with an enemy army in the field and around his reluctance to assume the frontal assault. Confederate maneuver in the East and some resulting victories in the early stages of the war were impressive, but the end results were the same. Moving with smaller armies than McClellan, Lee was unable to sustain maneuver or maintain his army in the field, or destroy an army following a tactical victory. Lee, through experience, found that the same military factors that checked McClellan's mobility also forced him to fight a war of strategic position and tactical confrontation.

Early strategic mobility in the western theater was achieved with smaller armies using the extensive river system over a larger geographical area. Once the western armies could no longer use the rivers, but had to turn to overland movements, maneuver faltered. Sherman's distinctive movements were made with smaller armies than the Army of the Potomac, and the benefit of much painfully learned experience about supply organization, particularly the inadequacy of the Napoleonic standard, a lesson to which McClellan's experience contributed. Sherman and other commanders late in the war moved with a more mature military organization in all respects. Grant, with experienced personnel and efficient organizational procedures, would still not maneuver successfully against Lee until Lee's field transportation gave out. McClellan's tactical and ultimately strategic decisions against a war of attrition in favor of maneuver, even when overcautious and influenced by political or other motives, were consistent within the history of his own military thought and practice, and within the contours of theory, doctrine, and organization available to early Civil War field command.

McClellan reflected the strategic dilemma imposed by the ascendancy of the entrenched defense coupled with the organizational problems affecting strategic movement. As Herman Hattaway and Archer Jones observe in their study of Union strategy, McClellan's early campaigns with the Army of the Potomac, as well as his role in the West as general in chief, confirmed strategic limitations to which he probably was predisposed. The course of early campaigning reinforced what McClellan, as well as most Union field commanders and members of the high command, had anticipated from the beginning: maneuver was an organizational monster. And maneuver with large green armies in American terrain offered little hope of fulfilling Jomini's principal strategic end, namely, the destruction of the enemy's army.

Even the First Battle of Manassas, despite small armies and a limited field of operation, was a strategic foreboding of what was to follow. McDowell's relatively well-executed turning maneuvers were stopped by Beauregard's Confederate defenders, who had the mobility to move and meet them. It was difficult to outmaneuver even green troops owing to the reorganization of armies into a hierarchy of smaller, more mobile units as the result of French army reforms during the Revolutionary and Napoleonic periods. The unwieldly mass that had made armies of the past so vulnerable in tactical defeat was relegated to history. The introduction of the railroad facilitated retreat along interior lines. The beginnings of modern signals organization, which the Confederates during the Battle of Manassas were the first to exploit on the field of battle, further aided retreat.

The Confederates, in turn, lacked the organizational means to move from their interior lines to the exterior lines of communication necessary to exploit their tactical victory at Manassas. Moreover, to do so would have made the Confederate victors vulnerable to McDowell's Union army fighting on interior lines. McDowell, similarly unable to move against the interior lines of the Confederates, retreated with impunity on his own interior lines.

During the Peninsula and Maryland campaigns, McClellan experienced on a large scale the strategic problem Manassas had anticipated on a smaller stage: Union forces had little chance of destroying the enemy's armies by maneuver. To flank a competently led army and force it to attack in defensive positions to protect its communications was an unlikely prospect. The advantage in mobility fell to the army in retreat along interior lines. If defeat of the enemy's army by maneuver was not feasible, the remaining option was to employ offensive assault tactics or attrition. And McClellan, from the beginning acknowledging the superiority of the entrenched defense, ruled out these options as realistic alternatives. Lincoln as well as Halleck in the West agreed with him.

Lincoln's occasional pressure to attack was his realistic response to political and public opinion, not his lack of appreciation for military realities. The president was militarily astute and a fast learner. By the time McClellan left the Army of the Potomac, Lincoln had come to accept the strategic position to which McClellan, as well as Halleck and their mentor Mahan, had always been predisposed, namely, that the goal should be to occupy the enemy's territory and defeat him by waging war on his communications and resources. Battle would be sought as a means to secure these objectives. Tactical victories, if they could not destroy the enemy's armies, could force them to retreat and abandon territory, communications, and resources.

Hattaway and Jones convincingly argue that from early in the war, McClellan, Lincoln, and Halleck concurred loosely about Winfield Scott's so-called Anaconda strategy, developed during his brief tenure as chief Union strategist. The plan called for the constriction of the Confederacy through the blockade of the coast and, most important, the penetration of the river systems that reached into the heart of the South. Focused on the Mississippi River, this strategy would gradually strangle the Confederacy's logistical capacity to sustain its armies in the field. McClellan in particular was influenced by Scott's advocacy and Mexican War example of turning movements making use of water transportation, together with the possibilities that the railroad now offered to concentrate large numbers of troops quickly and to change lines of operations. McClellan was not as nervous as Lincoln and Halleck with respect to turning movements using exterior lines of communication. He thus saw the eastern theater as a more feasible field of execution for a strategy of constriction against Confederate resources, communications, and territory.

McClellan's removal and Lincoln's eventual appointment of Halleck to replace him as general in chief altered the strategic role of the Army of the Potomac. McClellan and his generals thought that the army should pursue occupation and war against the enemy's communication and logistical resources from the Virginia Peninsula. Lincoln was always nervous about the exposure of Washington with a strategy that forced the Army of the Potomac to fight on exterior lines. Following the dismissal of McClellan, Lincoln acted as his own general in chief, asserting himself increasingly in the strategy in the East. The appointment of Halleck secured him a general in chief who both accepted the fact of Lincoln's involvement in eastern strategy, and, more significantly, accepted Lincoln's reservations about exterior lines. When Halleck ordered the Army of the Potomac from the Peninsula to check Lee's raid into Maryland, he signaled a change in the army's strategic role. The strategy of exhaustion subsequently would be pursued in the West. Halleck and Lincoln had decided that Union armies could not take Richmond, and the advantage of taking Confederate territory was not worth the risk of giving the Confederate armies a path to Washington. In adopting a strategy of simultaneous advances east and west, Halleck and Lincoln redefined the role of the Army of the Potomac to hold Lee's army in place so that it could not send reinforcements to the West. At the same time, they ordered the field command of the Army of the Potomac to destroy Lee's army, preferably by maneuver, to set up the circumstances for a decisive blow in the West.

The field commanders were shocked. The revised strategy was first presented to the army in Lincoln's final order to Ambrose Burnside and follow-up orders to Joseph Hooker. Loyal to McClellan and his strategy, the general officers of the Army of the Potomac were skeptical of their new role. They realized from their Civil War experience to date, as did Lincoln and Halleck, that there was little chance of destroying Lee's army, and that the order was in contradiction to experience and the direction of strategic thinking. They also no doubt realized that their new strategic role placed heavy organizational burdens on the capacity of the Army of the Potomac to sustain its mobility against a Confederate army that had demonstrated its capacity to maneuver. Removed from the sea, dependent on its ability to move overland in difficult terrain against an enemy that could use the river systems as defensive barriers, the army would spend 1863 coping with organizational challenges to move and to fight.[71]

3

More Reorganization

The Army of the Potomac

THE FLYING COLUMN AND STRATEGIC MOBILITY

If the Army of the Potomac was to keep Lee's army on its front, or attempt large-scale flanking movements, it would have to increase its logistical capacity away from its base of supply. Major innovations in this direction began to materialize in the spring of 1863. Ambrose Burnside had inherited from McClellan the beginnings of a realistic view of supply and transportation when he assumed command for the Fredericksburg campaign. By late March, 1863, however, the Army of the Potomac had only 53,000 horses and mules and 3,500 wagons. Of the horses, 10,000 belonged to the cavalry, and perhaps 500 more had to be exempted for line officers and other uses. Of the wagons, about half were available for forage and subsistence.[1] In the meantime, the numbers of the Army of the Potomac had swollen from an aggregate of some 125,000 men at the time of Fredericksburg to 163,000 men.[2]

Available transportation fell short of the necessary requirements to move so large an army. Since 3,500 wagons using four-horse or six-mule teams required at most only 21,000 animals, at least 22,000 mules were left for use as pack animals. These mules could carry the equivalent of about 1,800 wagons,[3] which gave the Army of the Potomac a total carrying capacity of about 5,300 wagons at a standard of 33 wagons per 1,000 men. This could allow the army, with 163,000 men and existing transportation standards, five or six days' time away from its railheads. Foraging on the route of march would extend the time it could stay away, but the necessity of scattering so enormous an army to forage would slow the march. To attack Lee south of the Rappahannock, General Hooker, now in command of the Army of the Potomac, would have to pick up his tail and move it to depots on Acquia Creek, where he could use the Falmouth Railroad in the vicinity of Fredericksburg.[4] Such a move would require seven or eight days. The problem remained, therefore: how to break the logistical chains to resume the offense.

A scenario that had begun more than a year before, on January 2, 1862, began to provide at least a temporary answer. On that date, Montgomery Meigs, the quartermaster general, had circulated a sketch of the logistical organization of a flying column in the French army.[5] The author was Alexis Godillot, the largest manufacturer of clothing and equipment for that army. The soldier in a flying column carried eight days' compressed rations, including desiccated vegetables, on his back. He carried a blanket but no overcoat. The men were divided into squads of eight, one of whom was to carry a covered cooking kettle, another a large mess tin, another an axe, another a pick, and one a shovel. One man in each company carried the hospital knapsack. Each man carried his share of a shelter tent. The cavalry were similarly equipped, but they also carried pickets and grain for their horses.[6] On March 7, 1863, general headquarters of the Army of the Potomac passed down Special Order no. 85, establishing a board to make recommendations on "the practicality and means of carrying an increased amount of rations . . . over the three days usually carried," having in view "the marching of troops without encumbrance of extra clothing or shelter tents, the use of desiccated vegetables or flour, and the carrying of fresh beef on the hoof, and the omission, in consequence, of beef or pork from the ration."[7]

This board, "after numerous experiments, and from . . . previous experience with troops in the field," to quote its report,[8] not only increased the ration but slightly reduced the individual soldier's load. By carrying beef on the hoof, eliminating all additional clothing except one extra shirt and one change of underclothing and socks, eliminating either the blanket or overcoat, dividing up the shelter tent so that each man carried a small portion, and using desiccated vegetables, the individual soldier should have enough room left in his knapsack and haversack to carry a maximum of ten and an average of eight days' rations.[9] The total weight of knapsack and haversack (with blanket) would be nineteen pounds, compared to twenty pounds previously carried (with blanket and overcoat). In its experiments, the board made a discovery that increased the carrying efficiency of the soldier. It found that carrying a fully loaded knapsack was less fatiguing than carrying a fully loaded haversack, and the board consequently recommended that the bulk of weight be shifted to the knapsack.

The board further concluded that if two pack animals per regiment could accompany the march to carry camp kettles, rice, beans, and desiccated vegetables, the ration could be stretched two additional days. Since officers of the line carried no knapsacks, the board recommended that they be required to employ the servant for which they were paid. Since the servant would not have to carry shoulder arms, ammunition, etc., he could easily carry both his own requirements and the knapsack of the officer. The officer himself was to carry his blanket and two days' rations in his haversack, "it being understood his necessary baggage and mess-chest should be carried in a reserve column of transportation."[10]

The recommendations of the board were immediately implemented in preparation for an eight-day march designed to turn Lee out of his positions on the Rappahannock. Each corps, including the cavalry, was made into a flying column on the French model, with some modifications. In addition to the knapsack and haversack with blanket, the soldier carried his shoulder arms, sixty rounds of ammunition, accoutrements, and a piece of shelter tent. An extra pair of socks was allowed. In some instances soldiers carried both overcoat and blanket, although this was not intended. Unlike the French flying column, the American troops did not carry entrenching equipment on their persons. Reserve trains brought up the entrenching tools, although the pioneer troops mule-packed their equipment.[11] The soldier carried an average load of forty-five pounds.

Pack mules transported reserve ammunition, forage for their own consumption, and packed-up supplies from the reserve trains. They were drawn from the teams of ammunition and supply trains. Never more than two mules were drawn from a single team, however, which left a minimum of four mules to a team, sufficient to enable the train, when needed, to move with moderate loads. The wagon trains followed in the rear of the marching columns, each teamster carrying his own subsistence and forage for his horses.

Although not without its difficulties, this revolutionary march was a logistical success. On the second and third day the weather turned warm, and many of the men discarded their blankets and overcoats. The troops reportedly carried their loads easily, although many—one estimate was 25 percent—abandoned their knapsacks upon going into action. At no time was there a supply problem.[12] The concentration and redistribution of field supply on the model of the modern French flying column came to terms with the persistent reality of wagon and animal shortages. The reorganization exploited the limited means of transportation at this stage of the war to restore some semblance of strategic mobility to Civil War field operations.

In the aftermath of the Chancellorsville campaign, the Quartermaster Department acted on the lessons of Hooker's offensive with the flying column. Ingalls forwarded to Meigs, at the latter's request, suggestions for future campaigning. On the basis of the meticulous analytical reports of his corps quartermasters, Ingalls now decided that "the pack mule system cannot be relied on for long marches with heavy columns. I shall have few hereafter, and intend to make them auxiliary simply to wagons, for short distances over rough country, where there are few and bad roads." Ingalls also, on the basis of the Chancellorsville experience, reduced the animals and wagons allotted for supply transportation for the cavalry in an attempt to further increase that arm's mobility.[13]

The refinements of the flying column after Chancellorsville were put into effect in late June, spurred by information that Lee might be concentrating his army near Gettysburg. The army prepared to move from supply depots on the Orange and Alexandria Railroad to Union Bridge and Westminster on the Western Maryland Railroad, a seven-day march. The plan was to advance as a flying column with the reserve train in the rear. In accordance with his earlier recommendations, Ingalls substituted wagons for pack mules. General George Meade, having succeeded Hooker in command of the Army of the Potomac on June 28, ordered that "the personal attention of corps commanders must be given to the reduction of impediments."[14]

The Army of the Potomac continued to move with enormous numbers. Officers and men totaled some 142,000, approximately the same as for the Chancellorsville campaign. Ingalls calculated at this time that with the transportation and supply reforms, "one wagon to every 50 men ought to carry 7 days' subsistence, forage, ammunition, baggage, hospital stores and everything else." This translated into a standard of 20 wagons per 1,000 men. An army with total personnel of 140,000 thus would need 2,800 wagons. But the Army of the Potomac did not cut down to Ingalls's prognosis of its logistical needs. It marched with 4,300 wagons, a standard of 30 wagons per 1,000 men, and with 21,628 mules, 8,889 horses, and 216 pack mules, a ratio of 1 animal to 4 men.

Ingalls and Meigs were both troubled by the continuously heavy horse losses, particularly through abandonment. Although it was not a great problem at this time, their concern and strict enforcement of discipline about equine care reflected continuing apprehension about the durability of horses as draft animals. The increasing proportion of mules indicated that they were resolving the problem by gradually phasing out horses for the more durable mule.[15]

Ingalls's report of the Army of the Potomac's movement organized as a flying column for the Gettysburg campaign and the subsequent pursuit of Lee is the most revealing document on the logistical details of a field maneuver in the records of the Civil War:

> On this campaign, from the Rappahannock to the James, our trains, large as they were necessarily, being over four thousand heavy wagons, never delayed the march of a column, and, excepting small-ammunition trains, were never seen by our troops. The main trains were conducted on roads to our rear and left without loss of a wagon.
>
> On the morning of July 2, I arrived at Gettysburg. . . . Arrangements were made to issue supplies at Westminster, brought over the branch road from Baltimore, and at Frederick by the Baltimore and Ohio Railroad. . . . Ample supplies of forage, clothing, and subsistence were received and issued to fill every necessary want without in any instance retarding military movements. All stores thrown forward over these routes and not issued were returned to the main depot at Washington, and again forwarded on the Orange and Alexandria Railroad after the army had crossed to the south side of the Potomac. The First and Eleventh Corps opened the great battle of Gettysburg. . . . The wagon trains and all impediments had been assembled at Westminster, on the pike and railroad leading to Baltimore, at a distance of about 25 miles in rear of the army. No baggage was allowed in front. Officers and men went forward without tents and with only a short supply of food. A portion only of the ammunition wagons and ambulances was brought up to the immediate rear of our lines. This arrangement, which is always made in this army on the eve of battle and marches in presence of the enemy, enables experienced and active officers to supply their commands without risking the loss of trains or obstructing roads over which the columns march. Empty wagons can be sent to the rear, and loaded ones, or pack trains, brought up during the night, or at such times and places as will not interfere with the movement of troops.
>
> After the retreat of the rebel army from Gettysburg . . . the trains were directed to join their respective corps; all those that were at Westminster to headquarter were in Frederick the night of the 6th.

The army was moved on the 9th from Middletown to the vicinity of Boonsborough. The order of the day directed that no trains but ammunition wagons, medical wagons, and ambulances should accompany the troops. Supply and baggage wagons were to be parked in the Middletown Valley on the roads taken by their respective corps. No special guards were left with the trains. Every man able to do duty was required to be in the ranks.

It was here known to the general commanding that the enemy had not crossed to the south bank, as had been rumored, but was in force, and entrenched on the north bank from Williamsport to Shepherdstown, hence the precautions in regard to the trains and preparations for battle.

On the 10th, 11th, 12th, and 13th, the Army of the Potomac was engaged in taking up positions in front of the enemy and in making reconnaissances. During this time the trains remained in Middletown Valley. . . . The army was kept supplied with all that was absolutely essential and nothing more. At our headquarters, for example, we only had a few tent flies, blankets, a few small portable paper cases, and two or three days' cooked food.

On the night of the 13th, the rebel army crossed into Virginia. . . . He [the general commanding] issued orders on that day, moving the army on the 15th. . . . The trains to join their respective corps at their camps in the vicinity of Harper's Ferry and Berlin . . . on the night of the 15th.

On the 16th, orders were issued to the army to replenish its supplies from the depots which I had established at Berlin, Sandy Hook, and Harper's Ferry, and to be quickly prepared to continue the march with three days' cooked rations in haversacks, three days' hard bread and small rations in the regimental wagons, and, in addition, two days' salt meat and seven days' hard bread and small rations in the wagons of the supply trains. The army was supplied with clothing, fresh horses, and mules. Our lines of supply were the Chesapeake and Ohio Canal and Baltimore and Ohio Railroad. The supplies furnished here were expected to answer until we could reach the Manassas Gap road at Gainsville and White Plains, and the Warrenton branch at Warrenton.

The Third and Fourth Corps having crossed into the Piney Run Valley near Lovettsville, the rest of the army followed on the 18th and 19th.

The Second and Twelfth Corps crossed at Harper's Ferry, and the First, Sixth, and Eleventh Corps, Artillery Reserve, and headquarters at Berlin, each command followed by its own trains.

I left the army at Berlin, and went to Washington to make arrangements for supplies over the Orange and Alexandria Railroad. Having perfected the arrangements and submitted requisitions, I proceeded by rail to White Plains, on the Manassas Gap Railroad, on the 24th, and rejoined headquarters at Warrenton on the evening of the 25th. . . . The campaign ended here.[16]

The circumstances of the Battle of Gettysburg tended to rule out the use of the flying column in any attempt to achieve victory by strategic maneuver. Although the terrain was open to flanking maneuvers, the two armies came upon one another by surprise. Dispositions for battle were not particularly suitable for turning movements, and the improvised nature of the battle enhanced the difficulties of unplanned maneuvers—again the fog of war was a factor for caution and a battle of position.

Meade's pursuit of Lee after Gettysburg was disappointing. Heavy rains turned the roads to mud. Meade also ran short of food and forage, and his horse supply began to give out. Much of his army was barefoot, and the men were weary from battle. Meade recouped somewhat at the Potomac. He outmarched Lee during the first stage of the enemy's retreat from the Potomac and successfully maneuvered to attack Lee's flank at Manassas Gap. But the commander of the leading Union corps failed to push the attack, giving Lee time to prepare a defensive line near Front Royal. From there the Army of Northern Virginia slipped away in the night to take up positions at Culpeper Court House.[17]

Further action was taken to increase the mobility of the Army of the Potomac by reducing its train. On August 7, Henry Halleck issued a general order as general in chief that further decreased the standard of transportation. Essentially it extended the lessons of the Chancellorsville campaign. Rations, clothing, and equipage allotments were standardized as well. Where troops on the march could receive daily rations from the train, they were to carry only two days' supply.

This reduction of carried rations may have been a conservative concession similar in spirit to the reservation General Daniel Butterfield, chief of staff to the Army of the Potomac, expressed to Meigs. Noting that "when troops came into action the knapsacks were invariably thrown off, and in most instances abandoned and thrown away," Butterfield was dubious about putting a heavy load on troops going into action. Otherwise he thought the heavier load could "be carried with perfect ease." A less conservative response, and one called for by some field officers, would have been a more rigid enforcement of troop discipline while in action. Carrying the rations on the back was the innovative perspective, considering the stakes and the advantages of reducing the train. Butterfield's and Halleck's responses were overcautious. But this modification when in proximity to the train did not affect preparations to achieve self-sufficiency in the field for eight to twelve days.

Provision was made and standards formalized to convert the army into a flying column that would be self-sufficient for eight- and-twelve-day periods away from the base of supply. Contrary to Ingalls's recommendation, however, Halleck retained the pack mules, probably owing to a persistent shortage of wagons. The beef or mutton ration was to be driven on the hoof and gathered totally, or alternately supplemented where possible, by levying local contributions. Flour and meal also were to be levied, where possible. Also, "in the proper season, the bread ration may be partially dispensed with by substituting green corn, which can be foraged in the fields." The regulations even provided that "moveable columns in the fields should be furnished with hand and horse mills for grinding the grain which they procure in the country."

The order called for rigid enforcement of the new directives. The knapsacks of infantry troops were to be inspected at frequent intervals to ensure that the troops were abiding by regulations. Inspectors of armies and corps were to report directly to the adjutant general every violation, "certifying in their reports that they thoroughly inspected the several commands, and have reported therein every deviation from this order." Allowing for the ability of the individual soldier to improvise his personal logistics, and to get around much of what he did not like, there appears to have been less leeway for private initiatives in the Army of the Potomac than in any other Civil War army.

On August 21, Halleck issued a general order setting the following wagon standard:

- 6 wagons/1,000 men for baggage, camp equipage, etc.
- 7 wagons/1,000 men for subsistence, quartermaster, etc.
- 5 wagons/1,000 men for ordnance
- 2 wagons/1,000 men (3/1,500) for medical supplies.

Halleck had instituted Ingalls's recommendation for a standard of twenty wagons per 1,000 men.[18]

After three weeks of reorganization and recruitment, the Army of the Potomac, advancing along its lines of communications, crossed the Rappahannock on September 16 and took up positions around Culpeper Court House. Lee subsequently retired south of the Rapidan near the Wilderness. Meade began to feel out the enemy's fortified lines along the south bank of the Rapidan and to acquaint himself with the militarily relevant features of the sixty-two miles of the Orange and Alexandria Railroad from Alexandria to Culpeper Court House. The railroad, by Ingalls's estimation, could, if necessary, have supplied 300,000 troops. As an indication of the improvement in a year, the same railroad in November, 1862, could supply only 40,000 men. But Meade balked at experimenting with the mobility of his army within the reorganized flying column. He resisted a general offensive, arguing with Halleck that the risk was not worth the gain, because he would be in no position to pursue Lee even if he forced him from his positions.

Meade, owing to inadequate intelligence, was also uncertain of Lee's numbers. He further feared that Lee would counter any attempted flanking movement across the Rapidan by moving the Army of Northern Virginia to the north bank, placing the Confederates between the Army of the Potomac and Washington. When Lincoln and Halleck pointed out to him that the object of his campaign was to destroy Lee's army, not to capture Richmond, Meade made preparations to launch a turning movement. He again reverted to the defense when Halleck made it known that he intended to detach a corps of Meade's army to the West to reinforce Rosecrans.[19]

It was Lee who took the offense. Thrown temporarily on the defense, Meade, except for one frontal assault, fought from entrenched defensive positions through the ensuing campaign, which included actions at Bristoe Station, Rappahannock Bridge, and Mine Run. Lee's intention to try a turning maneuver failed to materialize after an ambush decimated two of his brigades and then his supplies gave out. When Meade overran the undermanned Confederate positions in a surprise night attack, Lee withdrew across the Rapidan. With Lee's offensive checked, Meade turned finally to the strategic possibilities of his reorganized flying column.[20]

The Army of the Potomac, organized as a flying column, attempted a flanking movement. Each man carried eight days' supplies. The reserve supply train, bringing up the rear, carried ten days' rations of subsistence and forage. The depots were broken up. Only one-half the ammunition wagons and ambulances accompanied the troops. The other trains were assembled in one park and were not permitted to cross the Rapidan except by special orders from the commanding general. While the army remained at Mine Run, it was supplied, as at Chancellorsville and Gettysburg, by bringing up wagons and pack mules in the night or when the roads were not occupied by troops on the march.

But there were delays because of slow marching on the part of one corps, insufficient pontoons as a result of an engineering miscalculation, and the taking of a wrong crossroad. By the time Meade felt out Lee's line, the Confederates, warned of the movement, had solidly entrenched strong defensive positions on the hills behind Mine Run Creek. Meade entrenched strong positions on the hills opposite. Persuaded by one of his corps commanders, General Gouverneur Warren, that an assault on Lee's positions would be suicidal, Meade withdrew into winter quarters north of the Rappahannock.[21] With Lee lacking the resources to launch an offensive, active campaigning in 1863 came to an end. The logistical

Inflation of T.S.C. Lowe's balloon "Intrepid" to reconnoiter the Battle of Fair Oaks. "Intrepid" was the Union Army's first observation balloon. *Library of Congress.*

Union Signal Corps observing Confederates on the south bank of the Rappahannock River at Fredericksburg, December 12 or 13, 1862. *Library of Congress.*

Union Signal Corps Station on Elk Mountain, Maryland, overlooking the battlefield at Antietam, October, 1862. *T. H. O'Sullivan, Library of Congress.*

Stone wall below Marye's Heights, Battle of Chancellorsville, May 3, 1863. *A. J. Russell, Library of Congress.*

Railroad destroyed by Lee's cavalry during his withdrawal from Pennsylvania, October, 1863. *National Archives.*

Military bridge built by Union troops across the Tennessee River at Chattanooga, October, 1863. Army transport steamer "Wanhatchie" in the foreground. *Brady Collection, National Archives.*

Wagon park, VI Corps, Army of the Potomac, harnessed and ready to move, either at Brandy Station in May, 1863 or during the post-Gettysburg campaign. *T. H. O'Sullivan, Library of Congress.*

Union Landing on the James River, 1864. *Brady Collection, Library of Congress.*

U.S. Military Railroad Construction Corps working on the Orange and Alexandria Railroad, 1864. *A. J. Russell, Library of Congress.*

Union Military Telegraph stringing lines for the Army of the Potomac, 1864. *T. H. O'Sullivan, Library of Congress.*

Union artillary behind fieldworks at Fair Oaks or Seven Pines, Virginia, 1864. *Mathew Brady, National Archives.*

Union trenches on the North Anna River, Virginia, 1864. *Library of Congress.*

Union entrenchments, New Hope Church Battlefield, Georgia, May, 1864. *Mathew Brady, National Archives.*

Sherman's lines near Atlanta, 1864. *George N. Barnard, Library of Congress.*

Trenches with headlogs and skids in Sherman's lines before Atlanta, 1864. *Probably George N. Barnard, National Archives.*

Chattahoochie Bridge, 780 feet long, 98 feet high. Rebuilt by the Military Railroad Construction Corps in four and one half days during Sherman's Atlanta campaign. *National Archives.*

reorganization of the Army of the Potomac had proceeded in 1863 from theory to practice. In the process, it demonstrated the close integration of operational planning and that of the general in chief and supply bureaus. In this one area, the development of a mature modern staff system was evident. Not until 1863, when experience began to complement reorganization and adequate staffing, did this coordination work effectively. The practical results indicated, however, that the army would have to coordinate factors affecting strategic mobility other than field transportation and supply before logistical reorganization would make an impact.[22]

COMMUNICATIONS, STAFF, AND COMMAND PROCEDURES

For the Fredericksburg campaign, Burnside had a maturing but still experimental system of communications. The Signal Corps supplemented the innovational semaphore system with cipher disks and the Beardslee field telegraph. There was also further experimentation with Professor Lowe's balloons for aerial reconnaissance. The Signal Corps made detailed arrangements prior to the Battle of Fredericksburg. It put the artillery divisions in contact with the assaulting troops, general headquarters, and one another. Burnside's headquarters had contact with the headquarters of the four artillery divisions. A signal station stood ready to open communication with the left wing of the army once it crossed the Rappahannock. "Signal officers were also sent to each of the principal bridges, with instructions to cross with the advanced guards of each grand division and to communicate with the stations on the other side." General headquarters also made provisions for guides and aides for each of the grand divisions. And Burnside had Lowe's balloons ready to ascend—one at his headquarters—once the battle began.[23]

The Union plan was to defeat Lee by strategic maneuver. It called for the Army of the Potomac to move along Lee's lines of communications down the Rappahannock, cross the river at Fredericksburg, and straddle the enemy's communication lines by placing itself between Lee and Richmond. Burnside had attempted to consolidate command by creating the grand division structure with the corps coordinated under three commanders. But even with this reform, the basic problems of communications, staff, and command procedures continued to plague the army. Inadequate staff and command procedures came into play in a misunderstanding between Burnside and Halleck about Burnside's plan of operations. The misunderstanding delayed the dispatch of the pontoon trains to the Army of the Potomac. Burnside was out of telegraphic communication with Washington, and it was some time before the trains arrived by raft at Belle Plain. When they did arrive, they were without wagons to transport them overland to Falmouth. (The commander of the pontoon trains had thought that no wagons would be needed.) A belated overland train encountered the bad luck of heavy rains that turned the roads to quagmires, forcing a rerouting by raft to Belle Plain, where the train arrived on November 24, seven days after the first two trains. As the Army of the Potomac stumbled over problems of organization and the elements, Lee was able to follow along the south bank.

By November 25, the pontoon trains were finally with the Army of the Potomac, though by this time Lee had concentrated his army on the opposite side of the river. Burnside was forced "to make arrangements to cross in the face of a vigilant and formidable foe." These preparations were not completed until about December 10. In the meantime, the troops were stationed "with a view to accumulating supplies and getting in readiness for the movement." Lee, for his part, was unable to oppose the Union crossing because Burnside's artillery commanded the hills that covered the point of crossing.[24]

Burnside still planned for a victory by maneuver. His first plan was to cross the river at Skinker's Neck, about fourteen miles below Fredericksburg, so as to interrupt the enemy's communications and force him to abandon his positions. But the Confederates soon spotted preparations for the crossing and prepared strong defenses. With the enemy distracted at Skinker's Neck, and with his army spread out down the river, Burnside decided that he would try for a surprise attack by crossing quickly under cover of darkness in front of or near Fredericksburg to seize a position that would cut Lee's lateral communications before he could concentrate. Burnside's plan was to "separate Lee's forces on the river below from those occupying the crest, or ridge, in rear of the town."[25]

But again there was a full day's delay. The bridges were only two-thirds built when dawn broke. Enemy skirmishers opened fire on the working parties, and a dense fog prevented artillery from silencing them. The Federal engineers had to cease work until about noon, when the fog lifted and artillery checked the fire. The bridges were finished about dusk. Lee, maintaining communications with his dispersed forces, quickly consolidated his troops.

Burnside was still determined to avoid a tactical confrontation. He crossed the Rappahannock during the night and constructed a line of rifle trenches which fronted the entire Federal position. He intended to use them as a defensive holding position while he maneuvered against

Lee's flanks. But Lee had selected positions that were difficult to maneuver against. The plain between the two lines was "interrupted by hedges and ditches," which provided good cover to the defenders and made tactical maneuver difficult. Burnside's plan was to use an available road to skirt the right of the Confederate positions and place the Federal forces on Lee's communications to Richmond. In order to do so, it was necessary to occupy the crest on the extreme right of the enemy positions.[26] Any attempt to turn Lee's positions made heavy demands on Union communications, staff, and command procedures.

The Army of the Potomac at Fredericksburg had, technically, the best field communications ever seen on a battlefield; but a heavy mist on the 12th and dense fog and smoke rendered them ineffectual for the movements preceding the battle. No visual communications could be opened until about 2:00 P.M. on that day. Telegraphic field communications took up some of the load. The Beardslee equipment proved its potential in both strategic and tactical communications even when under artillery fire. By 3:00 A.M. on December 11, the Signal Corps had opened a line with the Beardslee machine between the headquarters of Burnside and those of General Franklin on the left flank. The next day they extended it to General Summer's division, although this last line was dropped for lack of extra instruments when Summer's forces crossed the river. Second Lieutenant Alexander Wright laid out a line that connected one advance headquarters with "first one battery and then another, after running his line by 'hand bearers' across fields, at a crossing of the Rappahannock River, at which point, on one occasion, the line was extended across the river with the troops and then reeled up when the troops recrossed." A line was opened between Burnside's headquarters and the army's supply base at Belle Plain on the Potomac. But despite the success of the Signal Corps in establishing good communications, offensive maneuver failed as Lee, moving laterally on interior lines, was able to get into position and force Burnside to fight the tactical battle the Union commander dreaded.

On the day of the battle, the fog and smoke cleared, and communications were successfully resumed between all points. "Signal stations were liberally established as the various grand divisions advanced. They fortified lateral communications between corps, as well as between higher formations."[27] But command and staff procedures were inadequate to exploit the new communications technology. Burnside lost control over some movements by choosing to direct the battle from the opposite side of the river. The wording of his orders to Franklin—in command of the grand division on the Union left wing—to launch an attack was vague. Even Burnside's liaison officer was unable to understand its meaning. It did not occur to Franklin to check it by the telegraph he had at his disposal. Franklin mistook the order to launch a general advance for instructions to make a reconnaissance in force. Most of his troops never got into the fight.[28]

At Chancellorsville, there was an even more extensive and sophisticated attempt at tactical communication and intelligence gathering than at Fredericksburg. Lowe's balloons were employed to take compass bearings on the Confederate positions, observe movements, and read rocket signals from Union reconnaissance troops. Lowe proposed to expand his reconnaissance role and use signals from balloons as an additional means of tactical communication, but Hooker rejected the idea. Hooker supplemented visual signals with the most extensive use of telegraphic communications to date. And he revised his command procedures to exploit the telegraph by using his chief of staff, General Butterfield, at general headquarters on the other side of the Rappahannock as a clearing agent for transmissions between the various corps headquarters and Hooker. The Army of the Potomac did not abandon signal stations, but they fell into disfavor. Field command believed the enemy to be reading transmissions, even though the cipher system made this virtually impossible. The telegraph nevertheless was supplemented by signalers accompanying the troops and by a line of signal stations.

Hooker needed this signals system to work if he was to execute his plan calling for four corps to cross the Rappahannock and turn Lee's left flank near Chancellorsville. General Sedgwick, meanwhile, employing the VI Corps as a diversionary force, was to cross the Rappahannock below Fredericksburg on the Confederate right flank to prevent a Confederate concentration against the turning movement. To coordinate the various corps over such an extensive front would require accurate intelligence and good communications. The densely wooded Wilderness country compounded communications problems.

The critical phase of Hooker's turning movement was successful. Between April 28 and 30, the four corps crossed the Rappahannock and the Rapidan. They assembled near Chancellorsville on Lee's left flank and successfully turned the Confederate entrenchments. The diversionary corps under Sedgwick crossed the Rappahannock below Fredericksburg on the 29th, constructed bridgeheads, and on the 30th connected them with a line of entrenchments in preparation for a holding action.

But the limitations of the signals equipment, inexperience, and continuing apprehension about new technology and new procedures were problems from the beginning. From May 29 to May 30, the Signal Corps ran telegraph lines with the Beardslee equipment between general headquarters and the corps on the other side of the Rappahannock. In some instances, telegraphic tactical communications extended down to the division level. The inexperience of the signal corpsmen, over half of whom were completely new to the job of working with telegraphic equipment, combined with the limited (five- to eight-mile) range of the Beardslee equipment to produce immediate difficulties.

On April 30 and May 1, the Military Telegraph with its Morse equipment took over the key lines from the Signal Corps when the Beardslee equipment proved too weak to transmit over the distances involved. Hooker crossed to Chancellorsville on the evening of April 30, leaving his chief of staff, Butterfield, in charge of general headquarters to transmit intelligence reports and orders. There was an unexpected delay, however, in establishing telegraphic contact between general headquarters and Hooker. Until the Military Telegraph took over the line on May 2, communications between Butterfield and Hooker took three hours. A further hindrance was teamsters and overly curious troops who, despite guards, regularly broke telegraph wires. The competition without coordination between the Signal Corps and the Military Telegraph, both using different equipment, remained a problem.[29]

Although Hooker was not depending exclusively upon telegraphic communication, the Signal Corps was also frustrated in its attempts to use visual signals. The signalers who accompanied the various corps on their marches were unable to open signals communication with general headquarters because the roads, the only lines of visibility in the Wilderness country, were too congested with troops. The twenty-mile line of stations established by the Signal Corps to collect intelligence on enemy troop movements and to maintain tactical communications was seldom used for the latter purpose, because the field command thought that the enemy had broken their code and were reading their signals. As previously noted, this fear of interception indicated a basic distrust of the Signal Corps, since the innovation of the cipher disk using the telegraphic alphabet made interception nearly impossible.

Butterfield, who required hourly reports, did make good use of the signals for intelligence purposes. He also utilized Lowe's balloons. One balloon gathered and transmitted information from Fredericksburg throughout the 29th and 30th on the number of troops opposite Sedgwick's front. Another was used at corps headquarters at Bank's Ford to relay information about troop movements on the Confederate left. Hooker's communications also benefited from his possession of accurate topographical data compiled during the previous campaigning in the area.[30]

At the crucial moment, however, intelligence and communications

breakdowns, combined with the controversial issue of Hooker's inde-
cision, undermined the Union offensive by causing hesitation at the
moment when the Army of the Potomac could perhaps have won a
victory through strategic maneuver. Early on the morning of May 1,
Hooker advanced to take up a line of battle before launching a simultaneous assault along the extent of the Confederate line. He had hardly
gotten underway when he ran into spirited resistance from the small
holding force Lee had sent to check him until Jackson could bring his
corps into position. Hooker's information was inadequate to give him
an accurate estimate of how many of the enemy currently faced him,
or how many were moving to meet him. Intelligence overestimated
enemy numbers. There is controversy over whether Hooker realized
this and used it as an excuse to support a failure of nerve at the crucial
moment. Organizational factors certainly gave him reason to pause.

Since the telegraph line linking Hooker with general headquarters
had not yet been put into operation, he could not receive rapid transmissions on enemy movements or swiftly coordinate the movements of
his army. Communications with headquarters took at least three hours.
Also, telegraphic connections were not satisfactorily established with
Sedgwick's corps on the Federal left wing at Fredericksburg, which was
to act in coordination with the turning movement on the right.

Hooker thus found himself fighting a blind uncoordinated offensive
in very difficult terrain. He countermanded his original order for an
offensive and fell back on the unentrenched line of the night before.
A council of war met to consider possible courses of action. "One was
to choose a position and entrench; the other, to choose our point of
attack, and advance with our whole force of five corps upon it," reported
General Warren, the chief engineer of the Army of the Potomac. Ignorant of both the enemy's numbers and the extent of his movements,
blind in the Wilderness, and temporarily without the communications
necessary to coordinate an offensive, Hooker decided caution was in
order and took the defensive. He withdrew his right wing to a line that
rested at one end on a clearing in the Wilderness which "bore the
pretentious name of Chancellorsville, though it consisted of only one
residence and its outhouses." Here Hooker ordered his army to dig in
to await the expected assault.[31]

Communications problems frustrated Hooker's one last attempt to
win the battle by maneuver. Barely surviving a brilliant turning movement by Jackson against the Union right flank, Hooker responded to
the setback by ordering General Sedgwick to turn the Confederate right
flank. A breakdown in tactical communications hampered movements
from the beginning. Coordination with Hooker on the other flank and

with Butterfield at general headquarters proved impossible. Retreating Union troops had disrupted the telegraph line that the Military Telegraph had finally laid on May 2 between general headquarters and Hooker. The line was not reopened until May 3. High winds kept the balloons down and interfered with telescopic observations.

Sedgwick's major communications difficulties occurred on his own front. On May 3, the Signal Corps followed him with a telegraph line as far as Fredericksburg. But when Sedgwick advanced beyond Fredericksburg, he had to rely on the signal stations to transmit messages to and from general headquarters. This means of communication stopped when Sedgwick received orders from Butterfield to cease sending signals because the Confederates were deciphering them. Sedgwick consequently did not receive the crucial information that the enemy had recaptured Marye's Heights on the 4th. As it turned out, it was Butterfield's intention that Sedgwick cease sending only torch signals that might reveal his positions. Captain B. F. Fisher, future chief signal officer in the Union army, noted on the occasion: "The signal corps is distrusted and considered unsafe as a means of transmitting messages."

Sedgwick's corps did drive Jubal Early's undermanned defenders from their entrenchments in the opening engagement of the turning maneuver. This might have been the Army of the Potomac's opportunity for victory by strategic maneuver had Sedgwick had the communications system and staff procedures to exercise effective control over the battlefield. But the defeated Confederates were able to withdraw, establish a second defensive line, and receive reinforcements before Sedgwick could attack again. Sedgwick's forces had suffered heavy losses in the original attack, succeeding only on the third assault. His battle-weary and depleted corps could not carry the second Confederate line of entrenchments.[32]

Inadequate field communications played a crucial role in the failure of Sedgwick's maneuver. Never before had field telegraph been used to such an extent over such distance. As in most experiments of this nature, technical problems occurred, partly because of the inexperience of the troops who continually cut the lines. The limitations imposed upon the speed of transmission by the crude nature of the equipment proved a major pitfall. Inexperienced in the use of field telegraph, Hooker sent too many messages. Also, he, Butterfield, and the signals officers did not always formulate clear orders. General headquarters, the relay center, was swamped with messages. The incapability of the Beardslee equipment to transmit over the distances involved, and the subsequent takeover of a number of lines by the civilian Military Telegraph reflected the experimental trial-and-error character of the use of field telegraph in the Chancellorsville campaign. The terrain also interfered with semaphore signaling as an alternative to telegraphic communications, although the signal stations were used effectively to gather intelligence.

Despite any distrust of both the new Signal Corps and the Military Telegraph, it was not feasible to return to conventional methods with mass armies in American terrain. The traditional courier service, although used, was unable to compensate for the breakdown in telegraph or semaphore communications. The distances involved were simply too great for the use of couriers, and only Stonewall Jackson among Civil War commanders had shown the foresight to employ his staff for tactical coordination.[33]

As the Army of the Potomac under Hooker's successor, General George Meade—another commander with an engineering background and Mexican War experience—embarked on the Gettysburg campaign, it showed that it had absorbed some lessons about communications from Chancellorsville. In the march to Gettysburg, the signals system successfully relayed transmissions between the scattered army corps, enabling their concentration at Gettysburg.[34] Sensitive to the problems of tactical communication, Meade ordered his corps commanders, while waiting for the enemy to reveal his intentions, "to familiarize themselves with the roads communicating with the different corps." Signals were skillfully complemented with a more traditional courier relay using cavalrymen.[35]

One lingering organizational problem was the jurisdictional dispute between the Signal Corps and Military Telegraph. Despite early success, particularly at Chancellorsville, the Signal Corps' Beardslee portable telegraph continued to suffer technical problems. Difficulties with the simplified letter indicator telegraph instruments that made the Beardslee equipment operable without the need for the highly skilled and scarce Morse operators forced Myer to replace them with Morse keys and sounders. His advertisements in competition with the Military Telegraph for the limited supply of Morse operators were regarded by Stager as an encroachment.

The jurisdictional conflict reached its crisis point at a time when the two services were reaching a practical and functional accommodation. The Chancellorsville campaign was their first well-coordinated effort. The Signal Corps handled tactical communications in the field, while the Military Telegraph relayed to army and corps headquarters the reports of the interconnected Signal Corps stations. It was toward some such formal coordination of tactical and strategic communications that Myer would secretly, if unsuccessfully, approach Stager in late 1864.

The dispute came to a head when Lincoln, on November 10, 1863, with Stanton's urging, gave jurisdiction for all field telegraph to the Military Telegraph. The Beardslee equipment was ordered turned over to the Military Telegraph, which abandoned it for conventional lines. That did not end the controversy. Some departmental commanders directed that the Beardslee equipment be returned for temporary use. On such occasions it was always operated by the Signal Corps.[36]

The Military Telegraph with its Morse equipment had largely taken over telegraphic field communications during the Gettysburg campaign. It connected Meade's headquarters to the headquarters of all corps and divisions. The Army of the Potomac set organizational precedent when, "for perhaps the first time in military history the commanding general of a large army was kept in communication during active operations with his corps and division commanders." Meade set a precedent in command procedures when he brought the signal officers to the conference table for consultation on the plan of battle. And in the course of the battle, Meade had the practical advantage of a signal station on top of Little Round Top which kept him posted on Confederate movements.[37] Improvements in tactical communications were utilized at Gettysburg in support of a battle plan of strategic position and tactical entrenchment rather than in aid of strategic maneuver. Gettysburg displayed how the comparative simplicity and advantage of organizing the existing state of field communications for static defense, rather than for the complexities of strategic maneuver, was contributing to the development of trench warfare.

TACTICS

McClellan's successors in command of the Army of the Potomac, with the exception of one incident on the part of Hooker, continued his commitment to a tactical organization that emphasized the place of battlefield entrenchment. McClellan's accompanying apprehension about the open frontal assault was at times accepted, at other times bent. General Ambrose Burnside, who succeeded McClellan in time to lead the Army of the Potomac in the Battle of Fredericksburg, was of a tactical mind with McClellan. It was Burnside who, when McClellan was under pressure to attack Lee's entrenchments during the Peninsula campaign, encouraged him to resist political pressure with the addendum that "you know as well as I that it is easier to turn a flank than force a front."[38]

Burnside, as noted, tried to avoid a tactical solution and win at Fredericksburg by maneuver. Only with the failure to "turn a flank," and with the dismissal of McClellan for failure to pursue the offensive no doubt weighing on his mind, did he revert to a more tactically compromising plan: a close-quarter holding-turning maneuver that depended upon the Union troops' occupying the crest on the extreme right of the Confederate positions. In the holding portion of the maneuver, Burnside showed all of McClellan's respect for the offensive use of field fortifications. He constructed a line of rifle trenches that covered the entire Union front. But when maneuver broke down for the reasons noted, the Battle of Fredericksburg deteriorated into a tactical bloodbath.

The frontal assault against the Confederate line floundered when tactical coordination broke down owing to inadequate command procedures. But the greatest hindrance to Burnside's assaults was the superiority of the entrenched defense over the frontal assault following the general introduction of the rifled musket. Burnside attacked Longstreet, the only commander in the Army of Northern Virginia to entrench his troops prior to the battle. It marked the first time the Army of Northern Virginia used entrenchments in the field. The close-order lines of the attackers quickly broke down. For the first time there was an indication that the combination of rifled infantry weapons, well-positioned artillery, entrenchments, and the difficulties of the terrain for offensive action were forcing a transition from traditional assault tactics to the predominance of the loose-order skirmish line.

The number of actions in which the skirmish line replaced the close-order line had escalated in 1862, and Fredericksburg carried this trend into a major battle.[39] For seven hours, assault after assault from two Union corps came to grief on the strongest section of Longstreet's line, the enfiladed stone wall at the base of Marye's Heights. The wall sheltered four lines of infantry armed with rifled muskets. Sharpshooters in rifle trenches and entrenched artillery directly covered and enfiladed it from the two terraces that rose behind it. The Union assault never got within 100 yards of the wall. One officer made his way to within 30 yards before meeting his death. Between his lonely body and the Confederate position, the ground was untouched. The sun went down on almost 3,500 blue uniforms stacked like so many abandoned potato sacks. The four Confederate brigades manning the wall had lost just under 800 men.[40] Firepower and entrenched defensive positions combined with terrain were pushing tactical thought to accept the obsolescence of traditional organization.

The sun came up on a new type of warfare as Lee followed Longstreet's example. During the night, Lee for the first time ordered the Army of Northern Virginia to entrench in the field. The Union troops, in turn, settled down in a ditch, which they proceeded to strengthen with entrenchments. Burnside directed preparations to be made for a renewed assault, then decided it was impracticable.[41] Jackson decided to make an offensive foray, but Union artillery quickly sent him scurrying for cover.[42] Fredericksburg was a victory for the entrenched defense.

On both sides, all enthusiasm for the offense waned. The two armies gazed expectantly at one another from their trenches across the snow-covered countryside and tried to keep warm. The first day after passed into the second. Passive trench warfare had made its appearance. Burnside, under the cover of darkness and a sound-erasing wind, recrossed the Rappahannock, drawing up his bridges behind him.

Burnside's last attempt at a long-range turning maneuver fell through because the Army of the Potomac was in no condition to move. A storm made the roads near-impassable for a plan to flank Lee by crossing the river above the Confederate positions. Trench warfare set in. Burnside returned to his positions at Falmouth and, together with Lee, transformed the rolling countryside into an unprecedented patchwork of trenches, parapets, and redoubts. Perhaps the troops and their commanders realized that at Fredericksburg they had seen their military destiny unfurl. The balance in Civil War tactical organization had taken one of its most dramatic shifts toward the dominance of the entrenched defense; and with the breakdown of maneuver, the Civil War slipped further into a static state of trench warfare.

In the subsequent Chancellorsville campaign, a breakdown in strategic mobility again reduced the Army of the Potomac to a tactical battle. While intent on a strategic offensive, General Hooker, who had succeeded Burnside, had not entrenched when fronted with Lee's army. But when a council of war made the decision to take the defense, he followed conventional doctrine and dug in to await the expected assault.[43] Hooker quickly entrenched the entire army behind parapets and breastworks of logs, supported by abatis entanglements.[44] At some points, at least, his troops constructed a triple line of entrenchments.[45] Later the same morning, Hooker moved two corps into the three roads leading to Fredericksburg and established an extensive entrenched line in the open country beyond the Wilderness.[46] Until he withdrew across the Rappahannock a week later, he fought his army constantly behind the cover of hastily improvised field works.[47] Although Hooker's use of field works on the defensive was within conventional doctrine, the extent and thoroughness of his preparations while in the open field represented a continuation of the tactical pattern that had set in for both armies during the immediate aftermath of Fredericksburg. Lee, in turn, refused to oblige Hooker by directly attacking his heavily fortified lines.

But Lee discovered a vulnerable point in Hooker's position. He found that Hooker's right flank "rested in the air" and was "not even covered by a curtain of cavalry."[48] In an entrenched holding-turning maneuver, Lee sent Jackson with his entire corps of 28,000 men against the exposed flank. Jackson took the enemy entrenchments by complete surprise, routing the defenders. Despite their disarray, the Union troops retreated in order to Fairview, where they threw up three lines of entrenchments in a near-impenetrable position.

Hooker lost the opportunity to turn the Confederate attack into a victory for the entrenched defense. Failing to sense its importance, he abandoned the key to the Fairview position, a place called Hazel Grove, from where E. P. Alexander's Confederate artillery enfiladed the Union positions. The Confederates combined artillery fire with their superior numbers on this flank to win a victory. A last-ditch Union stand without entrenchment near Chancellorsville quickly collapsed and withdrew when Alexander's artillery enfiladed it from three directions. But the Confederates' tactical victory could not be translated into strategic victory. Jackson's exhausted troops were unable to pursue. And even in victory, the casualty figures indicated how the frontal assault against entrenchments, even with surprise, was self-destructive. Even tactical victory was turning into strategic defeat through an attrition the Confederates could ill afford. The Confederate attackers had suffered 30 percent casualties in their frontal assaults against the Fairview position, compared to Union losses totaling about 15 percent of their paper strength and perhaps 18 percent of their troops in action.[49] The price of tactical victory was high.

The same lesson was learned on the other side when Hooker responded to Jackson's attack by ordering Sedgwick to turn the Confederate right flank. Sedgwick's corps drove Jubal Early's badly undermanned Confederate defenders from the entrenchments on Marye's Heights, but not before Early had beaten back two massed assaults and inflicted heavy losses on his assailants. Early withdrew his division to form a new line of battle about two miles to the rear, where General McLaw's division reinforced him. The battered Union forces were unable to follow up.

The successful Union assault on Marye's Heights was further evidence of the impact of the entrenched defense and the rifled musket on even successful innovations with assault tactics. The close-order line had given way to the skirmish line at this same place in the Battle of Fredericksburg. The Union field command now attempted to re-form while preserving traditional assault tactics. Some officers began to work out temporary command arrangements before an attack to reduce the disorder brought by the intermingling of close lines. The most significant development was a decision to shift the emphasis from the line to the column.

Major General John Newton, commanding the 3rd Division in Sedgwick's corps, devised the plan to attack in column, and Sedgwick approved. As Perry Jamieson, the historian of assault tactics, observes, Newton called for two storming columns

> placed at intervals great enough that the Confederates would not be able to shift troops to defend both points. The left column consisted of two regiments, and the right column consisted of two regiments supported by two others. Newton's two columns were supported by a line formation, consisting of one regiment deployed as skirmishers, followed by three other regiments deployed in line. Newton was supported on his left by three similar storming columns from the division of Brigadier General Albion Howe. Brigadier General Frank Wheaton, a brigade commander in Newton's division, was ordered to reform all the storming troops after they arrived at Marye's Heights, putting them into a two-line formation. The columns and supporting lines in double quick time carried the Confederate position.

But the slaughter was terrible. The VI Corps lost nearly 1,000 men in five minutes against an undermanned Confederate line that almost held.[50]

Though McLaw's division, upon joining Early, constructed no new entrenchments, it occupied entrenchments constructed at an earlier date. Sedgwick attacked again; and again the Confederates beat him back, inflicting heavy casualties. The firepower of the Confederate defenders shattered Union tactical formations. After the first assault, the Union assailants required rest and regrouping before they could undertake any follow-up action. With the repulse of Sedgwick's flanking movement, Hooker's plan to turn Lee's entrenched line of defense completely collapsed. He made the decision to withdraw the Army of the Potomac across the Rappahannock.[51]

Hooker's retreat indicated the extent to which tactical entrenchment had become a way of life for the Army of the Potomac when in the open field. Hooker covered every step of his pullback with entrenched positions. In a concentrated position fronting the river, the pioneer brigade, under the command of the chief topographical engineer of the Army of the Potomac, Brigadier General Gouverneur Warren, in less than forty-eight hours threw up five miles of the most formidable entrenchments yet constructed under battlefield conditions.

"Our engineers were amazed at the strength and completeness of the enemy's entrenchments," commented E. P. Alexander. "Impenetrable abatis covered the entire front, and the crest everywhere carried head-logs under which the men could fire as through loopholes. In the rear, separate structures were provided for officers, with protected outlooks, where they could see and direct without exposure." Any attack "would have to be made everywhere squarely in front," as both flanks rested upon the river, "and our artillery would be unable to render any efficient help."[52] Another of Mahan's star pupils had displayed his training.[53] Although he served as chief topographical engineer in the Army of the Potomac at Chancellorsville, it is significant that Warren had spent most of the war to date in command of a volunteer infantry brigade. He was to spend most of the remainder in command of a corps in the Army of the Potomac. The speed and relative ease with which the defeated Army of the Potomac stabilized and secured its front in accompaniment with the Confederate incapacity to pursue was further indication of the predominant role the entrenched defense was coming to assume as the two armies failed to overcome the obstacles to tactical and strategic mobility.

Hooker, by disposition an organizational innovator, introduced reforms in cavalry and artillery procedures. When he broke up Burnside's grand division structure to revert to direct control over the seven infantry corps, he consolidated the cavalry into one corps under Major General George Stoneman, giving the Union cavalry for the first time an effective structure to cope with the consolidated corps organization of Lee's cavalry. After Chancellorsville, Hooker reluctantly consolidated artillery organization, assigning brigades, under the command of an artillery officer, to the various corps. Each infantry corps received one, the cavalry corps two. Five brigades went to the reserve, doubling its size from Chancellorsville. This provided the centralized control and flexibility to match Lee's artillery reorganization. The Confederates had a smaller reserve owing to the lack of guns. As the fighting continued to drift toward a war of defensive entrenchment, these reforms would enhance the defensive role of artillery side by side with the rifled musket.[54]

General George Meade, having assumed command of the Army of the Potomac for the Gettysburg campaign, displayed a somewhat ambivalent attitude toward the relative merits of the frontal assault versus the entrenched defense. As previously noted, the circumstances of the meeting of the two armies at Gettysburg discouraged maneuver. Meade was personally anxious to launch an attack, only to be dissuaded by his corps commanders, upon whose advice he generally acted.[55] Meade also rejected an attack and took a defensive stance because he wished to rest

Sedgwick's VI Corps, which had marched all night to join the army. Uncertain of the exact position of the enemy, Meade wished Lee to develop his lines before he initiated any moves himself. He therefore resigned himself, at least temporarily, to the tactical defense. Meade strengthened his strong natural positions, complemented by strong fences, with breastworks of timbers, hastily piled stones, and in places earthworks.

The Union line held against Lee's assaults on Little Round Top on July 2. But despite some poor troop handling, poor tactical communications, and enormous losses, the Confederates did make gains. Though they had to fall back, they held ground taken on the extreme right of the Confederate line. And to demonstrate that offensive field fortification had come to the Army of Northern Virginia, the Confederate troops immediately made lodgements and threw up additional fortifications from which to renew the offensive.[56]

The Federal corps commanders had accepted the changed tactical balance in favor of the entrenched defense without question. But Meade was not convinced. After the fighting on July 2, he contemplated a frontal assault on the Confederate positions. He called his corps commanders to a council of war and posed the question: "It being determined to remain in present position, shall the army attack or await the attack of the enemy?" All opposed the attack.[57]

The ranks of the Army of the Potomac displayed their habitual conditioning in the changed tactical nature of warfare. A captain of the 60th New York Volunteers vividly described the ritual of Union troops on Culp's Hill after fighting on July 2:

> All instinctively felt that a life-and-death struggle was impending, and that every help should be used. Culp's Hill was covered with woods; so all the materials needful were at our disposal. Right and left the men felled the trees and blocked them up into a close low fence. Piles of cordwood which lay nearby were quickly appropriated. . . . All along the rest of the line of the corps a similar defense was constructed. Fortunate regiments, which had spades and picks, strengthened their work with earth. By 10 o'clock it was finished (started at six o'clock).[58]

When Lee attacked on July 3, the direct and enfilading fire of Meade's entrenched infantry and artillery tore apart the Confederate assaults. Having suffered 28,000 casualties, his army demoralized and deserting, almost out of ammunition, with local troops and cavalry hindering foraging, Lee made immediate preparations to withdraw across the Rappahannock.[59]

While tactical development displayed the defensive superiority of

entrenched infantry armed with the rifled musket, corresponding developments took place in cavalry and artillery tactics. On the side of
continuity, the most spectacular display of traditional cavalry tactics of
the entire war occurred during the Gettysburg campaign. The largest
cavalry battle of the war, fought on June 9 at Brandy Station, was an
hour and a half of textbook saber charges without skirmishing. Colonel
Percy Wyndham's cavalry brigade made six regimental and several smaller
charges. On July 3, saber charges took place in the cavalry battle east
of Gettysburg. Also on July 3, Brigadier General Judson Kilpatrick,
commanding a cavalry division on the Union left, ordered a brigade to
make a mounted charge in column against a Confederate position protected by stone walls. Kilpatrick's brigade was fortunate to escape with
only one-third casualties. More indicative of the changing reality of
cavalry tactics was the fact that units on both sides were initially deployed
dismounted. In the opening engagement of the Battle of Gettysburg,
Brigadier General John Buford's dismounted Union cavalry division
opposed Confederate Major General Henry Heth's infantry division.
Memories perhaps lingered of Stonewall Jackson's slaughter of a saber
charge in column formation by the 8th Pennsylvania Cavalry on May 2
at Chancellorsville.

The attempt to stem Jackson's offensive at Chancellorsville also reinforced the changing place of artillery in tactical organization. Massed
Union artillery made two successful defensive stands against Jackson's
infantry and artillery attacks: the first, a massing of about twenty guns
at Hazel Grove on May 2; the next, a massing of about thirty-four
guns at Fairview on May 3. Jackson managed to get about twenty-five
guns into the clearing at Fairview. But the defensive advantage of artillery prevailed, despite sloppy handling in the absence of Henry Hunt,
the artillery commander of the Army of the Potomac.

Hunt prevailed in a debate over his request, based upon the Chancellorsville experience, to further concentrate artillery organization. He
created artillery brigades assigned to each corps. This overcame a problem at Chancellorsville, where the batteries of uncommitted divisions
had gone unused. The reorganization also made the practical adjustment to a situation where the attrition of divisions was making the corps
the basic tactical unit. Hunt reorganized the division guns in new artillery brigades of from four to eight batteries, depending upon the size
of the corps, and retained a reserve of about one-third of the artillery.

The rolling open terrain of the Gettysburg battlefield invited the
use of artillery. The Army of the Potomac had the preferred positions.
The artillery duel that preceded Lee's assault emphasized the difficulty
of an offensive cannonade without good rifled guns or the technology

for indirect ranging and firing. The Confederate dispositions were bad. Confederate fire was generally perpendicular to the line of the Union guns. This called for pinpoint accuracy, and shells tended to go long. On defense, Union artillery was devastating. On July 2, about twenty-five guns held the Plum Run line on the Union left without infantry support. Hunt, acknowledging that the role of artillery was to defend against infantry attacks, hoarded his artillery during the Confederate cannonade to concentrate against the anticipated infantry assault. The Confederate artillery commander, E. P. Alexander, said he had never seen the Union artillery so reserve its fire for infantry. At long range, the Union artillery threw shot and shell; at short range, cannister. The Union infantry opened up at 300 yards to complete the slaughter.

Some Confederate artillery moved forward behind Pickett's infantry. This approach was as ineffectual as the offensive use of artillery by the Union in similar circumstances during the Battle of Fredericksburg. Alexander planned to advance nine howitzers in front of Pickett's assault, but he couldn't come up with the guns at the time of the assault. Evidence was accumulating that the offensive role of artillery was dead. Hunt showed his disdain when he ignored the fifteen to eighteen guns with which Alexander followed up the infantry assault to concentrate his fire on the Confederate infantry. Gettysburg was but one more progression in the growing superiority of the combination of concentrated artillery, rifled infantry, and the entrenched defense.[60]

In the aftermath of Gettysburg, Meade expressed his reluctance to repeat the error of Lee's frontal assaults. He hoped to force an engagement on ground of his choosing by turning Lee out of his lines. As he carefully felt out Lee's lines after Gettysburg, during his slow retreat, and in the movements that led to actions at Bristoe Station, Rappahannock Bridge, and Mine Run, Meade felt pressure from Halleck and Lincoln to engage the enemy. At the same time, they assured Meade that they did not intend for him to frontally assault strongly fortified positions, but to exercise his judgment. Yet Meade felt the weight of circumstances that discouraged maneuver and neutralized the advantages of his logistical organization as a flying column. His army was tired, and poor marching and poor coordination compounded several logistical problems. He was extremely nervous about the poor intelligence while stalking an enemy as dangerous as Lee. Halleck's detachment of a corps to the West increased his cautious disposition. With pressure for an engagement as a likely motive, Meade, accepting the unlikelihood of turning a flank, considered attacking Lee's lines on the Rapidan as the only alternative to stalemate. But his corps commanders proved even more cautious than Meade, five of six unqualifiedly rejecting his proposed assault in a council of war.[61]

Meade did launch one successful frontal assault, after his ambush of two of A. P. Hill's brigades forced Lee to abandon his own attempt at a turning movement and fall back on a fortified bridgehead on the north bank of the Rappahannock.[62] A surprise night attack, led by Emory Upton, carried by bayonet without firing a shot, but there is evidence that it benefited from the careless layout and construction of Confederate entrenchments.[63] Again, the advantage of movement fell to the retreating army; by the time Meade felt out the Confederate positions, Lee was solidly entrenched on the hills behind Mine Run Creek. Meade planned to attack, a decision that led the soldiers of the Army of the Potomac to perform perhaps an unprecedented ritual: each without comment pinned to his shirt a slip of paper bearing his name.[64] Gouverneur Warren, now a corps commander and a favorite of Meade, intervened to convince Meade that an assault would be suicidal.[65] It will be remembered that Warren, while in command of the pioneer brigade in his capacity as chief topographical engineer of the Army of the Potomac, had been responsible for the spectacular display of improvised field fortification during Hooker's withdrawal from Chancellorsville. He also had opposed frontal assaults on Lee's works during that campaign. The 1863 campaign of the Army of the Potomac ended with recognition of the supremacy of field fortification over the open frontal assault. With the acknowledgment of tactical as well as strategic stalemate, Meade, under cover of darkness, withdrew the Army of the Potomac and went into winter quarters north of the Rappahannock.

The Army of the Potomac that went into winter quarters for 1863 had the beginnings of an appreciation of tactical and strategic mobility in modern warfare. Despite some inconsistency in tactical behavior, the army from the field command through the ranks generally reinforced McClellan's early appreciation of the ascendancy of the entrenched tactical defense over the frontal assault. Where offensive assault tactics were used, there was a break with tradition to emphasize an extended use of the loose-order skirmish formation. McClellan's deployment of artillery was continued, with Hunt taking McClellan's concentrated artillery organization for defense one step further. The ambivalent tactical use of cavalry continued; but traditional saber charges were giving way to the increasing use of dismounted cavalry as mobile infantry. The reorganization of field transportation and field supply in the Army of the Potomac was a major change. Tactical and strategic communications continued to suffer from ad hoc organizational arrangements, technical problems, and jurisdictional disputes. But experience was contributing to increased efficiency within the technical and organizational limitations of the signals system. The organization of a staff system and command procedures to coordinate a mammoth modern army was perhaps the area of least development. Limited ad hoc innovation, such as Hooker's use of Butterfield, his chief of staff, to coordinate communications at Chancellorsville, Meade's planning councils with his corps commanders, and, for the first time under Meade, the inclusion of signal officers in the planning process, did bring some relief to what still remained improvised procedures. Only in logistics was there real movement toward modern staff organization.

ÉLAN, TRADITION, AND CHANGE IN CONFEDERATE VIRGINIA

4

Élan and Organization

Early Field Command in Virginia

CONFEDERATE DOCTRINE AND ORGANIZATION FOR WAR

Allowing for a veneration of military life in the South lacking in the North, early Confederate field command in Virginia nevertheless shared with its Union opposition the common theoretical, doctrinal, and organizational heritage of American military culture. The Confederate *Army Regulations* of 1861 were in the image of the U.S. *Army Regulations* of 1857; and the 1862 Confederate *Army Regulations* contained no significant organizational changes.[1] Confederate manuals and doctrinal disputes reflected, as could be expected, the traditions of the U.S. Army.

A common group of West Point-educated officers, many of whom attended the Academy together, served together, and were friends, carried their shared experiences to their respective posts. With early Confederate, like Union, field command in the East quickly centered around a single army and commander, the dialogue, frequently from different points of a common heritage, intensified. Lee and McClellan not only served together as engineering officers on Scott's staff in the Mexican

War; they also attended Dennis Hart Mahan's Napoleon Club at West Point. And both were commissioned in the tightly knit and elite Corps of Engineers, the institutional nexus for the continuation of West Point intellectual life into the officer corps of the regular army. The Army of Northern Virginia and the Army of the Potomac, in turn, gathered the highest proportion of West Pointers of any Civil War armies, forming a common culture down through divisional command, with the Army of Northern Virginia having a higher proportion of West Pointers at the corps and divisional levels than even the Army of the Potomac.[2] However, McClellan's immediate subordinates were heavily drawn from the Corps of Engineers, while Lee's were not.

One unanswered ideological question was how the economic, political, and general institutional world view of the Confederacy would compare with that of the Union in appreciating the need to centralize and coordinate the South's human and material resources to wage war, and how that response would affect tactical and strategic organization in the field.[3] A basic question of strategic doctrine was more easily answered, namely, how Confederate high command would interpret the principles of war applied to their objectives and their means to achieve them. Jefferson Davis, West Point graduate and Mexican War veteran, and Robert E. Lee, his early chief of staff and continuing advisor, as well as Joseph Johnston, who was involved in early high command decision making, similarly contemplated the problems of lines of operations, strategic points, and interior and exterior lines. Confederate, like Union, strategists were raised in the Jominian tradition emphasizing the destruction of the enemy's army, and like their opponents appreciated the difficulty of doing so in mid-nineteenth-century American circumstances. They recognized that the Union would attempt to penetrate the South using the river systems, the coast, and the Northern railroads, and that the objectives would be the political soft spot of the Confederate war effort, Richmond, and the penetration of Confederate territory and communications.

The Confederate strategists realized that they, in turn, must deny this penetration. Their consequent plan was a defensive line of operations behind which the Confederacy would pursue its ultimate strategic end: to wear down the will of the North to wage war, both at home and under the pressure of a foreign opinion hopefully sympathetic to the Southern cause. The means to achieve this would be an exploitation of interior lines facilitated by the new technology of the railroad and the comparative advantage that it gave the defense. At the same time, to protect Southern territory and communications, Confederate raids would disrupt Union offenses by threatening communications and strategic points in the Union lines of operations, as well as the Union's political soft spot, Washington. Against a Union strategy to disperse Confederate forces in order to concentrate against their parts, the Confederates, on defense, sought to concentrate against the dispersed parts of the Union army. Both sides danced to the same strategic tune. How well they danced depended upon how well field commanders adapted their tactical and strategic organization to the new conditions of warfare.

MANASSAS AND THE FIELD COMMANDS OF BEAUREGARD AND JOHNSTON

The skill with which Confederate field command in Virginia interpreted and adopted the common organizational heritage began to emerge as early as the First Manassas. Two significant tactical developments occurred: General P. G. T. Beauregard used field fortifications; and the Confederates preceded the Union in being the first to get a signals organization into the field. The signals system was largely attributable to the presence in Beauregard's army of E. P. Alexander, who eventually would achieve fame as Longstreet's chief of artillery. Alexander had worked with Myer in the prewar development of signals in the U.S. Army. At the outbreak of war, Davis appointed Alexander to set up a factory to manufacture signals equipment. This task completed, Alexander was ordered to Beauregard's staff in time to organize a signals service for Bull Run.[4]

When Alexander turned down the opportunity to head Confederate signals organization in favor of an artillery command, the position of chief signal officer passed to Major William Norris, appointed in the autumn of 1861 with the rank of colonel. Under the legislation of April 19, 1862, the Department of Signals became the Signal Corps, placed under the Department of the Adjutant Inspector General. Used for secret-service work, the Confederate Signal Corps had even more trouble gaining recognition as a tactical arm than its Union counterpart. Lacking the social and technological environment that would produce an adequate number and caliber of signal officers, it generally languished. The Confederacy used the same signals system introduced into the U.S. Army at the beginning of the war through 1864. They never introduced the cipher disk or otherwise attempted to change their procedures until October, 1864. Their signals were consequently vulnerable to interception, while the Union early developed a secure system.

The reasons for the failure of the Confederate Signals Corps to live up to its early promise and keep technological and organizational pace with its Union counterpart were present from the beginning. Surviving records render any attempt to do justice to the history of Confederate signals extremely difficult, any step-by-step reconstruction of development impossible. What material exists leaves the impression that despite Jefferson Davis's early interest in the Signal Corps, those responsible for military organization outside the corps itself generally neglected a modern signals system in favor of the traditional courier system.[5]

The low prestige with which Union officers associated an unglamorous addendum with no place in the traditional military branches seems to have been felt even more strongly in the Confederate army. The additional role of the Confederate Signal Corps as a secret-service organization could only have detracted further from its primary function. The extensive use of the corps for a variety of staff functions other than the working of a modern signals system seems similarly to attest to a lack of purpose, as does the seeming indifference to develop the technology to keep up with Union signals, even to the extent of devising a secure cipher system.[6] Speculation about the impetuous, impatient Celtic temperament at the basis of Southern personality and culture and its impact on the Confederate armies might have a place in reflection about how far the Southern soldier was willing to go in seeking technological refinement not directly translatable into the élan of combat.[7] From a strictly organizational standpoint, developing and manufacturing the signals technology was a serious problem, which there appears to have been no concerted effort to overcome.

The hit-and-miss organization of available telegraphic resources to create a system of strategic communications reveals the chasm in the Confederacy between disciplined military organization and free enterprise. William R. Plum, the contemporary historian of the Union Military Telegraph, believed that the "Confederates appear not to have regarded it [military telegraph] as so essential as did the Federals. Early in the war the South had resources enough for extending the telegraph from main line offices to all of her armies; but this was not done in western Virginia, southwestern Kentucky or, to any great extent, in Missouri." Though the Confederate postmaster general, Judge Reagan, was placed in charge of the lines of the two telegraph companies (American and Southwestern) that served the Confederacy, Plum concludes that laissez faire prevailed, and the postmaster general interfered with civilian operations "only as military purposes required." The Confederate States military telegraph supplemented the commercial lines, but it employed paid civilians and was under the postmaster general.

The Confederate Congress in July, 1861, authorized the president to seize all telegraph and to appoint agents to supervise it. But, concludes Plum, "there was no such thing as a military telegraph organization in the South, except at a few local points." Beauregard, for instance, had a "regularly organized system with a full corps of operators in and around Charleston. . . ." Plum further observed that

> the companies aimed to do the military telegraphing, even with the armies, and, to a great extent, succeeded. A few operators took service at the headquarters of the commanding officers and had a sort of military status, but they had very little to do in the Western departments, except when headquarters happened to be at some small station, where the company's operator was not able to do the work. It was quite usual, however, for operators to be associated with the principal cavalry chiefs, many as aides, yet others were soldiers. . . . Owing to the Northern operators leaving when the war began, and the enlistment of Southern operators in the armies, there was soon felt a great lack of such talent, and the only remedy lay in detailing operators from the ranks, which was done.[8]

The Confederates generally kept good telegraphic communications along their strategic lines, notwithstanding their ad hoc organizational structure.[9] During the Peninsula campaign, for instance, strategic communications were effective despite Union disruption that tried but failed to destroy the lines.[10] The Confederate postmaster may have intended to develop a field telegraph for tactical communications, only to give up the idea because of a lack of equipment and a shortage of wire, which was also in demand for mine warfare.[11]

But at Manassas, Alexander's organization did valuable service. It was an alert signals post that spotted the Union turning movement toward Beauregard's left flank. Alexander immediately signaled information of the maneuver, which Confederate infantry quickly moved to block. Aided by the heroic efforts of the Confederate signals officers, who maintained their positions under fire to transmit messages of enemy troop movements, the turning maneuver was stopped.[12]

In the other significant tactical development for the Confederates at Manassas, Beauregard challenged the ethos of the aggressive tactical offense and constructed field fortifications. Like Lee, Beauregard was commissioned in the Corps of Engineers after graduating second in his West Point class of 1838. He served with Lee as an engineering officer on Scott's staff in the Mexican War and was surely familiar with the tactical debates filtered through the experience of Mexico. At Manassas he maintained that he took a defensive stand because he considered himself badly outnumbered and hoped to induce McDowell to attack him. Despite strong natural positions occupied by his army, Beauregard entrenched. On the other side of his tactical outlook, Beauregard simultaneously gave orders calling for "great reliance—on the bayonet at the proper juncture."[13] In addition to entrenching his main line, Beauregard, in withdrawing his forces while under attack from Fairfax Courthouse to Manassas, fought his troops from behind abatis and rifle pits in each successive position. He even dug in his skirmish line. Beauregard's troops objected to the undignified nature of entrenching activity, complaining that they had not enlisted to do the work of Negroes, whereupon Beauregard enlisted slaves from the local plantations to do the entrenching.

Beauregard in 1863 would publish a brief guide for his officers, titled *Principles and Maxims of the Art of War*, which reflected the influence of Mahan's ideas on field fortification. Strategically, he displayed Jomini's influence with respect to concentration on interior lines. And perhaps reflecting his Mexican War experience, Beauregard placed heavy emphasis upon the turning movement to flank the opposing army as an alternative to tactical assaults. He backed up his position in this respect by taking directly from Napoleon's maxims, sometimes verbatim, sometimes modified, those principles he thought applicable to his field command in 1863. One modified maxim went beyond Napoleon in emphasizing the role of fortifications. This work and its author thus represented an interesting mesh of Mahan's tactical ideas with a particular reading of their place in the Napoleonic strategic legacy.[14]

General Joseph Johnston, in overall command of the Confederate Army of the Potomac at Manassas, originally espoused offensive tactical doctrine of the most traditional kind, though for the time being in the abstract, as Beauregard exercised tactical field command. Attributing Napoleon's success in 1813 to his large proportion of artillery clearing the way for cavalry, Johnston called for greatly increasing both arms. "For a battle I am sure that 3,000 or 4,000 cavalry in a field would be resisted by no Northern volunteers if they had artillery to open their way—I am confident from observations that Northern troops, like other raw soldiers, fear artillery unreasonably, and that one shall gain more by an addition of these guns than by one of a thousand men." This was surprising doctrine from the soldier who would go down in history as the Confederacy's most renowned defensive general.[15]

Johnston, though commissioned originally in artillery, had a distinguished record that took him through the Corps of Topographical Engineers as well as the cavalry and service as quartermaster of the U.S. Army with the rank of brigadier general. He led the storming column at Chapultepec in the Mexican War. He was also, like Lee, one of the few Civil War field commanders to graduate from West Point prior to Mahan's arrival.

Johnston refused to follow up the victory of Manassas by marching on Washington. A newcomer to the Manassas area and to the state of the army in the field at this time, he would have looked cautiously at the prospect of maneuver. Also, the former quartermaster correctly realized that his Confederate Army of the Potomac (renamed the Army of Northern Virginia when Lee took command the first of June) lacked the strategic mobility to continue the offensive. The Confederate supply system broke down under its own weight. Still in the process of getting organized, encumbered with inexperienced personnel and inadequate administrative organization, procurement and transportation collapsed. Also, Johnston's army was short of everything, including arms for the 20,000 additional men considered necessary to advance on Washington.[16]

The first test of Johnston's tactical outlook in actual field command would occur during the Peninsula campaign when McClellan, five miles from Richmond, entrenched to await the remainder of his army. Johnston would decide he must attack before McClellan combined his forces. He would contradict his earlier espousal of traditional assault tactics and order that entrenchments be turned and not frontally attacked.[17] Johnston's subsequent Civil War career would suggest that the other lesson to be learned in Mexico, as well as the other side of the tactical debate, made the greater impression.

As it turned out, Johnston had little control over tactical events. He had no plan of battle, and the familiar problem of command procedures and tactical coordination quickly surfaced. The Confederate attack was uncoordinated, as Johnston threw in divisions piecemeal. Despite his orders, his troops assaulted the Union entrenchments. Following the repulse of the first attack at the Federal entrenchments and abatis, the battle deteriorated into a large-scale firefight, with troops joining the battle as they arrived. As both sides improvised shelter, a Confederate unit took up positions behind a railroad embankment which "afforded natural rifle-pits." Confederate troops took advantage of rifle pits and abatis constructed by Union troops prior to the battle. The fog of early field command combined again with organizational deficiencies to take its toll. Offensive coordination against entrenched defensive positions broke down, and Johnston's assault at Fair Oaks failed.[18]

LEE, JACKSON, AND EARLY FIELD COMMAND IN THE ARMY OF NORTHERN VIRGINIA

When Lee succeeded the wounded Johnston on June 1, he showed no deference to tactical entrenchment or to the problems of tactical and strategic coordination in offensive operations. Lee's intellectual curiosity is a matter of some controversy; his diligence as a student at West Point, where he graduated second in a class of forty-six, is not. Lee did miss the intellectual volatility that Mahan and others brought to West Point in the 1830s, being one of the few Civil War field commanders to graduate before Mahan's arrival. But service with McClellan, among others, as an engineer officer on Scott's staff in the Mexican War, plus later participation in Mahan's Napoleon Club as well as the superintendency of West Point, should have precluded his losing touch with the continuing currents of American military culture.

In field command of the renamed Army of Northern Virginia, Lee quickly revealed himself to be an unqualified advocate of the offense. According to his military secretary, A. L. Long, he thought in terms of assuming the offense from the beginning of the Peninsula campaign. He never intended to defend Richmond by passively awaiting the advance of the enemy.[19] Even in what Lee considered the defensive phase of his strategy "to resist the regular siege of Richmond" in the face of McClellan's advance, he advocated only a limited use of field works. In orders of June 3 to the chief engineer of the Army of Northern Virginia, Lee, while on the one hand ordering that "I desire . . . the whole strengthened by such artificial defenses as time and opportunity may permit," on the other hand qualified his instructions by ordering that "it is not intended to construct a continuous line of defense or to erect extensive works."[20]

But even while on the defense, Lee was thinking of his positions as "a line that I can hold with part of our forces in front, while with the rest I will endeavour to make a diversion to bring McClellan out." Aware that Southern opinion called for the test of battle, Lee would demonstrate that he shared the Southern warrior élan. In his strategy, Lee recognized his dilemma in bringing McClellan to battle. "McClellan will make a battle of posts," he observed at the time. "He will take position after position under cover of his heavy guns, and we cannot be at him without storming his works, which with our new troops is extremely hazardous."[21]

Lee's decision to attack with sweeping turning movements against McClellan's rear in combination with frontal assaults revealed the organizational limitations of Civil War armies at this stage of combat. Lee did not make enough allowance for the undisciplined nature of his volunteers. He also overreached his capacity to maintain the tactical and strategic communications necessary for the coordination of the extended lines of mass armies.

Lee did introduce some organizational innovations into his army.

He made use of the telegraph to maintain strategic communications with Jackson as he maneuvered to join up with Lee's turning movement against McClellan, and also with General Benjamin Huger.[22] More significant, Lee made a move in the direction of modern staff organization for field operations when he improvised a staff system to move his troops. In general orders of June 24, he ordered the chief engineer of the Army of Northern Virginia to "assign engineer officers to each division whose duty it will be to make provision for overcoming all difficulties to the progress of the troops. The staff departments will give the necessary instructions to facilitate the movements herein directed."[23] Generally, however, inadequate staff and command procedures combined with inexperience to undermine Lee's ambitious turning maneuvers.

Lee found his options reduced to direct tactical confrontation. Despite reservations about the ability of green troops to execute assault tactics against entrenchments under McClellan's guns, he unhesitatingly chose to attack. Problems of coordination weakened the effect of the assaults. Lee also made poor use of his artillery. He adhered to the traditional dispersement of batteries through the army, and he failed to appreciate the difficulties of using artillery on the offense in difficult terrain under the concentrated guns and entrenched infantry of the enemy.[24] Lee's assaults from Mechanicsville through the Seven Days' Battles were disastrous. At Mechanicsville he suffered approximately 2,000 casualties, six times those of the entrenched Union defenders. During the Seven Days' Battles, the dense woods, hills, and swamps made it difficult for him to approach McClellan's well-chosen positions.

Lee's tactical communication and command procedures frequently broke down as Confederate lines made their way over the rugged ground. Again the fog of early Civil War command combined with organizational limitations to doom the offensive. Lee's one attempt to bring his artillery into play, at Malvern Hill, failed. The terrain made it nearly impossible for him to make offensive use of his batteries. On this one occasion when he did get them into action, he failed to concentrate them, in part, perhaps, because of the terrain, but also because of the dispersed organization of the artillery. McClellan's concentrated batteries on the defense drove the Confederate batteries to cover the moment they appeared.

Only twice during the Seven Days' Battles did Lee breach the Union lines. And the Confederate success at Gaines Mill was, as noted, a special case. The Union defenders had repulsed the Confederates at the Union entrenchments when the Union cavalry, moving to assault the retreating enemy infantry, charged between the Union artillery and infantry on the Union left flank. The heavy infantry fire and the cannonading threw the horses into confusion, and the bewildered animals turned about and dashed through the Union batteries. The Union cavalry was operating in this vicinity contrary to orders, and the Union gunners, convinced they were being charged by the enemy, scattered. Lee's infantry took advantage of the opportunity and successfully broke through McClellan's lines. But even with this unexpected turn of events, the price of victory by assault was high. Lee lost approximately 8,000 killed and wounded, to the Union losses of approximately 4,000. One Confederate division lost over 1,000 men in a single charge. The Confederates managed to breach a flank of the Union line at Frazier's Farm by sheer weight of numbers, three to one, in hand-to-hand combat, but McClellan quickly reestablished the line with reserves. When the Army of the Potomac slipped into its base on the James intact, the lesson would seem to be that the frontal assault was succumbing to defensive tactics aided by temporary field fortification.

Only in the use of cavalry—ironically, the one tactical area where his adversary, McClellan, was orthodox—did Lee indicate an innovative outlook. He removed cavalry from its traditional tactical role to concentrate it primarily for the strategic roles of reconnaissance, intelligence, attacking enemy communications, and guarding his own. Confederate cavalry organization combined with McClellan's failure to use his cavalry effectively resulted in Jeb Stuart's famous ride, unmolested, around the Army of the Potomac.[25]

Lee's strategic turning movements at Mechanicsville and during the Seven Days' Battles were overly ambitious for the state of his military organization. They called for the cooperation of as many as seven columns in unmapped and difficult terrain. Coordination depended upon good staff work and communications. However, as John English, the historian of Lee's field communications, noted, "the plan was not fully understood by all commanders. Some of Lee's orders were ambiguous. Details were probably omitted because it was assumed that everyone understood them. Too much discretion was given commanders who were not acquainted with a common doctrine."[26]

Also, Lee was working with the unwieldy divisional command system, where green commanders out of necessity were given considerable independence. There was insufficient provision for lateral communication between the divisions and for vertical communication between Lee and his division commanders. Lee's headquarters failed to make the necessary arrangements to maintain what communications there were. The courier and guide system was inadequately staffed. The assignments called for by army regulations could not be made. The Confederate divisions wandered about the Virginia countryside in a state that can only be described as lost and confused to launch uncoordinated piecemeal attacks against a coordinated and entrenched enemy. The Signal Corps was useless, since nobody knew where anyone else was in a terrain unfavorable to signals. As G. F. R. Henderson, the British military critic and historian, notes, Lee's staff was too small, inexperienced, and ill-trained to maintain communications in rough country.[27]

Lee's ready acceptance of such difficult turning movements suggests a reading of Jomini—if Jomini, in fact, supplemented Winfield Scott and Mexican War experience as Lee's tutor—to which, under the circumstances, the Swiss sage probably would have objected. Perhaps the antebellum South was more susceptible to military élan than to the cautious atmosphere of the Empire and Restoration period in which Jomini's attitudes and ideas took form. Élan, rather than a realistic appraisal of why he was unsuccessful, is the most likely explanation, at least, for Lee's observation in the aftermath of the Seven Days' Battles that he could have severely defeated if not annihilated McClellan's army if his plan had worked out. Whatever his passing thoughts on lost opportunities to defeat the Army of the Potomac, Lee's strategic thoughts now turned away from the destruction of the enemy's army to protection of Confederate territory and communications. In typical Jominian terms, he emphasized concentration to protect strategic points while diverting the enemy. At the same time, the tactical lessons of the Seven Days' Battles no doubt influenced his decision to pursue this strategy by turning the Union armies out of "strong and chosen positions" to fight on ground of Confederate choosing.

Lee, with the concurrence of Davis and Joseph Johnston, built his revised strategy around a movement across the Potomac to turn the Union forces and force them back out of Confederate logistical territory on the southern coast. At the same time, the invading Confederate army could live off the enemy's resources. It was a strategy, however, that left Lee with the same organizational difficulties that had accompanied maneuver during the Seven Days' Battles.[28] But Lee had absorbed some lessons from his initial campaign. Immediately after the Seven Days' Battles, he acted to establish better control in the field by a centralized reorganization of the command structure. Although he retained the divisional organization, he formed divisions into corps under Jackson and Longstreet.[29] He also streamlined and upgraded the courier system, which had broken down during the offensive against McClellan around Richmond, in part owing to the failure to staff it with sufficient numbers of qualified people. Lee had learned the lesson that efficiency in his courier service was essential for successful offensive maneuver.[30]

Placing Jackson in command of one of the corps was probably the greatest boon to command coordination, and consequently to tactical and strategic mobility, to come of the reorganization. Jackson was a painstaking perfectionist in the sphere of tactical coordination. And his emphasis upon organizational discipline began to bring early results. His concept of staff was more in the German than in the American tradition. He saw to it that officers or couriers from his efficient and well-organized staff were always present to give divisional commanders guidance with respect to orders or the plan of battle should they waver or be in doubt. He carefully posted guides so that the army was not held up at every crossroads while a conference decided which fork to follow. In one instance, he arrested a general who had failed to put a guide at a crossroads to prevent a brigade from taking a wrong road.[31] Jackson also made intelligent use of the telegraph for strategic communications with the other corps and with Lee,[32] and, wherever it was possible, he used semaphores for tactical communications.[33]

Lee got the opportunity to implement revised Confederate strategy in events that resulted in the Second Manassas or Bull Run campaign. This campaign grew out of both the Union and Confederate high commands' revamping the eastern strategy after the Seven Days' Battles. When Union high command turned its attention away from Richmond and the Peninsula and toward Lee's army, it sent General John Pope with the new Army of Virginia, a force of 50,000 men, to move overland against Lee. He was to be joined by most of the Army of the Potomac, which was to be withdrawn from the Peninsula.

Lee, seeing this advance from the north, with the Army of the Potomac inactive but still on the Peninsula, took the initiative. He sent an expedition of 24,000 men, consisting of Jackson's corps reinforced by A. P. Hill's division, to reach Culpeper and defeat the first Union corps before the remainder of Pope's army could arrive. But Jackson moved too slowly. Owing to an uncharacteristic breakdown in staff procedures, he failed to maintain adequate communications with his division commanders on his unfolding plans. Both Confederate and Union forces lost heavily in the disorganized battle that resulted. But the Confederates were now aware that Pope was launching a major offensive, and that the Army of the Potomac was moving to join him. This gave Lee the opportunity to concentrate his army of 80,000 on a single line of operations, with the advantage of interior lines, and the opportunity to implement his strategy of turning Pope's army out of Confederate logistical territory before the Army of the Potomac could reinforce it. His plan called for Longstreet's corps to hold Pope, while Jackson's corps turned Pope's right flank. Jackson would move north of the Rappahannock and occupy the supply territory that the Union army had been living off. Pope's army turned, Longstreet would follow to join up with Jackson.[34]

The results of army reorganization and the special talents of Jackson began to tell. With painstaking attention to detail, careful indoctrination of his divisional commanders in the plan of campaign, and skillful use of staff officers, couriers, and signals officers, Jackson maintained constant communication and coordination within his own corps and with that of Longstreet. At the same time, he was constantly aware of the position of the Union army under Pope. Jackson very neatly turned Pope's flank, destroyed his supply depot, and placed his corps on the enemy's line of communications between the Federal force and Washington. He then waited for Longstreet, with whom he was in communication, and who he knew would join him shortly.[35] Under sound leadership and with experience, the Army of Northern Virginia was improvising a functional command doctrine.

The newly formed Union Army of Virginia under the untested Pope was suffering all the anxieties of inexperience, inadequate training, and poor staff organization. Pope also had his problems compounded by an anti-Pope bias in the increasing politicization of eastern field command. Pope had never commanded in battle before, and he operated with limited knowledge of enemy movements and numbers. On August 13, for instance, the whole Confederate army had moved into position to attack without his being aware of it. Pope was first cognizant of the enemy's presence when one of his patrols captured Stuart's adjutant general with a copy of Lee's orders. During Jackson's maneuver to turn Pope's position, the Union signals station followed him from the beginning. But Pope misinterpreted the move. He was unaware that Jackson was turning his position until Jackson was sitting on his tail, having destroyed his supply depot and interdicted his supply line.

His position and his logistics disrupted, Pope had little option but to attack or leave the field. Lee had hoped to turn Pope out of the Rappahannock area without the risk or cost of battle. And Jackson's position was somewhat risky. Longstreet's corps was two days' march behind, giving Pope interior lines against Lee's spread-out corps. If he moved quickly, he could attack Jackson with a two-to-one numerical advantage. On the other hand, Jackson had the advantage of choosing his position and forcing Pope to attack him.

But Pope was having troubles discerning Jackson's movements and intentions. He first thought Jackson had taken up positions at Manassas and made preparations to attack. But Jackson had sent the divisions of Taliaferro, Ewell, and A. P. Hill in motion by different routes to the vicinity of Groveton. When Union troops approached the Confederate positions, the aggressive Jackson attempted to exploit their exposed flank with an assault. After bitter fighting with heavy losses on both sides, the Union force withdrew to Manassas. Pope misinterpreted their flight at Groveton as a Confederate delaying action to cover a retreat. He consequently attempted to concentrate for an assault on Jackson's outnumbered forces. The resulting Second Battle of Manassas or Bull Run again emphasized the ascendancy of the tactical defense.

Pope failed to attack before Lee, with Longstreet's corps, was able to join Jackson. The two corps spread out in a four-mile-long open V. The massed batteries of an artillery battalion under Colonel Stephen Lee commanded a ridge at their center and swept the open field before them. Jackson occupied positions behind an unfinished railroad bed complete with ties to serve as shelter and rifle rests.

Pope attempted to launch a turning movement against Jackson's left in coordination with frontal assaults. Both fell afoul of the terrain and a failure to sustain tactical coordination and discipline. Three successive frontal assaults were piecemeal and disorganized. But what they lacked in organization and discipline, Union troops attempted to make up for in determination. And the still-limited number of rifled muskets versus smoothbores at this stage of the war gave the frontal assault a fighting chance if it could stay out of the range of artillery. The combat was desperate, but the defense prevailed. A concerned Jackson called on Lee for reinforcements from Longstreet. But before they could arrive, Pope made the error of launching a massed assault across Stephen Lee's field of artillery fire. The Union infantry never reached the Confederate lines. One question left from the battle was whether or not the tactically aggressive Jackson was converted to the use of field fortifications on the field of battle, or whether he used them only because of the co-incidence of their availability, combined with the fact that he was out-numbered and assuming a deliberate defensive stance. Longstreet, by comparison, did not entrench.

Lee now encountered the disadvantages of the offense, while Pope reaped the advantages of the defense. Despite his tactical defeat, Pope was able to redeploy to cover his exposed flank, check Lee's strong counterattack, then retreat under cover of darkness. He also maneu-vered to cover an exposed flank against a second attempt at a turning movement. On the tactical defense, he beat back Jackson's assault by a numerically superior force. A third attempt by Jackson on September 1 to turn a Union flank again failed as the Union army maneuvered to block Jackson and beat back Confederate assaults prior to the Federal withdrawal.

But Lee was achieving the strategy he had devised with Davis and Joseph Johnston to clear the Union army out of Confederate logistical territory on the East Coast. And he was advancing toward the original goal of moving north of the Rappahannock. He had not avoided battle to the extent that he wished. Though his losses were favorably comparable to those of the Union—fewer than 10,000 to over 16,000 for the Union—they were losses that the Confederacy, with its more limited manpower base, could ill afford.[36]

ANTIETAM TO FREDERICKSBURG

The victory at Bull Run enabled Lee to continue his raid across the Potomac and into Maryland. This move would pin the enemy down in the North until the season was too late for another campaign into Virginia. The upcoming election in the North made it a good time to bring military pressure to bear for a peace settlement. And the Confederacy was still optimistic that a strong military showing would bring British recognition, which it was hoped would bring Northern recognition. A primary motive for Lee's move, however, was to supply his army from the resources available in Maryland.

Lee's early field transportation and supply standards cannot be determined. But the order of April 20, 1863, that called for thirty-four wagons per 1,000 men was a reduction from previous norms. Lee, therefore, in preparation for his movements out of Richmond north to the Potomac, may have aimed at a transportation ratio in the area of forty wagons per 1,000 men. As with later standards, which Lee acknowledged to be an objective adjusted to reality, it is more difficult to speculate on the actual facts. There is little question that Confederate, like Union, logistical practice never seriously attempted to live by Napoleonic criteria. Both sides probably moved toward comparable practical standards from the beginning, though the Confederacy, for obvious reasons, was less able to sustain them when its resource base deteriorated.

Lee absorbed himself in field transportation and supply problems from the day he assumed command of the Army of Northern Virginia. And the creeping logistical disintegration of that army by the time of the Maryland campaign heightened this concern.[37] To stay in Maryland through the autumn, he determined that he could not continue to live solely off the land. With no rail or water transportation, he intended his life line to be a wagon route to his army from Winchester, Virginia, through Harper's Ferry. Lee hoped that if he crossed the Potomac to threaten both Washington and Baltimore, he would force the Union evacuation of both Harper's Ferry and Martinsburg, enabling him to open up communications with the Shenandoah Valley and its sorely needed supplies. When the Union forces stayed put, Lee dispersed his army to send a force to take Harper's Ferry. With his army spread out, Lee determined that it was unprepared to continue its offensive and decided to withdraw it temporarily across the Potomac. But news of the fall of Harper's Ferry, and the possibility of reconsolidating his army, led him to continue north of the river.[38]

With reduced transportation and restricted use of animals, the Army of Northern Virginia moved with four separate commands marching along different routes. Employing a combination of couriers and semaphores, the separate columns maintained adequate tactical communications to coordinate operations successfully. But then chance intervened on the side of the Union. McClellan intercepted a copy of Lee's plan of operations—which Lee never missed—and acted accordingly. Well led and organizationally and administratively rejuvenated under McClellan's capable leadership, as well as being reasonably well drilled by Civil War standards, the consolidated forces from the Army of the Potomac and Pope's army took the offensive against the spread-out and highly vulnerable columns of Lee's army. Suddenly aware of danger, Lee scrambled to concentrate his troops. Turned out of his positions at Turner's Gap, he took up defensive positions at the base of the low range of hills overlooking Antietam Creek near Sharpsburg.

By the time skirmishing began late on the afternoon of September 16, the Army of Northern Virginia—with the exception of A. P. Hill's division, which Lee had left to receive the surrender of Harper's Ferry, which fell on the 15th, and McLaw's division, which in leaving Harper's Ferry on the 15th had to move slowly in the face of enemy resistance—was located in positions along Antietam Creek.[39] Lee did not wish to fight a battle so far from home. Badly outnumbered, his troops hungry and exhausted, his transportation and supply situation precarious, he now considered his only recourse to be the tactical defense.[40]

Tactical theory and doctrine, Mahan or pre-Mahan, called for an army when assuming a defensive battlefield position to entrench its front as well as its flanks and rear. Yet Lee did not give the order to dig in. Except for a conventional use of stone fences and rifle trenches to fortify a vital bridgehead at Antietam Creek, there was no fortification on the Confederate line when skirmishing began late on the evening of September 16.[41] Lee had the time and the equipment to entrench. His failure to do so suggests that he may have identified with an extreme tendency in American tactical thought opposing all fortifications on the open field of battle, on the grounds that they made green volunteer troops overcautious and destroyed discipline and the will to fight. There was another argument that such fortifications physically hindered the resumption of the offensive, even when the tactical defense was one's primary stance.

One divisional commander, seemingly on his own initiative, fortified that part of his line covering the exits from the woods through which the enemy would have to pass over open ground to attack. The fortifications consisted of a sunken road, stone fences, and breastworks of fence rails hastily thrown up to extend the barricade.[42] Otherwise the Confederate line was without fortifications. The toll in the Battle of Antietam, September 17, 1862, was the highest for a single day's fighting for the entire war. A total of 26,000 casualties littered the battlefield. The Confederate defenders suffered sightly more because of their greatly inferior numbers and their failure to entrench. But the defense held against Union assaults that suffered from the usual problem of coordination.

It was a tactical victory that further depleted Lee's manpower without accompanying strategic advantage. Lee could not exploit his victory. His raid was at an end, his army too physically and materially exhausted to continue. He had to withdraw from the field of battle, leaving the fruits of strategic victory to the Union.

Problems of authority in the Quartermaster and Subsistence departments combined with the failure of the procurement and transportation systems to further hobble Lee's battered army. On September 3, Lee had reported that his army "lacks much of the materials of war, is feeble in transportation, the animals being much reduced, and the men are poorly provided with clothes, and in thousands of instances are destitute of shoes." Lee was forced to gauge the possibilities of advance by the possibilities of foraging his animals and, to a considerable extent, feeding his men off the land. Previous campaigning had stripped the countryside of food and fodder.[43] Short of wagons and animals, the field transportation system was inadequate to forage for any army under the circumstances, let alone for one moving at Lee's pace in the face of an enemy.

Weary, hungry, and footsore, the soldiers of the Army of Northern Virginia straggled and deserted in ever-increasing numbers under the rigors of the long marches and nearly constant fighting. At the Battle of Antietam, fewer than 40,000 troops answered roll. Large-scale desertion depleted the ranks still further after the battle. At this stage Lee requested President Davis to have immediate legislation passed outlawing desertion and authorizing "the most summary punishment." Otherwise, he reported, he could not fulfill even his defensive design "to threaten a passage into Maryland to occupy the enemy on this frontier, and, if my purpose cannot be accomplished, to draw them into the valley, where I can attack them to advantage."[44]

The logistical problems that brought Lee's army to a halt had begun when the Confederates prepared for the Maryland campaign with an improvised and inferior procurement policy. This failure compounded problems caused by the inadequate bureau organization and transportation system of the Confederacy. The Quartermaster and Subsistence bureaus were decentralized and inefficient. Supply agents roamed the field without designated areas of forage. There was no demarcation of authority between the agents of the supply bureaus and the supply agents of the armies of the field. The field commanders, for the most part, did not appreciate or understand the problems of the supply departments; most were after all they could get for their own troops, with little consideration for the dimensions of the general problem. Some commanders made a habit of interfering with bureau arrangements for the procurement and distribution of supplies in their district. Early inexperience among bureau personnel, lack of responsibility among army supply personnel—many of whom played favorites—and much waste by undisciplined troops combined to retard both supply buildups and operations after the campaign was underway.[45]

Meanwhile, the government failed to face up to the problems involved in procurement policy. By the winter of 1861, Davis had finally abandoned the "King Cotton" concept to secure funds for foreign supplies. By this concept, the Confederacy proposed to wage war through the economic pressure of withdrawing cotton from the Union and European markets. Motivated by the laissez faire outlook of the time, however, Davis and the Confederate Congress failed to impose price controls on either foreign or domestic procurement. The results were hoarding, speculation, and inflation. While prices soared as a consequence, the Confederate Congress in its allotments to the War Department refused to face up to the cost of running the war. Even as Congress gradually became more susceptible to War Department requests, it forced the department to scramble in an atmosphere of uncertainty for allotments on a short-run basis. The department never had more than enough to meet minimum requirements to maintain the armies, let alone funds adequate to prepare an offensive campaign. But the patriotism of the Southern people came to the aid of a faltering government procurement policy. In this early stage of the war, massive voluntary contributions helped sustain the army.[46]

Faced with general shortages by the autumn of 1861, the commanders in the field began to resort to impressment without legal sanction. In

November the secretary of war gave the quartermaster general and commissary general official authority to impress, although only "if absolutely demanded by public necessities." At the same time, he extended the confiscatory power of field commanders. Incidents of impressment quickly assumed major proportions, although the railroads were exempted.[47]

But the loss of the resource-rich border areas and the second manufacturing city of the Confederacy, New Orleans, further set back the buildup for the 1862 offensive into northern Virginia and Maryland. Particularly vital was the loss of the beef and flour supply of these areas and the clothing and manufacturing facilities of New Orleans. By the summer of 1862, the supply bureaus and state governors began to pressure Davis to adopt a policy of trading through the lines, exchanging cotton for salt, meat, and clothing. In the face of impending disaster, a contraband trade already was springing up.

The supply of enlistments to fill the ranks also was causing headaches. In April, 1862, the Confederate Congress made a big step into modern military history when it passed the first conscription and exemption acts in American history. All men between eighteen and thirty-five years of age were eligible for three years' service. Substitutes were allowed, and certain categories of professionals and factory workers were exempted. The ranks were not filled with the numbers needed, as the exemptions were badly abused.[48]

The greatest error of government policy in preparation for the 1862 campaign, however, was the failure to regulate the railroads upon which the bureaus had to depend for distribution. The third session of the provisional Congress in the summer of 1861 "buried in committee a proposed bill to allow the government to regulate the railroads under the press of military emergencies."[49] In consequence, the railroad owners continued to operate their lines seemingly oblivious to the war, except as they could profit from it.

Moving his army from the railheads extended Lee's logistical nightmare to the crisis of field transportation. Though the census of 1860 indicates that a Virginia-based army had sufficient animals to begin a war, the source of resupply was inadequate by the 1862 campaign. The preferred source was understandably Virginia and North Carolina, because of both the distance and the relatively light burden on overloaded rail transportation. But this source had to be supplemented from the border states, since the lower South was not horse- and mule-breeding country, and Texas produced largely unsuitable mustangs. There was no difficulty procuring horses and mules in 1861; but the loss of territory in Missouri, Kentucky, western and middle Tennessee, and trans-Allegheny Virginia removed the principal source of top-grade horses. A large purchase of draft horses and mules in Texas early in 1862 got marooned on the far side of the Mississippi. To compound the problem of procurement, scarcity led to skyrocketing prices combined with a depreciation of Confederate currency. The Confederacy in April, 1862, finally adopted a policy of impressing horses under conditions of emergency, yet adhered to a policy of payment in cash. For a brief period, the Quartermaster Department supplied the draft animals and artillery horses requested by a reduced standard that probably was insufficient to maintain adequately an army in the field.

Field supply problems rivaled those of field transportation. Lee's operations in the summer of 1862 preserved the grain crop necessary for forage and subsistence; but by September, forage was scarce at a time when the animals, worn down by campaigning, most needed it. The fodder shortage compounded the horse supply problem. Seventy-five percent of Confederate horse losses came from starvation, disease, and abandonment when the animals were too weak to be of service.

By November, the subsistence standard for Lee's army was in crisis. An exchange between Secretary of War G. W. Randolph and Lee reflected the anxiety and frustration of all involved. Expressing concern about the insufficient supplies for the Army of Northern Virginia, Randolph, writing on November 14, reprimanded Lee for allowing an increase in rations from the previous reduction in April, 1861. Calling for Lee to adhere even more closely than before to the reduced standard, Randolph testily noted that the "supply of hogs is 100,000 less than it was last year; the failure of the corn crop in Tennessee and Northwestern Georgia renders even this supply to some extent unavailable." He went on to note that the beef supply was down in Virginia to less than one-half that of the previous year, and the corn crop of the Southern states was unavailable because of transportation difficulties.

Lee's biting reply noted that he had increased the flour and beef standard to one and one-eighth and one and one-quarter pounds because it was the exclusive subsistence of the men. "No other part of the ration could be furnished to the men except salt, nor could the men increase their fare by the purchase of bread, vegetables, etc." He noted that the lack of food was a cause of straggling and recommended to Randolph that the increased standard be maintained so long as flour and beef were available.[50]

The result of improvised policy and administrative measures combined with material shortages was that the Army of Northern Virginia undertook its 1862 offensive, as Lee noted, "short of its projected strength—fed on a monotonous diet ..., indifferently clothed and equipped, and short of arms and ammunition." Once the campaign had begun, the inadequate supply system was confronted with the even more traumatic problems of providing for a conscription-swollen—if still undermanned—army and the wastage involved in the fortunes of war. In an attempt to fill the ranks, President Davis, in late September, 1862, had Congress pass an act to extend the draft age from thirty-five to forty-five. This was followed in October with a revised exemption act which strictly qualified and defined exemption status. The vicious circle of increased numbers and inadequate transportation and supply took its toll.[51]

By the fall of 1862, the reserves of meat the Subsistence Department had stored up in 1861 in preparation for the campaign were exhausted, and the campaign was "too short for the commissaries operating in Lee's rear to gather sufficient supplies" to feed the troops. This predicament tied Lee to his communications.[52] By the winter of 1862, out of fodder and dependent on day-to-day rail shipments from North Carolina, the Army of Northern Virginia was concentrating more on its supply route than on the Army of the Potomac.

With the mobility, indeed the survival, of the army dependent on the efficient use of the railroads, the railroad owners responded with an assertion of their individual rights. They failed to cooperate. Government shipments were accorded low priority. The railroads over which the animals' feed had to be transported refused to use the space for bulk fodder. The breakdown of the railroad system led to a crisis in the supply of horses, mules, fodder, and subsistence. The Army of Northern Virginia was left hanging at the end of its lines of communications. The weight of this burden of waging war by improvisation within the confines of the Confederacy's social and political ideals helped break the back of Confederate offensive power.[53] The fact that Southern business elites escaped the institutional transition to modern warfare, while the lower orders of society who were the principal victims of America's first conscription laws did not, tells something of the character of Southern society and culture at war, particularly when coupled with heavy desertion from the ranks of Confederate armies.

With his badly outnumbered, undernourished, and ill-fitted army, Lee, after Antietam, had little choice but to take the defense. Retreating to the south bank of the Potomac, he found adequate forage and subsistence for his army. From there he could still fulfill his military objective of checking Union moves into Virginia. When the Army of the Potomac, after two months of preparation, finally moved down the Rappahannock to begin its attempted turning movement, Lee followed along the south bank. He believed from accounts in Northern newspapers that Federal strategy called for the Army of the Potomac to advance from Fredericksburg to Richmond. Anticipating that Fredericksburg would be a relatively certain point of concentration, he planned to slow down the advance the best he could. When the enemy crossed the Rappahannock, Lee felt he was unable to oppose the crossing. For the Battle of Fredericksburg, he had no choice but to fight from the tactical defense. In his own words:

> The plain on which Fredericksburg stands is so completely commanded by the hills of Stafford (in possession of the enemy) that no effectual opposition could be offered to the construction of the bridges or the passage of the river without exposing our troops to the destructive fire of his numerous batteries. Positions were, therefore, selected to oppose his advance after crossing.[54]

Lee subsequently positioned his army on a series of hills overlooking the Rappahannock. But much to the surprise of at least one of his staff officers, Lee, on assuming a tactical defense where doctrine called for fortification of his front, again failed to entrench.[55] He had his troops construct only a few minor earthworks at scattered positions. This despite Antietam and despite the fact that the rifled musket, with its greatly increased range and accuracy, was now in general use in the eastern theater. Jackson, similarly, showed that his use of cover on the field at the Second Battle of Manassas did not reflect any deep appreciation of the entrenched defense. Arriving in position at Fredericksburg a few hours before the Union attack on the morning of December 13, he neglected to fortify his line.[56] Activities a few hours later were to show that lack of time was not an explanation for his absence of entrenching activity. Jackson's first reaction was to suggest an immediate frontal assault on the position of the enemy, who had by now crossed the river and taken up entrenched positions arranged for crossfire effect. Jeb Stuart agreed, but Lee vetoed the idea.[57] He had decided that this was to be a defensive battle.

The incident did suggest that the command structure of the Army of Northern Virginia contained more than its share of what, at this stage of the war, could be considered extreme commitment to the frontal assault and against the virtues of field fortification under any circumstances. One is left to speculate about peer group reinforcement in the influence of the strong-willed Jackson and the dynamic Stuart, both deeply respected by Lee, upon Lee's tactical practice. Jackson, in particular, portrayed by his biographer, Frank Vandiver, as an aggressive "war lover" with an urge for the test of blood akin to what Thomas

Connelly detects in Lee, displayed a penchant for the offensive that dated from the Mexican War.[58] The support of a peer group from the Corps of Engineers was absent in the Army of Northern Virginia. Jackson, Stuart, and Longstreet were not, like Lee, commissioned in the Corps of Engineers, but in artillery, rifles-cavalry, and infantry respectively. To what extent was tactical doctrine a matter of collective professional pride to prove that one was correct in a heated professional debate? One can only speculate. Whatever the explanation, Lee took longer to learn from his experience that the frontal assault contributed only to attrition without victory than any other field commander in the Civil War.

It was not Lee but Longstreet who finally broke the tactical pattern. Although he occupied one of the strongest natural positions in the Confederate line, Longstreet ordered ditches, stone walls, and railroad cuts occupied and strengthened with rifle trenches and abatis.[59] The Federal assaults against his positions on Marye's Heights never got within a hundred yards of the stone wall. Behind the wall were four lines of infantry armed with rifled muskets, supported by sharpshooters in rifle trenches, and entrenched artillery that directly covered and enfiladed the wall from the two terraces that rose behind it. Their fire cost the Union troops 3,500 dead to their own losses of 800 men.[60] Lee watched the battle with Longstreet, overlooking Marye's Heights.[61]

Immediately after the fighting stopped, Lee ordered fatigue parties to entrench the heights. Despite their exhaustion after the battle, the men responded with enthusiasm. The 7th Georgia Infantry was representative of the troops' response. Although it took little part in the fighting, the regiment was close enough to suffer heavy casualties from artillery fire directed at its batteries and at the troops in the line of battle and on the flanks. That night its commanding officer reported: " . . . with light spades, six or eight picks, and a very few axes, it rendered its position impregnable to small arms, and to every kind of attack except one by artillery conducted on the principle of general siege. On the day of battle, it was without any artificial defenses, hence the casualties it sustained."[62] The Confederate army eagerly continued the construction of parapets into and through the next day.[63] "My Army," Lee reportedly said, "is as much stronger for these new entrenchments as if I had received reinforcements of 20,000 men."[64]

Jackson, obviously not too impressed with the previous day's proceedings, decided to launch a frontal assault against the entrenched and enfiladed Federal positions. The intended attack was barely out of the Confederate lines before Federal artillery fire sent his troops scurrying for cover.[65] Jackson finally asked for and received advice on entrenchment from Longstreet, which suggests that the latter perhaps enjoyed some reputation as an expert on temporary field fortification. If so, why did Longstreet not fortify at Antietam? Circumstances suggest that Antietam perhaps converted him to tactical entrenchment. Like any West Point graduate, Longstreet was educated in the construction principles of field works. All he needed was the incentive. In this respect, Jackson's solicitation of his advice may not have been out of respect for any special knowledge attributed to Longstreet but may have reflected Jackson's ignorance of the principles of field fortification construction. The subject of Jackson's inquiry, how to protect the men along his trenches from enfilading fire, elicited from Longstreet the standard solution that Jackson construct traverses.[66] Jackson could have obtained the information from readily available field manuals. Jackson's acknowledged distaste for military engineering as a student left some acknowledged gaps in his military education that he now called upon others to fill.[67]

When Burnside broke off action and recrossed the Rappahannock, Lee had the Army of Northern Virginia construct the most formidable entrenched positions yet seen on a Civil War battlefield. Ignorant of the enemy's movements, he feared that his army would be unable to prevent a crossing of the Rappahannock at some point along the extended Confederate line. Deciding that any attempt to block a crossing would prove too costly, he again selected his positions to resist the enemy once he had crossed.[68]

In the five weeks that followed the Battle of Fredericksburg, Lee fortified the extent of his twenty-five-mile line. "The world had never seen such a fortified position," General William Pendleton, Lee's chief of artillery, wrote to his family. "The famous lines of Torres Vedras could not compare with them." An awed opponent, Brigadier General Gouverneur Warren, chief topographical engineer of the Army of the Potomac, elaborated on the extent, strength, and sophistication of the Confederate lines in one of the most detailed and vivid on-the-spot descriptions of entrenchment to be found:

> The enemy occupied in strong force the heights south of the Rappahannock River . . . having continuous parapets throughout . . . , his troops being so disposed as to be readily concentrated on any threatened point. Interspersed along these lines of entrenchments were battery epaulements advantageously located for sweeping the hill slopes and bottom land, on which our troops would have to march to the assault, and which effectively protected the enemy's artillery from our own. Abatis, formed of fallen timber, and impassable swamps in places, still further strengthened his lines and reduced the number of assailable points. The crest

of the main hills, where the enemy had prepared to receive us, were from three-quarters to 1½ miles from the margin of the river, but this margin was strongly guarded by men sheltered behind rifle pits, which guard and its cover were made quite formidable at every available crossing place. In fact, every little rise of ground that could shelter our advance was entrenched and prepared for us. . . . About 2½ miles above Fredericksburg, the high bluffs on each side close in upon the river, having a height above it of perhaps 150 feet, with slopes generally well wooded, very steep, and deeply cut by side ravines. . . . A foothold on the opposite hills gave a command of all the enemy's lines. A place of such importance was guarded by the enemy with the utmost care. His earth parapets, placed so as to sweep with musketry every crossing-place and practicable slope, and traversed so as to quite protect the defenders from our artillery fire. It might be that these successive lines would be of little use after the first one was carried, as those who fled from the first would mask the fire of the other, so that pursued and pursuer might enter together. The tactics of the rebels, however, provided for this; the first lines generally surrendered when overpowered instead of running, and thus no confusion is produced in the succeeding lines. At Bank's Ford, moreover, two of these lines were so close to each other that both could in place bring their fire upon a party crossing the river, the rising slope permitting the rear lines to shoot over that in front.[69]

This was the line that Lee had failed to entrench prior to the battle. Field fortification had definitely found a place in the tactical organization of the Army of Northern Virginia.

5

Intimations of Modern Warfare

Lee and the Army of Northern Virginia

REORGANIZATION

The Army of Northern Virginia entered 1863 greatly deficient in all areas of supply. By February, the situation reached crisis proportions. The need to scatter the animals in order to feed them rendered the cavalry useless.[1] In addition, there were extreme shortages of footwear, clothing, draft animals, and wagons. Although not so desperate as the forage problem, subsistence during the winter of 1862–1863 was insufficient to resume active campaigning. Calorific standards from the severely reduced rations were adequate to sustain an army in encampment but inadequate for field operations. As an indication, employees on army rations engaged in manual labor for the Niter and Mining, Ordnance, and Engineer departments were getting too meager a diet to sustain them in their work.[2]

Lee, confronting cases of typhus and scurvy, made a plea for supplies in mid-April. He wrote to the secretary of war that the current ration "may give existence to the troops while idle, but will certainly cause them to break down when called upon for exertion."[3] As Lee sat behind his entrenchments on the Rappahannock, the Confederate government and supply bureaus began to show signs of confronting the problems of his army. Deprived of its resource-rich areas and New Orleans, and faced with the uncertainties imposed by the tightening blockade of the remaining Confederate ports, the Confederacy faced the alternative of perishing if it did not exploit its remaining resources.

Early in 1863, the Quartermaster and Subsistence bureaus were reorganized. The procurement wing of the Quartermaster Department was streamlined and centralized. It received exclusive control over purchasing, alleviating wasteful competition between the bureau supply agents and those of the field commanders. The new organization divided the Confederacy into eleven purchasing districts, for each of which there would be a purchasing officer and a central supply depot. Army quartermasters were restricted, except in enemy territory, to collecting forage and fuel only in crisis situations. Otherwise, they requested supplies through the quartermaster general's office. If the quartermaster general approved the requisition, he would instruct the appropriate district purchasing officer to meet it from his depot. Two exceptions to this structure were a supply agent in charge of leather procurement for four states and a supply agent who could procure forage where he could find it for the armies in Virginia and North Carolina. To improve the administration of field transportation needs, an inspector general of transportation, Major A. H. Cole, was appointed under the orders of the quartermaster general.[4]

In a series of general orders from April 12 to July 16, 1863—the first records available on his field transportation—Lee struggled to sustain the wagon standard of the Army of Northern Virginia.[5] Against the practical realities of campaigning in North America, the army saw its field transportation grow dramatically beyond the Napoleonic standard of twelve wagons per 1,000 men. Faced with a deteriorating supply base, Lee and his quartermaster personnel then struggled to bring the ratio down to achievable limits.

General orders of April 12, June 12, and July 16 indicate that the Army of Northern Virginia, like the Army of the Potomac, was attempting to reduce the wagon standard. General Order No. 58, on April 20, called for a decrease to approximately thirty-four wagons per 1,000 men.[6] Dwindling sources of subsistence, forage, and animals were the motives behind these reductions. But the fact that the Army of Northern Virginia never got its formal standard down to the twenty wagons per 1,000 men achieved by the Army of the Potomac's flying column by the end of the 1863 campaign suggests how the hard-pressed

Confederate armies might have benefited from experimenting with such a model themselves.

The headquarters standards at corps and divisional levels were reduced somewhat by general orders of April 12, June 12, and July 16.[7] General orders of July 16 set the ordnance standard at one wagon per 375 men—the bottom rung for the sliding regimental scale from 500 to 375 men—down from the April 20 ratio of one ordnance wagon per regiment. By comparison, the Army of Tennessee did not set the same standard until September 24. A general comparison with the Army of Tennessee, the only western Confederate army for which transportation records are available, indicates that transportation development, though similar, was not parallel. Eastern and western armies developed their field organization according to a common general norm, with variations for local definitions of needs and possibilities. There is no evidence of any central coordination of standards.[8]

General orders of July 18 further reduced the transportation allowance to approximately twenty-eight wagons per 1,000 men, including the reserve train and ambulances. The same general standard, though with some variation in particulars, was set for the Army of the Tennessee on September 24. To show the variations in the sequence of development in the two armies, three months after Lee had reduced his standard to twenty-eight wagons per 1,000 men, general orders of August 26 set the ratio for the Army of Tennessee at approximately thirty-five wagons per thousand. During 1863, Confederate armies decreased the load standard to approximately 1,800 pounds per wagon, probably to accommodate both a reduction in the size of teams with the shortage of animals and the capacity of the animals in situations where they were underfed.

There was an accompanying reduction in the baggage standard for officers. The men carried their own baggage, as in the Army of the Potomac. General officers in the Army of Northern Virginia had a standard set in general orders of April 20, 1863, at 80 pounds for general officers, 65 pounds for field officers, and 50 pounds for company officers. This was a drastic decrease from the formal standards set out in Confederate army regulations from 1861 through 1863.[9] Army regulations allowed general officers in the field 125 pounds, field officers 100 pounds, captains and subalterns 80 pounds. The forage allowance set for animals in army regulations was 14 pounds hay and 12 pounds oats, corn, or barley. There was no variation for horses and mules, but the Confederate armies were largely dependent upon horse transportation. The standard therefore can be assumed to be for horses. In the feeding of mules, the Confederates probably followed the common prewar standard shared with the Union army.

From 1861 through 1863, the daily Confederate ration standard set by army regulations consisted of three-quarters pound pork or salt beef plus eighteen ounces bread or flour, twelve ounces hard bread, or one and a quarter pounds corn meal per man. For every 100 rations, the following distribution took place: eight quarts of peas and beans, or alternately ten pounds rice; six pounds coffee; twelve pounds sugar; four quarts vinegar; one and one-half pounds tallow; one and one-quarter pounds adamantine or one pound sperm candles; four pounds soap; and two quarts salt. On a campaign or a march, the ration of hard bread was one pound per man. This averages at the lowest standard to slightly over two pounds per man per day in the field. Field orders provided for men to carry their baggage, but there is no instruction on subsistence. Presumably the whole was carried in the supply train. Casualties to the official standard came early. The coffee ration tended to be deleted by April 10, 1862. The supply of soap became sporadic, and candles quickly disappeared from supply records. Special orders became necessary to get candles by 1862.[10]

The Subsistence Department also underwent reorganization in the early months of 1863. Although the territorial losses of 1861 and 1862 had drastically reduced its subsistence base, the Confederacy had enough food to feed both its civilian and military population. Virginia was the only state without food surpluses. Since it was the scene of the eastern campaigning, however, it was also where surpluses were most needed. The problem lay in the efficient procurement and distribution of available resources.

The Subsistence Department, as previously noted, suffered from the same problems as did the Quartermaster Department, namely, inefficient district organization and the interference of field commanders. In early 1863, Subsistence centralized and streamlined procurement with a district organization similar to that of the Quartermaster Department. But unlike the quartermaster general, the commissary general did not receive authority to centralize distribution in his hands. The chief commissaries of the armies in the field submitted their requisitions instead to the chief commissary of the state or states in which their armies were located or through which they intended to pass, and commissaries of one state or district could borrow on the depots of others. Of greater consequence, the secretary of war failed to demarcate authority between the field commanders and the Subsistence Department, either in collection or in distribution. He merely told the army commanders to make necessary arrangements for procuring subsistence in each department. As the historian of Confederate logistics Richard Goff observes, the generals were not, as a rule, overly cooperative.[11] Consequently, conflicts between the commissary agents of field commanders and those of the Subsistence Department hampered efficient gathering of available resources. Although the revised organization for procuring and distributing subsistence was a definite improvement over what it replaced, it left more room for waste than the Confederacy could afford.

The commissary general's greatest burden was the failure of the railroads to cooperate in the distribution of food surpluses from other states to the Army of Northern Virginia. Neither the army nor the government exercised any control over the railroads. As Goff observed: "By the spring of 1863 the Subsistence Department . . . found itself in large part the victim of circumstances, harassed by too many imponderables to plan with confidence." Tied to the railroads; unable to build up a reserve; frequently uncertain whether or not their troops were going to be fed from one day to the next, field commanders understandably experienced a general loss of confidence in the Subsistence Department, accompanied by an increasingly defensive, railroad-oriented outlook.

In an attempt to alleviate the drastic shortage of meat, salt, and clothing, Davis, under pressure, in December, 1862, even rescinded the policy of denying cotton to the Union and sanctioned trade through the lines. This stopgap measure was a failure, however, as the Union tightened up on contraband trade. Some quartermaster goods were received through the lines, but there was practically no return in foodstuffs. Another improvised government measure to deal with the subsistence shortage was the "tax in kind," which was put into effect as part of a tax bill passed on April 24, 1863. The tax in kind, as Goff observes, "cut through the Gordian Knot of inflation, speculation, impressment, and hoarding by simply taking a portion of subsistence stocks of the country as taxes." A new, well-organized, and centralized branch called the Post Quartermaster was added to the Quartermaster Department to administer the "tax in kind."[12]

The failure to regulate shipping further hampered the alleviation of the supply crisis of the winter of 1861–1862. The tightened Union blockade increased the risk and consequently the overhead for blockade runners. As a result, blockade running came to be concentrated in fewer and fewer hands. The increasingly greater profits to be gained from bringing in goods for private consumption led to a shunning of government supplies.

By the winter of 1862, large-scale impressment began to anger the citizenry, local officials, and private contractors alike, as the civilian element was forced to compete with the supply bureaus for subsistence and for profit. Faced with this conflict between the prevailing laissez faire outlook and military necessity, the Confederate government opted for the former. It refused to pass legislation instituting price controls. Speculation, hoarding, and runaway inflation were the result.[13]

False hope for reprieve in the crucial area of rail transportation came on the last day of April, 1863, when Congress hesitantly, in the face of the impending starvation of the Army of Northern Virginia, granted the executive the authority to regulate the railroads. The laissez faire-minded Davis was as reluctant to accept this authority as the Confederate Congress was to bestow it. Here was the instrument to prevent a recurrence of the crisis of the past winter. It would enable through scheduling the interchange of rolling stock from one railroad to another. It also would enable the War Department, rather than the railroad owners, to decide on the priority of material to be transported. On May 1, 1863, Davis signed the bill into law. It was perhaps an omen of the future that, at the same time it granted Davis his regulatory authority over the railroads, Congress withheld the administrative machinery to make it effective. Congress failed to confirm the office of railroad superintendent proposed by the secretary of war, while at the same time it shelved the man whom he temporarily had appointed to hold this office while awaiting congressional confirmation.[14]

While Lee struggled with the interdependent areas of field transportation and supply, bureau organization, and the political labyrinth affecting logistics, he also brought changes to areas over which he exercised more direct control. A major tactical reorganization took place in his artillery during the winter of 1863. Lee had long been sensitive to the inefficiency of traditional decentralized artillery organization, which assigned individual batteries to brigades, scattering them throughout the army, and confusing lines of authority between infantry and artillery. His controversial chief of artillery, Brigadier General William Pendleton, had, on Lee's suggestion, drawn up a revised set of regulations in June, 1862. The new regulations centralized all batteries under a chief of artillery for each division. The chief had the additional authority to establish a divisional reserve to supplement the general reserve. This reform gave some independence as well as increased flexibility to artillery organization. But much of the advantage was lost because the individual brigade commanders assumed control of the batteries once they reported to brigade.[15]

The division reserve never assumed a formal place in the army.

Longstreet had formed a loosely organized reserve of ten guns at the Second Battle of Manasses, but no formal reserve had accompanied Jackson. And though the pooling of batteries at the division level gave the artillery a mobility lacking under the old brigade system, the parochialism of divisional organization now became the problem. There was no mechanism to mass guns from more than one division except by drawing from the reserve.

A further revision to tighten the organization and increase the mobility of the artillery took place in the wake of the artillery's success at the Second Battle of Manassas. Batteries were organized into loose battalions, with one battalion assigned to each division. A reserve was organized for each of the two army corps into which Lee, in November, reorganized the army. There was, in addition, the general army reserve. Though Pendleton had previously organized the general reserve into battalions, neither they nor the regular division batteries were integrated into the tactical organization.[16] This plan did not go into effect in time for Antietam. During the winter, the development of the first modern battalion system in artillery organization was carried through its final phase. The final reorganization was the work of Pendleton, Stapleton Crutchfield, Jackson's chief of artillery, and E. P. Alexander, Longstreet's chief of artillery.[17]

Pendleton on February 11, 1863, made a strong recommendation that the artillery be concentrated and placed under more centralized command rather than grouped under divisional command with batteries attached to brigades. He complained that brigade and division commanders were too burdened and preoccupied with infantry to give to artillery the minute supervision it required, especially under the pressure of battle. The existing command organization left the artillery officers with too little scope. Pendleton further complained that batteries permanently attached to division and brigade could scarcely be assigned elsewhere without producing some difficulty, "almost as if a vested right was violated." He thought the major deficiency of the existing system was that it hindered "unity and concentration in battle."

The recommended restructuring called for the organization of artillery in battalions, each to consist, for the most part, of four batteries. Though each battalion would ordinarily "attend a certain division and—report to and receive orders from it," the corps commander or commanding general could divide, detach, or otherwise dispose of the battalions as he saw best. Pendleton called for "all the battalions of each corps to be supervised by and report to the chief of artillery for the corps, as representing for his army the general commanding." He also asked that care be taken to respect the experience of batteries that had served together in the new assignments within the reorganization.[18] Lee authorized the new system on February 15, 1863. He completed the reorganization during the winter when he assigned a field-grade artillery officer to each battalion and reduced his artillery reserve to six batteries.

CHANCELLORSVILLE

As the Army of the Potomac, reorganized and fighting for the first time as a flying column, moved into position near Chancellorsville, Lee and his corps commanders looked over the enemy's entrenchments with mixed emotions. Jackson favored a frontal assault.[19] Arriving with his corps on the threatened flank, he ordered work discontinued on the trenches Lee had ordered Anderson to construct.[20] Fredericksburg, obviously, had not dissuaded Jackson from his belief in the primacy of the frontal assault and his accompanying lack of appreciation for the combination of the rifled musket and field fortifications.

Lee, however, had come to appreciate the entrenched defense. He considered that it was as impracticable for his army to attack the enemy's entrenched positions across an open field at Chancellorsville as it had been for Burnside to attack the Confederate fortifications at Marye's Heights during the Battle of Fredericksburg. The two engineers Lee sent to reconnoiter the Federal line also advised against a frontal attack.[21] But Lee had placed Jackson in command of the Confederate movement to check Hooker, and following his practice of letting subordinate commanders make their own tactical decisions, he did not interfere. Jackson himself decided against an attack on the basis of the information the engineers brought back regarding the strength of the Federal defenses.[22]

The Confederate course of action was determined when Fitzhugh Lee's cavalry discovered that Hooker's right flank "rested in the air," and was "not even covered by a curtain of cavalry."[23] Lee then decided to use the Confederate entrenchments that fronted Hooker's positions as a pivot to launch Jackson on a turning movement around Hooker's exposed flank. Concurrently, Lee, with the remaining troops, would launch a frontal assault to hold Hooker and prevent him from reinforcing that portion of his army under attack by Jackson.[24]

Jackson, as usual maintaining tactical communications by his use of staff officers to transmit and oversee the execution of his orders, briefed all divisional and brigade commanders and placed staff officers at intervals between the divisions.[25] Leaving Lee with some 14,000 troops to face Hooker's approximately 50,000 men, Jackson set out on May 2 with his entire corps of some 28,000 men to roll up the enemy flank.

The movement came at a convenient time. A heavy wind grounded the Federal observation balloons and interfered with good telescopic observation. "The distances involved were also quite great, and the Confederate forces had become rather adept in the art of camouflage. Furthermore, Hooker did not have the services of his cavalry on May 2."[26] Fitzhugh Lee's cavalry brigade was used as mounted infantry to screen the movement.[27] The dense, flat Wilderness afforded excellent protection against detection. Jackson emerged from the woods in successive deployed lines. The Federal defenders, taken completely by surprise, fled when Jackson's troops opened fire.

Effectively combining infantry and artillery, Jackson's attack rolled on. The Federal artillery checked the surge briefly, but then it too retreated to join the infantry at Fairview. Here the Union troops quickly threw up three lines of entrenchments in a nearly impenetrable position. The opportunity to check the Confederate advance fell through when Hooker, failing to sense its importance, abandoned Hazel Grove, the key to the Fairview position, to the Confederates. From this location the Confederate guns could enfilade the Fairview positions. Without the addition of the enfilading fire, Confederate frontal assaults probably would have produced another Fredericksburg-style massacre. But E. P. Alexander was able to make a rare effective offensive use of artillery. Working within Lee's artillery reorganization, he managed to concentrate twenty-five guns.

Blasted by Alexander's artillery from Hazel Grove, the Federal lines were vulnerable. Hooker's first line of entrenchment fell under the first attack. The second line beat back two massed assaults in rapid succession but out of exhaustion succumbed to a third. The Confederates were securing victory by combining superior numbers and artillery against a vulnerable point. The Federal artillery, which occupied the third line of entrenchments, was abandoned. The Federal troops attempted to make a stand without fortifications near Chancellorsville, but Alexander massed up to forty of his fifty guns and enfiladed the Union lines from three directions.[28] Under this punishment, the Union defense quickly collapsed and withdrew. Jackson's casualty-ridden troops were too exhausted to pursue, however, and activities on the other flank were soon to occupy Lee's attention.[29] For Jackson, the artilleryman who had won fame for his aggressive offensive use of artillery in the Mexican War, and who at the First Manassas managed to concentrate as many as twenty-six pieces in front of his infantry, Alexander's performance must have confirmed his tactical predisposition.

It was a great victory, but at great cost. The Confederate casualty list suggested that Lee could afford few such victories at the going exchange rate for frontal assaults against entrenched positions. The Confederate attackers had suffered 30 percent casualties in their frontal assaults against the Fairview positions. The entrenched Federals, on the other hand, had lost about 15 percent of their paper strength and perhaps 18 percent of their troops in action.[30] Jackson, mortally wounded by his own pickets, was not to have the opportunity to further evaluate the changing tactical balance in favor of the entrenched field of battle.

The loss of Jackson and the heavy toll of senior officers had far-reaching organizational effects on the Army of Northern Virginia. Without Jackson and with the absence of an apparent successor who could handle a corps of 30,000 men, Lee, on May 30, reorganized his army on a three-corps system. This, in turn, led to some artillery reorganization, in which E. P. Alexander played an instrumental role. Each of the three corps received three regular and two reserve artillery battalions. This required fifteen artillery battalions where only fourteen existed. Lee took the extra battalion from the general reserve, which had played no effective role at Chancellorsville.[31]

FROM CHANCELLORSVILLE TO GETTYSBURG

Victory at Chancellorsville still left the Army of Northern Virginia strategically immobile. Part of the problem was the condition of the animals.[32] But the larger issue was the general supply situation, which tied Lee to his supply lines. There was reason to doubt that the past policy of ad hoc improvisation without benefit of central regulation or direction would succeed in giving the Confederate army the logistical and manpower capability to maintain any degree of mobility. But would Davis and the Confederate Congress respond? Would they finally abandon the prevailing laissez faire outlook with respect to transportation and direct the nation's resources to the winning of the war? Ironically, the Army of Northern Virginia's victory at Chancellorsville and the relief of its subsistence and forage crises by spring vegetables and grass-fed cattle indirectly contributed to its strategic immobility. Improved conditions gave President Davis and the Confederate Congress the opportunity to forget about the emergency regulations they had been on the verge of putting into effect. Lee was unable to make good the losses of Chancellorsville,[33] leaving him with an inadequate number of men and animals to undertake the offensive during the following month.[34]

It was supply and transportation that again posed the most pressing problems. Although spring had ended the immediate crises, there was still a shortage of animals, wagons, and fodder. The Quartermaster

Department had to depend upon horses from Texas, California, and Mexico; and Abraham Myers, the quartermaster general, on March 4 complained of their poor quality. He expressed concern about the adaptability of mules from Texas because they were too small, while cautiously observing that horses from these areas were adaptable to cavalry service "if judiciously selected."[35]

On April 20, Lee, as noted, had reduced the transportation of the Army of Northern Virginia by a drastic cutback on the baggage train and by laying down a complete new standard of transportation. Yet he could not get the formal standard below approximately thirty-four wagons per 1,000 men. Despite the series of reforms to lower the ratio of wagons to move his army, Lee resigned himself to the gloomy prognosis that probably he would never again get the horses that he needed for even his reduced standards. They simply were not to be found. The Confederate quartermaster general shared his sentiments, noting early in 1863 that the Confederacy was consuming more horses per year than they were able to replace by natural increase.[36]

Lee was agonizingly aware that his formal standards were goals increasingly removed from reality. Even by his reduced standard, he reported on May 23 that he was unable to supply fresh horses for artillery, medical wagons, ambulances, and ammunition trains. An exchange with Pendleton, his chief of artillery, emphasized Lee's forage problem even if enough horses were available. In response to Pendleton's urgent requests for more artillery horses, Lee warned him not to increase his horse supply more than the forage permitted so as to avoid the consequences of malnutrition. He further told Pendleton that the new transportation standard was dependent upon an improvised stocking of supply wagons, with the standard adapted to what was available.[37] On June 30, Lee complained that he was still "deficient in general transportation for commissary, quartermaster, etc., trains."[38] The artillery had only enough horses available to service four guns per battery of horse artillery.[39]

Lee had other problems. Limited to two cavalry brigades, and unsuccessful in his attempts to acquire reinforcements, he was unable to protect his communications lines from the raids of the Union cavalry. Also, owing to a shortage in the supply of carbines, only part of what cavalry he had were armed adequately. On the positive side, by June 1, the Confederate conscription laws were beginning to yield some results. Lee's rolls showed 68,000 effectives out of an aggregate present of 89,000, men, of whom 74,000 were present for duty. At the same time, however, his large contingent of North Carolina troops was deserting in considerable numbers.

The increased strength of the Army of Northern Virginia also meant increased subsistence, transportation, and forage demands. Once spring had relieved the winter food crisis, Davis, never happy with the compromise to his laissez faire outlook contained in the power Congress had bestowed on the executive to regulate the railroads, reverted to his traditional beliefs. The railroads, in turn, continued their traditional policies. By this time, railroad equipment and rails were showing the signs of wear. Breakdowns were increasingly common, and replacements were not easily come by. Hampered though he was, Lee made plans for a summer campaign, hopeful that spring forage and vegetables and grain-fed cattle would enable him to build up a sufficient reserve so that, coupled with foraging on the march, he could take the offensive.[40]

How did Lee envision Confederate strategy at this time? On June 8, he wrote a confidential letter to James A. Seddon, the secretary of war, in which he maintained that the only sensible thing to do was to take the offense in an attempt to draw the Army of the Potomac out of its defenses to assail it on more advantageous terms. "Unless it can be drawn out in a position to be assailed," Lee noted, "it will take its own time to prepare and strengthen itself to renew its advance upon Richmond, and force this army back within the entrenchments of the city." Then, in an interesting comment reflecting his appreciation of the military situation and the probable fate of the Confederate war effort, he added: "This may be the result in any event." In another letter to Seddon, two days later, Lee made it clear that with the dwindling resources of the Confederacy matched against the growing strength of the Northern war effort, the only real hope was for the peace party in the North to gain the ascendancy.[41]

By mid-June, the Army of Northern Virginia finally was getting sufficient forage and subsistence to build up a small reserve. By the end of June, cattle and sheep were coming in, and Longstreet, who had been detached with a force prior to the battle of Chancellorsville to gather forage and subsistence in North Carolina, had returned with his spoils.[42]

GETTYSBURG

Carrying what supplies he could, Lee advanced from the Rappahannock into Pennsylvania, planning to live off the land once he exhausted what he carried. As noted, he aspired to a transportation standard of 34 wagons per 1,000 men for this period. At the same time, he acknowledged the difficulty of achieving this goal. The fact that he lowered the goal to 28 wagons per thousand on July 12 leaves room to speculate that for the Gettysburg campaign, he probably achieved a standard of around 30 wagons per 1,000 men, for a total of 2,950 wagons. The assumption is that Lee's objectives bore some resemblance to deteriorating realities. With 89,000 men aggregate present at the start of the campaign and hence dependent on the transportation and supply system, by John Moore's calculations Lee had near exactly the capacity, with standard rations and forage, to move his army—provided he didn't send empty wagons back for resupply but refilled them off the land, which was his plan. And with numbers declining through the campaign owing to desertion, the demands on the transportation and supply system lessened.

Lee at least partially overcame the problem of the increased number of wagons needed to forage when he anticipated the organization for foraging that Sherman would develop, apparently independently, for his march to the sea. When on June 25 Lee completely abandoned his supply lines, rather than sacrifice the troops necessary to guard them, like Sherman in his 1864–65 campaigns he marched his men in columns in the fields on each side of the turnpikes. The supply trains moved on the turnpikes, facilitating their access to the troops while allowing foraging parties to sweep the areas between the columns. This organization speeded the movement of the army while shielding the foraging parties. One cannot determine whether this was Lee's standard organization or whether he first introduced it for the Gettysburg campaign. The fact that he marched with his columns spread out during the Maryland campaign perhaps implies the former.

The evidence suggests that by Gettysburg, and probably before, Lee understood that speed and the logistical organization it required were the keys to living off the thinly spread resources of the American countryside. Sherman had a higher transportation allowance while living completely off the land with a smaller army during his marches to the sea and through the Carolinas. But even Rufus Ingalls, the talented quartermaster of the Army of the Potomac, bemoaned the unnecessary standard of living expected by the Union soldiers, a dilemma, it appears, in Sherman's army, as well. The Union soldier could have cut down his logistical burden and still have marched and fought efficiently, if less comfortably. With the 1863 reforms in the Army of the Potomac, in fact, the transportation ratio was reduced by August 21 to twenty wagons per 1,000 men. And the Army of the Potomac moved during the Gettysburg campaign with approximately thirty wagons per 1,000 men. Though Lee's army lacked the elaborate field transportation and supply reforms necessary to achieve this level with any degree of comfort, its standard for the Gettysburg campaign was adequate, providing forage and subsistence was available on the land and the ever-vulnerable horses of the supply trains held up.

As it turned out, forage was in rather short supply. Lee sent his lead corps into Pennsylvania to forage while the remainder of the army held the Army of the Potomac in place. But Union militia and partisans made their task difficult. Nevertheless, when Lee marched, his army, when it could take advantage of good roads, probably averaged about ten miles per day.[43]

In the aftermath of Gettysburg, Lee maintained that unless attacked, he had not intended to fight so far from his railhead. When he stumbled upon the whole enemy army, however, he considered a withdrawal through the mountains too difficult and dangerous, particularly since he was then without the reconnaissance services of his cavalry. But he believed he could not await an attack since the country was unfavorable for collecting the supplies he needed to survive. The enemy could hold the mountain passes with local and other troops, as well as limit Confederate foraging parties. Moreover, unless Meade took the offensive, Lee decided that he would have to take the initiative and launch a frontal assault. Should Meade oblige, however, Lee, out of respect for the enemy's positions, expressed a preference for remaining on the tactical defense.[44] Yet Lee's initial failure to entrench his positions adds to conjecture that at Gettysburg Lee may have welcomed, if he did not seek, the test of combat. Or his motive may have been to lure Meade to attack.

In the face of Meade's hesitancy to attack, Lee reluctantly planned a frontal assault.[45] Longstreet, in opposition, proposed a turning movement around the Federal left flank. This would have interposed the Army of Northern Virginia between the enemy and Washington, and forced Meade to attack the Confederates in their positions.[46] Lee dismissed Longstreet's strategy. There were certainly great risks and difficulties in such a plan. Without Stuart's cavalry, which had become separated from the army, such a move would have had to be made without reconnaissance and screening in the face of an enemy force estimated to be twice their number. This included a cavalry force numbering almost 20,000 men.[47] Thus, the risks of maneuver led Lee to seek what he had come to reject: tactical victory by frontal assault. The assault was not to be undertaken in ignorance of the possible consequences, but because circumstances forced the issue.

Apart from the entrenched enemy on the hills opposite, the principal obstacle to success was probably the coordination of the extended line of attack. For the army that had executed the movements that won the Second Battle of Manassas and Chancellorsville, that might have been a manageable obstacle. But, this was not that army. In particular, gone was Jackson, the major architect of command coordination. Without him, the absence of the staff coordination and communications required by a modern army became obvious. With new division and brigade commanders exercising their commands in a major action for the first time, even coordination between general and corps headquarters was inadequate. Part of the problem was a lack of confidence in the Signal Corps. Reservations about Confederate signals were legitimate. Unlike the Union Signal Corps, the Confederates had not developed a visual system secure from interception, which led to almost total reliance on verbal and written orders carried by couriers and staff officers; another was that in the haste of taking up their extended positions, all of the line "was not well studied, and the officers of the different corps had no opportunity to examine each other's ground for chances to cooperate."[48]

Despite some poor troop handling and tactical communication, Lee's assaults on July 2, at tremendous cost, did take and hold some ground on the extreme right of the Confederate line. Despite being thrown back at the line of defense on Little Round Top, Longstreet's troops held ground taken by positioning themselves behind rocks, trees, a stone wall constructed on the field of battle, and then strengthening positions with breastworks.[49]

The day's fighting buoyed Confederate morale. In his official report, Lee wrote: "The result of this day's operation induced the belief that, with proper concert of action, and with the increased support that the positions gained on the right would enable the artillery to render the assaulting columns, we should ultimately succeed; and it was accordingly determined to attack."[50] Other factors contributed to Lee's optimism. Reinforcements arrived. General George Pickett's division was fresh, and Stuart had curtailed his wanderings and arrived with his cavalry.[51] Lee's aide-de-camp, Taylor, stated that "an overweening confidence possessed us all."[52] Alexander perhaps caught the mood in his comment that "there seemed to be a prevalent feeling that fortune now favoured us and that victory or defeat now depended solely on ourselves."[53]

But "overweening confidence" turned to despair. Both the "proper concert of action" and the "increased support that the position gained on the right would enable the artillery to render the assaulting columns," upon which Lee was depending for success, failed to materialize. Unclear orders, tardy couriers, and a legitimate hesitancy to use signals for fear of Federal interception left the July 3 assault disjointed and uncoordinated.[54]

The performance of Lee's reorganized artillery reinforced the diminishing role of artillery on the offense. Anticipating European artillery reorganization after the Franco-Prussian War, Lee had broken up what remained of his reserve after Chancellorsville.[55] The concentrated Confederate cannonade brought 142 guns to bear.[56] The rolling open ground invited the use of artillery, but in the haste of preparing for battle, the Confederate artillery took positions from where their fire was generally perpendicular to the line of the Union guns. The state of artillery development could not provide the pinpoint accuracy their positions required. In addition to the shortage of ammunition, the Confederate artillery in the Army of Northern Virginia, as elsewhere, continued to have problems with the quality of shells.[57]

E. P. Alexander maintained that Lee placed too much faith in the Confederate artillery:

> It seems remarkable that the assumption of Colonel Long [former secretary to Lee and now chief of artillery in Ewell's corps] so easily passed unchallenged that Confederate guns in open and inferior positions could suppress Federal artillery fortified upon commanding ridges. Our artillery equipment was usually admitted to be inferior to the enemy's in numbers, calibres and quality of ammunition. Moreover, here, the point selected and the method of attack would certainly have been chosen for us by the enemy had they had the choice.[58]

For reasons not explained, the Confederate artillery was not entrenched.[59] To make matters worse, once the attack was launched, Long, by his own admission, scattered his fire over the whole field instead of concentrating on key points, for the most part overshooting the enemy's positions.[60] The Confederate ammunition shortage also kept their artillery from maintaining a persistent cannonade.[61]

But most responsible for the failure of the Confederate offensive was the direct and enfilading fire of the fortified Federal artillery and infantry. This fire tore apart the Confederate assault by successive deployed lines. Alexander's attempts to bring up artillery to support Pickett's legendary charge were ineffectual.[62] In what amounted to a sideshow to the Battle of Gettysburg, the nearby cavalry battle on July 3 was one of the few in which Lee's cavalry employed conventional cavalry charges. Initially, however, the cavalry continued a pattern they had established early in response to terrain and the rifle: they deployed dismounted in a skirmish line.[63]

POST-GETTYSBURG

Having suffered 28,000 casualties, his army demoralized and deserting, almost out of ammunition, with local troops and cavalry hindering foraging, Lee prepared to withdraw to the Rappahannock. In one of the most remarkable displays of the limitations the new conditions of warfare were imposing on strategic maneuver, Meade, in the best campaigning season, was unable to exploit his victory to prevent the Confederate retreat. Despite the fact that Lee was some two weeks' march into Federal territory, without communications, living off the land, his field transportation in bad shape owing to the deterioration of his horses, and his army soon reduced to about 35,000 by desertions, Lee successfully made a slow and arduous ten-day withdrawal to the Rappahannock. Faced with Meade's pursuing army, he crossed unmolested. With Meade pursuing on interior lines, Lee proceeded to make a twelve-day march southeastward down the Shenandoah Valley to south of the Rappahannock at Culpeper Court House.

As he recouped at Culpeper Court House, Lee adhered to his original strategic hope that the Federal army could be brought to fight on ground of Confederate choosing. But if not, he chose to attack Meade where he stood. He wrote to Jefferson Davis: "As soon as I can get the vacancies in the army filled, and the horses and men recruited a little, if General Meade does not move, I wish to attack him." But the familiar problems of supply frustrated any aggressive designs Lee may have held. The countryside stripped by his stationary army, Lee was hit with another acute shortage of forage and subsistence, the railway owners again failing to respond to the supply needs of the armies in the field, and Davis failing to respond to the need for regulation. The forage problem put both the Confederate cavalry and artillery out of business, since the horses had to be widely scattered for their survival. In the first week of August, Lee had to allot a portion of his transportation to the Commissary Department to collect grain. And in early August, a shortage of weapons left 1,700 men in the Army of Northern Virginia unarmed. The offensive capacity of Lee's army was exhausted.[64]

The chronic shortage of wagons and animals worsened. The latter situation was sufficiently desperate to drive the Confederate inspector general of field transportation, Major A. H. Cole, to request, on July 2, permission to purchase animals in Union territory. To make matters worse, the destructive disease glanders infected the horses of the Army of Northern Virginia.[65]

To add to his problems, Lee could not replenish his manpower. Despite concerted efforts to bring the Army of Northern Virginia to offensive strength, by the end of August the aggregate present exceeded that of August 10 by only 4,000 men, climbing from 68,000 to 72,000 officers and men, compared to an aggregate present of 89,000 at the time Lee had launched his offensive into Pennsylvania. The Army of the Potomac numbered 90,000 aggregate present. Any hopes Lee had for an offensive were dashed for the time being when Longstreet's corps was detached to bolster the Confederate forces in Tennessee, thus reducing the Army of Northern Virginia to an aggregate present of 54,000 men.[66] Lee retired south of the Rapidan near the Wilderness, which brought him back to where he had begun his offensive into Pennsylvania three and one-half months before.

Despite his manpower, supply, and transportation problems, Lee decided to launch an offensive when a corps of Meade's army was detached to the West to reinforce Rosecrans, in response to the Confederate detachment of Longstreet to reinforce Bragg. In part, the motive for the offensive was to prevent Rosecrans from receiving additional manpower from the Army of the Potomac.[67] By October, the corn crop allowed Lee to feed his limited horse supply more or less adequately, which temporarily gave him the mobility to try to push Meade back to the line of Bull Run.

Lee prepared for the campaign with an improved logistical organization. Brigadier General A. R. Lawton, appointed quartermaster general in August, imposed a more diligent supervision over the railroad supply of subsistence and forage. This gave the Army of Northern Virginia minimal relief, although the supply was never sufficient.[68] Lawton was more willing than his predecessor, Abraham Myers, to use the railroad control law; but he acted only when directed, and restricted his actions to specific cases. He did not advocate its general use.[69] Major Cole, the inspector general of transportation, issued a general order on October 30 which attempted to establish some centralized authority, together with clear procedures to regulate the use of field transportation and artillery horses.[70]

In the ensuing campaign, which included actions at Bristoe Station, Rappahannock Bridge, and Mine Run, all the new features of trench warfare combined to produce complete tactical and strategic stalemate. The signs began to appear in skirmishes leading up to the confrontation at Bristoe Station. Both sides used their cavalry extensively as mounted infantry fighting from cover. In one instance, the Federal cavalry fought from rifle pits.[71] As the campaign unfolded, the trend toward intensified trench warfare continued. Except for one offensive stance, Meade fought from entrenched defensive positions throughout the campaign. Circumstances soon combined to force Lee to follow suit. At Bristoe Station, Lee surveyed Meade's strongly entrenched positions and immediately ruled out a frontal assault in favor of a turning movement.[72]

But at this juncture, chance intervened to disrupt both strategic and tactical expectations. General A. P. Hill carelessly marched into an entrenched ambush. Two of his brigades were decimated, and the loss of men, to say nothing of morale, was a serious blow to Lee's already depleted army. A much greater setback than Hill's defeat, however, was the loss to the blockaders of the imported clothes and footwear upon which the Confederate forces were depending for the winter campaign. The Quartermaster Department could not immediately get funds out of the inflation-ridden Treasury Department to buy the cotton to pay for additional supplies in England or on the Continent. Demoralized and without sufficient human or material resources to continue the offensive, Lee, again without serious interference, fell back from his fifty-mile penetration and fortified a bridgehead on the north bank of the Rappahannock.[73] There is evidence that the Confederates carelessly laid out and constructed their works.[74] Meade, no doubt anxious to silence loud criticism of his failure to disturb Lee's retreat from Gettysburg, launched a surprise night attack, which overran the Confederate positions.[75]

With an extended front and the possibility of being pushed back into the Rapidan, Lee again withdrew across the river to his starting point of a month before. When Meade failed to attack, Lee decided to assault the Union left flank in an attempt to turn the enemy positions. The attack found empty entrenchments. Meade had withdrawn the night before to go into winter quarters north of the Rappahannock.

Although the Confederate Quartermaster and Subsistence departments had begun to meet the minimum needs of the reduced Army of Northern Virginia, they were unable to build up any reserve, forcing Lee into winter quarters and the daily ritual of watching the railroads.[76] Lee fought the post-Gettysburg campaign painfully aware of his strategic limitations. Ruminating on his fate, he observed that to turn Meade's position would merely induce the Army of the Potomac to retreat. The Army of Northern Virginia could not pursue because the quest for supplies would carry it too far from Richmond. Besides, he observed that the army was too poorly provided for to contemplate such a campaign; the condition of the men too destitute to even stay on Meade's front if the latter remained quiet.[77] That he undertook what he did, considering his reservations, is remarkable, lending some credence to psycho-historical speculation about Lee's aggressive neurosis as a strategic motive, or to the culture and personality theory pertaining to the aggressive Celtic battle leader. After six months of tactical and strategic stalemate, active campaigning in 1863 thus came to an end exactly where it had started, behind fortifications on opposite sides of the Rappahannock and Rapidan in the vicinity of the Wilderness.

By the end of 1863, the Army of Northern Virginia had established an organizational history in tactics and strategy that reflected both the heritage it shared with the Army of the Potomac and its own variations on the common theme. Whether Lee's belated conversion to the tactical role of field fortifications and the obsolescence of the frontal assault was attributable to the influence of his two corp commanders, to youthful doctrinal influences in the cra before Mahan, or to his own neurotic aggressive personality or Celtic warrior élan is conjecture that the historian must risk. On the evidence, all of the above probably played a role in his tactical outlook. Whatever his motives, Lee's respect for the entrenched defense after Fredericksburg brought uniformity to the tactical pattern in the eastern theater. Only at Gettysburg, faced with the alternative of attacking or retreating because of his precarious logistical situation, did Lee break the prevailing pattern to make an open frontal assault against entrenched positions without the advantage of surprise.

Though McClellan was the Civil War innovator who broke with doctrine to concentrate his artillery, Lee followed. He acknowledged the failings of a decentralized and dispersed artillery command at the brigade and divisional levels to concentrate his artillery at the corps level, both for ease of concentration by the artillery chief and commanding general and to give artillery officers more control over their own operations. Lee also created the modern battalion organization to give artillery greater ability to move and maneuver.

The Army of Northern Virginia also abolished the artillery reserve, partly in recognition that its offensive use was obsolete. Lee, like Joseph Johnston, Jackson, and most Confederate artillery officers, was slow to acknowledge the diminished offensive role of artillery. Early reorganization for offensive concentration did not acknowledge the lessons of the Peninsula campaign and Fredericksburg. Although McClellan's artillery did play an offensive role at Antietam, as did Alexander's during Jackson's turning movement at Chancellorsville, these were anomalous incidents. The defensive role of Confederate artillery at Fredericksburg seemed to have been overlooked as the significant positive lesson for the Army of Northern Virginia in 1861–1862. The poor quality of shells and lack of devices for indirect ranging and firing on the offense, together with the range of the rifled musket, supported by the Napoleon, on the entrenched defense, imposed the changing tactical balance at Gettysburg. Nowhere was the futility of artillery on offense more conspicuous than in Alexander's frustrated attempt to get his guns into the field to support Pickett's charge at Gettysburg.

In cavalry organization, Lee early appreciated what the field command of the Army of the Potomac was particularly slow to note: that the predominant role of cavalry was to be strategic, not tactical. The concentration of cavalry for raiding and protecting lines of communication, as well as its deployment for reconnaissance and other staff functions, was an early part of Lee's military organization. Jackson's use of cavalry to facilitate his staff and command procedures for strategic coordination revealed exceptional foresight. Lee's organization of a separate cavalry corps was perhaps the most dramatic organizational recognition of the revised strategic role for cavalry.

Cavalry battles, where they occurred, were incidental both to the cavalry's primary role and to the course of tactical development. Lee's cavalry, when it fought tactically in the line, from the beginning of the war fought dismounted. Mounted combat did occur, but it was anomalous except when following up an advantage gained while fighting dismounted. The changing tactical role of cavalry was another reflection of how, by the end of 1863, the Army of Northern Virginia, like its opponent, had arrived at a war of tactical entrenchment dominated by infantry armed with the rifled musket, and supported by the defensive deployment of smoothbore artillery.

The reorganization of Lee's Army of Northern Virginia into three corps after the Peninsula campaign, combined with the centralization of his artillery command, was an early recognition of the need for greater centralization in command procedures to coordinate a mass modern army under existing conditions. Jackson was the locus of an improvised set of command procedures in the Army of Northern Virginia that resembled a modern staff system. But the system was too personalized to survive the deaths of both Jackson and so many field officers experienced in the use of Jackson's procedures during the Battle of Chancellorsville. Lee and his corps commanders had recurring problems with command coordination thereafter.

The promising early introduction of a Signal Corps seemed to receive a less than enthusiastic follow-up from Lee. Belated efforts to work out a signaling system that could not be read by the enemy were perhaps a commentary on the role of signals envisioned by Lee, who gave indications that he preferred the traditional courier as a source of communications. Shortages of both telegraph wire and a pool of technical talent from which to draw operators were sufficient reasons by themselves to discourage extending the telegraph from strategic to tactical communications.

Lee's strategic mobility away from his base of supply disintegrated around a shortage of animals. The early loss of the major horse-raising areas of the Confederacy, combined with ideological and structural failures to organize the supply system, was an insurmountable strategic burden. The failure to subordinate the railroads to military needs, contrasted to the organization and administration of railroads in the North, was a continuous logistical hindrance as Lee anxiously awaited subsistence, fodder, animals, and wagons over a railroad system upon which he could not depend.

Field transportation and supply standards in the Army of Northern Virginia, as in the Army of the Potomac, quickly expanded beyond Napoleonic norms to meet the realities of American conditions. Lee's basically ad hoc standards were comparable to those of the Army of the Potomac prior to Union reforms that led to the flying column. The Army of Northern Virginia increasingly had to live with less than Lee's downward-shifting standard, owing to the failures of Confederate supply organization combined with real shortages, while the Army of the Potomac, faced with the contrary dilemma of largess, developed the dramatically reduced standard of the flying column. Lee, in practice, probably came close to that standard, but without the organizational benefits of the Union flying column.

Belated Confederate moves to centralize and specialize, such as the creation of the post of inspector general of field transportation, brought some results. But the government's aversion, shared by some quartermaster personnel, to subordinate commercial free-enterprise activity in the economy in general and the railroads in particular frustrated internal reforms in supply organization. Cooperation, let alone integration of planning, between the quartermaster of the Army of Northern Virginia and the supply bureaus was not good.

Though subsistence and forage were available if the economy and the supply system had been able to organize their procurement, there were not enough animals. Even had he enjoyed adequate organizational support, the shortage of animals was sufficient to make Lee's spectacular raids logistical gambles. That he achieved what he did toward his military objective of keeping the Union army out of Virginia was a tribute to his logistical daring and insight.

Lee was hampered by the general organizational chaos in logistics, but he sensed what was necessary to move his army in the field. While he seemed to lack the creativity to emulate the Union flying column with a reorganization of his field transportation and supply structure, he showed exceptional ability in exploiting the standard system. Confederate logistics lacked the efficiency, creativity, and cooperation that Montgomery Meigs provided in molding the bond between bureau and army logistical organization in the Army of the Potomac—which is to say that Lee lacked what in this one area the Union had: the anticipation of a modern staff system to coordinate operational planning with bureau and strategic planning. Lee did appreciate early that the secret of strategic mobility was organizing to live off the land. From the beginning, he seems to have appreciated that the key to living off the land while maneuvering with a large army was to move quickly. And he anticipated Sherman in the logistical organization of his army to move quickly while sweeping the path of his army for supplies. The terrible deterioration of his army when on the march was the price of moving with a transportation and supply system pushed beyond its limits. But arguably, it was the price that he had to pay to prevent the greater military disaster, namely, Union penetration of Virginia and the consequent loss of essential communications and supplies. The results indicated that he achieved his strategic objectives through Gettysburg. The consequences for his army indicated that to sustain this type of strategy under the same or deteriorating logistical circumstances would destroy that army.

CONTINUITY AND CHANGE WESTERN STYLE

6

Maneuver and Tactics

The First and Second Lines of Confederate Defense

THE WESTERN ARMIES

The 1861–62 campaigns in Tennessee, Mississippi, and Kentucky began with several impressive strategic movements. The small armies, which until the summer of 1862 seldom numbered more than 30,000 men, did not assure greater strategic flexibility in the western theater. The western armies suffered even more than the large eastern armies from basic problems of organization. But they benefited from circumstances that reinforced their small size. They were fighting in a relatively resource-rich area. And the Federal forces had the advantage of good communications with Illinois and Ohio, making the procurement of food, fodder, horses, and wagons for an army of 30,000–40,000 men less of a problem than it was with the large armies of the East. But the early success in the West was most attributable to Union accessibility to the river systems as routes of supply and avenues for strategic turning movements.

For various reasons, the Confederacy chose to assume a defensive posture in the West. With the pursuit of political recognition their ultimate objective, the formulators of Confederate strategy believed this end could best be achieved through denying Federal forces access to Confederate territory. Economic and logistical considerations forced the Confederacy, with its limited resources, to guard the rich resource area of the West, particularly after the loss of the border states. Another factor to consider, as in the East, was inferiority in numbers. Thus, a strong defensive line to secure the western perimeter of the Confederacy was in order.

The Confederates anchored the western extremity of their line of defense at Columbus, Kentucky, on the Mississippi River, with alternate forts downriver toward Memphis. Columbus was occupied by an army under the command of General Leonidas Polk, who threw up enclosed bastioned earthwork fortresses to close the Mississippi River.[1] The center of the defensive line was a strongly entrenched position at Bowling Green, Kentucky, a railroad junction from which an army under Albert Sidney Johnson controlled the Louisville Railroad—a potential invasion route—which branched at Bowling Green to connect with the principal railroads of the Confederacy.[2] Bowling Green was also the best position from which to cover Nashville, the base of supply for this line of defense.

Running parallel and close together, the Tennessee and Cumberland rivers penetrated the Confederate line between Columbus and Bowling Green. To obstruct this entry, the Confederates built Fort Henry to guard the entrance to the Tennessee. A short distance away, and connected with Fort Henry by a good road and a telegraph line to enable mutual support,[3] they constructed Fort Donelson to control the Cumberland and protect the railways connecting Bowling Green, Columbus, and Memphis.

Both Donelson and Henry were enclosed bastioned pentagons with irregular features supported by outworks of rifle pits and by heavy abatis to protect the land approaches.[4] The eastern end of the Confederate line was anchored by an entrenched camp at Mill Springs, Kentucky. It guarded Cumberland Gap, the traditional entrance by way of the Cumberland River through the Alleghenies into the Tennessee Valley. The defenders entrenched the camp on three sides and threw up abatis. The fourth side was protected by the high bluffs on the south bank of the Cumberland. On the north side of the river, the Confederates constructed a line of entrenchments about one mile in length between the Cumberland and White Oak Creek.[5] The Confederate railroad network and the Cumberland, in theory, at least, permitted relatively easy concentration at any position on the line. In fact, the lack of rolling stock and of steamboats greatly restricted the use of these interior lines.[6] The Union war effort in the West confronted the tasks of penetrating and driving the Confederates out of this defensive line, destroying Confederate communications, occupying Confederate territory, and, if possible, destroying the enemy's army.

In spite of their smaller size, the western armies in the first stages of the war were as unwieldy as those in the East. Missing was the hard core of professional officers and regular regiments that bolstered the eastern armies. Although some states' militia institutions were better than others—for example, Indiana and Kentucky—and many militia officers were competent, the Federal forces nevertheless were lacking in consistently well-trained officers, as the Union failed to follow the Confederate practice of dispersing regular officers to their home states. But in the Confederacy, as well, professional officers were heavily concentrated in the East. Divisional commanders without prior military experience were relatively common. Below the divisional level, militia officers were the rule. Where regular officers were available, they sometimes were sacrificed to the electoral system of selecting officers or to political patronage at the regimental level and above. In the early stages of the fighting, there was consequently a serious lack of military discipline. Added to this was a general ignorance of conventional staff and command procedures. Such innovations as a Signal Corps, let alone telegraphic communications, were viewed with even more suspicion, particularly at lower command levels, than in the eastern armies.[7]

Officers with engineering experience were so rare that they were treasured and passed around. Not unrepresentative was the plight of the Confederate General F. K. Zollicoffer, who prior to an action at Barboursville, Kentucky, in mid-September, 1861, reported: "My only engineer officer understanding military engineering has resigned and gone home." Grant had one engineer officer and no engineering troops at the Battle of Shiloh in April, 1862.[8]

Organizational problems abounded. There were no topographical maps, the road system was inadequate for tactical or strategic coordination, and the terrain was even more rugged than that in the East. For the most part, the western infantry began the war with long rifles, flintlock muskets, and shotguns taken from cabin walls. To make matters worse for the Union forces, there was no unified command in the West. Upon taking over as general in chief early in 1862, McClellan concluded that "utter disorganization and want of preparation pervaded the Western Armies."[9]

Despite these early hindrances to movement, there were certain modifying influences. Owing to the comparatively small numbers of the western armies in the early phase of the war, the food and fodder problems, especially since the fighting was in a good resource area, were not as serious as in the East. The smaller western armies were also better able to live off the land during the growing season. Nor were the problems involved in coordinating the tactical movements of these small armies as formidable as with the mass armies of the East, although the poorer performance in tactical communications was a leveling influence. And on the Ohio and Upper Mississippi, the Union busily fitted out a river fleet of transports and armored gunboats. The Confederates could not match this effort because they lacked the heavy industry in the West to turn out either engines and parts or armor. Union exploitation of the river system offered the best possibility for sustaining a war of strategic maneuver.

It was January, 1862, before the Union forces could consider an offensive against the Confederate line, and even then preparations were inadequate for a sustained winter campaign. As could be expected, there was an even greater shortage of experienced supply personnel than in the East. The setting up of an effective logistical organization dragged out through the early stages of the war in the West.

The greatest initial problem affecting mobility in the West, as in the East, was the shortage of wagons and horses. Every field commander voiced despair.[10] Inadequate staff procedures compounded by jurisdictional disputes plagued organizational efforts to get enough animals. And rail transportation was not adequate to meet early animal and wagon needs. Subsistence was given priority over quartermaster supply when the railroad system was not capable of serving both equally.[11] Typical of the improvised scramble to field armies, the Department of Ohio resorted in late July, 1862, to the requisition of horses, wagons, teamsters, and wagon masters from the city of Louisville, taking the Eighth Street stables and those who worked there, lock, stock, and barrel.[12]

Quartermaster statistics give a general indication of early problems. On July 1, 1862, the entire Union army had on hand 14,842 horses, 16,899 mules, 1,727 oxen, 4,645 army wagons, and 149 light wagons. On July 1, 1863, the supply system had improved the figures to 45,755 horses, 46,226 mules, 1,276 oxen, 10,729 army wagons, and 1,263 light wagons.[13] Though incomplete and low, these statistics give some sense, after subtracting the total for the Army of the Potomac alone, of the straits in which the Union armies in the West went through the early campaigns, as well as their dependence upon requisitioning wagons where available.

Yet, in the spring of 1862, there was a brief period of largess in field transportation for at least the Army of the Mississippi. In the western as in the eastern armies of the Union, there was, as Meigs acknowledged, no fixed doctrine on transportation standards in the early stages of the war. Standards were established in part by the political push and pull of field commanders competing for existing resources, and in part by the availability of resources close at hand. One of the more successful in acquiring field transportation was General William S. Rosecrans in his early command of the Army of the Mississippi. Rosecrans, by March, 1862, had accumulated just under 2,000 wagons, sufficient for the very high ratio of 50 wagons per 1,000 men for his army of 40,000 men. A shortage of available animals, approximately 1,900 horses and 5,700 mules—1 animal for almost every 5½ men—kept the ratio down to 35 wagons per thousand. The problem of unserviceable animals may have reduced this to a working standard as low as 30 wagons per 1,000 men except when the army was moving in the field with good foraging conditions.[14] By April, Rosecrans had acquired almost 12,000 animals. This made up the deficiency of the previous month to provide sufficient animals to achieve a ratio of 50 wagons per 1,000 men, with 1 animal for approximately every 3½ men. Allowing for unusable animals, Rosecrans had a working standard at worst of approximately 45 wagons per 1,000 men.[15]

Whereas the Army of the Potomac did not begin to phase out the horse for the less vulnerable mule until late 1863, the mule was dominant in the western armies from the beginning. The erratic fluctuation in the ratio of mules to horses suggests that convenience of supply more than concern about their relative merits was the cause. For example, the ratio of mules to horses for the Army of the Mississippi fell to two and a half to one in April, 1862, recovered to three to one in July, fell dramatically to three to two in August, and then came back to two to one in September.[16]

Not until July did the Army of the Mississippi's transportation standard begin to fall as resources were redistributed elsewhere. A slight reduction in June led to a drop of the standard in July to 40 wagons per 1,000 men with available animals. The decrease was in wagons, down from almost 2,000 in March and April to under 1,600 in July. Rosecrans had enough surplus horses and mules, however, to compensate for any problems with unserviceable animals. The train probably utilized the surplus, as was the practice, as pack animals. This slightly increased the transportation standard.[17] By August, Rosecrans's wagon supply fell to 957 wagons, a ratio of 24 per 1,000 men, with over 2,200 horses and approximately 3,300 mules.[18] Rosecrans had enough animals to sustain as high as a 30 percent loss of horses if his mules remained relatively healthy. With the use of his surplus for pack animals, Rosecrans had the makings, with a moderate loss of horses, of a standard of around 25 or 26 wagons per 1,000 men.[19]

For the Confederate armies in the West, there was early disorder and step-by-step improvisation and development of field transportation and supply standards. Beauregard, for example, after succeeding to the command of the Army of the Mississippi following General A. S. Johnston's death at Shiloh, complained of a shortage of haversacks. In a special order, April 10, 1862, he ordered haversacks to be made, if necessary, "of old tents." Plagued with the familiar burden of chaotic baggage organization, Beauregard further ordered that all loose transportation "not private or attached to battalions" be collected at once by the chief quartermaster.[20] Just before Shiloh, Johnston, in a special order, April 3, 1862, had established a standard of one wagon to two companies for the Army of the Mississippi.[21] Braxton Bragg, upon succeeding Beauregard, also attempted to cut down on baggage. In general orders of June 14, 1862, he eliminated all trunks and boxes in the personal baggage of officers and men, and set standards for tents and files.[22] Bragg, in a special order June 13, 1862, established a standard for ordnance of two wagons per regiment.[23] General Earl Van Dorn, commanding the Army of the West, in special orders of May 10, 1862, set a standard of one wagon for pioneer companies in each brigade.[24] There was also a serious problem with the organization of the train. For example, as late as July, 1862, there was uncertainty as to where in the general train of the army to place the baggage train and how to integrate private wagons.[25] The western armies of the Confederacy, like others at this early stage, were improvising from experience.

There are some interesting and unexplained variations between the early subsistence standard of the Army of the Mississippi at Corinth in April, 1862, and the standard set in army regulations.[26] One is left with the impression that the official norm was a guideline, adjustable to local surpluses and shortages, as well as to a general Confederate pattern of local improvisation in logistics. There seems to have been a general tendency at this early stage of the war to push subsistence supply above the limits of army regulations.

In early January, 1862, there still was not sufficient transportation to build up an adequate network of Union supply depots.[27] By mid-January, the western armies of the Union had swollen to around 90,000 men, allowing for the difficulty of determining real numbers in the West in the early stages of the war.[28] The supply problem grew accordingly, and was made worse by the lack of forage in the winter season.

Training the thousands who poured into the Union camps contributed further to the immobility of the Union forces. The lack of military experience exacerbated the task. "I am in the condition of a carpenter who is required to build a bridge with a dull axe, a broken saw, and rotten timber," wrote Henry Halleck from his western command in the first week of January, 1862. "It is true I have some very green timber, which will answer the purpose as soon as I can get into shape and season it a little."[29] Commanders bemoaned the shortage of good staff officers.[30] Attempts to coordinate strategic planning between the two military departments under Henry Halleck and Don Carlos Buell were ineffective, owing to both human failings and the lack of an adequate staff and command structure. But politicians and, to a lesser extent, even the generals were impatient. In mid-January, the ill-equipped, ill-provisioned, and ill-trained Union forces made their first serious attempt to dent the Confederate defense.

STRATEGY AND TACTICS
IN EAST TENNESSEE

Union thinking recognized that the waterways were the surest avenue to strategic success. The rivers had served as principal routes of commerce. It was to be expected that they would continue to be used in wartime to transport troops and supplies. In November, 1861, Grant, under orders from McClellan to make a demonstration against Columbus to prevent reinforcement from there to Missouri, had launched an amphibious operation from his base at Cairo, Illinois; but the first serious assault on the Confederate line of defense was a land operation against General F. K. Zollicoffer's entrenched camp at Mill Springs, Kentucky, in January, 1862.

General Don Carlos Buell, a Mexican War veteran commissioned in infantry, was in command of the department centered in Kentucky east of the Cumberland. Buell gave in to pressure from Lincoln, exerted through McClellan, to relieve Unionist East Tennessee. He reluctantly concentrated 14,000 men in southeastern Kentucky under General George Thomas. Buell had complained in December that his inadequate field transportation and his supply problems prevented an advance into East Tennessee:

> The movement on East Tennessee attacks their rear, and if properly supported, promises great results. The first 12,000 must probably be followed by others, particularly as it will be unsafe, if not absolutely impossible, to carry along the outfit for 10,000 men. With it the column would employ some 1,200 teams of all descriptions and occupy a stretch

of road that the troops could not protect, to say nothing of the difficulty of foraging so many animals in a country which affords but scanty supplies.[31]

By mid-January, Buell was still having great difficulty collecting the trains he needed. McClellan told him that Meigs had sent the 400 wagons requested and that he should hire or, if necessary, seize private teams if those proved insufficient.[32]

Thomas had brought up the idea of descending the Cumberland by boat to Mill Springs, but enemy positions along the river ruled out that possibility.[33] The alternative land route revealed how ill-prepared the western armies were to launch an overland offensive. Although Thomas's force numbered only 14,000 men, with two artillery batteries and a brigade of cavalry,[34] his supply system could support a winter march only under the most strained circumstances. Thomas's army made most of its march on half-rations. Part of the problem was the shortage of supplies, part a shortage of transportation. With the 400 wagons that McClellan sent, he had a generous standard for so small an army of almost 29 wagons per 1,000 men. But the wagons got spread over extended supply lines in a manner that created a transportation crisis. A lack of transportation seemingly reduced the regimental trains to the point where they could not carry adequate supplies. The general supply train was inadequate, on the one hand, to stock an intended depot in proximity to the campaign. On the other, it was inadequate to carry sufficient supplies from the more remote depots, because the size of the train would have increased with the distance between the army and the supply base. Of equal if not greater importance were the winter rains that rendered the roads nearly impassable for army wagons.[35] The successful completion of Thomas's march can be attributed in large part perhaps to the hardy character of the western farmers who predominated in the ranks.

Thomas was seeking a tactical confrontation rather than a turning movement. Under the circumstances, he had little choice. His tactical decisions quite possibly reflected the teaching of Mahan, since the reflective Thomas was a West Point graduate, as were some of his subordinates. Thomas was reluctant to attack Zollicoffer's well-placed and -constructed entrenchments, and plans were made to draw the Confederates out for an open battle. This decision had nothing to do with the new rifled muskets, since none were present. In fact, there were only a limited number of regulation smoothbore muskets. The Confederate defenders saved Thomas from making a decision when their Council of War decided that they were outnumbered and incapable of withstanding a strong attack. The Confederates had eight regiments of infantry, six pieces of artillery, and two companies of cavalry, but effective strength for the battle was only 4,000 men.[36]

The ensuing battle, at least from the Union side, could have come from Mahan, or from untutored common sense. The presence of competent West Pointers, who official reports indicate made the tactical decisions, suggests the former explanation. When the two forces met near Logan Cross Roads, Thomas covered his line "throughout its entire extent by the fence separating the field and woodland and by the timber and thick undergrowth adjacent thereto."[37]

General George Crittenden, who assumed command of the Confederate force after Zollicoffer was killed, positioned his line in a deep protective ravine, extending around the ridge at the head of the ravine and onto the hill occupied by the enemy. The Confederates forced the battle by moving against Thomas's army. The conflict quickly deteriorated into a firefight, vividly described in Robert McCook's official report for his brigade:

> I ordered the Second Minnesota Regiment to move by the flank until it passed the Tenth Indiana and the Fourth Kentucky, and then deploy to the left of the road. I ordered the Ninth Ohio Regiment to move through the first cornfield on the right of the road and take position at the farther fence, selecting the best cover possible. . . . The Ninth Ohio's position checked an attempt on the part of the enemy to flank the position taken by the Second Minnesota, and consequently brought the left wing almost against the enemy where he was stationed behind straw stacks and piles of fence rails. Another regiment was stationed immediately in front of the Ninth Ohio, well covered by a fence and some woods, a small field not more than 60 yards wide intervening between the positions. The enemy also had possession of a small log house, stable, and corn-crib, about 50 yards in front of the Ninth Ohio.
>
> Along the lines of each of the regiments and from the enemy's front a hot and deadly fire was opened. On the right wing of the Minnesota regiment the contest at first was almost hand to hand; the enemy and the Second Minnesota were poking their guns through the same fence. However, before the fight continued long in this way that portion of the enemy contending with the Second Minnesota Regiment *retired in good order to some rail piles, hastily thrown together*, the point from which they had advanced up on the Fourth Kentucky. This portion of the enemy obstinately maintaining its position, and the balance remaining as before described, a desperate fire was continued for about thirty minutes, with seemingly, doubtful result.[38]

A significant tactical development saw Colonel Frank Wolford, in command of Thomas's cavalry, fight with his men dismounted beside the infantry, while using his mounts to change position.[39] By contrast, the cavalry was dismounted comparatively late in the East. Crittenden also maintained that he attempted to use his cavalry in the line in conjunction with artillery, but the problem of topography prevented their getting into position.[40]

When the Confederates fell back to Mill Springs, Thomas deployed in line and advanced to positions on a summit overlooking their entrenched camp. A Military Telegraph line that he had ordered completed as far as Somerset, some seventy miles from where the Battle of Logan Cross Roads had been fought, kept up strategic communications during the pursuit to Mill Springs. Tactical communications were executed, however, without the advantage of a signals organization of any kind. Respectful of entrenched defensive positions, Thomas ordered his two batteries of artillery, which had been fighting in the line throughout the battle, to bombard the defenses prior to a frontal assault. Thomas's guns kept up a barrage of shot, shell, and spherical case until dark. The Union assault found the Confederate entrenchments empty. Crittenden, weighing his inability to counter the range of the Union Parrot guns, the insufficient numbers to man his entrenchments, his shortage of provisions, and his overextended line of communications, had abandoned his positions.[41]

Although the undermanned Confederate force soon collapsed and scattered in panic, Thomas was unable to pursue. The Quartermaster Department had failed to come up with enough horses, mules, and wagons to support a continued offensive, and the subsistence shortage required the tired Union troops to remain on half-rations. To make matters worse, after a brief period of relief, winter rains set in again to make the dirt roads nearly impassable.[42]

The fall of Mill Springs gave the Union access to the Upper Cumberland, exposing Bowling Green and rail communications along the length of the defensive line. Eastern Tennessee, with its valuable niter and coal fields in the Cumberland Mountains, was uncovered. Although the conditions of the roads and the lack of transportation and forage prevented the Union forces from advancing into eastern Tennessee,[43] the threat weakened the Confederate defenses by forcing General A. S. Johnston, in command in the West, to thin out his already overextended army. The fall of Mill Springs prompted Johnston to detach several regiments from Bowling Green to protect East Tennessee.

On February 1, Buell informed McClellan that he did not have the logistical means to undertake a campaign into East Tennessee. In explaining his decision, he noted that he was some 200 miles from his depots. Buell observed that a continuous supply train from the army to the base of supply would be the only way he could move. He estimated that he needed 1,000 wagons "constantly going" to sustain 10,000 men under such poor foraging conditions, a standard of 100 wagons per 1,000 men and 1 horse approximately for every 2 men. He didn't have the wagons, and if he did, he observed, he would need to corduroy the roads before they could take the load. This would require five regiments working full time.

Buell hesitated to enter the vicious logistical circle. There was "too much to be undertaken on the whole route to East Tennessee. If the number of troops and consequently the amount of hauling is increased, the difficulty is increased in a greater proportion. The limited amount of forage on the route will be speedily exhausted, as besides provisions for our men we must then forage for our animals." Buell estimated that it would take three divisions totaling 30,000 men at effective strength to penetrate East Tennessee, two to penetrate the countryside, and one to keep open communications, and he envisioned an impossible logistical situation for an army one-third that number.[44] By late January, however, the attention of Lincoln and McClellan turned from Buell's department to that of Henry Halleck.

Halleck, while working diligently to bring order to his department, which stretched westward from the Cumberland to the Mississippi and included politically divided parts of Missouri, also developed a western strategy. In accord with McClellan and Lincoln, he early saw the western war as a struggle to push the Confederates out of their territory by waging war on their communications and logistics. Halleck, like Buell, believed that the place to break the Confederate line, in the best Jominian tradition, was at the middle. And the middle was a perpendicular line that coincided with the Tennessee and Cumberland rivers. Halleck planned to take advantage of water transportation to capture Forts Henry and Donelson, which commanded the Confederate line on these rivers, before they could be reinforced. He could then break the Memphis and Ohio Railroad, costing the Confederates their mobility on interior lines, and move up the Tennessee and Cumberland rivers to turn the Confederates out of Columbus and Bowling Green.[45]

To execute his strategy, Halleck selected General Ulysses S. Grant. He discussed the plan with Grant, who strongly endorsed it. Grant moved his army by river steamer in two trips and debarked about five miles below Fort Henry. From there he intended to invest the fort from its land side while the gunboats of Flag Officer Andrew Foote shelled it from the river. Grant left his supply and baggage trains at Paducah, Kentucky, to be brought up by river steamer. He outfitted his army of some 15,000 men with three days' rations and forage, had them carry their camp and garrison equipment, and restricted each regiment to a maximum of four teams. His wagon standard cannot be determined. The familiar problem of restricted mobility returned. Coordination collapsed when the almost impassable roads delayed Grant for several hours.

But in this instance, Confederate incompetence in constructing Fort Henry compensated for the breakdown of land movement. Seemingly unfamiliar with the principles of river defense, the Confederate engineers had built the earthen fort so close to the river that the large Dahlgren guns of the Federal gunboats could demolish it. The location of the fort on low ground also denied its guns a plunging fire on the Federal gunboats, while the iron-armored sides of Foote's vessels protected them from all but plunging fire. Without waiting for Grant's arrival, Foote opened the attack. By the time Grant belatedly put in an appearance, Fort Henry had fallen. The garrison, which the Confederate commander had placed in a safe place outside the fort because he thought the men were so inexperienced that they would be useless in its defense, made good its escape to Fort Donelson twenty miles away. Grant, following Halleck's orders, cut the Memphis and Ohio Railroad at the bridge over the Tennessee River.

Grant then proceeded to Fort Donelson. The move, though short, was not easy. Snow followed by rain turned the ground to deep mud. Grant was not fitted for a winter campaign. His green army had no signals organization. Most difficult, he moved without his supply train, which Foote was to transport by water. He continued to travel with his stripped-down transportation and supply standard. Neither tents nor baggage was taken, except as the men could carry. Troops carried forty pounds of ammunition in their cartridge belts. They carried two days' rations in their haversacks, with three days' additional rations in wagons to follow but not impede the progress of the main column. Grant's logistical plight worsened when the regimental trains that had been left behind were forwarded but did not arrive, owing to a breakdown in transportation procedures in the field. And then several of the regiments Halleck had sent by raft and water to reinforce him came without wagons. Grant later complained that this had cost him what little mobility he had.

Grant's logistical organization was so spare that he moved without a quartermaster. On the supply side, the contractors for fresh beef had the cattle needed, but were unable to procure transportation to get them to Grant, who unsuccessfully scoured the countryside to compensate. The need to live off salt meat caused an outbreak of dysentery.

Grant was learning the logistical limitations and possibilities of strategic movement. His move from Fort Henry to Fort Donelson, twenty miles away, took seven days. That was a discouraging sign for overland winter campaigning.

After Donelson, Grant limited officers to 100 pounds each in wagons, including mess kits. He limited each company to one wagon for camp and equipage and officers' baggage, while he provided for three extra wagons to each regiment for headquarters, medical, and quartermaster supply. Grant's experience as a quartermaster may in part account for his early confidence and improvisational skill in the organization of field transportation and supply, to say nothing of his logistical daring. It also no doubt contributed to his emphasis upon logistical reform and the establishment of efficient standards as essential to strategic mobility.[46]

With reinforcements, Grant's army outnumbered the Confederate defenders two to one. Nevertheless, he believed the occupying Confederate force to number 29,000 men. Yet he failed to entrench.[47] In answer to later criticism, Grant insisted in his *Memoirs* that though "the troops were not entrenched . . . the nature of the ground was such that they were just as well protected from the fire of the enemy as if rifle-pits had been thrown up. Our line was generally along the crest of ridges. The artillery was protected by being sunk in the ground. The men who were not serving the guns were perfectly covered from fire on taking position a little back from the crest."[48] Grant's explanation is weak, considering his thin line and the fact that he was not as familiar with the terrain as was the enemy, that he could not bring his siege artillery from Fort Henry, and that he could have expected the inadequately provisioned and isolated garrison to attempt a breakout. More telling, perhaps, is Grant's earlier acknowledgment, in a letter to General John Fremont, September 5, 1861, pertaining to the entrenchment of his lines in the vicinity of Cairo, Illinois: "On the subject of fortifications I scarcely feel myself sufficiently conversant to make recommendations." Grant approved of good fortifications, but felt the need for engineering help. In the above instance he finally assigned to engineering duty Joseph Webster, a former captain in the Topographical Engineers who had resigned to go into business and returned to the army as the paymaster of a volunteer regiment.[49]

Shortly after that incident, at the Battle of Belmont in November, 1861, Grant again indicated an appreciation for fortification on the field of battle. At the beachhead where he disembarked, and from which he would retreat if necessary, he posted a guard in a ditch, which, he noted, formed "a natural entrenchment," and from which it "could hold the enemy for a considerable time."[50] He further indicated an appreciation of tactical doctrine regarding entrenchment by criticizing the Confederates' failure to protect their position at Belmont with more than a single artificial construction, an abatis of felled trees.[51] While General Pillow had chosen to fight an eighteenth-century battle by leaving his covered positions and forming his line of battle in the open field, Grant had put his troops behind the trees on the field's edge and raked the exposed enemy troops.[52] These incidents leave room for speculation that by the time of Fort Donelson, Grant, though appreciative of covering his troops, was still not comfortable with constructing artificial entrenchments, and avoided them when he had the advantage of strong natural positions.

Fort Donelson was a more formidable obstacle than Fort Henry. Donelson was well located on high bluffs somewhat back from the river. Its water batteries, strongly protected in positions cut into the bluffs, had the advantage of descending fire. Foote's gunboats could not bring their guns effectively to bear on the elevated and well-protected Confederate gun positions. After receiving a severe pounding from fire, which registered over sixty hits on his flagship, Foote withdrew down the river. His two strongest gunboats were disabled and could not render assistance for almost two weeks. Grant's investing army was feeling the effect of a severe cold snap. Many of his green troops had discarded coats and blankets on their march. None of them had tents, and all were finding it difficult to keep up their fires. The river arm of their strategic maneuver paralyzed, Grant and Foote jointly decided that the land forces had no alternative but to entrench for a siege while the flotilla was repaired.[53] Grant could be supplied by way of the river. With the naval arm immobile, position had won at least a temporary victory over maneuver.

But before he could entrench in accordance with siege doctrine, chance and inexperience intervened. An attempted Confederate breakout collapsed, leaving the defenders in confusion and destroying their morale. To effect the concentration for the breakout, the Confederates had drained the troops from the ring of rifle pits that were the key to the Donelson-Dover position. Grant quickly rallied his forces and drove them over these outer defenses before the Confederates could redistribute their men. With the Union troops encamped within their lines, the Confederates surrendered. The heavy losses inflicted on Grant by the attempted breakout cast doubt on the wisdom of his not entrenching his investing force. Even Grant admitted that only hesitant leadership prevented the Confederates' exploiting the confusion of the green Union troops to escape.

The fighting produced a significant incident in the development of assault tactics to cope with the entrenched defense. Colonel Morgan Lewis Smith's 5th Union Brigade abandoned conventional assault tactics to advance by rushes. Smith deployed eight companies in a skirmish line that took advantage of the underbrush and forest. When his two regiments came under fire in a clearing, he had them lie down while the skirmishers occupied the enemy. When a lull occurred in the enemy's line, the two regiments rushed to absorb the skirmishers. This pattern was repeated several times until the brigade finally closed to carry the enemy works as a heavy skirmish line. Smith's innovation resulted in casualties that were only half those of a successful assault in column by a brigade near the same sector of the line.[54]

With the loss of the Cumberland and Tennessee rivers, the whole Confederate defensive line crumbled. Nashville was abandoned. Johnston ordered Polk to withdraw from Columbus. The Confederate armies fell back to Corinth, Mississippi, and their second line of defense. Southern failure to defend their interior lines, despite unified command in the West, was in part the product of poor strategic vision and poor generalship in the field. As Hattaway and Jones note in their study of western strategy, the Confederates failed to see the defensive line as a whole. They lapsed into a cordon defense, with each of the separate detachments in the department committed to defend a particular point or locality. Instead of using the Cumberland River and the railroads to concentrate at a threatened point, each of the Confederate commanders thought only of his individual responsibilities.

> This state of mind infected the department commander, Albert Sidney Johnston, who not only had no plan for a coordinated defensive, but so focussed his own attention on defending the Bowling Green line against Buell that he gave little consideration to the remainder of his department. A similar myopia afflicted . . . Polk, in whose district precariously nestled Forts Henry and Donelson. Polk's fixation remained Columbus, and he determined not to weaken it.[55]

Johnston's poor generalship was compounded by that of John B. Floyd in command of the Donelson reinforcements.

Discernible in the early contest of position versus maneuver were elements that potentially could give the western war quite a different character from that of the war in the East. The most important of these was the strategic role of the waterways. The rivers were the most accessible routes into the heart of the Confederacy, and conversely the focus of the Confederate lines of defense. The first head-on confrontation on the river systems, though influenced by the extraneous factors of inexperienced troops, questionable Confederate generalship, and an engineering failure at Fort Henry, suggested that the offense had the upper hand. At a stage in the evolution of warfare when problems of maneuvering large land armies in rugged terrain were giving the advantage to the entrenched defense, strategic movement by water and coordinated envelopment by land and naval forces suggested a solution to the threat of the new positional war.

While the prevailing state of military technology did much to contribute to the breakdown of movement on land, on the rivers it proved a boon. The comparatively slow development of efficient rifled artillery and exploding shells meant that the smoothbore was still used in river defense. And smoothbores could not pierce the iron armor of the gunboats, except under such extreme circumstances as when Foote's flagship took over sixty hits at under 400 yards. Unless the Confederates could take the initiative, or overcome their industrial incapacity to build ironclads on the western rivers to challenge the Federal flotilla, the Union's armored vessels, with their ability to run past the river defenses, stood to gain the strategic advantage on the western rivers.

SHILOH AND CORINTH

With their base of supplies and their transportation net shrinking, the western armies of the Confederacy fought increasingly from a precarious defensive posture to protect what remained. The influx of recruits to swell the armies strained existing resources still further. The Confederates found themselves boxed into the limited area in which they could secure supplies, and the shortage of transportation and their inferior numbers accentuated their defensive orientation.[56]

With the loss of his first line of defense, Johnston concentrated most of his force at Corinth to check Grant's anticipated thrust down the Tennessee River into the heart of the Confederacy. Corinth was the junction of major east-west and north-south rail lines through the western half of the Confederacy. Beauregard, in charge of the Mississippi defenses, fortified Island No. 10 and the nearby village of New Madrid. Since these positions about eight miles below Columbus were outflanked by Grant's army whenever Grant was free to turn his attention to them, Beauregard considered them only a stopgap. He constructed the main line of Mississippi defenses on the bluffs above Memphis, which were connected by rail with Corinth, the Confederate base of operations.[57]

Grant, meanwhile, using the Tennessee River as his supply route and Savannah as his depot, began a buildup of men and supplies at Pittsburg Landing and Crump's Landing, which Halleck had selected as a base of operations for the campaign against Johnston's army entrenched nearby at Corinth. The Confederate entrenchments were constructed on the principle of continuous lines, which were considered most advisable for undisciplined troops. They consisted of strong redoubts connected by curtains of breastworks of earth and wood. The redoubts covered prominent positions and the roads that converged at Corinth, a town surrounded by marshes covered with woods.[58]

An organizational act and a military action potentially added to the efficiency of the Union army as it prepared for the coming campaign in the West. On March 11, Lincoln put Henry Halleck in command of all forces west of the Alleghenies to assure better coordination between the two principal armies under Grant and Buell. Previously these two armies had been directly under orders from Washington. The defeat of Van Dorn's Confederate army in the trans-Mississippi theater relieved Federal anxieties about Missouri. It also eventually enabled the Union forces to meet the combined Confederate forces when Van Dorn brought his trans-Mississippi army to reinforce the combined forces of Bragg and Johnston at Corinth. But Van Dorn would not arrive until after the impending battle, leaving Johnston with 40,000 effective troops.[59]

While Grant was building up his forces at Pittsburg and Crump's landings, Halleck on March 12 ordered Buell to join Grant with the Army of the Ohio. Following the railroad, Buell made his way to Columbia, Tennessee, where the rain-swollen Duck River required him to reconstruct a railway bridge upon which his army was dependent for its supplies. Buell now found it necessary to march his 20,000-man army eighty miles without major rail or water transportation to link up with Grant.

With Grant's assurance that the depot at Savannah could support Buell's army and supply a pontoon bridge to cross the Tennessee River, Buell left his own supply train behind to join him later. Stripped down to the wagons required to carry ammunition, rations, and forage to reach Savannah, he left Columbia on March 31. The advance force of the Army of the Ohio reached the banks of the Tennessee on April 5.[60] Buell's land movement, covering approximately fifteen miles per day, emphasized the comparative advantage of moving with a small army in rich forage, contrasted to circumstances in the eastern theater.

But Johnston had decided to take the initiative. Upon hearing that Buell was moving to reinforce Grant, Johnston chose to attack Grant before Buell could reach him. Without Buell, the two armies were approximately equal in number. There is some evidence that Johnston's decision was in part determined by a report that the enemy had constructed no fortifications at Pittsburg Landing.[61]

To undertake a campaign twenty miles from his base of supplies, Johnston stripped down his transportation and supply, carrying five days' rations (three in haversacks, two in wagons) and 100 rounds of ammunition per man, 200 rounds for each piece of artillery, and two tents per company.[62] Entrenching equipment seems to have been left with the reserve train. Once again, the limited size of the army involved was facilitating strategic mobility.

Johnson gave no indication that he was contemplating maneuver. Strategic maneuver against Grant's army was no doubt out of the question, since any attempt to turn Grant's position at Pittsburg Landing would have required crossing the Tennessee and striking at Savannah. With the Union gunboats controlling the Tennessee, it would have proved impossible to throw down and maintain pontoon bridges. Also, that would have exposed the Confederate army to Buell, exactly what Johnston was attempting to avoid. Moreover, Johnston did not have a pontoon train. Johnston's army also consisted largely of raw recruits led by inexperienced officers, and lacked adequate command procedures to coordinate movements in heavily wooded country. Envelopment was out of the question, as Grant's flanks rested on the river. Since Johnston knew that Grant had failed to fortify his positions, a direct tactical confrontation was his best and only alternative.

Beauregard, Johnston's second in command, drew up a plan for a surprise frontal assault, which was not inconsistent with his respect for the entrenched defense. Surprise was always doctrinal grounds for the tactical offense. When he thought that surprise was lost, Beauregard wanted to give up the offensive in anticipation of Grant's having had time to entrench. Johnston, Bragg, Polk, and Breckenridge all wished to attack regardless.

Grant's failure to entrench his position harks back to the seeming ambiguities in his attitude toward the role of fortification on the field of battle. While he acted in accordance with tactical doctrine when he fortified his beachhead at Belmont, at Donelson he omitted to entrench his investing force. Now again at Shiloh, despite Halleck's orders to fortify,[63] Grant did not entrench his army—this despite the fact that he was situated with his back to the river and with what he mistakenly believed to be an army of 100,000 men only twenty miles away. In answer to criticism of his failure to fortify at Shiloh, Grant later wrote: "When all reinforcement should have arrived I expected to take the initiative by marching on Corinth, and had no expectation of needing fortifications, though this subject was taken into consideration." He continued:

Col. J. B. McPherson, my only military engineer, was directed to lay out a line to entrench. He did so, but reported that it would have to be made in rear of the line of encampment as it then ran. The new line, while it would be nearer the river, was yet too far away from the Tennessee, or even from the creeks, to be easily supplied with water, and in the case of attack these creeks would be in the hands of the enemy. *The fact is, I regarded the campaign as an offensive one* and had no idea that the enemy would leave strong entrenchments to take the initiative when he knew he would be attacked where he was if he remained.[64]

"The fact is, I regarded the campaign as an offensive one," is perhaps the key to Grant's attitude on army doctrine for the tactical use of field fortifications. Although Mahan advocated that undisciplined troops—which Grant's certainly were, three of the five divisions engaged on the first day undergoing their baptism of fire almost totally devoid of training[65]—be fought from behind entrenchments under all circumstances, Gay de Vernon's text and official army regulations were geared to experienced regulars and did not make this qualification. This situation left considerable latitude for a conflict in tactical doctrine. While on the defense, Gay de Vernon and army regulations advised the entrenchment of the entire line; on the offensive, the army was to entrench only the flanks and the rear. Grant's attitude was consistent with, if not motivated by, this doctrinal outlook; his flanks and rear were protected by the river.

Why, then, should Grant have escaped the influence of Mahan? Although it is true that Grant had taken Mahan's senior-level course in military engineering, he had not seen active duty in Mahan's major support group, the Corps of Engineers. No military intellectual; out of the service for a considerable time previous to the war; and out of the mainstream of military life since the Mexican War, Grant, in all probability, was out of touch with the main currents of military thought. And Sherman's later observation that Grant was short on theory but long on common sense is compatible with Grant's erratic behavior by the standards of military theory and doctrine.

Grant's Mexican War experience may have left an ambivalence in his outlook that he carried with him to the Civil War. While on the one hand, as noted, he expressed an appreciation for Scott's use of field fortification in aid of holding-turning maneuvers, as well as an aversion to losses in frontal assaults; on the other hand, his Civil War actions suggest that Zachary Taylor's successful use of assault tactics against Mexican fortifications was perhaps the greater influence.[66]

Grant's further contention that his green volunteers would draw greater benefit from the discipline instilled through drilling rather than entrenching reflects either an indifference to or a complete rejection of Mahan's *Treatise on Field Fortification.* One possible influence was his young intellectual corps commander William Tecumseh Sherman. At this stage of the war, Sherman rejected Mahan's emphasis on the role of field fortification. In his *Memoirs,* Sherman, who was on record as being versed in Mahan, supported Grant's failure to entrench at Shiloh. He maintained that field fortification there "would have made our raw men timid." Interestingly, Sherman, like Grant, did not serve in the Corps of Engineers. Sherman further noted that "at a later period of the war, we could have rendered this position impregnable in one night. . . . At this time we did not [entrench], and may be it is well we did not."[67] Sherman's attitude suggests that his appreciation for the extended use of fortification on the field of battle came from experience rather than from Mahan; or that both Grant and Sherman were still thinking up arguments to justify what came to be considered a major tactical blunder.

With the possibility of turning movements ruled out, and with the tactical use of fortification playing no part, the Battle of Shiloh had little relevance itself to the evolution of trench warfare. Many now-familiar factors hindering tactical mobility and strategic maneuver were present. Lack of tactical coordination reduced the battle to a large-scale firefight, frequently between isolated segments of the two armies. Command procedures broke down in the wooded terrain, and both sides paid the price of an overabundance of green troops. The Confederate line of attack broke and intermingled, with all loss of tactical order. Corps lines became so badly intermingled that informal command agreements replaced the corps command system.[68] The contrast of Johnston's meticulous and detailed order for a battle in conventional tactical formation and the reality of Confederate performance was a striking slice of American military culture in the early stages of the Civil War.[69]

The improvised organization of artillery and cavalry and their coordination with infantry emphasized the organizational disorder while at the same time producing moments of practical insight. Both sides, for instance, again dismounted cavalry and fought them as skirmishers, in the case of the Confederates on Beauregard's orders. At the same time, he ordered his cavalry to prepare to support infantry in the line. The Confederates used their cavalry not only to mask artillery, but also to support them in offensive action by dismounting and fighting as skirmishers. Anticipating a more mundane but increasingly prevalent auxiliary role, both sides employed cavalry to round up stragglers. Grant also used cavalry in the rear of infantry as file closers.[70]

Confederate and Union artillery, conventionally used in line and on the flanks, fought both from behind and in front of the infantry line.

It was detached at times to search out the most advantageous positions to join in the battle. One Union battery commander even threw up breastworks to hold an offensive position. Both sides deployed artillery about equally against infantry and artillery. Beauregard after the war said he had intended his corps commanders to use masses of twelve guns at a point on the offense to clear the way for his infantry. This Napoleonic-era tactic was still feasible, since few infantry at this time were armed with the rifled musket. Brigadier General Daniel Ruggles did mass a collection of Confederate batteries, which helped reduce the Hornet's Nest; but the general pattern of battle saw cavalry and artillery conspicuously subordinated to the flow of the infantry.[71]

The coordination of the two Union armies as Buell moved to reinforce Grant was an example of organizational development in the strategic use of Stager's Military Telegraph. Grant was in telegraphic communication with Buell from the time he left Columbus, Kentucky. Under the duress of the first day's assault, Grant hung on, encouraged by the awareness through his telegraphic link that Buell would reinforce him the next day.[72]

The Shiloh campaign was the first shakedown for Buell's signals organization in the field. Buell had received three Signal Corps sections for the Army of the Ohio during the winter. The first, in the judgment of J. Willard Brown, the contemporary historian of the Union Signal Corps, was qualified to go into service by February 6. But a shortage of equipment prevented the organization from taking the field until February 25, during the course of Buell's march to Nashville. When Buell reached Nashville, another camp of instructions produced additional signal officers. At this early stage, signals were still transmitted by flags and torches. The cipher was not introduced in the West until late in 1862. The Signal Corps' portable field telegraph had not as yet made its way into the western armies, but Stager's Military Telegraph was maintaining strategic communication as well as occasionally extending their lines to the field of battle. Buell paid close attention to the state of his strategic telegraphic communications, and strongly implied during his movement to join with Grant that the latter would be well advised to do likewise to improve the coordination of the western armies.[73] While Buell was criticizing Grant's neglect of telegraphic communications, Grant was simultaneously complaining of his difficulties in command procedures to coordinate his army.[74] The incident presented another interesting example of the problem of ideas, doctrine, organization, and the military outlooks of field commanders in a somewhat distended state.

Various problems prevented the Signal Corps from being of use during the Battle of Shiloh. One was the dense woods. What terrain didn't disrupt, early apprehension about the role of the Signal Corps did. There was a lack of cooperation between brigade commanders at crucial times when signaling was most urgently required. Brigade commanders also routinely called back officers detached for signaling. A general problem in early Union signals operations saw equipment frequently turned in by order of the quartermaster and other officers not responsible to the Signal Corps, and lost. This problem was alleviated but not eliminated by a War Department order on June 18, 1862, making all signal officers responsible to the signal officer of the army. Only the adjutant general of the army could relieve them from duty. The mobility of the Signal Corps was greatly restricted because of the early failure to provide it with horses. An order after Shiloh attempted to rectify this problem, but the next shipment of horses was diverted to the line. Brown, allowing for his stance as an involved advocate, is critical of both Buell and Grant for actions that disorganized the Signal Corps.

In an incident that reflected the novelty of the Signal Corps in military organization, General George Thomas, in attempting to establish communications while encamped between Pittsburg Landing and Corinth, asked Sherman where his Signal Corps was. When Sherman informed Thomas that he not only didn't have one but didn't know what one was, Thomas detailed to Sherman some of his own signalers. The Union Signal Corps was so weakened by the withdrawal of officers for line duty that it was unable to participate in action leading to the Confederate evacuation of Corinth. The Confederate Signal Corps, for its part, was well located at Corinth to observe Union movements. But sloppy signaling reduced its effectiveness, while reflecting early organizational problems.[75] Sherman's mystification over the Signal Corps reflects in part the sporadic organization of signals in the West. While Buell's army had a signals organizaton from February, 1862, not until November of that year did orders call for the organization of the Signal Corps in Grant's Army of the Tennessee. And the first signals detachment was not ready to take the field until the end of March, 1863. Grant was no enthusiast about the Signal Corps. He would be one of the commanders who made it necessary for the War Department to issue the special order of January 22, 1863, which formally instituted the detailing of officers and men for signal duty. Grant reluctantly complied. As late as May 19, 1863, the Signal Corps was still trying to get his subordinates to comply with the order. To add to the list of Grant's ambivalent acts, however, in early May, 1863, he would ask for six of the experimental field telegraph trains.[76]

With respect to tactical development, there remains the question of why

Beauregard, who took command at Shiloh with the death of Johnston, did not entrench after the toll of the first day's fighting. He had entrenched at the First Battle of Bull Run, and his writings emphasized the role of tactical entrenchments. The fact that Johnston seems to have left the entrenching tools behind in his stripped-down offensive move is one probable reason. The troops were also disorganized and exhausted after their long forced march and lengthy battle. They lacked the habit of entrenchment which would have made such considerations irrelevant later in the war. One can also speculate that the Southern warrior ethos, after several months of defeat and retreat, was not psychologically willing in this instance to go over to the entrenched defense.

In the aftermath of the battle, Grant ordered abatis to be constructed.[77] There were now some grounds for taking a defensive attitude, which Grant may have conceded called for fortifications. Another motive could have been compensation for his disobedience of Halleck's orders to entrench before the battle and the resulting casualties. The future would tell what effect the heavy casualties inflicted on his unentrenched troops would have on Grant's tactical outlook.

For the immediate future, however, attention passed to Halleck, who took over command in the field himself after the near-disaster at Shiloh. Whereas Grant had failed to entrench at all, Halleck proceeded to put on what in many ways was the most extraordinary display of entrenchment under offensive conditions witnessed in the entire war. The Union army, which with reinforcements now numbered some 100,000 men, dug its way from Shiloh to Corinth. From start to finish, the Federal lines were always behind entrenchments. Reconnoitering parties cleared the way for the advance, and were under orders not to bring on a general engagement. The army moved by corduroyed roads from one line of entrenchment to the next as it was laid and made ready. To enable the troops to concentrate in case of attack, Halleck also constructed crossroads to each new position.[78]

Buell's reaction to Halleck's orders to entrench revealed that he was following traditional tactical doctrine rather than following Mahan. When ordered to entrench, he fortified only his flanks. When Halleck reprimanded him for failing to carry out orders to entrench the extent of the line, Buell was surprised that that had been Halleck's intention.[79]

Halleck arrived at Corinth to find that Beauregard, who had kept close to Halleck's front during his advance, had evacuated the city, retreating south by railroad the day before. In so doing, he gave up not just Corinth but the crucial logistical link for the Confederacy that Halleck coveted, the Memphis and Charleston Railroad. Beauregard had considered himself outnumbered and the enemy's entrenchments too formidable for his inexperienced troops to attack. He had found it difficult to supply his army—which the influx of the Alabama, Mississippi, and Louisiana militia had swollen to 75,000 men present for duty. With his communications threatened, and Halleck indicating that he intended to conduct an investment and siege, Beauregard had seen no alternative but to retreat.

The reasons for Halleck's actions probably were twofold. For one thing, he was a disciple of Mahan. In his *Elements of Military Art and Science*, Halleck repeated Mahan's dictum that undisciplined militia or volunteer troops should always be fought from behind entrenchments. And, professional perfectionist that Halleck was, he considered Grant's army—with some justification—a raw, undisciplined mob. Nervousness induced by near-catastrophe at Shiloh probably accentuated his desire to take extra precautions. Halleck also had a major transportation problem. With Beauregard barring the way to the Memphis and Charleston Railroad, Halleck had to advance on a wagon transportation line. The poor state of the roads meant that he had to build miles of corduroyed roads to support his wagon line from a base on the Tennessee River. Beauregard's presence on his front prevented his foraging what little he may have found on the land.[80]

This early phase of the western campaign, dominated by river maneuver and small armies engaged in land operations, came to an end when the Union navy collapsed the second line of Confederate defense anchored on New Madrid, Island No. 10, and New Orleans. River maneuvers, successful land movements by small armies, and the ambiguous tactical lessons of the early fighting in the West were potentially deceptive experiences. The growing size of the western armies by Shiloh and Corinth, with their attendant problems of tactical and strategic mobility, was a sign of coming realities in the West. And though the rivers still would have a role to play, the problems of overland movement with the growing size of the western armies would increasingly occupy the attention of western field commanders.

7

The Emergence of Trench Warfare

The Third Line of Confederate Defense

THE DECLINE OF UNION MOBILITY

The Confederate forces in the West fell back to defensive positions at Vicksburg on the Mississippi and to a line from Chattanooga to Cumberland Gap in the eastern part of the theater. Beauregard, and then his successor as western commander, Braxton Bragg, rebuilt and reorganized the Army of the Mississippi (later Army of Tennessee) at Tupelo, Mississippi, while Edmund Kirby Smith's small army held the line from Chattanooga to Cumberland Gap.

With the closing of the lower Mississippi, Vicksburg was the last significant supply route from the trans-Mississippi. It was now the central depot for transshipment from West to East. Though well positioned and well constructed, the city's defenses were subject to being run past by both the seagoing fleet under Farragut and the river fleet.[1] Isolating Vicksburg was more difficult. Surrounded by swamps and marshes that were intersected only by easily defended watercourses and too shallow for navigation during dry weather, it presented the most formidable challenge to joint land/water envelopment that the Union forces on the Mississippi had yet encountered.[2]

But Halleck's plans centered not on Vicksburg, but again on the middle of the Confederate line. He accordingly prepared to advance along the Memphis and Charleston Railroad to Chattanooga. For various reasons, the Union army was slow to move. One setback was the growing size of the western armies, with the accompanying problems of transportation and supply. Halleck's combined forces on June 1 numbered 150,000 aggregate present (202,000 aggregate present and absent, 120,000 present for duty).[3] Although the roads would be in good condition, the Union forces could not take full advantage of them until they overcame the animal and wagon shortages. Large-scale desertion of wagon drivers aggravated the situation. The lack of quartermasters and commissary officers continued to be a problem, the Army of the Potomac absorbing almost all available. The staffing and organization of the supply bureaus in the West at this stage of the war were abominable. The Union forces also were suffering from a serious shortage of fresh water. The muddying of water by spring runoff rendered it unfit for animals to drink, and artesian wells were polluted. Unsanitary conditions led to a mounting sick list.[4]

Grant and Buell spread their forces to occupy their overextended fronts and overextended lines of communication. To undermine their strength still further, the enlistments of the one-year volunteers recruited after the First Battle of Bull Run ran out, resulting in another influx of green troops to be trained. During the drought, the Union army also was hard hit by illness along the fever-ridden banks of the Tennessee. In pursuing their offensive into the heart of the Confederacy the Union armies in the West had necessarily so overextended their fronts and lines of communications that they had forced themselves into a defensive posture—a posture hardened by a sudden strengthening of the Confederate defenses.

By early July, hit-and-run warfare by partisans and the cavalry of Nathan B. Forrest and John H. Morgan, supplied and informed by a sympathetic populace, began to turn Union attention almost exclusively to the critical problem of guarding communications. Forrest's destruction of the crucial intermediary supply depot at Murfreesboro—unentrenched and caught sleeping—and the cutting of rail and telegraph lines were a particularly severe blow to Union logistics.

The second development to bolster the Confederate defensive line occurred when the defenses of the Mississippi River finally held. On June 28, Farragut's gunboats ran by the Vicksburg defenses to join with the river fleet under Porter, but to no avail. Unlike in New Orleans, this did not isolate the river defenses. Farragut needed the cooperation of a land force against the difficult approaches to Vicksburg, but Halleck was unable to spare the troops for such an undertaking. Meanwhile, Van Dorn, now in command of the Mississippi defenses, fortified Port Hudson on the Mississippi River below the Red River basin. This threatened Farragut's communications with New Orleans. The appearance below Vicksburg of the Confederate ironclad *Arkansas* forced Farragut to return to a point below Vicksburg, which severed his communications with Memphis. Under the impact of heat and malaria, the Federal forces abandoned an attempt to dig a canal across the neck of land that separated the river fleet and Farragut, thereby completely bypassing Vicksburg.

Their morale raised by the Confederate victories in the eastern theater, and their numbers increased as a result of the first conscription act, the western armies of the Confederacy rebuilt and reorganized. The cavalry raids of Forrest and Morgan forced Buell to distribute his army along his lengthy communications lines, leaving him vulnerable to a concentrated thrust at any one point. Though Bragg wished to take the offensive to fend off an expected invasion of East Tennessee, his shortage of transportation, artillery, infantry weapons, and ammunition, together with the absence of his cavalry, prevented him from immediately doing so. While Bragg waited for the expected transportation convoy and artillery train to reach him by land across the mountains dividing East from West Tennessee, his ordnance chief and Josiah Gorgas, the efficient chief of Confederate ordnance, managed to build up munitions stocks sufficient for an extended offensive campaign.[5]

In the Union camp, Buell's army continued to deteriorate. Sickness and the shortage of forage and food took their toll. By the first of August, the stationary Federal forces had exhausted the countryside of forage and provisions. Inability to keep the supply routes open forced Buell to put his army on half-rations. Bragg, by contrast, felt that his Confederate army "has much improved in health and strength and has progressed rapidly in discipline, organization and instruction."[6]

Fearful of an offensive that would threaten the Union's vulnerable communications, Halleck—first as western commander, and from July as general in chief with the divided commands of Buell and Grant— grew frustrated in his attempt to seize the initiative. His most aggravating source of delay was Buell's slow repair of the badly damaged Memphis and Charleston Railroad, his route to Chattanooga. Halleck's impatience was kindled by the fact that General Ormsby Mitchel, operating south of Nashville, had captured nearly intact the major section of the railroad from Stevenson, near Chattanooga, to Tuscumbia, close to Corinth. But Buell had cause for concern, with poor intelligence of the enemy army, and partisans and Confederate cavalry constantly cutting his communications. He was also short of locomotives and rolling stock, and his field transportation deficiency made foraging to complement his rail communications difficult, especially in country that Mitchel had already foraged heavily.[7]

Buell from July through September had a field transportation standard of between only twenty-three wagons per 1,000 men while moving with animals spread to forage, and eighteen to twenty wagons while stationary, when the greater attrition of animals would leave some available wagons without teams. His Army of the Ohio suffered the disadvantage of being the only western army to have slightly more horses than mules in the early stages of the war. The erratically fluctuating horse/mule ratios for all western armies suggest, as noted, that at this stage of the war, at least, the reason was probably the availability of local supply rather than preference, as exemplified by the earlier-mentioned requisition by the Department of Ohio, in late 1862, of horses, wagons, teamsters, and wagon masters from the city of Louisville.[8]

Bragg reorganized as well as refurbished. His first general order after he took command of the Army of the Mississippi, interestingly, was that each corps organize "a company of cavalry of not less then fifty effective men assigned to their headquarters to act as escort and couriers." This early development of an extensive courier organization in Bragg's command procedures no doubt played a role in his successful maneuvers. Bragg would also centralize the command structure of his army with the subordination of the corps to a wing command system, an organizational change that may, nevertheless, have had dubious results because of the difficult personal relations between Bragg and the wing commanders.[9]

CONFEDERATE MANEUVER AND TACTICAL ORTHODOXY IN TENNESSEE AND KENTUCKY

While Buell slowly advanced toward Chattanooga, hugging his rail lines and intermediary depots, Bragg began his major raid to undermine the Union line. A harsh disciplinarian and organizational perfectionist, he showed talent in organizing and moving an army. Feigning a movement toward Grant's position on the right of the Union line, Bragg moved to turn Buell's flank. To do this, he secretly moved 35,000 men by six rail lines on an almost 800-mile circuitous route south through Mobile to get in front of Buell at Chattanooga. Kirby Smith, meanwhile, in accordance with Bragg's plan, moved from Knoxville, pushed General Morgan from the Cumberland Gap, which the Confederates had lost in June, and broke out into Kentucky. Bragg slowed at Chattanooga to wait for more field transportation to be supplied and then moved north with some 28,000 men. He planned to cut Buell's communications and force him to abandon Middle Tennessee. A simultaneous advance by Van Dorn and Price in Mississippi would hold potential reinforcements to Buell from Grant or, if they were sent, would allow the Confederates to occupy West Tennessee.

The Confederate raid left Buell's communications in a precarious state. The lack of engines and rolling stock prevented his effective use of the Memphis and Charleston Railroad. Buell was precariously connected to his main supply depot at Nashville by a single line, and his intermediary depots between Nashville and his army near Chattanooga were exposed. Kirby Smith, in addition to threatening Lexington and Louisville, also threatened Buell's vulnerable 500-mile supply and telegraph line from the Ohio River, a single line running through partisan-infested territory.

Bragg quickly took possession of the Knoxville and Nashville Pike, which gave him a supply route from eastern Tennessee, and an offensive route into the heart of Tennessee. Moving swiftly along the pike, he took possession of Carthage, which gave him control of both banks of the Cumberland. The pursuing Buell was disadvantaged by Bragg's early start and unknown destination. Kirby Smith defeated the only organized Federal forces in Kentucky, while Morgan's destruction of the tunnel on the railroad between Nashville and Louisville eliminated the threat of Buell's moving a force by rail to intercept him. Kirby Smith occupied Lexington in early September.[10]

But the Confederate raid began to stall logistically as the Union defenders hastily fortified their vital positions. The invading army began to experience the anxieties of a logistical breakdown and living off the land. The heavy escorts needed for his large convoy severely reduced Bragg's fighting strength. The inherent advantages of a war of position in friendly territory close to one's supply base over offensive maneuver in hostile territory quickly reasserted themselves—this time for the Union.

While Bragg and Buell engaged in a race for Nashville, James St. Clair Morton, the young engineer and prewar theorist on fortification, had hastily fortified Nashville, an adjacent hill, and the bridge across the Cumberland, without the main army.[11] Using the railroad and good turnpikes, Buell had slipped past Bragg into the fortified city. Bragg, finding Nashville occupied, and deciding that "an assault on the enemy's . . . force, well fortified at Nashville, gave no promise of success," moved to sever Buell's communications with the North to prevent his taking the offensive against Kirby Smith at Lexington.[12]

By mid-September, as he moved toward Louisville, Bragg did not have the logistical capacity to maintain his offensive. His supply reserves began to dwindle by late summer. The Confederacy, East and West, began to feel the material consequences of the loss of New Orleans and Union-occupied Tennessee. Particularly apparent was the shortage of quartermaster supply. As early as August 21, Kirby Smith wrote that his men were "ragged and barefooted." In mid-September, Bragg described his men as "somewhat destitute."[13] The Confederate offensive, while taking the army farther from its intermediate bases and its central supply base at Atlanta, reduced Buell's logistical vulnerability by allowing him—in fact, forcing him—to draw his army closer to his base of operations at Nashville and his source of supply in the Ohio Valley.

The undernourished Confederate troops also suffered from sickness and exhaustion. On September 17, Bragg received the surrender of the Federal garrison at Munfordville, an obstruction that held up the advance on Louisville long enough to allow Buell to make some gain in the race for that city. This minor success was to be Bragg's last. Buell, using the functioning parts of the Louisville-to-Nashville line and the good turnpikes in the area, was marching on Bragg's army from Bowling Green. Bragg entrenched his army. But in "hostile country, utterly destitute of supplies," Bragg, with his sick, "much jaded and somewhat destitute" army and only seven days' provisions, was in no position either to take the offensive or to remain long on the defense.[14]

Unless the defenders left the commissary reserves to be captured— which was highly unlikely—for Bragg to capture Louisville with an army out of provisions might be a disaster. Limited transportation, supply bureau inefficiency, and distance made it impossible to build up a reserve from the supply base at Lexington sufficient to sustain his army immediately upon entering Louisville. Also, communications between Louisville and Lexington would be exposed to Buell's army advancing from the south. With his back to the Federally controlled Ohio River without so much as a pontoon train—assuming the Federal troops blew up the bridge before letting the city fall into Confederate hands—Bragg would be isolated with Buell's army between him and his supply sources.

If Buell refused to attack him within a very few days, Bragg had no alternative but to seek subsistence. Coming within range of the Confederate army, Buell entrenched. He refused to rise to Bragg's bait to launch an attack on the Confederate positions. "Reduced . . . to three days' rations . . . ," exclaimed Bragg, "we were—compelled to give up the object and seek for subsistence. Orders were sent for a supply train from our depot at Lexington to meet us in Bardstown, and the march was commenced for the latter place."[15] Bragg later stated that his preference was to attack, but it was impractical. In addition to his precarious supply situation, Bragg believed that the exhaustion of his troops ruled out a tactical offense. He further calculated that he had little to gain even if he won a tactical victory. Bragg observed that Buell, if defeated, would merely have retreated to prepared positions at Bowling Green, and the Confederates lacked the logistical capacity to pursue and besiege him.[16]

Buell, his army scattered *en echelon* to forage, slipped unopposed into Louisville. His 110-mile march from Nashville had taken only fourteen days, a fairly impressive average of eight miles a day for so large an army foraging with such limited transportation in this early organizational stage of the war. Buell's transportation standard did not exceed twenty-four wagons per thousand. Even allowing for the use of functioning parts of the Louisville-to-Nashville railroad to complement his foraging, Buell was learning the logistical art of extending limited field transportation through the combination of widespread foraging and rapid movement.

Somewhat ragged and badly in need of footwear, Buell's army was refurbished from the stocks collected at Louisville from the Ohio Valley. Buell integrated into the veteran regiments the poorly disciplined volunteers hurriedly thrown in from Illinois, Indiana, and Ohio to defend the city. By October 1, he ordered his rested and revitalized army, numbering 75,000 aggregate present, to march as a light column at "half baggage," each man carrying the standard three days' rations, with the reserve supply to be carried in a reserve train.[17]

Buell was now marching with a transportation standard of approximately thirty-three wagons per 1,000 men, having recouped from a decrease in July, August, and September to between approximately eighteen and twenty-four wagons per thousand. By November, he would increase his standard to approximately thirty-seven wagons per 1,000 men.[18] Erratic field transportation ratios appear to have been endemic for the western armies during the summer and autumn of late 1862, even allowing for a redistribution of resources to fields of action. The Army of the Mississippi, as noted, appears to have drifted from forty-seven to twenty-four wagons per 1,000 men as it sorted its field transportation between June, July, and August, 1862.[19]

In contrast to Buell's improving circumstances, Bragg, in addition to being shoeless, tired, and hungry, in mid-September was despairing of the failure to recruit from the surprisingly reluctant population. Not only was he unable to increase the size of his army, he was unable to replace more than one-half his losses. Over 15,000 stands of arms remained unused. On the other hand, he was unable to supply the troops he had, let alone reinforcements.[20]

At the same time that Bragg ordered the supply trains from Lexington, he instructed Kirby Smith to rendezvous for combined operations on Louisville once the armies were refurbished. Owing to the delay in communication, Bragg did not realize that Kirby Smith had sent his army in an attempt to check a Federal breakout at Cumberland Gap, thus preventing the junction of the two Confederate armies. The supply apparatus failed to build up a reserve of provisions at the place of rendezvous sufficient for the immediate resumption of the offensive.[21] The country surrounding Lexington provided sufficient subsistence to build up an adequate food reserve. But Bragg's transportation shortage prevented the transfer of a provision reserve from Lexington to an intermediary depot before Buell, in early October, took the offense and forced Bragg to fight the Battle of Perryville.[22]

The Battle of Perryville began as a firefight. It was brought on by the engagement of pickets, with the two armies joining in piecemeal. Communications, intelligence, training, troop discipline, and terrain combined to rule out for Buell the feasibility of strategic maneuver with so large an army. The commanders had limited control of the tactical course of the battle. The Union army, for instance, to facilitate foraging, was marching on several roads without lateral communication. The first corps commander of the army's left wing failed to inform Buell that he was being engaged early in the morning by what turned out to be the main Confederate force. Consequently, the remainder of Buell's army was not aware of this fact until late in the afternoon. Poor lateral communication then delayed concentration.

What coordination there was in the Union field command during the course of the fighting owed much to the improving performance of Buell's signals organization. During this campaign, the Signal Corps began to assume an ordered place in his army. In the main battle at Perryville, Buell's signals organization maintained communications between the corps commanders and between corps commanders and Buell. Buell would commend the Signal Corps in his report of the campaign. The Military Telegraph maintained good strategic communications throughout the campaign but did not play a role in tactical communications.[23]

The main battle saw both sides fight primarily from orthodox formations, assaulting and counterassaulting in line across an open field in relatively good order. Parts of the lines typically intermingled and broke down, with tactical order deteriorating into a large-scale firefight. Artillery and cavalry were again used in an ad hoc organization to back up the infantry. During the battle, Union cavalry dismounted and fought as skirmishers in support of infantry units. Cavalry also commanded some artillery batteries, masking them while moving them around to exploit situations during the course of the battle. Union and seemingly Confederate artillery, in their supporting roles to infantry, again fought both from behind and in front of the infantry line, as well as with cavalry, and were deployed against both artillery and infantry. The commander of the Union I Corps did order his batteries to stop dueling the enemy's artillery when no infantry was present in order to save ammunition. On one occasion, a Confederate battery took the offensive in the open field, with no infantry backup, and effectively shelled Union infantry that were temporarily without artillery support. It was an incident made possible only by the shortage of rifled muskets in the West in the early stages of the war.[24]

Neither side entrenched. This was explicable in part because neither side had sufficient warning to construct artificial fortifications before battle was joined. Both sides did take advantage of natural cover and on occasion fought from behind stone fences. The 3,300 casualties suffered by the 14,000 men of the Union I Corps, which bore the brunt of the fighting, and almost equally heavy losses by Bragg, suggest that artificial entrenchments would not have been out of place.[25]

Bragg's tactical victory came to naught with his discovery that Buell's main army was in front of him. With heavy losses and the arrival of an additional Federal corps on his exposed flank, Bragg retreated to a defensive line at Harrodsburg. Despite the fact he hoped to draw Buell into an attack, he failed to entrench. Refusing the invitation to attack, Buell moved instead to cut Bragg's communications with the Cumberland Gap. Bragg responded by falling back to offer battle at Bryantsville, an intended intermediary depot that had only two days' rations.[26] Buell again failed to attack, this time contenting himself with the destruction of the mills and other sources of breadstuffs. The Confederate army, in addition to being threadbare and shoeless, was now destitute of any accumulated provisions supply. "The necessary concentration of my forces rendered accumulation from the small country mills impracticable, and our supply was reduced to only four days' rations. To attack and rout an enemy largely superior in numbers (for simply to cripple him would not suffice) or to evacuate the country in which we could no longer subsist became now an imperative necessity. Moreover," continued Bragg,

> I was informed that still another force was moving on my right flank from Cincinnati in addition to the overwhelming one with which I was

already contending. The season of autumnal rains was approaching, the rough and uneven roads leading over the stupendous mountains of Eastern Tennessee and Kentucky to and through Cumberland Gap would then become utterly impassable to an army. Should I remain till then and meet with a reverse the army would be lost. Had the foregoing considerations permitted a doubt to remain in my mind as to the course of duty it would have been entirely removed upon receipt of the intelligence of our disaster in North Mississippi [Grant's defeat of Van Dorn at Corinth] by which the whole country in our rear was left open to the enemy's victorious forces there.

"Jaded, hungry, and tired," Bragg's army withdrew through the Cumberland Gap, draining the countryside of what resources remained. The pursuing forces soon turned back to the railroad to procure supplies.[27]

Confederate field commanders in the West faced an accumulation of factors that affected strategic mobility. They suffered the logistical consequences—particularly in clothing and subsistence—of the loss of Middle Tennessee and New Orleans, as well as the effects of the inadequate organization and staffing of the Quartermaster and Subsistence bureaus. They were hobbled by the lack of locomotives, rolling stock, and rails owing to the absence of an industrial base, as well as by the ever-present shortages of horses and wagons. Terrain and distance also were problems. When stalled by the fortified defense in combination with other frustrations, strategic mobility collapsed.

There was little change in the role Union and Confederate commanders envisioned for fortifications on the field of battle. With Halleck removed from the scene, Buell, except for defensive entrenchments near Munfordville, stopped fortifying his front. Nor did Bragg or any other field commander construct offensive entrenchments. Bragg's entrenchments near Munfordville were prompted by his decision to take a tactical defensive stand owing to logistical considerations and to the poor condition of his troops. Under such circumstances, tactical doctrine called for fortification. As noted, however, on occasion even defensive positions went unfortified. The works at Munfordville, and the fortifications at Nashville and Cincinnati, though impressive, were what one would have expected under existing doctrine. From the beginning of the war, even the western commanders displayed little reluctance to adhere to doctrine dictating the fortification of static positions of strategic significance. Bragg's failure to entrench his army before the Federal fortifications at Munfordville, however, was a violation of even traditional tactical doctrine.

Although conduct might have been the same regardless of the circumstances, there were common-sense reasons for the limited appreciation of fortification on the field during the Confederate offensive into Middle Tennessee and Kentucky. The armies frequently fought in thick forests with readily available natural cover. The construction of artificial fortifications possibly appeared somewhat superfluous, at least until the test of battle decisively gave evidence to the contrary, as on the open battlefield at Perryville. The fact that the troops on both sides— until the Union forces began to operate off their supply base at Louisville—generally came to the battlefield exhausted, hungry, footsore, and in many cases ill, discouraged the expenditure of energy to construct field works. The rifled musket would overcome this hesitancy regardless of circumstances, but early in the war the smoothbore was still the dominant infantry weapon in the West.

Bragg's ambivalence in constructing field works at Munfordville but not thereafter comes against a background that offers some room for speculation on his tactical thinking. Even when he came to accept entrenchments in 1863, Bragg is quoted as having little faith in them, believing that they demoralized troops. There is evidence that he was greatly influenced by his Mexican War experience, particularly by the model of Zachary Taylor and his successful use of frontal assaults against fortified positions. Bragg drilled and disciplined his troops against rigorous professional standards and got good results, though he paid the cost in popularity. He attempted with as much if not more vigor than any Confederate field commander to meet the standard of a regular army. A somewhat microscopic military professionalism may have left him temperamentally unsuited to realistic expectations for a raw Civil War army.[28]

MANEUVER, POSITION, AND TACTICAL CHANGE IN MISSISSIPPI

Along Grant's front at the other end of the Union line in the autumn of 1862, an equally dramatic scene was being acted out on the theme of position versus maneuver and the entrenched defense versus the frontal assault. Neither Grant nor his opponent, General Earl Van Dorn, considered his army strong enough to assume the offense. After Bragg requested that Van Dorn launch an attack to divert the Union forces from the Confederate offensive in Tennessee and Kentucky, Van Dorn in mid-September moved to join Sterling Price's army of Missouri volunteers at Iuka, Mississippi. From Iuka they would advance on Corinth.

Uneasy about meeting the combined Confederate forces in his undermanned and overextended defensive works, Grant decided to send two columns to envelop and defeat Price's army of about 14,000 at Iuka before Van Dorn put in an appearance. Grant divided his offensive columns, which numbered about 15,000 men. He ordered Rosecrans, with about 9,000 men, to leave the railway at Iuka to cut Price's communications and line of retreat from the south.[29] On the other flank, General Ord was to move south of Iuka to Burnsville by railway, and from there north by road to the rear of Iuka.

Grant's plan was ambitious under prevailing conditions. The field transportation standard was adequate for small offensive columns; Rosecrans moved with about twenty-four, and General Edward Ord with thirty wagons per 1,000 men.[30] But once more the topography was unknown. Heavy rains had broken up the roads, and Rosecrans's route was impeded by rain-swollen streams, swamps, and dense forests. The two forces were not in strategic or tactical communication except by courier. Grant, fortunately, was notified that Rosecrans was not going to be able to rendezvous in time. He arranged for the attack to begin when Rosecrans signaled his arrival in position by cannon fire. Before Rosecrans could deploy from the narrow road along which his army was strung out, Price launched a surprise attack. The wind was blowing the wrong way, and Grant did not hear the cannon signal. Keeping control of the road necessary to advance upon or to retreat from Iuka, Price withdrew his army. Another turning movement having stumbled, the Union forces fell back to their defensive positions at Corinth. An informative tactical incident occurred during the Iuka action when Grant ordered a column that arrived early to entrench, indicating that he had not let Shiloh pass unnoticed.[31]

Van Dorn and Price now attempted an offensive solution. Van Dorn, who took command of the combined Confederate forces, planned to concentrate the entire army of some 22,000 men against Rosecrans's army of some 20,000 defending Corinth. Corinth, the vital link in the Federal line, was a most formidable obstacle. Beauregard had constructed works in May for over 60,000 troops to protect the east side of the town, and Halleck had extended these works for 100,000 men. With his reduced army, Grant looked upon these as advanced works and built an enceinte around the town on lines that could be held by his smaller army. The enceinte consisted of redoubts connected with curtains of rifle trenches, strengthened by abatis wherever the lines passed through the forest. Grant placed emphasis on the north and west sides of the town, which Beauregard and Halleck had fortified inadequately, and protected roads and railways with detached works.[32]

In the first day's action on October 3, the Confederates drove the Union defenders, who had not completed concentrating their forces, from the outer works with massed frontal assaults in line formation. The Federal troops fell back to within a mile of Corinth, where they made another stand from behind fences, heavy woods, and underbrush.[33] But the assailants pushed them back into the main line of works. When darkness brought fighting to a halt, the Confederate attackers slept on their arms without fortifying. The collapse of the outer defenses had set off feverish activity in the main line of entrenchments. Federal troops, aided by fugitive Negro labor, spent the night throwing up a new redoubt and obstructing all the forest roads with breastworks. Before daybreak they had reconstructed their entire defensive front.[34]

In the bitter fighting of the following day, this line generally held, though a contingent of the assaulting force did penetrate as far as Rosecrans's headquarters before reserves drove them back and restored the line. The combination of entrenched infantry and artillery on defense displayed its advantage over the most determined frontal assaults, even when supported by a heavy advantage in numbers. There was some artillery preparation for the assaults, but generally, Price was unable to get his guns effectively into the action. Attempts to bring artillery forward quickly fell victim to Union guns; well placed along the line to sweep the rear and flanks as well as the front, they took a heavy toll on the Confederate assaults. Rosecrans's artillery reserve, organized to cover movements on the rear and flanks, checked a major Confederate breakthrough by moving into position and sweeping the front over which the advancing infantry attempted to turn the Union positions. The Union infantry quickly moved to rout the stalled Confederate attack.[35] The cavalry, in turn, displayed its increasing irrelevance in battle within traditional tactical organization. The two cavalry arms fought a mounted skirmish on the flanks and played peripheral roles thereafter.[36] Unsuccessful in his assaults, and turned out of the line he had established in the other works when the Federal artillery enfiladed his positions from neighboring heights, Van Dorn retreated.

Grant pursued along the railroad until the Confederates crossed the Hatchie River. But logistical problems again intervened. Complaining that he was encumbered by excessive baggage trains, Grant was unable to catch the retreating army. He discontinued his offensive, arguing that it was impractical to attack the enemy in his fortifications at Holly Springs, and that his troops "would have suffered for food and suffered greatly from fatigue."[37]

Rosecrans objected to Grant's decision to discontinue the pursuit. Revealing an awareness of the interrelated impact of supply and field fortification on the growing tendency toward positional trench warfare, Rosecrans, on October 7, 1862, wrote to Grant:

>We have defeated, routed and demoralized the army which holds the Lower Mississippi Valley. We have the two railroads leading down toward the Gulf through the most productive parts of the State, into which we can pursue them with safety. The effect of our return to old positions will be to pen them up in the only corn country they have west of Alabama . . . and permit them to recruit their forces, advance and occupy their old ground, reducing us to the occupation of a defensive position, barren and worthless, with a long front, over which they can harass us until bad weather prevents an effectual advance except on the railroads, when time, fortifications, and rolling stock will again render them superior to us.[38]

But Grant, "on reflection," decided that it was "idle to pursue further without more preparation."[39] Rosecrans, in a dispatch to Grant dated two hours after he proposed to continue the pursuit, contradicted himself when he noted a severe ration shortage. He also complained of communications problems, and called for telegraph lines to be strung.[40] The incident was a vivid expression of the factors restricting tactical and strategic mobility, and the frustration of being incapable of doing anything about them.

Neither Van Dorn nor Price had entrenched during the offensive on Corinth. When it was the intention to launch an assault, as previously noted, doctrine for veteran troops did not call for entrenchments. Only against bastioned works, which those at Corinth were not, were counterentrenchment and approach by parallels dictated. Even when the Confederate troops "slept on their arms within 600 yards of Corinth," they did not entrench.[41] Price had advanced behind moving hemp bales against the fortifications at Lexington, Missouri, in one of the first actions of the war. Subsequent entrenchment under fire suggests that he was not unappreciative of the use of fortifications on the field even during an offensive.[42] His early activities had also been in accordance with Mahan's dictum to entrench green volunteers. At Corinth he fought with seasoned troops. One is left to speculate on Price's tactical reasoning. Van Dorn's entrenchment of his camp at Holly Springs, from where he launched his expedition against Corinth, and his entrenching activities on the tactical defensive during his retreat from Corinth, suggest that he too may have acted in accordance with prevailing doctrine for veteran troops. Confederate casualties at Corinth again indicated the increasing cost of the frontal assault against entrenched positions. The assault on Corinth, by his own returns, cost Stirling Price's two divisions over 3,000 casualties.[43]

The collapse of the Confederate offensive in both Kentucky and Mississippi once again reversed the roles of the two armies in this campaigning area. Their offensive capacity exhausted, the western forces of the Confederacy fell back to their fortified defensive line. The Union forces, meanwhile, began to gather the means to restore strategic mobility and challenge this line of defense.

Reinforced by a new Federal call for troops, Grant, in early November, prepared to make his move on Fort Hudson and Vicksburg. The presence of Van Dorn's and Price's forces, now under General John C. Pemberton, in northern Mississippi ruled out Grant's undertaking an amphibious operation with his entire army against Vicksburg from Memphis. Such a move would uncover his entire line of defense and expose Tennessee. Grant's only choice was to advance his recruit-swollen army of 72,000 men aggregate present against Vicksburg by land, moving down the Mississippi Central Railroad and using Memphis and Holly Springs as his base of supply. This required that he repair and protect the railroad while he coped with Pemberton's army as he advanced. Spreading out his army to protect his communications, Grant moved an offensive force of about 31,000 men with a transportation standard probably under twenty wagons per thousand.[44]

Intent on fighting a defensive delaying action, the outnumbered Pemberton did what both doctrine and common sense dictated: he entrenched a defensive line behind the Tallahatchie River across Grant's route of march and fortified all crossing places.[45] On the north side of the river, the Confederates threw up "two circular field works, four to six embrasures each . . . occupied in force."[46] There is no evidence that Grant entrenched his offensive line. He was failing even to entrench his camps.[47] On the other hand, there was no doubt in his mind that the enemy was retreating. Joined by Sherman with 16,000 men from Memphis, Grant considered the Tallahatchie defensive line too formidable to carry by assault. If the enemy did not abandon the line, he proposed to turn it.[48]

When the small Union trans-Mississippi army crossed the Mississippi and cut up the railway line along which he was being supplied, Pemberton abandoned his Tallahatchie position. He briefly halted behind the Yalobushu River, hastily fortified two divisions in advance of the river to cover his positions, and finally withdrew his small army away from the railways into the interior of Mississippi to live off the land. Grant's army in the field with the addition of Sherman's troops numbered about 47,000 men. Unfamiliar with the foraging conditions in central Mississippi, and with winter rains turning the roads to mud, Grant dared not pursue.

Grant now had to hold Pemberton in check to keep him from moving into Vicksburg. Prompted by Halleck, he decided to send Sherman with about 30,000 men, in cooperation with Porter and Farragut, against Vicksburg by way of the Mississippi. Sherman's plan was to ascend the Yazoo, where it ran into the Mississippi just above Vicksburg, and place himself between the fortress and Pemberton. This plan would enable Grant to join up with Sherman to isolate Pemberton from Vicksburg. Confronted with the combined forces of Grant and Sherman, the small Vicksburg garrison would have a strong inducement to surrender. If Pemberton held out, Sherman was prepared to attack the fortress.[49]

Sherman's orders revealed that either he had revised his opinions since Shiloh on the use of fortifications in the field, or his postwar support of Grant's failure to entrench at Shiloh was merely loyalty to a friend and respected colleague. In special orders, he gave his divisional commanders the radical instruction to entrench a succession of prearranged offensive lodgments during the advance toward the rear of the Vicksburg fortifications.[50] Sherman strongly emphasized the importance of having a sufficient supply of axes, picks, and shovels, which were to be carried in the divisional trains. On the other hand, Sherman's tactical orders did not require the entrenchment of infantry when they encountered the enemy on the route of advance. He did, however, call for the entrenchment of his artillery under such circumstances, the infantry furnishing the working parties. His infantry were to rush the entrenched infantry and artillery positions that he expected to encounter.[51]

This strategic offensive went aground on the twin obstacles of logistics and entrenchments. Van Dorn and Forrest destroyed Grant's supply depot at Holly Springs and ripped up large sections of the railway over which he was receiving a portion of his rations. Grant got enough from foraging to feed his army until the railroad was repaired. From the start, he had been feeding his animals, and for the most part his troops, off the countryside. Halleck had been unable to provide him with an adequate number of locomotives to more than partially supply his army by rail. But now the land was exhausted, and his inability to depend on the railroad forced Grant to tell Halleck that he could advance no farther south. Halleck agreed, and ordered Grant to fall back and hold his defensive line.[52]

Grant had no telegraphic communication once he left Memphis. Sherman was unaware of the collapse of Grant's offensive, or of the arrival of a portion of Pemberton's army at Vicksburg. The failure of strategic communications with Grant was accompanied by a makeshift organization for communications in the field. As noted, the Army of the Tennessee did not get its first Signal Corps detachment into the field until the end of March, 1863. The reassignment of two signal officers from other duties in Sherman's command brought this total to six for the combined land and river operations. They maintained constant communication between the division generals and with the fleet admiral during the passage down the river. After Sherman landed at the mouth of Chickasaw Bayou, the terrain made further communication by visual signals impossible.[53]

Sherman, moving with a transportation standard probably under twenty wagons per 1,000 men,[54] arrived with his army of 30,000 to find the Yazoo and its tributaries defended by entrenched infantry and artillery.[55] An attempt to approach Vicksburg by way of an old channel of the Yazoo called Chickasaw Bayou ran into entrenched artillery with crossfire positions, and sharpshooters and regular infantry entrenched in multiple lines of rifle trenches and breastworks on hillside positions. Sherman could not circumvent these positions in the swamps. His artillery was seldom able to set a good position because of the terrain and generally suffered badly from the superior Confederate gun emplacements. Sherman resorted to an unsupported frontal assault against this obstruction, with his troops "massed as close as possible." This attempt to get more punch from mass failed with heavy losses.

Sherman turned back to the Yazoo. If he could take Drumgould's Bluff, the first defensive position on the river, the bottleneck on Chickasaw Bayou would be bypassed. Sherman planned to attack Drumgould's Bluff in combination with Porter's fleet under cover of darkness. Fog prevented the launching of the assault the night planned. When a late-setting moon prevented it again the following night, Sherman abandoned the plan. When torrential rains turned the river banks into quagmires that made it impossible to disembark, Sherman, on January 2, 1863, withdrew.[56] It was not with any sense of deep regret that he abandoned the projected attack on Drumgould's Bluff. The massacre of his troops in the assault on the defenses at Chickasaw Bayou—which in retrospect he implied was a mistake for which he took full blame—had made an impression. He observed "that even in case of success the assault of the batteries of Drumgould's Bluff would have been attended with a fearful sacrifice of life."[57]

A defensive force of 3,000 men in entrenched positions had repelled an army ten times its number, inflicting 2,000 casualties in the process. Thus, terrain and logistics once again frustrated strategic maneuver to force a tactical decision. And the tactical outcome contributed to the ascendancy of trench warfare. This time there was the added significance of raising doubts in Sherman's mind about the frontal assault while increasing his respect for the value of entrenchments. In his summary of the campaign, Sherman noted: "I attribute our failure to the strength of the enemy's position, both natural and artificial. . . . We are unable with present forces to remove the obstruction at Vicksburg."[58]

POSITIONAL WARFARE AND TACTICAL ENTRENCHMENT IN TENNESSEE

Trench warfare also was emerging in Tennessee. Following the collapse in September of the Confederate offensive into Kentucky, the Union Army of the Cumberland, now under Rosecrans, encamped behind the Nashville defenses, while Bragg took up positions near Murfreesboro. Bragg, at this state, was more concerned with replenishing depleted supplies than with an immediate winter campaign against Nashville, 180 miles away.[59]

Rosecrans had no immediate alternative but to sit and wait until the rebuilding of the Louisville-to-Nashville railway made it possible to build up supplies for a winter campaign against Chattanooga. Another inducement to Federal caution was the threat to communications posed by the large cavalry forces under Morgan and Forrest, which were running wild in central Tennessee and Kentucky. The number of front-line Federal troops was at times reduced to one-half the total forces, owing to the necessity of garrisoning the communications lines. The rebuilding of the Louisville and Nashville Railroad enabled Rosecrans by late December to build up a supply reserve at Nashville sufficient for a winter offensive. A daring long-range Federal cavalry raid in force under General Samuel P. Carter helped Rosecrans's cause when it severely damaged Bragg's communications by destroying the railroad to Virginia beyond hope of immediate repair.

Picking a time when Morgan and Forrest were involved in Kentucky and western Tennessee, Rosecrans, with the capacity to move if not maneuver, put his army of some 45,000 men on the march along the railroad to Murfreesboro. An inadequate number of muddy and narrow roads in densely wooded country hampered movement. In addition, there was a shortage of wagons that provided a very low, difficult-to-discern wagon standard, tying Rosecrans closely to the railroad. Rosecrans had also neglected to map the Murfreesboro area during the months he occupied it. The flat and wooded nature of the terrain made it impossible to effect communications by semaphore signals, though the Signal Corps maintained a line between the two columns of the army until they combined. Rosecrans had little choice but to seek a tactical confrontation.[60]

Rosecrans's advance caught Bragg off-guard with his army stretched over an unentrenched thirty-five-mile front. Bragg withdrew to prepare for battle at Stones River, just northwest of Murfreesboro. Without the capacity to maneuver, Bragg also prepared for a tactical encounter. The two armies came face to face at Stones River, in the vicinity of Murfreesboro. Rosecrans planned for the right of his line to engage the Confederate left and hold it in check while he massed his own left to throw the Confederates off the heights that constituted Bragg's right flank.[61] From these heights, the Federal artillery could enfilade the entire Confederate line. The inability to use signals because of the terrain contributed further to the positional battle of direct confrontation. An attempt to connect the Union line by signals failed.[62]

There was limited entrenchment in the opening phase of the battle. Rosecrans's plan called for massed frontal assaults. Rosecrans was one of the group of young engineering officers who had been picked by McClellan for high command. As a former engineering officer who graduated near the top of his West Point class and later taught at West Point, he would have been closely exposed to Dennis Hart Mahan. Yet in his rejection of the active entrenched defense for massed frontal assaults with an army containing a high proportion of raw recruits, he rejected Mahan out of hand. His general order prior to the battle was an extreme throwback to traditional assault doctrine with emphasis on the bayonet:

> Keep ranks. Do not throw away your fire. Fire slowly, deliberately. . . . Close steadily in upon the enemy, and, when you get within charging distance, rush on him with the bayonet. Recollect that there are hardly any troops in the world that will stand a bayonet charge, and that those who make it, therefore, are sure to win.[63]

Rosecrans's failure to fortify his flanks and rear was a violation of the precepts of even conventional doctrine. On the other hand, as he noted, "this whole country was a natural fortification."[64] But the natural cover was not sufficient cause for the omission to entrench, particularly in the relatively open area of the battle.

The spirit of Mahan was not completely rejected. The pioneer brigade of the Army of the Cumberland, in addition to its regular duties, was serving in the line as an infantry brigade, complete with an artillery battery. Upon taking up its position on the Union left flank, it constructed an abatis along a portion of the front.[65] The pioneer commander was James St. Clair Morton, as noted, an influential prewar theorist and publicist of the tactical outlook of Mahan. There is evidence that other units hastily improvised breastworks of fence rails and used standing fence in forming their lines of battle.[66]

For his part, Bragg assumed a deliberate tactical defense. "Fully aware of the greatly superior numbers of the enemy . . . , it was our policy to await attack. The position was selected and the line developed with this intention." Bragg selected what was a relatively weak defensive position, because, he maintained, he considered it the only place where he could concentrate his army while he covered the roads to Nashville.[67]

Bragg had at least part of his line fortified. There is some question as to how much and who ordered the fortifications. Rosecrans refers to Confederate "works" without elaboration. One of Bragg's officers observed later, in April, 1863, that "General Bragg has never shown much confidence in them [field works]—Murfreesborough, for example." Yet Polk's report notes that one badly exposed brigade in his line "had thrown up a slight rifle-pit." And there is evidence that perhaps most of the Confederate line threw up breastworks made from fence rails, including at least three of the four dismounted cavalry regiments fighting in the line as infantry. One Union regimental commander reported moving into line of battle on the 29th "within sight of the enemy's rifle pits."[68]

Rosecrans failed to launch a frontal assault on December 30 as expected, but rather made movements that led Bragg to believe he was being flanked. Bragg, in an attempt to roll up the enemy's line, ordered an attack against the Union right with the same emphasis on the bayonet as at Perryville.[69] The Confederate assault collapsed Rosecrans's right flank, threatened his communications, and forced him to stop his offensive and turn his attention to the force advancing from the rear against the center of his line.[70] Well positioned in trees and behind rocks, Philip Sheridan's infantry and concentrated artillery checked eight Confederate assaults before Rosecrans could reinforce him.[71] A Confederate attack on the Union flank was unsuccessful. Bragg's exhausted and battered troops fell back to recuperate.

During a two-hour lull, part of Rosecrans's weary army—possibly motivated by common sense induced by the heat of the battle, but perhaps incidentally in accordance with tactical defensive doctrine— took up positions behind a railroad embankment that extended along the Federal line. The Union infantry and massed artillery had strong defensive positions where rough ground and cedar growth hindered the assaulting infantry and rendered Confederate artillery nearly useless. From here the artillery threw back the next series of Confederate assaults. Generals Breckenridge and Hardee finally refused to slaughter any more troops against the railroad embankment.[72]

An incident affecting the deployment of Bragg's artillery, though of doubtful consequence for the outcome of the battle, nevertheless again reflected how the inadequate staff and command procedures of Civil War armies affected tactical coordination in battle. General Breckenridge and Captain Felix Robertson, in command of Breckenridge's artillery, got into a debate over Bragg's orders with respect to the line of artillery command as well as over artillery tactics. Breckenridge wanted the artillery to accompany the infantry assault. Robertson argued that Bragg intended the infantry to advance alone, with the artillery to follow and occupy the high ground in front after the infantry pushed the enemy off. Breckenridge wanted Robertson to deploy the artillery between the two lines of infantry; Robertson refused, because he considered this poor tactical organization. The outcome of the debate was that the artillery finally followed immediately to the rear of the infantry, where terrain largely eliminated its effectiveness. Bragg also had difficulty coordinating his infantry assaults. The close-order lines tended to intermingle. There was a further loss of order and discipline as the lines had difficulty getting through the cedar breaks.[73]

Ten hours from the initiation of action, the two exhausted armies gave up the battle and entrenched. Requiring provisions, ammunition, and rest, Rosecrans assumed the tactical defense.[74] Though he planned to take the offensive once his forces were replenished,[75] Rosecrans succumbed to tactical doctrine while on the defense and entrenched. His troops constructed not only earthworks and breastworks but redoubts, as well. General McCook, commander of the Union right wing, led the way when late in the afternoon he fortified part of his line behind barricades which, he believed, "could well have been defended by single lines."[76]

Bragg, in turn, accepted the futility of further assaults on the enemy positions, deeming it "unadvisable to assail them as then established." The Confederate army likewise assumed the tactical defense and entrenched at least part of its line. The extent and origin of Confederate entrenchment are again difficult to determine. One of Breckenridge's brigades entrenched behind "a low and very imperfect breastwork of earth and rails" following its repulse during the battle.[77] McCook observed that the enemy opposite him on the Union right had "barricades [which] extended fully three fourths of a mile beyond the Franklin Road." The commander of the first battalion of the Union pioneer brigade, positioned on the Union left, refers to the enemy falling back after a brief skirmish "behind his entrenchments."[78]

Union use of entrenchments was erratic. When Bragg had left the heights on his right unoccupied in moving his line to the left the day before, Rosecrans had extended his lines to occupy these hills. But his troops failed to entrench. Breckenridge's division on the Confederate right launched an innovational assault. It advanced in heavy columns on a battalion front behind a double line of skirmishers accompanied by three artillery batteries. The attack succeeded in routing the Union infantry, which was supported by only a single battery. But it then advanced into redirected artillery, which, combined with rifle fire, enfiladed their approach and tore them apart. The Confederates lost about 1,500 men in less than three-quarters of an hour. After this defeat of the Confederates' right wing, the Union troops repossessed the heights, and this time they quickly entrenched.[79]

In both armies there is some question of whether or not corps, division, and even brigade commanders were instrumental in making the decision to entrench. When on the defensive, regulations allowed corps and divisional commanders to make that decision independently. There is no explicit indication that Bragg and Rosecrans ordered entrenchment. And there is evidence that a corps commander and—in the case of James St. Clair Morton and probably one of Breckenridge's officers—even brigade commanders independently ordered entrenchments. The source of orders, though ambiguous, probably came from other than Bragg and Rosecrans.

Just as tactics continued to be dominated by infantry and the defensive organization of artillery, so Murfreesboro witnessed the continuing practical adjustment of cavalry in the western theater to its role in the battlefield. The Confederate and Union cavalry commands of Generals Joseph Wheeler and David Stanley effectively performed strategic roles of reconnaissance, raiding, and protecting supply lines, while concurrently moving in and out of the battle to fight in the line. There were some mounted engagements, including two charges by the Union cavalry. And there was some hand-to-hand mounted fighting. But the principal tactical role played by both cavalry forces was dismounted, organized as skirmishers, and using available cover in the form of fence rails.

Both cavalry forces displayed tactical presence about whether to deploy mounted or dismounted. In one major engagement, the Union cavalry, encountering the Confederate cavalry advancing in skirmish line against their positions on the Union flank, similarly dismounted and deployed in skirmish order. When the larger Confederate force turned their flank, they mounted and retreated to a better position. When the situation favored them, the Union cavalry again remounted and successfully charged the Confederate line. The Union cavalry also made good use of their flexible tactical possibilities by having mounted troops scout and guard the rear of their dismounted colleagues. The reports of both cavalry forces reinforce the pattern in the West where the cavalryman had no delusions about a dramatic mounted role on the battlefield, while at the same time appreciating the possibilities of the cavalry arm in a prominent support role.[80]

Rosecrans abandoned plans to extend the turning movement when rain made the ground too soft for campaigning.[81] Bragg then found it impractical to remain in position:

> On Saturday morning the 3rd, our forces had been in line of battle for five days and nights, with but little rest having no reserves; their bags and tents had been loaded and the wagons were 4 miles off; their provisions, if cooked at all, were most imperfectly prepared, with scanty means; the weather had been severe from cold and almost constant rain, and we had no change of clothing, and in many places could not have fires. The necessary consequence was great exhaustion of officers and men, many having to be sent to the hospitals in the rear, and more still were beginning to straggle from their commands, an evil from which we had so far suffered but little. During the whole ... day the rain continued to fall ... and the rapid rise of Stones River indicated it would soon be unfordable. ... I ... received the captured papers of Major-General McCook ... showing their effective strength to have been ... near ... if not quite 70,000 men. Before noon, reports from Brigadier-General Wheeler satisfied me the enemy instead of retiring, was receiving re-enforcements. Common prudence and the safety of my army, upon which even the safety of our cause depended, left no doubt on my mind as to the necessity of my withdrawal from so unequal a contest.[82]

Rosecrans, in turn, went into winter quarters along a defensive line near Murfreesboro. From there he could replenish his army by way of the Nashville-to-Murfreesboro railroad and await a more favorable season to resume the campaign. In the three weeks from December 26, 1862, to January 16, 1863, Rosecrans lost 2,100 animals and captured 400, a loss which alone was sufficient to hobble him for the considerable length of time necessary to replace them.[83] Acting in accordance with doctrine for a deliberate tactical defense in a state of encampment, Rosecrans entrenched.[84]

Unable to sustain his army in Middle Tennessee, Bragg retreated to take up winter quarters and to disburse his army near the more abundant food and fodder resources of the southern part of the state. His retreat from Murfreesboro was a major logistical disaster. It interrupted meat-packing operations for the winter; and, as it turned out, it deprived the Confederacy of the valuable resources of Middle Tennessee for the duration of the war.[85] This additional contraction of their resource areas restricted still further the offensive capacity of the Confederate armies.

The entrenched tactical defense had experienced a boost in prestige. That the massed assault and unfortified defense were exacting too high a price to be regularly paid was attested by approximately 11,000 Confederate casualties at Murfreesboro (out of a force of 38,000)—more than 9,000 of them either killed or wounded—and by approximately 9,500 dead and wounded Federals, with another 3,700 prisoners or missing.[86] Murfreesboro was the most costly battle in terms of percentage killed and wounded to that date. The rifled musket, with which the majority of western troops were now armed, began to register its impact. As the general introduction of the rifled musket accelerated the tactical ascendancy of the entrenched defensive, and strategic maneuver failed to remove military decisions from the realm of tactical solutions, trench warfare showed signs of becoming the predominant feature of war in the West as well as in the East.

At the end of the 1862 campaign, the supply situation of the Confederacy rendered its armies in both theaters incapable of extended strategic movement. The meat reserves gathered in 1861 were exhausted. The principal resource areas in Virginia and Tennessee were lost. Although the blockade was not particularly effective, the Confederacy was reduced to two ports, which had to be held at all costs. The Confederacy lacked the material and men to reclaim the lost resource areas of Virginia and Tennessee, and an offensive that risked defeat would also risk losing still more of the remaining resources.

The most practicable strategy was to hold and make efficient use of what remained. These resources, if properly exploited and supplemented by imports, would be adequate to support both the civilian and military population. The need for caution was accentuated in the case of the Confederacy by a manpower shortage that made it increasingly less practical to pay the mounting price of the frontal assault, particularly when the Confederacy's grand strategic end—recognition through wearing down the Union's will to sustain the war effort—could be attained by a defensive as well as by an offensive strategy. The inability of the Union armies to resolve the problems that prevented victory by strategic maneuver as an alternative to tactical confrontation promised to contribute further to the development of positional trench warfare.

8

Trench Warfare
and Maneuver

VICKSBURG: STRATEGIC MANEUVER
AND TACTICAL ENTRENCHMENT

The western armies of the Confederacy began 1863 on the defensive.
The Army of Tennessee under Braxton Bragg protected eastern Ten-
nessee and the approaches to Atlanta, while an army under General
John Pemberton watched over the Mississippi River from Vicksburg.

Union field command in the West, with Halleck's endorsement, developed a plan to offset the interior lines of the Confederate armies.
As the Confederates became increasingly difficult to defeat on their
interior lines, the western commanders focused even more intently on
a strategy of exhaustion against their logistics. The expectation was to
turn the defenders out of their positions protecting Middle and East
Tennessee as well as the Mississippi River at Vicksburg. Grant's results
at Vicksburg were to exceed expectations.

In the aftermath of the failure of his overland expedition against
Vicksburg in 1862, Grant had turned again to the water route from
Memphis. He ordered General Banks, with his small army of about
13,000 men, to prepare to make his way upriver from New Orleans to

join with the Army of the Tennessee at Vicksburg, a plan that entailed the reduction of Port Hudson en route. The Federal army, with an effective strength of about 45,000 men, was transported downriver to Milliken's Bend, ten miles above Vicksburg, where Grant in early February established his base of operations.

Grant spent the next two and one-half months in winter camp making the buildup by water from his central depot at Memphis and waiting for spring forage. Sherman's experience in the Yazoo River expedition in December had discouraged approach to the Vicksburg defenses from the north. Grant decided to approach from the south, where he could invest and perhaps successfully assault the defenses. His attempt to avoid running the river past the Vicksburg batteries, by renewing the canal project undertaken the year before to bypass Vicksburg, fell through when the river flooded.

To avoid another stalemate, Grant, with the subsiding of the river and the emergence of spring forage, in mid-April undertook a daring maneuver. He marched his troops down the west bank to below Vicksburg; ran gunboats and transports past the Vicksburg batteries; crossed to the east side of the river ten miles below Grand Gulf, a fortified position more than twenty miles below Vicksburg; and, to eliminate having to guard his communications, cut himself loose from his supply line to march against Vicksburg with only three days' packed rations, 120 wagons of hardtack, coffee, salt, and sugar, and 2 wagons of ammunition per regiment. During the next twenty days, until it invested Vicksburg on May 19, the Army of the Tennessee lived on its meager rations and what it collected from the land. In rich country with readily available livestock, the Union force found sufficient forage, corn, bacon, and beef to provide regular rations. Shortages of bread began to appear by the time of the investment, but by then the army was receiving supplies by water through Haines' Bluff.

Sherman learned from Grant's logistical daring. During the planning stage, he feared that the contemplated movements would overextend logistics. Grant ignored Sherman's fears. Sherman was greatly relieved when, during his eighty-three-mile march from Haines' Bluff to join Grant's army advancing on Vicksburg, he discovered that Grant was correct. Sherman lived comfortably off the land, despite a shortage of wagons and provisions at the start of his march. Sherman also had reservations about the ability of the logistical organization to supply Vicksburg by the river route. He noted that Grant "is entitled to all the credit, for I would not have advised it."[1]

The addition of its first modern signals organization improved the mobility of the Army of the Tennessee as it left Memphis. As noted, the army's first Signal Corps detachment was not ready for the field until the end of March, 1863. Grant left Memphis on April 1 with a detachment of seventeen officers and thirty-seven enlisted men. Brown thought that "probably a better or more thoroughly equipped party had never been sent into the field for signal duty. They rendered excellent service during the campaign, most of them receiving honourable mention from time to time in official reports."[2]

Grant's swings between orthodoxy and change occurred again during the Vicksburg campaign, with, on the one hand, his destructive interference with Signal Corps organization, contrary even to War Department special orders, and, on the other, his request for six of the Signal Corps' controversial and experimental field telegraph trains. Although he requested the trains in early May, they did not reach Memphis until June 20 and were not ready for the field until after the fall of Vicksburg. By the end of 1863, the Army of the Cumberland and the Army of the Tennessee had between them eleven of Myer's field telegraph trains.[3]

Grant had now placed himself between the two parts of the Confederate army under Pemberton at Vicksburg and Joseph Johnston at Jackson, fifty miles east. Grant's relatively secure interior lines, with all his communications north of Vicksburg on the Mississippi River, combined with the logistical and manpower plight of the Confederate armies, prevented the defenders from reacting. And General Benjamin Grierson's Union cavalry raid put one of the two railroads, upon which Johnston was depending to build up and supply an army at Jackson to lift the investment, out of operation for over a month. The two corps of Sherman and McPherson, during their advance on Vicksburg, further disrupted Johnston by driving him out of Jackson. They wrecked his railroad facilities in that city and the line that led to Vicksburg, and destroyed all materials of war they could find. With his inadequate wagon supply, this railroad was Johnston's only means of approaching Vicksburg unless he could forage off the land. By the time he had gathered a respectable-sized army with some facility to move, Grant had stripped the land.[4] Moreover, Johnston could have moved only directly against the Federal army; Grant's lines of communications through Haines' Bluff were inaccessible to assault by land. Pemberton, for his part, brought his army out of Vicksburg to check Grant's advance in the open field. He intended to cut the enemy's line of communications, if possible, and to save his own communications with Johnston. After a brutal battle at Champion's Hill, Pemberton retreated behind his Vicksburg defenses.

From the standpoint of the tactical use of field fortifications, the

numerous actions during the Federal advance on Vicksburg were revealing. Neither side entrenched in the major encounter at Champions
Hill. Pemberton's unsuccessful defensive stand cost him about 3,000
of his 20,000 troops, against approximately 2,000 Union casualties from
a total force of about 30,000 men.[5] Apart from Johnston's previously
prepared works at Jackson, which were of little use to his small force
of about 6,000 men, field works were scarce. They appeared only once
prior to the investment. Pemberton fortified a bridgehead on the Big
Black River with an extensive semicircular line with both flanks resting
on the river. But this bridgehead was also part of the outer works
protecting the immediate approaches to Vicksburg, behind which the
Confederates planned to make one last stand before retiring to the
main line of defense.[6] Under such circumstances, doctrine explicitly
called for fortification. The Federal troops carried the undermanned
bridgehead by rush assault.[7] A shortage of tools perhaps in part explained the failure of either the Union or Confederate troops to entrench; Pemberton had only about 500 with his army. Although the
train carrying Grant's entrenching tools was left behind to facilitate
movement, there were pioneer troops with entrenching equipment.[8]
The fact that Grant left his tools behind and never used his pioneer
troops to entrench suggests that he had reverted to the traditional
doctrine of not digging in while pursuing a tactical offensive, an attitude
perhaps encouraged by his underestimation of the enemy's numbers.

Grant's operations against the main Vicksburg fortifications constituted "a conflict," to quote the Comte de Paris, "between two entrenched armies rather than a siege in the strictest acceptance of the
term." The two chief engineers of the Army of the Tennessee agreed
with this analysis.[9] The entrenched line on which Pemberton fell back
was not, as the Federal engineers and Pemberton himself noted, particularly impressive. It was a light system of works consisting of small
lunettes, redans, and redoubts connected in most instances with rifle
trenches. Many rifle pits, however, stood unconnected between the works.
These fortifications, constructed the previous fall and winter, were badly
eroded.[10] The main line of defenses, which Pemberton considered to
be "the shortest defensible line of which the topography of the country
admitted," extended for about eight miles.[11] Pemberton distributed
15,500 men behind this line and left the remainder of his effective force
of approximately 22,000 in reserve.[12] In a misunderstanding of Pemberton's orders, again reflecting problems of staff and command procedures, an outer line of defenses was thrown up about 600 yards in
advance of the main line. Pemberton abandoned this line rather than
further overextend his army. With more than 20,000 men, he was in a

good tactical position behind his works if Johnston could relieve him before Grant had time to augment his army.

Under the direction of engineer officers, fatigue parties immediately began to repair and strengthen the main line. They connected rifle pits and obstructed approaches to the works with ditches, abatis, palisades, and entanglements of pickets and telegraph wire. They constructed platforms and embrasures for artillery. Annoyed by the enfilading fire of sharpshooters and artillery, the Confederate engineers constructed numerous traverses and arranged for covered approaches from the rear.

Since Pemberton had a total of only about 500 entrenching tools, his troops were incapable of performing any extraordinary feats of entrenchment on short notice. Even when strengthened, the Confederate fortifications still did not constitute a heavy system of works. As the chief engineers of the Army of the Tennessee noted, the line

> consisted of small works on commanding points necessarily irregular from the shape of the ridges on which they were situated; in only one case (that of a redoubt 30 yards square) closed at the gorge; of weak profile . . . and connected by lines of simple trench. Vicksburg was, then, rather an entrenched camp than a fortified place, owing much of its strength to the difficult ground, obstructed by fallen trees in front, which rendered rapidity of movement and ensemble in an assault impossible.[13]

Arriving before the Vicksburg defensive lines on May 19, Grant attacked. He was encouraged by the hoped-for demoralization of the roughly handled Confederate army and by the general enthusiasm of his own officers and men to continue the offensive that had brought them such success over the previous twenty days. Grant also underestimated the enemy's numbers.[14] The defenders easily drove the assailants back.

When another assault was planned for the 22d, Sherman, the day before, issued the revolutionary tactical order that "the skirmishers along our whole front will, during the night, advance within 100 yards of the enemy's works, and will, with the spade or ax, prepare pits or fallen trees, so as to give them cover from which to kill artillerists who attempt to load the guns, also to keep down the fire of the enemy's infantry in the rifle-pits during the assault."[15] It was the most impressive appreciation of offensive entrenchment displayed to date, the more significant because it came from the man destined soon to lead the western armies of the Union.

The Federal assault failed. Weak though the Confederate positions were in profile, their compensating natural strength, combined with the firepower of the rifled musket, rendered them quite satisfactory for a

defensive stand. An interesting incident in Union assault tactics occurred when Brigadier General John Stevenson, initially advancing his
brigade in column, ordered it to lie down until fire let up. He then
unsuccessfully attempted to carry the Confederate works with a rush
in skirmish order. The assault was reminiscent of fellow brigade commander Morgan Smith's attack by rushes at Fort Donelson, a precedent
with little follow-up in Grant's army until now.[16]

Convinced that frontal assaults were futile, officers and men of the
Army of the Tennessee accepted the necessity of a siege.[17] Both sides
dug in. Grant called in Porter's fleet, with which he had signals communication,[18] to support the bombardment with its mortars and Dahlgren guns.[19] Although the investment was completed on May 22, the
besiegers could not begin large-scale entrenching activity until a week
later, when the train carrying entrenching tools finally made its way to
the battlefield. "In the meantime the most was made of the few [en-
trenching tools] that could be gathered together around camp and from
the pioneers."[20] On May 24 the besiegers thwarted Pemberton's attempt
to extend his works to the river. Failing to secure his flank in this
manner, Pemberton, on the 25th, started a line along the river, extending from the right extremity of his front and connecting with the
batteries at Vicksburg. Several new batteries were constructed, and work
to repair and strengthen the defenses continued along the length of
the line.[21]

The Federal execution of siege operations was a showpiece of improvisational ingenuity. When the siege began, Grant had two officers
on engineer duty. That he managed to acquire one more is one indication of the state of engineering organization in the western armies.
Aides-de-camp and line officers with engineering training at West Point
were posted to engineer duty and assigned to headquarters of corps or
divisions. There were no engineer troops. The three regular and the
improvised engineering officers instructed them on the spot. Pioneer
companies, in divisions where they were present, were used as engineer
troops. They and fugitive Negroes did most of the sapping and construction of parallels. In accordance with practice in siege operations,
work performed by infantry details was comparatively minor.[22]

The ad hoc engineering organization of the Army of the Tennessee
rose to the challenge. Faced with a shortage of materials, it used what
was at hand. Grapevines were used for gabions.[23] When these were
found to be too heavy, an aide-de-camp who was serving as an engineering officer experimented with crushed sugar cane, which proved
far more satisfactory. Crushed cane was also used for fascines.[24] Bales
of cotton from neighboring plantations and rails and "timber from the

nearest barn or cotton house" reinforced the parapets. At first there was some difficulty in building sap rollers for protection from infantry fire that were not too heavy to push across the rugged ground between the lines.[25] One of the regular engineer officers solved this problem by using two barrels head to head for the hollow core around which he built cane fascines. In accordance with practice when constructing siege approaches, "whenever an approach gave opportunity for fire, loopholes were either formed in the parapet, made by using sand bags, or in timber laid along the parapet." At close quarters the gunners used plant shutters to keep the embrasures closed to rifle fire. Where the approaches had to cross ravines enfiladed by the enemy's artillery, the siege parties constructed traverses by placing tree trunks on top of one another.[26]

Improvising and learning through practice, the sappers pushed forward their approaches and advanced their parallels closer to the enemy's lines. "The weather is now very hot," wrote Sherman, "and we are digging roads and approaches so that it tells on our men, but they work cheerfully and I have approaches and parallels within eighty yards of the enemy's line. . . . Any man who puts his head above ground has his head shot off."[27]

The work progressed steadily but slowly. Although highly laudatory of the ingenious improvisation and of the adaptation of untutored officers and men to siege techniques, one of the chief engineers of the Army of the Tennessee felt that the lack of an adequate engineer corps had delayed the pushing of the approaches close enough for an entrenched assault line by two to three weeks.[28] The besiegers were fortunate in that the fire of the defenders was slight. Owing to the feebleness of the Confederate artillery, the thickness of the Federal parapets seldom exceeded six to eight feet.[29] An acute shortage of percussion caps combined with a lack of heavy artillery pieces to prevent the Confederates from conducting a vigorous harassment of the besiegers.[30]

As the enemy pushed his approaches and parallels increasingly closer, the Confederates, in accordance with doctrine, constructed retrenchments at threatened points along the line.[31] On June 24 they built a retrenchment under fire to protect a heavily shelled redan. At the same time, they prepared the ditch of the redan for riflemen to form a double line at this position. When on June 13 Union artillery firing from a parallel at close range destroyed the parapet of another Confederate redan, the defenders promptly constructed a second redan a few feet to the rear of the first.[32] During the night of June 14, the Confederates constructed new rifle pits to envelop a threatened stockade and the redan that protected it. After June 15, under orders from their chief

engineer, Confederate working parties constructed retrenchments behind all salient works against which the Union troops were extending
approaches and undertook countermining.[33]

The Union sappers exploded a mine beneath a redan on June 25,
but the defenders stopped the ensuing assault from retrenchments that
they had constructed some fifteen feet to the rear. On July 1 the Union
sappers exploded a 1,500-pound powder charge, which completely destroyed another redan, leaving a crater twenty feet deep and thirty by
fifty feet across. The besiegers understandably did not attempt to push
an assault through this giant hole. During the night of July 2, the Confederates laid out eleven mines to be exploded when the Federal saps
came within their range.[34] Their effect was not to be known. Without
provisions, informed by Johnston that he could not relieve the siege,
and believing his enfeebled army physically incapable of attempting a
breakout, Pemberton surrendered on July 4.[35] Grant had achieved the
ultimate victory: the surrender of the enemy's army. In the process, the
Civil War had witnessed its most extended and in some ways most spectacular display of trench warfare to date.

The failure of the Confederate armies under Johnston and Pemberton to mobilize sufficiently to break the siege was an essential part
of the Vicksburg campaign's tactical story. There were several reasons
why Johnston, only fifty miles away, was unable to use the army he was
collecting to lift the siege by cutting Grant's communications, by attacking his rear, or by supporting a breakout by Pemberton. Grant's
communications through Haines' Bluff were inaccessible by land. Grant
discouraged Johnston from attacking his rear by entrenching a force
of about 30,000 under Sherman on a strong line of circumvallation
from Haines' Bluff to Big Black River,[36] holding Pemberton on his front
with the remaining troops, which, with heavy reinforcement, numbered
another 30,000 men. Grant also had the countryside stripped so that
Johnston could not support an army.[37]

But Johnston's mobility was so hampered by other factors that he
was unable to budge his army before July. His strained resource base,
the general transportation hindrances to logistical buildup, Grierson's
destruction of the railroad south of Jackson, plus the drain of Lee's
offensive campaign had left Johnston's new army of some 25,000 men
deficient in artillery, ammunition for all arms, and wagons and animals
for both field transportation and artillery. Johnston was also conscious
of the futility of attacking an entrenched army that he correctly estimated to number about 60,000 men.[38] When in early July he finally
acquired limited mobility, the best he could do was to propose a rendezvous with Pemberton, if the latter could break out of Vicksburg.

The inability of a Confederate army to disturb Grant's entrenched army, deep in Confederate territory, and with proportionate numbers, was still another example of the impact the prevailing conditions of warfare were having on strategic mobility, particularly for the Confederates.

The siege of Vicksburg also led to a psychological side effect of extended periods in the trenches: fraternization. On occasion, what began as exchanges of news at close quarters ended in discussions with the lines thoroughly mixed.[39] This reflected a phenomenon that was to become more familiar as armies increasingly came to spend long periods in proximity to one another across entrenched battlefields: men detaching themselves from the motivations that inspired them to fight one another to react as men tied by the bond of a common isolation, a common struggle to survive. A feature of World War I, it became a part of modern warfare during the Civil War. Almost all accounts of the captivity of the Confederate army after its surrender and before its parole comment on the surprising good will and mutual respect that characterized the relations between the ranks of vanquished and victor.

SHERMAN AND THE ORIGINS OF TOTAL WAR

The fall of Vicksburg had immediate repercussions. The 4,000-man garrison of Port Hudson some 150 miles downriver surrendered to the lengthy siege by General Banks's army of 13,000 men. This removed the last obstacle to Federal control of the Mississippi. Joseph Johnston immediately extended and strengthened the fortifications of Jackson in anticipation of a move against him. Sherman, in the ensuing campaign against Johnston, began to experiment with the theory of warfare that would characterize his strategy for the remainder of the war.

The development of Sherman's thoughts on total war began when he assumed command of the District of West Tennessee, with headquarters in Memphis, on July 21, 1862. Sherman had previously held conventional views on civilian neutrality. As he witnessed Southern profits from Union commerce going to support Confederate armies, he decided that it was necessary to wage war against civilian resources and morale, which, he believed, would also demoralize men in the enemy ranks because of problems centered on the homefront. By October, 1862, Sherman had decided on a philosophy of total war against the civilian population as well as the armies of the Confederacy.[40]

To wage total war, Sherman had to develop a logistical organization that would sustain him in the face of the enemy army deep in Confederate territory. He turned to this problem as he advanced on Johnston's position at Jackson. Sherman traveled light. On Grant's orders, "all baggage, tents, and encumbrances of any kind" were left behind. The baggage standard was reduced to three wagons per regiment, and the wagons saved were transferred to the supply train. Five days' rations were carried in haversacks and regimental wagons. Each company had one pack mule to carry water. The wagon standard was probably about forty per 1,000 men.[41] Sherman sustained his position before Jackson by building up a sufficient number of wagons and animals to run a supply line between Jackson and an intermediary depot on the Big Black River.[42]

Sherman coupled the strategic mobility achieved through logistical reorganization with his commitment to defend the enemy by maneuver rather than by tactical attrition. Refusing futile assaults against Johnston's field works,[43] Sherman held the enemy in his entrenchments while he directed his cavalry toward Johnston's communications. He intended to lay siege as soon as his ammunition train brought sufficient supplies for such an undertaking.[44] At the same time, he completely destroyed the resources of the countryside. Sherman's troops tore up over 100 miles of the railroad running north and south through Jackson upon which Confederate supply depended. They stripped the countryside of food and forage, turning fields of green corn into pasture for their animals, and hauling away what they could not eat.

"The wholesale destruction to which this country is now being subjected is terrible to contemplate," observed Sherman of the havoc he was causing, "but it is the scourge of war."[45] Sentiment regarding social ethics in warfare had moved a considerable distance from the comparative humanity that in the early stages of the war had attempted not to involve civilians. The hostility manifested in Confederate guerrilla activity, combined with Sherman's observation of the economic and logistical cost of a policy of political conciliation, shifted the motive from conciliation to terror. Sherman reduced the population of the area to dependence on the largess of the Union army for its survival. It was difficult for the Confederates to sustain a cavalry or infantry force of any size for any length of time on the devastated countryside.[46] Having reduced interference with his investing force, Sherman could pursue his holding-turning movement against Johnston's entrenched army with relative impunity.

On July 17, Johnston's army, its communications in peril, abandoned the Jackson defenses and withdrew along the railroad eastward toward Meridian and the interior of Mississippi. The hindrances to strategic movement discouraged pursuit. Johnston had the advantage of a head start and the railroad, which he tore up behind him. More important, in the intense summer heat, Sherman's war-weary and fever-ridden troops, feeling the effects of being too long in the trenches on the banks of the Mississippi without leave, were clamoring for furlough, a reprieve that Sherman granted. The entire army badly needed to reorganize and to absorb the large numbers of troops who had joined during the Vicksburg campaign.[47] Sherman would have time to reflect on the early organizational lessons of his strategy to concurrently wear down the enemy's will through his resources while wearing down the enemy's army on his front. Most important, he would have to solve the logistical puzzle of how to follow the Confederate army into the heartland of the South.

ROSECRANS AND MANEUVER IN TENNESSEE

While Grant tended to Confederate defenses on the Mississippi, William S. Rosecrans and his Army of the Cumberland prepared to challenge Braxton Bragg for control of Middle Tennessee and the route to Atlanta. But Rosecrans first raised some interesting strategic questions about the efficacy of Halleck and Lincoln's strategy of simultaneous advances with respect to an advance on Bragg's positions covering East Tennessee. Supported by Generals George Thomas and, significantly, the aggressive "Fighting Phil" Sheridan, Rosecrans raised the prospect that Bragg could draw him deeper into the Confederacy, cut his communications, raze the countryside, then join Joseph Johnston in Mississippi. While Rosecrans argued a losing case for staying on the defense to hold Bragg where he was,[48] he also struggled with the organizational problems of preparing for a major maneuver detached from his supply base.

Rosecrans and Meigs spent the winter and spring engaged in a revealing dialogue on field transportation and supply in relation to the strategic mobility of the Army of the Cumberland. Rosecrans argued that he needed animals for transportation to forage depleted countryside in the face of the enemy while 220 miles from the nearest supply base at Louisville. On March 31, 1863, Rosecrans's quartermaster reported that for 60,000 men he had 3,747 draft horses and 23,859 mules in the army and at depots. He noted, however, that one-quarter of the horses were worn out and unfit for service. This number was all that had survived from 19,164 horses available on March 23. The number of mules, by contrast, remained constant over this period.

The quartermaster commented on the vulnerability of the draft horses, noting the substitution of mules for most of the limited number of horses that he reported. Rosecrans observed that the heavy mortality was due to the lack of long forage, and requested an additional 10,000 cavalry horses to mount infantry to forage. On March 23, he reported that only one-third of all animals were serviceable.[49] Meigs responded with a lengthy lecture to Rosecrans on how to care for his animals and organize his field transportation. But the horse mortality problem was endemic to the Union army for reasons that even Ingalls, in the Army of the Potomac, determined to be a mystery. As noted, it may have been attributable largely to the inadequate feeding standard for horses.

Meigs also had a combination of insight in perceiving another problem and shortsight in overcoming it. From the beginning, as noted, Meigs had appreciated the difficulty of foraging a static army. As Rosecrans exhausted his environs, Meigs wrote:

> Our armies, it appears to me, are encamped too much in mass. How Napoleon divided his troops during every period of inaction, bringing them together only the day before or night before a battle and scattering them for subsistence the moment the blow was delivered! Look at the Army of the Potomac—a solid, inactive mass of men and animals for the past five months . . . it has drawn nothing from the countryside it occupies, except wood.

The foraging area required to do this in the American countryside as contrasted with France, as noted, and the consequently greater problems of communications and command to bring them together if threatened, made Meigs's suggestion impracticable. It was even more impracticable until the spring corn crop. In this instance, as in others, bureau personnel continued to lean somewhat toward abstract Napoleonic models, while the field command continued to face uncomfortable realities.

Meigs correctly identified one self-defeating logistical circle in his criticism of Rosecrans's request for more cavalry horses to facilitate foraging. "Had it been possible to furnish so many men with horses," Meigs observed, "it would have been necessary to furnish more horses still to transport forage for these, and the difficulty of feeding them would have been greater and greater. I doubt the wisdom of building up such masses, which crumble under their own weight." Rosecrans completed the circle when he noted why the cavalry horses were essential to maintain his position. Noting that only half those horses were serviceable, he argued that these numbers were "effectively not half that required for a permanent garrison of infantry equal to that of this army," and that the cavalry "has to furnish pickets, scouts, couriers, for Fort Donelson, Clarksville, Nashville, Gallatin, Carthage and the front of his army from Franklin to this place, 28 miles." He further argued that the long forage, for which he needed additional cavalry horses to mount infantry, was necessary "owing to the impossibility of getting transportation, either by water or rail—we are 220 miles from our base of supplies at Louisville." If he was going to compete with the enemy for scarce forage, Rosecrans contended that he needed the mounted men requested. Meigs accepted Rosecrans's argument insofar as he acquiesced to Rosecrans's request.[50]

Rosecrans's problem was in building up the provisions necessary to move. Once underway, he could supplement and replace the supplies he carried by foraging. There is room for conjecture on whether Rosecrans as yet fully appreciated what all field commanders were simultaneously learning, namely, the advantages of foraging when on the move as compared to when stationary, especially for the health of the animals. On the other hand, to begin his advance without adequate provisions would have been contrary to practice as well as unwise. Forage was scarce, the country having been stripped by the Confederates. He would also have had to spread his army so widely as to leave himself vulnerable to Bragg's nearby army and the more imminent danger of the deadly Confederate cavalry as well as partisans. Rosecrans had little choice but to begin his move well provisioned. He could then supplement and replace supplies off the land, which meant he had to wait for spring crops, especially corn.

On June 23, Rosecrans moved. And for a general who, like McClellan, was accused of being slow, he moved in spectacular style. His thinking was to avoid another tactical bloodbath with no accompanying strategic advantage. He consequently planned to turn Bragg's communications at Tullahoma. By getting behind Bragg and cutting his route of retreat, Rosecrans planned to force him to fight on ground of Union choosing, and to inflict a severe if not annihilating defeat on his army.

Rosecrans failed in his attempt to get to Bragg's rear. Torrential rains turned the roads to thick mud, slowing his advance. More significant, Bragg, taking advantage of his rail communications, fell back quickly out of Rosecrans's grasp. Bragg rejected Joseph Johnston's idea that he exchange bases with Rosecrans. The Union move of eighty miles turned Bragg out of Middle Tennessee, but the muddy roads made pursuit extremely difficult. Bragg also stripped the countryside in his retreat, making it necessary to await the repair of the railroad to resupply the Army of the Cumberland.

It is difficult to calculate Rosecrans's transportation standard for the Tullahoma campaign and his subsequent maneuver to turn Bragg out of Chattanooga. But it is possible that for Tullahoma, he moved with an extraordinary standard that may have exceeded sixty-nine or seventy wagons per 1,000 men. Rosecrans also moved with 45,000 animals, the highest proportion of animals to men of any campaign in the war. The 1864–65 average in the Union army would be 2 men to 1 animal.[51] Rosecrans's success and the speed of his movement made a case for the virtues of careful preparation and an abnormal transportation standard, though there is a legitimate question as to whether or not he needed his standard to achieve the results that he did.

Rosecrans's speed of movement was remarkable, considering that he had to cope with torrential rains that turned the roads into quagmires. He moved approximately eighty miles in only nine days, for an average of nine miles per day. Subtracting thirty-six hours that he halted at Hoover's Gap and sixty hours in front of Winchester, he averaged over sixteen miles a day.[52] This rate exceeds Sherman's averages of between twelve and fifteen miles a day in his raid to Savannah and around nine miles a day through the Carolinas. Though Sherman, like Rosecrans, had encountered arduous conditions, he also had better forage. There is room for the conclusion that Rosecrans was an extremely well-organized and disciplined field commander with a competent quartermaster department.

Rosecrans's penchant for thorough organization again came into play as he paused for six weeks to await railroad repairs necessary for resupply. His plan was to continue his maneuver against Bragg's flank, this time to cut his communications at Chattanooga. Rosecrans again prepared to live off the land, supplemented by a long wagon route over bad roads in rugged terrain. When Rosecrans began his maneuver on August 16, the train of the Army of the Cumberland was in excellent shape. Meigs observed that "most of the wagons and mules had been long enough in service to be thoroughly tested and trained." So prepared, Rosecrans made his long trek across the mountains with, as Meigs observed, "very little loss or injury."[53] From departure August 16 to the beginning of the Battle of Chickamauga in mid-September, Rosecrans moved approximately 130 or 140 miles in thirty days, for an average of just over 4 miles per day.

The best explanation for his slow movement compared to his average in the Tullahoma maneuver is that the greater distance tied him closely to his wagon supply line to supplement his foraging from the land. For the Tullahoma campaign he was able to move free of the supply lines, living off the land to supplement what he carried. And the faster he moved, the more forage he could gather, especially with his large capacity to forage. His maneuver to Chattanooga, by contrast, could not be achieved without a supply line. The forage on the land was too thin and the distance too far. Rosecrans was consequently tied to his wagon supply line to supplement what he carried and could forage. Even then, he moved faster than Sherman would subsequently move on his march with a mobile railroad that followed him from Chattanooga to Atlanta.

Rosecrans facilitated his movement by widely dispersing his army, both to ease his passage through the mountains and to collect what forage was available. He assumed this risk in the face of the enemy partly because, after turning Bragg out of Chattanooga, he mistakenly believed that Bragg was retreating to Georgia. Rosecrans's intelligence suffered owing to an inadequate number of cavalry available for scouting and reconnaissance. Bragg also did an excellent job feigning his intentions. Bragg, in fact, was moving to join a concentration to protect the railroad into North Georgia. It was his intention to resume the offensive. Simon Buckner's army, brigades from Joseph Johnston, and Longstreet's corps were all en route by rail to join him and challenge what the Confederate high command considered the weakest link in the Union line. Rosecrans, caught by surprise in a situation reminiscent of Lee's at Antietam, was, like Lee, able to concentrate his army in time to meet Bragg's combined forces for the Battle of Chickamauga. Though Rosecrans was outnumbered 70,000 to 60,000, his strategic movement gave him the tactical advantage. Bragg had to take the tactical offensive to recover his communications.[54]

In defense of the approaches to Atlanta, Braxton Bragg struggled with the same problems as Rosecrans. While Rosecrans argued his case for careful preparation through the winter and early spring of 1863, Bragg complained of insufficient field transportation to make even short-range movements in the presence of the enemy, let alone large-scale turning movements away from his railway supply lines. He argued that he lacked enough transportation to forage.[55]

The first evidence of Bragg's transportation standard, his general orders of August 26, 1863, indicates that he may have been somewhat hesitant to accept the realities of field transportation available to Confederate armies at this stage of the war. His allowance provided approximately thirty-five wagons for 1,000 men.[56] Lee, earlier in April, also had set a standard of approximately thirty-five wagons per 1,000 men, but in July had reduced it drastically to about twenty-eight per thousand. A month later, in his general orders of September 24, Bragg brought his transportation allowance in line with Lee's, dropping the standard to approximately twenty-eight wagons per 1,000 men. This may have been induced in part by Longstreet's arrival from the East without any field transportation. Bragg at the time complained, with justification, that his transportation predicament made even short-range movements in the presence of the enemy difficult. The reduction came largely through a drastic cut in the general supply train for rank and file from one wagon per 100 men to one wagon per 200 men present for duty, and a cut in ordnance wagons from two for every 250 men to two for every 375 men present for duty.[57] On the supply side, Bragg was deficient in blankets, tents, and shoes, with inadequate stock to replace them. By August, he would be short of meat and grain.[58]

There was also a suggestion of disorganization contributing to Bragg's problem. General E. P. Alexander, arriving with Longstreet's corps, considered Bragg's army so disorderly and ill-armed as to be incapable of assuming the offensive. About one-third of Bragg's men were still using the .69 caliber smoothbore musket. The opposing Union troops, on the other hand, were completely equipped with rifles. Some units were even armed with repeaters. Alexander considered Bragg's army an inefficient military machine "whose power for offense was scarcely fifty percent of what the same force would have developed upon the defense."[59]

This comment from an officer as critically observant as Alexander must be taken seriously. It observed the price Bragg paid for his earlier offensive and the problems of rebuilding, especially with the malfunctioning and deprived Confederate logistical system. It also may have reflected the relative standards achieved in the western and eastern armies of the Confederacy. In part, it may have been Alexander's reaction to the "western style." Even Bragg, organizer and disciplinarian that he was, could not make an army that mirrored the style of the Army of Northern Virginia. There is also the question of whether Alexander's rating of the offensive versus the defensive merits of Bragg's army did not increasingly apply to Lee as well.

Bragg's concentration both to check Rosecrans's advance and to prepare for a counterthrust was, despite Alexander's comments, a tribute to his organizational skills with limited resources. Bragg conducted a well-organized and skilled withdrawal from Chattanooga. He successfully hid his intentions while spreading rumors of panic and low morale. He played for time while the carefully veiled strategic reinforcement by rail secretly brought him Buckner, Longstreet, and reinforcements from Johnston. Bragg maneuvered to force a favorable battle with the intention of using it to his advantage to turn Rosecrans. On September 16, Bragg concentrated to cut through Rosecrans's front. He planned to place himself between the Union army and Chattanooga, then move southward to drive the defeated army into McLencore's Cove, where he hoped to destroy it. It was an ambitious plan with what

Bragg acknowledged was limited transportation for even short-range movements in the face of the enemy, to say nothing of the difficulties of tracking the enemy's army through dense forests.[60]

CHICKAMAUGA: NEW DEVELOPMENTS IN TRENCH WARFARE

Too many factors mitigated against victory by maneuver as the two armies finally came together to fight the Battle of Chickamauga. The opposing armies were hampered by exceedingly difficult wooded and undulating terrain. Both sides were unfamiliar with the country, and both suffered from breakdowns in tactical communications.[61] Large numbers of raw recruits further weighed down the two armies. In the Confederate case, several newly organized divisions were strangers to one another.[62] And Bragg, as noted, suffered from a transportation shortage.

Circumstances drew the two armies to a tactical battle, as they stumbled into one another near Chickamauga Creek. Entrenchment was implemented by degrees. The failure to entrench extensively at first was due in part, at least, to the natural features of the terrain. Rosecrans's strategic decision "that the battle . . . be for the safety of the army and the possession of Chattanooga" led him to take a tactical defensive stance.[63] But he also decided that, owing to the natural strength of the position, "concealed in a dense forest," he would require only "slight breastworks of timber and abatis."[64]

Bragg, unwilling to accept a stalemate, decided to attack. As an alternative to a frontal assault, which was unpopular, Generals D. H. Hill and Breckenridge planned turning movements with their divisions to take the Federal entrenchments from the rear. Hill was unsuccessful. Breckenridge, surprisingly, succeeded in getting his entire division beyond the Union flank and part behind their positions. But his force was too small, and Union reinforcements quickly drove him back.

Bragg now reverted to the remaining alternative to a stalemate, ordering a successive frontal assault from deployed positions for September 19 from right to left along the entire Union line. When the Confederate infantry moved into their assigned positions, a significant tactical development took place in the Army of the Tennessee: it constructed breastworks of fallen timber and stones in close proximity to the Union lines.[65] This construction of field fortifications during a tactical offense other than a siege was a departure from conventional doctrine and a significant signpost when the field commander was Braxton Bragg.

The Federal line repulsed the Confederate attack, a single line assault unsupported by artillery.[66] That night Longstreet arrived with two divisions to reinforce Bragg. The Union army, meanwhile, deciding that the gifts nature afforded their defensive line could be done greater justice by human endeavor, further strengthened their lines and terminated each end with fortified wings that extended well to the rear. Particularly impressive were the works General George Thomas, an early practitioner of field fortification, had thrown up on the Union right. "All during the night, the noise of his axes had been heard felling trees and building breastworks of logs," commented E. P. Alexander, "and work was kept up until the Federal right occupied a veritable citadel, from which assault by infantry alone could scarcely dislodge him."[67] After his failure on the 19th, Bragg at first decided to revert to the tactical defense, but then he decided to try another series of successive frontal assaults along the entire line.[68]

Chance now came to Bragg's aid in the form of a breakdown in Union communications and command procedures. A misinterpretation of unclear orders from Rosecrans led to the mistaken withdrawal of a Federal division to support another area of the line. The result was a gaping hole through which Longstreet quickly ordered his command. Part of the force in the center of the Union line fled from the field and withdrew to Chattanooga. From his heavily fortified crescent-shaped position on the Union right, Thomas held off the entire Confederate army, until Longstreet forced him to withdraw by putting eleven guns in a position to rake the left of the Union positions from the flank and rear.[69] Bragg's victory had been won at great cost. Nearly 50 percent of the effective strength of his army was on the casualty list. The figures again suggested the increasing impracticality of the frontal assault against entrenched defenders. The fire of two of Thomas's brigades armed with repeating rifles had been particularly devastating.[70]

Bragg in later reports stressed his troubles with field transportation and supply in accounting for his failure to pursue Union troops after Chickamauga or to assault Chattanooga. The emphasis on his supply problem would grow when his failure to pursue the offensive became a matter of later controversy. But the immediate reports and correspondence in the aftermath of battle strongly suggest that Bragg's real motives were his enormous losses at Chickamauga and a reluctance to lose still more blood by attacking the strong defensive positions at Chattanooga. In subsequent reports, Bragg also explained for the first time his decision not to invade Tennessee after his victory at Chickamauga largely in terms of his lack of field transportation. There were additionally no pontoons, the bridges over the Tennessee were out, and the river was flooding, making fords subject to sudden rises. Bragg's mixed motives emphasized how the twin dilemmas of field transportation and supply and the cost of the frontal assault against field fortifications increasingly haunted western as well as eastern field command.[71]

One of the tactical incongruities at Chickamauga was the performance of Longstreet. In the eastern theater, he had established himself as an advocate of the entrenched tactical defense. At Fredericksburg he had become the first Confederate commander in the East to employ the entrenched defense in the field. At Gettysburg he had vigorously opposed Lee's decision to launch a frontal assault. At Chickamauga he seemingly departed from form. He was consistent in advocating a turning movement against Thomas's position, but came out strongly against the tactical defense. Not only did he take the frontal assault in stride, but he wrote James Seddon, the secretary of war, sharply criticizing Bragg's original decision to assume a tactical defense. He went so far as to say that "our chief Bragg had done but one thing he ought to have done since I joined the army. That was to order the attack."[72] How much of his change of mind was due to his good luck in his own frontal assault is, of course, speculation.

Longstreet did show development in his tactical thinking as he employed the massed column in an attempt to counter the entrenched defense. In the assault by his left wing on September 20, Longstreet deployed his brigades and divisions in lines arranged along so narrow a front that they constituted a large column. Although the attack was successful, the Confederates encountered the familiar problem of close assault lines intermingling, with consequent loss of order and tactical control.[73]

The Confederate attempt at Chickamauga to make offensive use of artillery also played an ambiguous role in the outcome. Following in the rear of the center brigades, the artillery advanced with the infantry. On occasion, batteries got within 100 yards of the enemy's lines. Some credit fell to the artillery for diverting Union reinforcements, and on one occasion they established an offensive position that enfiladed parts of the entrenched Union line. The general pattern, though, saw the difficult topography prevent the artillery from keeping pace with the advancing infantry, the woods and the troops in front obstructing fire.[74]

Chickamauga again emphasized the subordination of artillery and cavalry to the infantry. Problems of terrain and mobility greatly reduced the supporting role of artillery on offense and defense, and cavalry increasingly fought dismounted as a mobile infantry force. Both Confederate and Union cavalry units did play important reconnaissance roles. Wheeler's Confederate cavalry corps was particularly efficient, sending back to army headquarters several full reports each day on the location and movements of the enemy, while Stanley's Union cavalry guarded communication lines. There were still a few mounted confrontations in line—on one occasion there was a column attack by Wheeler down a road; on other occasions, the cavalry even successfully charged infantry. But these were anomalies. The cavalry on both sides was used predominantly as infantry fighting in skirmish line, frequently complete with breastworks of logs and fence rails. In a striking diversionary action, Wheeler dismounted his entire command and made an approach on the Union flank that was mistaken, as intended, for an attack in force, drawing off Union reinforcements from elsewhere in the line. In one action, a Union cavalry regiment successfully executed a mixed holding-turning movement on the Confederate infantry, half attacking in a dismounted skirmish line while the other half turned the Confederate flank. In battle there was little distinction between the Union cavalry and the mounted infantry regiments, the latter sometimes fighting under cavalry command. Artillery, meanwhile, was more than ever subordinated to infantry as terrain made it extremely difficult for the Union artillery to unlimber and find positions to check the Confederate assaults. On the offense, artillery was well handled and not without its moments. But the Battle of Chickamauga was even more than usual a day for the infantry.[75]

Rosecrans, pursuing the only course his logistical vulnerability left open to him, took up defensive positions in the Chattanooga Valley astride his lines of communications. Here he strongly entrenched a double line of lunettes, redans, redoubts, and even an occasional bastion and half-bastion. All these works were connected with rifle trenches.[76] Even the picket lines entrenched.[77] To overcome the problem a double line might create in the eventuality of a retreat by the first line, Rosecrans directed that openings be left in the inner line of works through which to pass artillery when withdrawing from the outer line. He camouflaged the whole by ordering bushes placed in front of the inner line so that the enemy would not be able to detect what kind of works were being constructed.[78] The Union defensive preparations reflected the extent to which entrenchment was becoming habitual. There was hardly a soldier who did not have a trench shelter. Even the railroad-building parties dug in.[79] As if to demonstrate how a soldier could be of two tactical minds, Rosecrans ordered Sheridan "to . . . drive away the rebels reported to be constructing the bridge by a bayonet charge."[80] Since Rosecrans had ordered a bayonet attack during the Battle of Stones River, it seems that he remained ambivalent about the impact of the new infantry weapons on traditional assault tactics.

The Confederate line ran along the crests and slopes of Lookout Mountain and Missionary Ridge. Its profile was strong in outline. Like the Federal line, it contained redans, redoubts, lunettes, and occasionally bastioned forts and half-bastions, connected with rifle trenches and breastworks of logs and stone. Picket lines were entrenched farther down the slopes from the main line and sometimes extended into the valley.[81] All this was done in spite of evidence of a general shortage—or even the complete absence in parts of the line—of entrenching tools. There was only a single overworked engineer, and the usual shortage of pioneer troops. Although certain sections of the resulting line were poorly laid out and inadequately entrenched,[82] the Army of the Tennessee was acknowledging the changing realities of warfare.

STALEMATE AND SHERMAN'S EXPERIMENTS WITH FIELD TRANSPORTATION AND SUPPLY

Rosecrans arrived at Chattanooga in relatively good logistical shape. He had lost few wagons at Chickamauga, and his supply situation was good. As Montgomery Meigs noted: "Forage and subsistence for some time still remained in the wagons." The wagon trains that maintained the supply lines were inconvenienced when the Confederates destroyed a bridge, cutting communications with the supply base at Nashville. Although they were forced to take a circuitous route, there were sufficient animals and wagons to do it, and the "corn which remained standing upon the abandoned plantations which lined the banks of the Tennessee supplied some forage to the animals and some food to the men of the trains." But rain that began in early October made the roads impassable.

By October, logistical considerations began to render the Army of the Cumberland both strategically and, to a considerable extent, tactically immobile. The Confederates held positions on the north slope of Lookout Mountain and thus controlled both the Tennessee River and Rosecrans's rail communications with his main supply depots. Rosecrans's predicament worsened as the problem of a large stationary army quickly asserted itself. The exhausted countryside increasingly could not provide forage. Rosecrans had been told in late September that there was an abundance of forage in the Sequatchie (Hog Trough) Valley, but he complained of insufficient wagons to forage and of a lack of adequate horses to mount his cavalry to keep open the lines of communications. When the early October rains virtually closed down the roads, the loss of forage supplies created mass starvation among the animals. To make matters worse, a Confederate cavalry raid against a supply train bogged down in the mud cost the Army of the Cumberland another 1,800 animals as well as 300 wagons.[83] Ration and harness shortages added to Union problems. By October 14, the Army of the Cumberland was on three-quarter rations, and shortly thereafter on half-rations. The animals were too depleted to be of service without rest and forage.[84] Grant, on October 27, requested 4,000 sets of harness to replace worn-out equipment in the Army of the Cumberland.[85]

For the six weeks extending through October, all that stood between remaining in the field and the necessity of retreat was "a long [seventy miles] mountainous and almost impasssable road from Stevenson, Alabama." By the end of the month, more than 10,000 animals had perished in supplying half-rations over this route. Soon after Grant took command of the combined western armies, he commented that horses and mules "had become so reduced by starvation that they could not have been relied on for moving anything. An attempt at retreat must have been with men alone, and with only such supplies as they could carry." Such a retreat, Grant observed, "would have been almost certain annihilation."[86]

Beginning the end of October, a series of developments revived the offensive capacity of the Union forces in Chattanooga and provided them with an incentive for a tactical offense. A well-executed campaign from October 27 through 29 by Hooker's two corps, which had arrived from the Army of the Potomac by rail, recaptured the positions on the south side of Lookout Mountain, which commanded the rail communications with the south side of the Tennessee River. The near-investment was lifted.[87] In early November, Sherman brightened Union prospects further when he arrived with the XV Corps from the Army of the Tennessee plus an additional division.

Sherman had marched the whole way from Memphis, a distance of approximately 200 miles direct distance and over 250 actually traveled. He lived off the land and received supplies from the railroad and the Tennessee River. He also levied from the local populace and from the readily available supply of refugee Negroes to "drive teams and do other useful work." The chief quartermaster of Sherman's corps, Lieutenant Colonel J. Condit Smith, reported that Sherman's force arrived "amply provided with subsistence, forage, and means of transportation; the animals of the train in good condition."[88] Data are lacking on the details of Sherman's transportation standard, but limited available evidence suggests that the Army of the Tennessee probably had approximately forty wagons per 1,000 men.[89]

The march of a portion of Sherman's corps, with additional troops from the Army of the Cumberland, subsequently would extend to Knoxville and back in relief of Burnside's Army of the Ohio. This was another 200 miles direct distance, and probably about 250 to 300 miles actually traveled. In this latter march, the train was left behind. The troops carried four days' rations, drawing supplies en route from river steamers. Otherwise, they lived off the land.[90] Condit Smith, Sherman's quartermaster, noted that rapid movement was the key to living off the land. Sherman was working out the system of field supply and transportation that eventually would take him through the heartland of the South.[91]

CHATTANOOGA

Confronted with the arrival of Sherman to join the Union forces concentrated in the vicinity of Chattanooga, Bragg called a council of war to discuss strategy. Longstreet proposed a sweeping strategic movement of the entire army against the enemy supply lines, to be followed by a move into Middle Tennessee. But again field transportation and supply problems intervened. This plan was opposed, to quote one of those present, General Hardee, "on the ground that our horses would starve before they could forage for their subsistence; that the country over which we should have to pass was a barren wilderness, and that we could not rely on any supplies for man or beast before reaching Duck River." Upon being told that the horses would be at least five days without forage, Longstreet agreed that the idea was impracticable. The plan arrived at as most feasible was to invest Rosecrans and to send Longstreet with a force of at least 15,000 men into East Tennessee to destroy Burnside's small army. Thus, the logistical situation dictated a tactical solution. Not confident that they could assault Grant's numerically superior and entrenched army, the Confederates continued to work on their fortifications.

The detachment of Longstreet against Burnside provided Grant with an immediate incentive to attempt a breakout, or at least to press Bragg's army sufficiently to compel him to recall Longstreet. Grant realized that Burnside did not have the transportation to retreat from East Tennessee without losing most of his army. Also, he preferred that Burnside, until he could be reinforced, hold Longstreet in the Knoxville area in order to deplete his army sufficiently to render it incapable of resuming the offensive that winter.[92]

To force Bragg to recall Longstreet, Grant prepared to attack the Confederate line as soon as Sherman arrived and the Union forces could build up their supplies and replenish the animal shortage.[93] The plan called for Sherman to cross the Tennessee River and combine with

General Thomas, who on October 17 had succeeded Rosecrans in command of the Army of the Cumberland, to make an advance along the whole line. Hooker was to turn Bragg's left flank on Lookout Mountain. Sherman, who succeeded Grant in command of the Army of the Tennessee when Grant took over the consolidated western command on October 17, was to assault his right on Missionary Ridge, and Thomas was to command the central force connecting with Hooker and Sherman on his flanks.

It was a daring plan. It had to overcome an entrenched but badly overextended enemy in elevated hill positions in country where maneuver was extremely difficult. The Federal army had no detailed maps.[94] There was the ever-present problem with tactical communications with limited means, as well as with staff and command procedures. Yet the plan worked; and in its execution, Sherman, Thomas, and Hooker all rejected conventional tactical doctrine to construct field fortifications while engaged in a tactical offensive.

On November 23, Thomas advanced from his fortifications and drove Bragg's pickets from their rifle pits, securing an elevated position for the Union troops. Planning to resume the offensive in combination with Sherman and Hooker the following morning, Thomas had his working parties spend the night fortifying his new position and bringing up his artillery. His troops now held an entrenched line a mile beyond that which they had occupied in the morning.[95]

Sherman put on an equally impressive show of offensive entrenchment. "Spades were handed to many of us," wrote a company commander in the advance force that was to establish a bridgehead on the opposite shore of the Tennessee River. "We did not ask what for, we knew too well. . . . In a half hour we were up the opposite bank and creeping along through the thicket, a spade in one hand and a rifle in the other.[96] Daylight found 8,000 men fortified in rifle trenches on the south side of the Tennessee."[97] This incident and Sherman's order prior to the May 28 attack on Vicksburg that his skirmishers entrench 100 yards from the enemy's defenses were probably the first instances of troops' carrying entrenching equipment on their persons into battle. On the 24th, the remainder of Sherman's forces crossed over. By nightfall he controlled the whole northern end of Missionary Ridge as far as the railroad tunnel. Sherman's troops that night entrenched with earthworks and logs a line of battle from which to launch an assault the next morning.[98] During the same night, General Hardee similarly fortified a division behind breastworks of earth and logs to withstand Sherman's expected assault the following morning.[99] Thomas, in the center of the Union line, had spent the 24th repulsing Confederate attempts to retake the positions he had taken the day before. Hooker, on the Union right, had turned the Confederate defenders out of their positions on the northern slope of Lookout Mountain. Deeming an advance that night into the valley imprudent, Hooker strongly entrenched his force preparatory to resuming the attack the following day.[100]

Union offensive success was at least in part a result of good tactical communications and improved staff and command procedures. Well briefed by Grant with detailed instructions regarding their individual movements and the junction of the three forces; and making efficient use of the Signal Corps and roads for lateral communication, Sherman, Thomas, and Hooker converged on schedule for the planned general assault of the 25th.[101] Rosecrans's report on the Chickamauga campaign noted the growing esteem for the Signal Corps. The dense timber combined with smoke and dust largely removed the corps from the battle itself, though it did sustain communications with the flanks and rear as well as with departmental headquarters. It also managed the occasional line to the front, including one from Thomas's headquarters on the 21st. During movements leading to Chickamauga, the Signal Corps' telegraph train successfully, if not flawlessly, maintained tactical communication between the parts of Rosecrans's army. In situations where terrain and the cutting of the telegraph lines so necessitated, couriers were used effectively in combination with or as an alternative to the field telegraph. The corps also sent valuable information from Lookout Mountain on Confederate troop movements leading to the battle.

At Chattanooga, the Signal Corps was more effective in battle, maintaining tactical communication with the portable field telegraph, semaphores, and torches between Thomas, Sherman, and Grant, and between Sherman and some corps and divisional commanders. It also provided valuable information on troop movements and topography in an area where the Union had no maps. Working with a captured book of Confederate signals, the Signal Corps read Bragg's communications from Missionary Ridge to Lookout Mountain. After Chattanooga, the corps was to be more routinely accepted in tactical and strategic organization. It worked with increasing efficiency and acceptance, though the shortage of personnel continued to be a problem.[102]

Perhaps of greater importance in maintaining mobility was the growing sense of teamwork that the reports and correspondence suggest among able commanders and the parts of their commands. It was a process similar to the improvisation of command procedures within the Army of Northern Virginia prior to the deaths of Jackson and so many veteran senior officers at Chancellorsville. Union teamwork no doubt benefited from the 1863 army reorganization that made the corps rather than the division the basic strategic unit. Having only three subordinate commanders eased Grant's problem of command and coordination.

The Union advance on the 25th again showed the developing role of fortification on the battlefield. The plan called for Hooker to attack the entrenchments on Missionary Ridge from the rear, while Thomas launched a holding assault. Sherman was to assault the positions facing him on the north slope of Missionary Ridge. When the entrenched Confederates stopped him short of their fortifications, Sherman accepted a tactical stalemate. He did not, however, retreat to his previous line. Reminiscent of the entrenchment of his skirmish line prior to the May 22 assault at Vicksburg, Sherman had his troops fell trees and fortify the positions where they had taken cover behind rocks and other obstacles close upon the enemy's positions.[103]

This was probably the first time a commander had entrenched his line to hold territory taken during an assault while still under close fire. The two entrenched forces continued to exchange desultory fire with little damage. Neither side resumed the offensive. The incident was perhaps the most striking portrayal to date of the increasing role of field fortification, as tactical evolution responded to the increased firepower of the new weaponry. Sherman was emerging as perhaps the most advanced tactical thinker on the use of field fortifications in the Civil War armies.

Elsewhere along the line, however, the unexpected turned the course of tactical development topsy-turvy. The unforeseen chain of events began with a four-hour delay of Hooker's turning movement when the Confederates, evacuating Lookout Mountain, burned the bridge across Chattanooga Creek.[104] Thomas consequently launched his assault against the entrenchments on Missionary Ridge without the benefit of the planned distraction. Marching as if on drill parade, Thomas's troops overran the entrenched skirmish line and, finding resistance unexpectedly weak, scrambled up and over the hill in an unplanned attack to break the main line. In the light of past events, one asks why such a potentially strong entrenched position collapsed so quickly. E. P. Alexander, Longstreet's artillery chief and one of the most insightful historians of the Civil War, placed the blame on a combination of factors. He listed a shortage of entrenching tools, faulty engineering owing to the presence of only one, consequently overworked, engineering officer, poor troop dispositions, and a faulty tactical plan of battle.

Although it is difficult to gauge whether it significantly affected Thomas's success, the entire Union front in the assault on Missionary Ridge advanced using Mahan's recommended offensive tactical formation that combined lines and small columns. Chattanooga was the first battle where the Union extensively employed Mahan's system. Brigadier General Thomas Wood also used the formation in the successful assault on Orchard Hill on November 23, as did the supporting division of Brigadier General Adolph von Steinwehr.[105]

An amazingly long delay in laying out the line at the position attacked—induced in part by the absence of the engineering officer, and in part, the length of the delay suggests, by negligence—resulted in the Confederates' not beginning to entrench the main line on Missionary Ridge until Thomas began his preliminary attack on the 23d. And then they suffered from "a very insufficient supply of tools."[106] Hard and rocky ground slowed work. When Thomas launched his main attack on the 25th, the Confederate entrenchments were only waist-high. The engineer who had laid out the line left many ravines and hollows protected from its fire.

The Confederates made the additional mistake of dividing their already overextended forces. Half the troops were located in an entrenched skirmish line at the bottom of the hill. The main line at the top could present only a single line to the assailants, with the result that loading time further reduced the fire effect of the defenders' resistance. To make matters worse, the skirmish line was under orders to retreat to the main line after it fired a single volley at 200 yards. This was not time enough to escape in good order. The Confederate defenders in the main line confronted Federal assailants and retreating Confederates moving upon them together.[107]

After throwing the Confederates off the summit of Missionary Ridge, Thomas's troops tore down the defenders' hastily constructed log breastworks, moved them to the other side of the ridge, and formed an improvised defense against possible counterattack.[108] But Bragg had had enough. He withdrew his army from the field. Bragg's dead and wounded totaled a low 2,500 compared to the Union's loss of 5,500 men, which again indicated the price of the frontal assault, even when successful. But over 4,000 Confederate missing, a high percentage probably deserters, as compared to 300 for the Union army, more than balanced the books.[109]

Despite the chance success of Thomas's frontal assault, the Battle of Chattanooga strikingly portrayed the developing pattern of habitual entrenchment, whether on the defense or offense. The combination of rifled musket and defensive use of artillery was taking its toll.[110] Following the Union victory, Grant again fell victim to the usual logistical problems that discouraged pursuit and withdrew from the field to give his animals a much-needed rest.

KNOXVILLE: FURTHER DEVELOPMENTS IN TRENCH WARFARE

The same pattern, meanwhile, was emerging in East Tennessee. Burnside, made aware that Bragg had sent Longstreet's corps against him, decided in consultation with Grant to stand at Knoxville. The objective was to deplete Longstreet so that he couldn't resume the offensive that winter. The Knoxville garrison consisted of 600 men poorly equipped with entrenching tools. Its light defenses had been constructed "only to hold the place against a cavalry clash."[111]

Burnside had prepared for the 1863 campaign with transportation and supply problems similar to those of Rosecrans and other western field commanders. His horses, like those of Rosecrans, suffered terribly. By April, 1863, Burnside complained that the number of unserviceable animals from want of forage had increased from one-quarter to one-third.[112] As with Rosecrans, Meigs criticized Burnside for not taking care of his horses, accusing him of unnecessarily "tasking them beyond their strength."[113]

Burnside's movement was severely restricted. He had no rail or water transportation to make an advance from Kentucky into East Tennessee, while the Confederates could use the railroad to bring reinforcements to bear on any advance. In defeat, a Union retreat would have been difficult and potentially disastrous. And Confederate cavalry raids further distracted Burnside.

When Burnside finally moved, the former commander of the Army of the Potomac (who brought the IX Corps of that army to the West) probably marched with the standards of the flying column. One similarity was that his troops carried eight to twelve days' supply on their backs. Burnside stripped down his supply trains to ambulances, medical wagons, and absolutely necessary cooking utensils. Knapsacks were put in empty wagons, the men carrying only a blanket and change of underclothing. If shoes were not in good order, the soldier was to carry an extra pair. Burnside's field organization lacked the finesse Ingalls had established in the Army of the Potomac. There was a problem of road jams amid ad hoc procedures for movement. There were also problems with respect to the appropriate location of supply trains in relation to the marching columns and to the army during battle.[114]

When Longstreet moved against him, Burnside retreated to Knoxville. He fought a series of delaying actions that gave the Union army time to get its supply trains into Knoxville and the garrison time to prepare its defenses. The nature of the countryside and the difficulty of maintaining visual communications, with the point of command constantly shifting, eliminated the use of signals during Burnside's move-ment into Knoxville. Once in Knoxville, the advantage of the static defense for signals communications asserted itself, and the Signal Corps rendered good service.[115] In each delaying action, Burnside forced the enemy to turn his position. He then withdrew to take up another line of resistance. During this series of holding actions, Burnside did not entrench, if for no other reason than that Longstreet had captured what little entrenching equipment he had.[116]

Burnside moved his army into Knoxville on the night of November 16. "As soon as any portion of the force arrived and was placed in position it was put to work to entrench itself." Owing to the extreme shortage of equipment, the construction of defenses was slow. The only supply of tools available was that brought from Kentucky by the engi-neering battalion.[117] In a gallant stand from fortified positions about a mile from Knoxville, Colonel Sanders's cavalry division held back the advancing Confederates for two days. This gave Burnside's army time to extend its works from a single line of light rifle trenches and two previously constructed forts of moderate dimensions, to a strong line containing redans, lunettes, and redoubts. At its most vulnerable po-sition, the defenders constructed an interior line of rifle trenches, an-choring the extremities with strong batteries. The parapets were fronted by a ditch about eight to ten feet wide and from four to six feet deep with almost perpendicular sides.[118] By the time Longstreet was free to turn his attention to these still-uncompleted works, they were strong enough to discourage attack. The Confederates entrenched behind a continuous line of rifle trenches about a mile from the Federal lines. Sharpshooters went forward, dug rifle pits, and annoyed the unceasing Federal entrenching activity. Under the fire of the Confederate line, the Union defenders constructed another fort and greatly extended their rifle trenches.[119]

Longstreet, less enthusiastic about the offensive than when he had earlier criticized Bragg for his lack of offensive initiative, was reluctant to launch an attack against these works. But Bragg suggested that he bring the enemy to battle. Then word arrived of Bragg's defeat at Chat-tanooga, and that Sherman was marching for Knoxville. With the al-ternatives of immediate attack or retreat, Longstreet reluctantly chose to attack.[120] He decided to combine a frontal assault with a turning movement against the rear and flanks of the Union line. The plan for the frontal assault called for the offensive use of entrenchments. Almost simultaneously on different battlefields, traditional doctrine for the of-fense gave way to the use of entrenchments. Under the cover of dark-ness, Confederate sharpshooters were ordered to entrench themselves in rifle pits 200 yards in advance of the Federal works. From there, combined with artillery, they were to keep down the enemy's artillery and musketry fire during the main assault in column, which was to jump off from a line close behind the rifle pits of the sharpshooters.[121]

The Confederate sharpshooters' covering fire was effective in keeping down fire from the area to be attacked, but the artillery failed to quiet enfilading works on the Confederate left. The complaints of Longstreet's artillery commander, Alexander, echoed the complaints of Brannen, the artillery chief of the Army of the Cumberland, and emphasized again the problems weighing against the effective use of artillery in attack. As he attempted to bombard the enemy lines in preparation for the attack, and then cover the assault, Alexander complained that his shells were "frequently exploding in the guns causing great chaos in the batteries, not exploding at all, and those that got fired were tumbling, destroying all accuracy." To compound his technological troubles, Alexander was also short of ammunition, artillery horses, and horseshoes.[122]

The assailants discovered that they had underestimated the depth of the ditch that fronted the Union works. They found they could not get across it without ladders, which they had not brought up, believing that they would not need them. To make the stalemate complete, the turning movement against the Union flank and rear collapsed. Further assaults proved unsuccessful.[123]

Codification by habit continued without interruption in the tactical use of cavalry as mobile infantry, particularly for diversionary and flank attacks. The cavalry of both sides fought dismounted in skirmish line, mounting only to pursue infantry retreating in disarray.[124] The strategic use of cavalry in force for reconnaissance and raiding continued the pattern set in earlier campaigns in the West. Burnside further used cavalry to protect his telegraph lines.[125]

Longstreet faced the threat of Sherman's advance up the south side of the Tennessee River. He also suffered a transportation shortage that made it impossible to collect supplies to sustain his position before Knoxville. He finally broke off the action and withdrew into winter quarters in northeastern Tennessee. Dependent on river transportation for supply, Sherman was in no position to pursue.[126]

Tactical development from Murfreesboro through Vicksburg, Chickamauga, and, in the final stages, Chattanooga and Knoxville, witnessed the growing dominance of the infantry and the increasing acceptance of the role of field fortification under all circumstances, even to the use of offensive entrenchments to hold every foot of territory taken.

The latter trend was best, though not exclusively, demonstrated by Sherman at Vicksburg and on Missionary Ridge. Chattanooga and Knoxville were the first battles in which the acceptance of offensive field fortifications became the general pattern.

The final incentive to the general extension of field fortification to the tactical offense was the common-sense observation that rifled infantry weapons made it impossible to do otherwise if one was to hold one's position on the field and avoid unacceptable casualties. The tactical tendency toward an infantry war of entrenchment grew, with artillery proving itself effective on defense but not in attack, while cavalry in the West from the beginning accepted their tactical role as mounted infantry in support of the line.

The 1863 campaigns in the West were a showcase for the development of strategic maneuver as an alternative to direct tactical confrontation without strategic advantage. As the Union armies sought to wage a strategy of exhaustion against the resources of the Confederate armies, they also incidentally forced the surrender of a Confederate army at Vicksburg. Water routes still played a role for Grant at Vicksburg, as well as for Sherman's long marches along the Tennessee River. But more significant, the Union field commanders, forced to move away from water, were honing their organizational skills in the science and art of maneuver while living off the land. Rosecrans's movements were breakthroughs that the growing largess of the Union increasingly could afford to support in animals and wagons. The Confederates, by contrast, were failing in their attempt to use raiding maneuvers to hold their defensive line and protect their diminishing resources.

The rich documentation of Meigs's 1862–63 dialogue with Buell and Rosecrans on field transportation and supply indicates the recurrence of some common logistical themes in the two theaters. The individual field commanders in their experimentation leaned strongly on their own practical experience and inclinations. And Meigs tended to deal with individual armies. For example, there is no evidence that Grant, Sherman, or Rosecrans was involved in the experiments by the Army of the Potomac in 1863 with the flying column, experiments closely supervised by Meigs and Halleck. Yet there is some evidence that the Army of the Ohio, under a former commander of the Army of the Potomac, Ambrose Burnside, did adopt at least some of the reforms of the flying column. There is no question that the coordination and cooperation between Meigs and the western field commanders did not measure up to staff coordination in the East. Early neglect of the western armies no doubt fostered the independence that continued to characterize the logistical behavior of western field commanders. Yet by late 1863, the increased attention to the field transportation problems of the growing western armies brought Meigs more into western decision making. What coordination existed between Meigs, Halleck, and the individual western and eastern field commanders could not help but cross-fertilize thinking on logistics.

Improvements in the organization of command and control procedures began to play a role by the end of 1863. Experience combined with organizational and, in the case of signals, technical improvement, all added to the increased mobility of the western armies. Change in this as in other organizational respects had been slower in the West because of the smaller armies and the advantage of waterways to ease mobility early in the war. The comparative lack of professional officers, signals personnel, and equipment had hindered early development of improved command and control procedures. By the end of 1863, however, signals organization in the West was increasingly parallel to that in the East, and command and control procedures, like other areas of tactical and strategic organization for field command, moved further into the emerging forms of modern warfare in mid-nineteenth-century America.

ORGANIZATIONAL IRONY

9

Loss of Legitimacy

*The Peculiar Fate of Engineering
Organization*

By the end of 1863, a significant institutional development in Civil
War military organization was the decline of the elite Corps of Engineers
and the Corps of Topographical Engineers in their engineering capacity—the two corps were merged by an act of Congress in 1863 before
the Chancellorsville campaign, but orders were not issued uniting them
in the Army of the Potomac until after Chancellorsville. Following impressive beginnings in the construction of the defenses of Washington
and Richmond, regular engineering organization languished as the Union
and Confederate armies took to the field.[1] Engineer officers were, of
course, educated to assume command roles. And the need for these
officers for field command, as well as normal ambitions to pursue such
opportunities, was an obvious problem in supplying engineering personnel. But the decline of regular engineering organization reflected a
more fundamental change in American military culture during the Civil
War. A month-by-month, year-by-year observation of the reorganization
of Civil War armies to fight an unanticipated major war in a period of
change not only diverted the engineers from their technical roles as
professional officers, it also broke their organizational and intellectual

hold on American military culture. Their narrow mechanistic professionalism largely gave way to the practical need for broader perspectives
in organization for war. Both the difficulties of sustaining the regular
engineering organization, and the subsequent pattern of ad hoc improvisation were arguably signs of the decline of the legitimacy and
authority of the engineers as a command elite.[2]

The frustration of the declining recognition of engineering needs
in field operations was probably greatest among professional officers
with engineering backgrounds. They, more than others, were likely to
have formulated a view of warfare that recognized the importance of
an extensive engineer organization. McClellan, for instance, in envi-
sioning a war dominated by field fortification, also recognized the consequent need for good engineers to plan and direct entrenching activity.
Mass armies in American terrain needed expanded engineer organization for other activities, ranging from the construction of roads,
bridges, and depots to topographical surveys in the largely uncharted
campaigning areas. McClellan must have had nostalgic memories of the
prestige of the engineering officer on Scott's staff in Mexico.

The field commanders of Civil War armies found themselves ham-
strung not just by a general shortage of engineering officers and troops,
but also by a civilian outlook—with some military support—hostile both
to a war of entrenchment and to the technically oriented military professionalism of the Corps of Engineers. The engineers, as noted, were
singled out as the source of a defense-oriented elite more inclined to
digging than fighting. Even Lee, another field commander commissioned in the Corps of Engineers with service on Scott's Mexican War
staff, was derisively labeled in the Confederate press as the "King of
Spades," with respect to defensive works to protect Richmond. And,
as previously noted, even so distinguished a Confederate general as
Richard Taylor questioned Lee's willingness to fight for the reason that
he was from the Corps of Engineers. The fact that Taylor was not a
graduate of West Point or a professional officer makes his critique that
of a citizen soldier, albeit a lieutenant general. This mood of a Civil
War fought by citizen soldiers understandably undermined attempts to
establish a regular engineering organization, as did public expectations
on both sides for quick and dramatic victory through the test of battle.

McClellan spent considerable time trying to build an engineering
organization adequate to the tasks of modern warfare. He experienced
frustration in his efforts to cope with the dispersion of many engineers
to line duty and to military and civilian tasks at times peripherally related
to the war. Attempts to reestablish any engineer organization, whether
regular or improvised from the volunteer forces, met with the politi-

cians' reluctance to sacrifice manpower for engineering duties. The Union army's Corps of Engineers and the Topographical Engineers could not begin to meet the needs. For the first two years of war, engineer officers were in such short supply that they could not be detailed permanently even to corps headquarters in the Army of the Potomac, which got most of the engineers on duty with a field army.[3] The shortage was even more desperate in the West. Grant, for instance, undertook the siege of Vicksburg in mid-1863 with three engineering officers and no engineering troops. Line officers with engineering backgrounds improvised and led dual military lives, organizing and training pioneer troops and working parties from the line on the job.[4]

In addition to the loss of thirteen officers to the Confederacy,[5] and the need to assign fourteen others to nonengineering duty in staff and line command,[6] the Union army sent some engineer officers to maintain its extended system of fixed, mostly coastal, fortifications, while others continued their prewar civilian function in building bridges, running surveys, and other internal improvements. These civilian demands continued to be met during the Civil War. Despite the increasing need for engineering personnel in the field, as many as one-third of the officers in the Corps of Engineers remained assigned until the end of the war to coastal defense or to internal improvements.[7]

The Civil War emphasized how the engineering elite was caught between two professional roles. While there was supportive public and political opinion which understood that the principal role of West Point was to turn out the professional officer corps created by the army reforms of 1821 to complement the militia system, another point of view justified the Academy chiefly in terms of its role as the primary source of civilian engineers for internal improvements, particularly in times when the need was high. This role for army engineers began in 1824. Civilian needs declined during the 1840s, but picked up again with the opening of the Far West. The conflicting pushes and pulls of society and culture, as noted, created a debate about the nature of military professionalism, in the context of strict military roles versus mixed military and civilian careers, that occupied some space in antebellum military literature.[8]

At the time of the First Battle of Manassas, only twelve officers in the Corps of Engineers were assigned to engineering duty with a field army.[9] Trained engineer troops were in even shorter supply, their pattern of dispersion paralleling that of their officers. The Union army began the war with but a single company of 150 troops.[10] Despite the pleas of McClellan, Lincoln and Congress were reluctant, in the uncertainties of the early stages of the war, to sacrifice for engineering duty manpower needed in the line. The congressional act of February 28, 1861, that called up the militia provided for the addition of six officers to both the Corps of Engineers and the Corps of Topographical Engineers,[11] as well as three additional 150-man companies of troops for the Corps of Engineers, each to be commanded by an engineer officer; one for the Corps of Topographical Engineers; and one company of sappers and miners.[12] But recruitment of these companies received low priority in the early scramble to fill the ranks. By July 1, 1862, only 276 of the 600 men allotted for the engineer brigade had been recruited. The brigade did not have its full complement until November.[13] By that time McClellan had organized the Volunteer Engineer Brigade of the Army of the Potomac, which consisted of two volunteer engineer regiments that would be regular units for only a few months in 1863. There being no provision for engineer troops in the volunteer forces, McClellan asked for permission to detail infantry for engineering duty.[14]

Congress, in an act passed on July 17, 1863, accepted the improvised measures that McClellan already had put into effect. Commanding generals received authority to recognize, on the same footing in all respects with engineers in the regular army, units like those that McClellan had already mustered into service as volunteer engineers, pioneers, sappers, and miners, as well as those units mustered as infantry but assigned to engineering duty.[15] In failing explicitly to provide for the creation of new engineer units, however, Congress left the western armies standing naked. Their commanders had not followed McClellan's creative lead. Thus, as noted, Grant fought the Vicksburg campaign with an engineering organization improvised on the spot.

By the end of 1862, the introduction of the rifled musket had completed the transition to extensive fortification on the field of battle; while the difficulties of achieving victory by maneuver had intensified the evolution of positional trench warfare. Yet not until mid-1864 would the Union Congress begin to react more promptly to requests for an expanded engineering organization in the field to meet, among other needs, the demands of trench warfare.

The history of requests from field commanders of the western armies of the Union indicated that they were only slightly less tardy than Congress in seriously considering the need for a permanent engineering organization. It is perhaps significant in this respect that these commanders, with the somewhat ambiguous exception of General George Thomas, were late converts to the obsolescence of orthodox tactical doctrine. Even Sherman, a brilliant practitioner once converted, was slow to come around. It is also perhaps significant that of the early western field commanders, only Halleck and Rosecrans were from the

Corps of Engineers, and, other than Thomas, only Halleck paid much early attention to engineering organization.

On May 20, 1864, Congress would pass an act granting General Thomas's request to raise an additional ten-company volunteer regiment of engineers in the Army of the Cumberland.[16] In March of 1865, Congress would allow Thomas to expand this regiment by two companies, and would provide for the establishment of six additional volunteer regiments.[17] The first regularly organized engineer regiment would join the Army of the Tennessee on August 31, 1864.[18] The Army of the Cumberland would have an engineering officer detailed from the ranks for each corps, each division, and nearly every brigade. Not until May, 1864, would a regular engineering officer be assigned. The position until then would be filled by an officer with an engineering background detailed from the line for temporary duty, with authority to organize a volunteer engineering regiment.[19] But by 1864, the western, like the eastern, armies would have improvised, with volunteer units, including pioneers, carrying the engineering load.

In June of 1864, the regular Union Corps of Engineers would number eighty-six officers, of which Grant's combined forces operating against Richmond had twenty-one and Sherman nine.[20] The improvised and volunteer units for the most part performed increasingly well with experience. In a few instances, led by regular officers with engineering backgrounds—sometimes officers temporarily detailed from the line, sometimes former engineer officers in foreign armies—as well as by volunteer officers with civilian engineering backgrounds, they added to the legitimacy of the citizen soldier even in such technical military duties as engineering. Their large role in engineering organization, coupled with their competent performance, emphasized how the flux of Civil War military organization displaced the Corps of Engineers and the Topographical Engineers even in their technical role on the battlefield.

The Confederate army began the war with an even more desperate shortage of engineers. The Confederacy inherited only thirteen regular engineer officers, seven of whom were soon detached. The others had limited experience. The Confederate, like the Union, Corps of Engineers assigned many officers to coastal and interior defenses. The Confederates fell back on the officers of the provisional Corps of Engineers, drawn in large part from civilian civil engineers, many of whom, in the opinion of Colonel Jeremy F. Gilmer, the chief of the Confederate Engineer Bureau, "had no experience in military construction up to the date of appointment, and had therefore much to learn at the same time they were called on to reduce it to practice."[21]

The Confederate army showed perhaps more flexibility than the Union in meeting this shortage. Despite inheriting only 13 engineer officers, the Confederates made an impressive attempt to improvise an organization of some size. In September, 1862, the Confederate Congress provided for the Confederate Corps of Engineers to be increased from 50 to 100 officers.[22] By 1865, there were many more Confederate than Union engineers. While the Union Corps of Engineers never numbered more than 86 officers,[23] the Confederate corps numbered 13 regular officers, 115 provisional officers, and 188 officers assigned to engineer troops.[24]

On the other hand, the quality found among the Union engineers seemingly was lacking in the Confederate army. After the increase of the Confederate Corps of Engineers to 100 officers, Colonel Gilmer, the chief of the Confederate Engineer Bureau, complained that only about a dozen of the appointees could properly be called engineers.[25] Allowing for the possibility of a jaundiced appraisal from an officer who had spent his career as an engineer, including a period as an instructor of engineering at West Point, so extreme a condemnation of quality must be weighed seriously.

The Confederate army lagged behind the Union in establishing engineer troops. Colonel Gilmer, in December, 1862, requested that 4,000 troops be selected from the ranks for their skills in some mechanical branch of labor.[26] The secretary of war supported Gilmer's recommendation in his end-of-the-year report;[27] but it was March, 1863, before Congress acted. On March 20, Congress approved the appointment "from each division of infantry in service, one company of engineer troops, to consist of one hundred men," to be commanded by a captain and three lieutenants. Officers were to be taken "from the Engineer Corps if practicable, and where not, . . . from the line or staff of the army, reference being always made to their qualifications as engineers." The act also provided for mounted engineer troops to be selected from the cavalry and organized on the same basis as the other troops.[28] Thus, until March, 1863, engineer troops were detailed from the line as required,[29] in contrast to McClellan's de facto creation of permanent troops in the Army of the Potomac prior to congressional approval. At the same time, the act failed to provide the Confederate army with the pioneer troops that Seddon had requested.[30] So while the Confederate army made greater provision for the engineer officer in its military organization, in balance it went further even than the Union army in improvised organization.

Ironically, the success of improvised solutions by a mass army of amateur citizen soldiers, meshed with a small professional cadre, partially reinforced the view of preindustrial society that any citizen with basic intelligence could learn to play multiple social roles. It was an attitude that could not but help challenge the professional ethos of the engineers. And the Civil War decline of the antebellum definition of military professionalism embodied in the Corps of Engineers was perhaps most visible in the decline of Civil War engineering organization itself.

The Civil War forced the regular officer—whether from the engineers, infantry, artillery, or cavalry—to reconsider his professionalism from a broader intellectual and organizational perspective. The changes in warfare that he had to bring under control required that he adopt a more open, flexible, and historical, and less static, mechanistic, and absolutist military world view. Otherwise he would fail in his effort to create at least a working doctrine and organization to move, maneuver, and fight Civil War armies. The development of the American officer corps after the Civil War emphasized that change in war requires time for digestion before lessons are converted—if they are converted—into theory and then doctrine. The West Point curriculum would not change appreciably in the postwar period. The Corps of Engineers would retain its elite status in the postwar army, as indicated by branch assignments, based on general order of merit of West Point graduates through the mid-twentieth century. Even Sherman failed to change the status quo, despite his open scepticism about the outlook, power, and arrogance of the Corps of Engineers, and his prestige and power as Grant's successor as general in chief, a position he held until 1883.[31] Yet from 1861 to 1865, the Civil War introduced the face of modern warfare for American and general military culture to contemplate.

NEW
THRESHOLDS OF
MODERN WARFARE

10

Position and Attrition

From the Wilderness to Richmond

MANEUVER VS. POSITION

The emergence of trench warfare by the end of 1863 was a fore-warning of the next two years. Yet, as the Army of Northern Virginia and the Army of the Potomac observed one another from entrenched winter quarters on opposite sides of the Rappahannock, there were probably few in their numbers who foresaw the extent to which trench warfare would dominate their lives in the days ahead.

Lee's strategic outlook remained the same as for the Gettysburg offensive. With spring forage, he planned a campaign to prevent the enemy from concentrating against his enfeebled army.[1] But the government failed to regulate railroads. Moreover, rails and rolling stock were nearly depleted. The need to bring grain from Georgia with the exhaustion of supplies in Virginia and North and South Carolina made it impossible to gather the provisions Lee needed to launch his projected May offensive.[2]

Having spent the winter preparing for an early spring campaign, the Army of the Potomac also had to postpone its offensive when April rains made the roads impassable.[3] This delay allowed Lee to take advantage of the new forage to feed his animals and, by the end of April, to achieve a temporary strategic concentration.[4] Before he could take the offensive, however, Grant, who had been waiting for the roads to dry, began to move, ending four months of inactivity in the eastern theater.

The fighting of the next two months produced a repetitious pattern as the two armies fought over the small area from the Wilderness to Spotsylvania, to the North Anna, to Cold Harbor, to Petersburg. Grant moved to turn Lee's right, while Lee maneuvered to place his forces between the Union army and Richmond. The failure to turn Lee's flank, and alternately Lee's success in continually blocking the enemy's movement, resulted in a series of brutal battles during which the Civil War soldier developed the tactical lessons he had learned to date.

Grant's ambivalence about maneuver and tactical bloodletting remained a part of his outlook and, perhaps more fundamentally, his personality. This skilled exponent of maneuver in pursuit of a strategy of exhaustion, the field commander who turned Vicksburg, arguably had his moments of bloodlust. Though some of his aggressive tactical behavior can be rationalized within strategic and political considerations, the overall pattern and tone of his correspondence and reports suggest that his decisions taken as a whole were prompted by at best mixed motives. Prior to becoming general in chief, Grant did propose to Halleck a raiding strategy of exhaustion in the East as well as in the West for the winter of 1863–64. Halleck rejected Grant's recommendations on strategic grounds, and stayed with his eastern strategy to hold Lee and do damage to his army. Apart from its strategic merits, Grant's plan was impracticable, because reenlistment furloughs reduced the numbers of the Army of the Potomac to below those he considered necessary to achieve his objective. Grant also made his recommendations for the East from the safety of the West. When he became general in chief, he abandoned the plan he had recommended to Halleck for a raid into North Carolina and for a strategy of exhaustion in Virginia. He lined up behind Halleck's and Lincoln's strategy to do damage to Lee's army while holding it in place for the western armies to pursue this strategy of exhaustion.

Grant's motive in accepting the challenge of chivalrous combat with Lee seems at times to have been more than acquiescence to the political expectations of Washington and the eastern media, though these were not inconsiderable pressures. He at times seemed driven by the warrior's need for the test of blood. Grant did weigh more ambitious maneuvers, but there is room to question how seriously he did so. His lack of familiarity with the Army of the Potomac and the eastern campaigning area appears to have been a restraining influence, as does his lack of confidence in his army as a vehicle for maneuver. As he became familiar with both the soldiers and the headquarters of the Army of the Potomac, Grant appears to have accepted the more pessimistic judgment of the army as strategically conservative. And it is reasonable to assume that the presence of Lee on the other side of the battlefield struck a note of caution in even the victor of Vicksburg. Grant, like all field commanders, particularly at this stage of the war, recognized the unlikelihood of maneuvering successfully against an army with interior lines fighting on the defense—let alone an army led by Lee. If Grant accepted the improbability of damaging Lee by maneuver, and if he acknowledged the political need for a chivalric test against Lee's army, then there was good reason to fall back on Halleck's and Lincoln's strategy. And accepting the difficulty of maneuvering against Lee, the most feasible option was attrition. Despite his sometimes expressed aversion to the sacrifice of life, Grant did in fact sacrifice life, in great quantity and, at times, with questionable judgment for any motive other than combat for the sake of combat—or attrition. There is a striking statement in Grant's official report summing up the 1864–65 campaign in which he acknowledges, albeit in retrospect, that attrition had been part of his strategic outlook.[5] Grant's motives seemingly reflected the range of factors affecting strategic decision making with a mature mid-nineteenth-century army, fighting under American circumstances, at this stage of the Civil War. As the comparative maneuverability of modern armies on the defensive, especially one so competitive and well-led as the Army of Northern Virginia, rendered strategic victory by maneuver unlikely; as the material expectations of the Union's citizen soldiers expanded the logistical trains in terrain near-devoid of forage; as nationalistic fervor called for the test of combat; and as mid-nineteenth-century weaponry made attrition feasible against an undermanned and vulnerable enemy, Grant took early modern field command down one possible strategic path.

It was the logistical organization of the Army of the Potomac for 1864 that above all, perhaps, suggested a conservative outlook on strategic maneuver. On the one hand, the technical ability of the army to perform within Grant's goals for 1864–65 was exceptional; on the other, Grant's indulgence of a high supply standard, his abandonment of 1863 field transportation and supply reforms, and the limited attempt to maneuver all implied conservative goals.

Several developments increased the army's potential for maneuver by the end of 1863. The condensation of rations and the streamlining of the trains that had been going on since 1862—culminating in the flying column—all increased the mobility of the army away from its base of supply. Bureau and field organization in supply and transportation developed a high level of efficiency through experience. And the Union's resources were well organized to meet the army's needs. The organization of field transportation continued to improve with experience. By spring, 1864, Meigs had responded to the greater durability of mules by restricting purchases of horses to artillery and cavalry.[6] Quartermaster personnel administered the wagon trains with the efficiency of a mass-production assembly line. The details of standard specification, interchangeable precision parts, maintenance routines using portable maintenance equipment manned by artisans and mechanics, and the assurances of the Quartermaster Department that "it is seldom necessary to abandon a wagon on the march," are far removed from the family farm but probably akin to the commercial organization of wagons in large American cities.[7]

While on the one hand, the rivers that penetrated the eastern seaboard between Washington and Richmond bisected the approaches to Richmond, on the other, they allowed Grant to establish advance depots supplied by a combination of water and railroad. The general who had learned to exploit the rivers of the West appreciated the advantage the eastern rivers now offered to move from supply base to supply base, and to launch turning movements against Lee's right flank.[8] The mobility of the Army of the Potomac in 1864 and 1865 was even more dependent upon efficient supply and transportation because the campaigning area was largely devoid of supplies. Food and forage came by rail and water. The only times the system left the army short were during a grain-and-hay shortage before Richmond in late November, 1864, and again in January of 1865.[9] On the latter occasion, as a reminder that common sense could still lapse even amid general efficiency, Colonel Charles Thomas, the assistant quartermaster general, suggested to Ingalls that he follow Sherman's example of camping the cavalry and trains at some distance from the main body of the army, changing camps as forage was exhausted. Ingalls went through the roof, pointing out what he thought was obvious, that the country was destitute. Ingalls put the animals on half-rations, stating that he didn't think he could do any more.[10]

The Army of the Potomac drew provisions for the Wilderness campaign and for the move to Spotsylvania from depots along the Rappahannock, primarily Rappahannock Station and Brandy Station. The Orange and Alexandria Railroad supplied these bases from Washington and Alexandria.[11] The same depots first resupplied the army at Spot-sylvania. In addition, bridge material was forwarded to Grant up the Rappahannock. Arrangements were made for wagons to relay supplies the short distance from the Acquia Creek depot if the Richmond, Fred-ericksburg, and Potomac Railroad, which connected this depot with the Rappahannock, was not open.[12] The move to Spotsylvania also linked the army with the Piney Branch and Spotsylvania Railroad.[13]

On May 10, the third day at Spotsylvania, Grant shifted his supply base to Fredericksburg, which received shipments via both the Rich-mond, Fredericksburg, and Potomac Railroad and the Rappahannock River. He drew his provisions for the move to the North Anna from Belle Plain on the Potomac, which was only about five miles from the Rappahannock. As he moved to the North Anna, Grant advanced his supply base farther along the Rappahannock to Port Royal, which could be reached by both water and the railroad. The move from the North Anna to Cold Harbor was to the advanced depot at White House on the Pamunkey River, also supplied by rail and water.[14] At Cold Harbor, Grant decided against a favorable opportunity to turn Lee's left flank, partly because "if we work this route all we did would have to be done while the rations we started with held out."[15]

The five-day, fifty-mile[16] move from Cold Harbor to south of the James River was to the advanced depot at City Point on the James, which at first was supplied only by water. By the time the Union army was established before Petersburg, it also was supplied by rail.[17] Grant facilitated his movement when he used water transportation to transport one corps from Wilcox Landing on the north bank of the James to south of Petersburg.[18] Some sense of the efficiency of the Army of the Potomac is found in the contemporary observation of Colonel Theodore Lyman, Meade's perceptive aide-de-camp, on the crossing of the James River:

> —A pontoon bridge, 2,000 feet long, was made in ten hours, and over this passed a train of wagons and artillery thirty-five miles long; more than half the infantry in the army and 3,400 beef cattle; besides 4,000 cavalry; all of which was chiefly accomplished within the space of forty-eight hours! In civil life, if a bridge of this length were to be built over a river with a swift current and having a maximum depth of eighty-five feet, they would allow two or three months for the making of plans and collecting of materials. Then not less than a year to build it.[19]

The Army of the Potomac's wagon and animal supply was more than adequate for the necessary movements. The army began the 1864 campaign with 3,500 wagons and 50,000 horses and mules for 90,000 men.[20] This constituted a standard of 40 wagons per 1,000 men, the standard that Grant had reached for the Army of the Tennessee before he left its command. On May 24, Burnside's IX Corps, which until that time had been operating independently under the direct orders of Grant, was assigned to the Army of the Potomac under Meade, increasing the army to 120,000 men. This added 600 wagons,[21] for a total of 4,100, and presumably a proportionate increase in animals to the above totals.

Burnside's IX Corps was an anomaly. With only 600 wagons for some 30,000 men, it had a standard of 20 wagons per thousand, the final standard achieved by the flying column in late 1863—increasing speculation that Burnside may have organized the Army of the Ohio on the model of the flying column. There is no evidence that Grant ever raised the standard of Burnside's corps to that of the remainder of the army. Why Grant excluded this corps from the increase in wagon standards is open to conjecture. There were sufficient mules to make up the difference in a pack train. But the fact that Ingalls didn't like pack trains, and in 1863 recommended against their use except for short distances over rough country, supports speculation that probably the army did not use them. On the other hand, Halleck in 1863 had over-ruled Ingalls and retained the pack trains, though perhaps because of the persistent shortage of wagons at the time.[22]

The command of the Army of the Potomac thought the army had the capacity to carry eight days' subsistence and forage in the supply train.[23] Grant, to increase the mobility of the marching column, left the subsistence trains behind to be brought up in the general supply train. The men packed three days' full rations in haversacks and three days' small rations in their knapsacks or blankets—compared to eight days' average and ten days' maximum in the flying column. Three days' beef accompanied on the hoof. Grant stripped each corps to march with only about one-half its supply train, the remainder to be brought up in the general supply train.[24]

For the Army of the Potomac other than Burnside's corps, Grant backed away from the standard of some thirty wagons per 1,000 men for the Gettysburg campaign, fought with an army of approximately 140,000, and the further reduction after Gettysburg to a standard of twenty wagons per thousand. Even before the reorganization of the Army of the Potomac as a flying column, McClellan had marched his army of some 160,000 men for the ten-day expedition from Antietam to the vicinity of Fredericksburg on a standard of approximately thirty-five wagons per 1,000 men. The smaller the army and the shorter the movement, the lower the wagon ratio needed. And the Army of the

Potomac organized as a flying column in 1863 numbered approximately half as many men again as Grant's army, including Burnside's corps, and was organized to move up to ten days. Although the area of campaign was now almost completely devoid of supplies, it had not been much better for the 1863 campaign. For 1864, Grant evidently was unwilling to sacrifice the army's standard of living, security, or both below a conservative level.

Meigs, who well into 1863 still pushed hard for the Napoleonic standard of twelve wagons per thousand, now informed Grant that he could give the Army of the Potomac additional wagons. Grant turned down the offer. Meigs's actions throughout 1864–1865 with respect to the Army of the Potomac seemed to reinforce the consensus that the army was not seriously organizing for long-range maneuver. With the animals for artillery and cavalry as well as the trains, Grant's army averaged one animal for every two men. The organizational standard for field supply and transportation in the Army of the Potomac for the remainder of the war was in place by late spring of 1864.[25]

Ingalls bemoaned the excesses imposed on him by the field command of the Army of the Potomac, while he resigned himself to the reasons why the standards of the flying column would not return. Ingalls throughout the 1863 campaign, it will be remembered, had defended the standard for the load carried by troops in the flying column. In reply to critics who noted that troops tended to throw away knapsacks and overcoats, particularly before going into action, Ingalls, after Chancellorsville, sided with those who recommended the enforcement of troop discipline.[26] Now he reversed himself, conceding that either the soft and fat Union soldiers would not accept the more vigorous standards, or the field command of the Army of the Potomac would not demand the necessary discipline.

Observing that "our troops are undoubtedly loaded down on marches too heavily even, for the road, not to speak of battle," Ingalls called for a reduction of the soldier's load "consistent with his wants and the character of service." While he did "not think the knapsack should be dispensed with altogether, for it should, ordinarily, form a part of the equipment," Ingalls nevertheless recommended that "on short campaigns, and on the eve of battle, and when near the supply train, a blanket rolled up and swung over the shoulder and looped under the arm, is sufficient without knapsack or overcoat." In eliminating the overcoat, Meigs conceded the most frequently violated standard of the flying column. Meigs further urged that "the soldier can carry three days' cooked food in his haversack. If necessary, he can carry two or three days' bread and some underclothes in his blanket."

Ingalls complained that "our men are generally overloaded, fed and clad, which detracts from their marching capacity, and induces straggling." Then, in resignation, he gave in: "I do not propose any modifications, however, as our commanders understand these matters better than I do, probably; at any rate they know what they want, and have the power to make such changes as they may deem proper."[27] Ingalls captured the logistical dilemma of the army that would not, against an undersupplied and vulnerable opponent, undertake a strategic maneuver of more than five days or farther than ten miles a day. Its norm was far less.

In proclaiming strategy after the fact, in his report on operations of the Armies of the United States, March, 1864, to May, 1865, Grant declared that it had been his intention "to hammer continuously against the armed force of the enemy and his resources until, *by mere attrition,* if in no other way, there should be nothing left to him but . . . submission. . . ."[28] Whether justification after the fact for his difficulty in defeating Lee by maneuver, Grant's proclamation certainly captured the reality of the war of attrition that he in part fought.

An incident concerning a proposal for a condensed marching ration suggested the conservative strategic mood behind the complacency in field supply and transportation of which Ingalls complained. The Union army experimented with and evaluated such a ration from the spring of 1864 through the end of the war and after. Proposed by Professor H. A. Horsford, what became known as the Horsford marching meat and bread rations, if successful, had the potential to revolutionize field transportation. Horsford claimed that his marching ration would reduce the bulk of existing rations by three-quarters. Grant established a board to study the proposal. Experiments in the field saw the bulk reduced from two and one-half wagons for conventional rations to one wagon for Horsford's.

The Horsford ration substituted roasted and ground wheat or self-rising flour for hard bread and replaced salt pork or salt beef with boiled or roast beef sausages, dried and compressed. After extensive experimentation and expert evaluation through field and bureau staff, it was rejected by the army board. The board acknowledged the reduction in transportation. It also conceded that no other ration could be issued as quickly or produced less wastage. The experiment died on the conclusion that the ration did not contain sufficient nutrients, had an unpleasant taste, and was susceptible to spoilage through dampness and heat.

The extensive and prolonged dialogue on the Horsford ration serves as a case study in the modern use of bureaucratic decision making to resist change in other than crisis situations. The case against the condensed ration seems more convincing as a bureaucratic gang-up than as a critical evaluation of costs and benefits. There appears to have been an atmosphere that exaggerated problems rather than a practical attempt to surmount them. The evaluation leaves the impression that merits outweighed demerits, and that the benefits would have greatly increased strategic mobility in the field at the expense of some limited discomfort.

One is left to speculate. Were demands of the Army of the Potomac for its creature comforts coupled with Grant's implicit strategy of attrition, a strategy feasible within existing transportation standards, the hidden agenda for the board that rejected the proposed ration? Grant's influence over the decision seems even more apparent when weighed against a plea from the army during the earlier flying column experiments for what Horsford's ration now provided. As early as May, 1863, the chief of staff of the Army of the Potomac, General Daniel Butterfield, had called for a ration such that "the troops without carrying an extra load could carry ten days' ration in a concentrated form." As if to accentuate the mood that rejected the new ration, Montgomery Meigs dismissed out of hand, with flimsy explanation, Horsford's related proposal for an improved canteen to consolidate and lessen the weight and bulk of cooking and eating utensils, even though the same board that rejected Horsford's ration recommended that the canteen be adopted.[29] Considering Meigs's early history as an advocate of transportation reform, one is led to the conjecture that Grant may have imposed his conservative attitude about the Army of the Potomac's limited capacity for strategic movement upon Meigs and the Quartermaster Department.

The Army of the Potomac, insofar as it did move with its logistical weight, moved with increasing coordination. During its flanking maneuvers, it maintained constant telegraphic communications between general headquarters and the headquarters of each corps, as well as with the supply depots. Either Grant's ambivalent attitude toward telegraphic communications in the West had matured, and blended with general acceptance by this stage of the war, or he simply accepted the mature signals organization that he had inherited in the Army of the Potomac—or both. On the 50-mile move from Cold Harbor to the James, for instance, the army strung more than 350 miles of telegraph line.[30] It had become a stolid, efficient organization.

But Grant did not display the mobility to turn Lee's flank. The Army of Northern Virginia, badly undernourished and deficient in everything, matched the Army of the Potomac's rate of march. One reason was that Lee's army, with its smaller numbers and less cumbersome supply and baggage trains—less cumbersome through scarcity—was easier to move. General orders for April, 1864, do not indicate a significant change in the transportation standard for the Army of Northern Virginia from July, 1863, when it was approximately twenty-eight wagons per 1,000 men.[31] But Lee had noted that the standard was a guide to be modified by circumstances, and circumstances were extreme. There is no further record of his changing standard. Based on the approximate parallel of transportation and supply standards in the Army of North Virginia and the Army of the Tennessee for 1863, one can speculate that the parallel probably continued. Standards for the Army of the Tennessee were dropped from approximately twenty-eight wagons per 1,000 men in September, 1863, to approximately nineteen per thousand on August 9, 1864, and to approximately sixteen per thousand by November 3.[32]

Confederate army regulations for 1864 drastically reduced daily subsistence from the 1861–63 standard of three-quarters pound pork or bacon or one and a half pounds fresh or salt beef, to one-half pound pork or bacon to troops in movement or at hard work and one-third pound to stationary troops. There was a corresponding reduction in transportation requirements from a minimum standard for total subsistence of slightly over two pounds per man per day for 1861–63.[33] And standards, as Lee noted, were guidelines to be adjusted downward when necessary.

Although inadequate diet no doubt hindered Lee's marching efficiency, high morale, in part induced by the religious revivals in the army during early and mid-1864, helped drive his men on.[34] In addition, Lee had the advantage of interior lines and a shorter route of march. His judgment in anticipating Grant's moves also was excellent.

Chastened by past experience on the folly of the tactical offense, and logistically incapable of offensive movement, Lee chose to exploit the possibilities of defensive maneuver. He stated his campaign strategy "to engage him [Grant] when in motion and under circumstances that will not cause us to suffer from this disadvantage." Lee ruled out offensive maneuver because "neither the strength of our army nor the condition of our animals will admit of any extensive movement with a view to drawing the enemy from his position."[35]

Lee's strategic movements even on defense were considerable feats with the logistics of the Army of Northern Virginia. Trouble with the supply system, free-enterprise priorities, and the failure of railroads to run on anything resembling a schedule were continuing problems. An exception was the Industrial Bureau, which sustained the production of ammunition and clothing, some of which even got to the battlefield under top-priority designation. But lack of funds collapsed domestic procurement, and incompetency in established overseas procurement policy reduced relief from that quarter. Lee's army went through its third winter of belt tightening.[36]

In 1864, the shortage of animals and wagons for field transportation did more to hobble Lee's army than production troubles. Poor organization and administration were the major problems. The administration of field transportation ranked with the administration of rail transportation as the great failures of the Quartermaster Department. It is arguable that the shortage of animals defied any organizational solution. The Quartermaster Department bungled an opportunity to supply mules from Mexico in the summer of 1864. But whether Mexican mules could have made much difference is doubtful. To make matters worse, the Quartermaster Department operated a poor infirmary system for its animals. They were not sent back until they were too exhausted to recover. To compound his problems, Lee, owing to his horse shortage, was too short of mounted infantry and cavalry to protect his supply lines.[37]

Lee did gain some advantage from his Richmond-Petersburg line, which shortened rail links with his supply sources in the Carolinas and Georgia. There was also some food and forage immediately south and west of Richmond. But there was little grass or clover in the area the army occupied.[38] Without horses, Lee's cavalry could not guard the army's flanks. Logistics tied the Army of Northern Virginia more and more helplessly to the defense.[39]

Lee never got the animals he needed. Farmers and state officials refused to cooperate with impressment. Faced with the option of defeat or losing what few agricultural animals remained to the war effort, they chose, at least implicitly, defeat. Procurement in Mexico, and finally even behind enemy lines, was not effective, partly because Major Cole, the inspector general for transportation, never received the necessary funds in a bankrupt Confederacy. A personal appeal by Lee to the citizenry helped only marginally.[40] With spring, Lee couldn't move and he couldn't stay. Worn down by attrition and logistical exhaustion, particularly in the horse supply, the Army of Northern Virginia failed to make the next move, and Grant finally succeeded in turning its flank.

THE TACTICS OF ATTRITION

Lee's prolonged success in the use of strategic maneuver on defense turned the 1864–65 campaign between the two armies into a trench war of tactical attrition. The extended close-quarters fighting from the Wilderness to Petersburg was a final testing and problem-solving phase for the tactics of trench warfare. Field fortification grew more intense and sophisticated as, for the remainder of the war, the eastern armies entrenched one battlefield after another. The densely wooded countryside contributed to the final results by making offensive coordination and maneuver exceedingly difficult.

The priority Grant accorded entrenching equipment in the Union supply trains reflected the increased respect for hasty entrenchment after the 1863 campaign. In preparation for the 1864 campaign, Grant ordered one-half the wagons carrying entrenching tools placed at the head of the supply column of the leading division of each corps.[41] Perhaps he had learned his lesson at Vicksburg, where the equipment had been left behind in the general supply train, making it impossible to dig in during the advance, and delaying entrenchment before the Vicksburg defenses. The engineers were in charge of the entrenching tools.[42] Troops in the eastern theater do not appear to have carried such equipment on their persons. Most lines for entrenchment, even, as a rule, under the most urgent circumstances, were probably laid out by the engineers until Cold Harbor. Thereafter, the troops increasingly chose where to dig in.[43]

From the first encounter in the Wilderness, there was an acceptance of offensive entrenchments from which to launch frontal assaults as close to the enemy as possible, as well as to hold ground captured. This practice built on the lessons of 1863. Although the 1864 campaign witnessed the intensification of entrenchment whenever an army stopped, not all commanders immediately accepted this change. There were momentary hesitations followed by acceptance of the prevailing pattern as early as the first clash in the Wilderness on May 5. The two armies reacted differently to field fortification on that first day in the Wilderness. On the Confederate side of the battlefield, no fortifications were constructed along the line of battle previous to engaging the enemy. By contrast, the length of the Union line was entrenched before the Federal assault.[44]

General Hancock entrenched his Union corps behind a triple line of breastworks of logs and earth immediately upon taking up positions.[45] During the battle, Ewell had his Confederate corps throw up slight works.[46] That night Ewell strongly entrenched a line about 300 yards to the rear of his first hastily fortified position.[47] Two divisions of General A. P. Hill's corps, under Generals Henry Heth and Cadmus Wilcox—which constituted the remainder of the Confederate army engaged the first day—did not have time to entrench, regardless of what the views of Hill or his division commanders might have been on the subject.

The enemy attacked almost before they could get into line of battle. Bearing the brunt of the assault, they had no time to fortify, as they repulsed wave after wave of Federal assaults.

Lee's failure to entrench prior to battle presents a problem of motive. Lee had been consistent since Fredericksburg in his appreciation of field fortifications. His assault at Gettysburg had been motivated by what he considered strategic necessity despite tactical misgivings. Did he believe that failing to entrench would draw the Army of the Potomac to attack to his tactical advantage? Were Longstreet's absence and the presence of the offensively aggressive Hill a factor in influencing Lee? Did Lee, as was his procedure, leave the decision on entrenchment to his corps commanders, with Hill taking the opportunity to challenge recent history in a binge of aggressive behavior? Did Lee's critical military intelligence give way to what Thomas Connelly has interpreted as his latent aggressiveness, or McWhiney and Jamieson as his Celtic warrior élan?

Whatever the explanation, as darkness brought fighting to a halt, Hill still did not entrench his battered line. After bearing the brunt of the assault, the lines of Hill's two divisions were in disarray and so close to Hancock's line, which hastily dug in, that the opposing troops accidentally intermingled. Since it was impossible to straighten out the front of Hill's two divisions in the darkness because of the dense forest and close proximity of the enemy, Lee decided to replace them with Longstreet's fresh corps, which was scheduled to arrive about midnight. Lee subsequently had a line drawn slightly to the rear of Wilcox and Heth, which Longstreet was to entrench upon his arrival. When Wilcox and Heth requested instructions from Lee, he told them to remain in position where they were, and that Longstreet would relieve them about midnight. Their troops exhausted and assured of relief, neither Hill nor his division commanders ordered the construction of entrenchments.

Owing to communication problems, Lee was not informed by an aide until 10 P.M. that the head of Longstreet's corps would not arrive until daylight. When Longstreet did not show up by 3:30 A.M., Wilcox finally ordered the pioneers of Hill's corps to the front to entrench the line. By the time they reached the front it was daylight, and Federal sharpshooters quickly drove them off. Hill's troops obviously had not come as yet to appreciate the role that bayonets, mess kits, and canteens were soon to play in hasty entrenchment. The lack of fortification on Hill's front almost led to disaster. Longstreet took a wrong road and failed to arrive before the Federal assault. The Union assault routed the unentrenched Confederate line. Only Longstreet's belated but opportune arrival saved Lee's army from a possible defeat.[48]

The battle produced no further failures to entrench. By 10:00 A.M. on the morning of the 6th, after a series of Federal assaults and Confederate counterassaults that began at daybreak, stalemate set in along a temporarily stabilized front, with the Federal troops driven back somewhat beyond their original line of battle.[49] It was a grim form of warfare. Infantry could not see one another until they were almost nose to nose. Artillery was useless. At these close quarters, infantry exchanged their deadly fire. It is not particularly surprising that one Texas brigade lost nearly two-thirds of its numbers in the morning assaults.[50]

Both sides accepted the tactical stalemate until they could formulate new plans. At 10:35 A.M., Meade ordered the engaged corps—those of Warren and Sedgwick—to break off action and throw up fortifications to hold their positions. Warren immediately had the engineer officers lay out the line and ordered up the engineer troops. They quickly went to work constructing the new lines of log and earth breastworks, while at the same time strengthening old works.[51] The Confederates fortified their positions in the enemy's captured first line of entrenchments.[52]

But neither side had yet abandoned the offense. Meade made it known at the time he ordered the construction of the new line of entrenchments that he intended another attack. In fact, Meade's actions on the 6th showed that his early enthusiasm for the tactical offense had not yet abated. He now had the aggressive Grant instead of the conservative council of war that had restrained him in the past. It is well to remember that Meade had been inclined toward a tactical offensive against fortified positions during the Gettysburg and Bristoe Station—Rappahannock Bridge—Mine Run campaigns, and that he had been dissuaded by his corps commanders, particularly Warren. In orders for the Federal offensive on the morning of May 6, Meade gave instructions to "spare ammunition and use the bayonet."[53]

While Meade was planning another attack, Lee found a plank road to turn the Union line. This time, however, there was not a repeat of Jackson's success at Chancellorsville. After rolling up a section of the line, the troops in the turning movement had to be regrouped before they could pursue the retreating army. The delay gave General Hancock time to rally his troops behind breastworks he had constructed the day before.[54] This time, unlike at Chancellorsville, the Army of the Potomac did not retreat from its secondary defenses. The Confederate offensive stalled.

The Confederates followed with a turning movement on the left. This maneuver also foundered on Federal entrenchments. The Union army secured its right flank when the Confederate General Jubal Early failed to accept the word of one of his brigade commanders that the

Federal right flank was exposed. By the time Lee arrived and heard the brigade commander out, the enemy had entrenched his flank.[55] The fighting in the Wilderness cost Grant approximately 18,000 casualties,[56] while Lee had lost 8,000 men with little hope of replacing them. But with 61,000 men, Lee had stopped an army of 100,000.[57] Expecting further assaults on his right wing, Lee constructed strong entrench-ments during the night of May 3.[58]

But the familiar pattern of extended tactical and strategic stalemate in one position was not to be repeated, at least not in the Wilderness. The two armies remained in their trenches the day of the 7th. But Grant had decided that the Confederate positions were too strong to attack. In a precedent-setting maneuver on the night of May 7, Grant, while holding the enemy on his front, moved the corps on his right across the rear of his positions and toward Spotsylvania, a night's march away. The right wing of his army safely underway, the remaining corps fol-lowed. If he could race Lee to Spotsylvania, Grant would cut Lee's communications with Richmond, while the Army of the Potomac could be resupplied from its original bases, as well as from the Acquia Creek depot. But Lee anticipated Grant's destination. The Confederate cavalry fought a well-executed delaying action made possible in part by Sher-idan's inexperience in handling the Union cavalry corps. After a rapid march over a shorter distance on interior lines, Longstreet's corps— now under General Richard Anderson, Longstreet having been wounded—won the race.

After an initial letdown by Warren's corps, entrenching activity sur-passed even that in the Wilderness. Arriving near Spotsylvania on the morning of May 8, after an all-night march, Warren was immediately ordered to attack, while Sedgwick supported him in reserve. Warren, surprisingly, in the light of his past actions, did not entrench his troops before going into battle. The correspondence and official reports for that day strongly suggest that the reason was the fatigue of the troops after their all-night march; Warren probably decided not to further exhaust his men before their attack. Another possible explanation is that there was not enough time to entrench between Warren's arrival and the time of the ordered assault. Warren's past advocacy of forti-fications on the field of battle, which dated at least from Chancellorsville, suggests that he was not motivated by any tactical ambivalence. The Federal troops, in part probably because of weariness, but also, no doubt, remembering the Wilderness, showed great reluctance to assault the Confederate fortifications. Under cover of the dense woods, the Confederates came out to meet the Federal advance. After grim fighting, frequently hand to hand, Warren's troops withdrew and quickly entrenched.[59]

After heavy fighting on the 8th, both armies spent that night and the 9th strongly digging in their lines. As in the Wilderness, General Hancock led the Federal corps commanders in fortifying, once again throwing up three successive entrenched lines.[60] Sedgwick ordered working parties detailed from each brigade to entrench his corps' positions.[61] The Confederates were as busy, anticipating that Grant intended to fight it out on the Richmond line. Lee decided that unless an excellent offensive opportunity presented itself, his limited human and material resources restricted him to fighting the remainder of the war from a defensive posture.[62] General Anderson continued to develop his fortifications on the left of the Confederate line, while Ewell did likewise in the center. Lee personally laid out a strong defensive line on the 9th for Hill's corps to occupy when it arrived. With Lee's decision to exploit the supremacy of the tactical defense as the basis of his strategy, the specter of a long war of entrenched stalemate became still more ominous.

Lee's army now held a semicircular line. It was about three miles long, on a ridge, and resting on the Po and Ny rivers. But it had a weakness. It was necessary to include in the line an elevation in the open field from which the Federal artillery, if they occupied it, could command the Confederate positions.[63] The position was especially vulnerable to assaults. Thick pine forest came to within 200 yards of its works. The salient was about a half-mile wide and almost a mile in depth. Fearful, the defenders strongly entrenched. Heavy logs surmounted the earthworks, "underneath which were loopholes for musketry." Abatis fronted the positions, and artillery were carefully placed and protected by traverses. In addition, there were traverses at intervals along the entire work. In accordance with doctrine for exposed areas of a defensive line, there was a second line of retrenchment about 100 yards to the rear, though it was only partially completed on the 9th.[64] Lee was in favor of constructing a line of retrenchment across the base of the angle, and reportedly issued orders to begin work. But this line was neglected, supposedly because the woods at the base of the salient needed to be cleared to prevent the enemy's approaching unobserved. This was too long and arduous a task. Also, many officers believed the main line was not strong enough to hold the enemy until there was time to spare the labor properly to prepare the base line.[65]

The Confederate defensive works were not a departure from existing doctrine or past practice. What was extraordinary was that such an extensive and sophisticated line was constructed in such a brief time.

As Freeman aptly noted: "The strength of the line was the more re-markable when it is remembered that it was not laid out at leisure but was started from the positions taken up by the infantry on May 8 and was then developed to make the most of the natural advantages of the adjacent terrain."[66] The line was far stronger than in the Wilderness. It "was exactly adapted," wrote G. F. R. Henderson, "to the numbers he had at his disposal; in order to turn the position his adversary would have to cross one of the streams, and so divide his army giving him an opportunity of dealing with him in detail."[67]

When Lee checked a half-hearted attempt to turn his positions,[68] Grant and Meade, to maintain the offensive in their present positions, had little choice but to attack. On May 9, the Confederates fought off several assaults on their left. About 6:00 P.M., Federal artillery began to bombard the salient from the nearby woods. Then came Colonel Emory Upton's assault with a brigade of the VI Corps. Upton attacked with shallow, mobile columns four lines deep and three regiments wide.[69] His blend of firepower and mass with shallow, highly mobile columns bore a striking similarity to Jomini's post-Crimean recommendations to cope with the increased range and accuracy of the new infantry weapons.

Upton was at first successful. The combination of firepower and bayonet—the latter, in a rare instance, being effectively used by both sides—quickly carried his columns over both the enemy's first and second lines of works. The division that was to exploit the opening failed to arrive, however, and the Confederates quickly moved in from both sides to close the breach. Failing to receive reinforcements, Upton had to withdraw.[70] The next two days saw relative quiet, disturbed principally by sharpshooting that prevented any but the most careless or curious from exposing any portion of his body from behind his entrenchments. Both sides, meanwhile, extended and strengthened their fortifications.[71] The quiet came to an abrupt end on May 12 in one of the most gruesome trench battles of the war, the encounter in the "Bloody Angle."

Lee, having received false information that Grant was moving around his left, had withdrawn his artillery from the salient. He realized his mistake when the dawn of the 12th brought news that the Federal infantry had broken through on the salient. Many defenders found that their rain-soaked cartridges would not fire. Confederate reinforcements quickly drove the breakthrough back, but not out. The Federal infantry stopped on the outer side of the Confederate parapets, turning them against the counterattacking infantry. The Confederate counterattack got stranded on the opposite face of the parapet, it being impossible to withdraw safely to the gorge to form a second line. Attacks along the remainder of the line failed. The "Bloody Angle" became the focus of the battle.

When Lee found Federal entrenchments blocking flanking maneuvers to force a Federal withdrawal from the salient, he ordered the entrenchment of the line he earlier had considered constructing across the gorge of the salient.[72] Until it could be completed, Lee ordered the troops in the salient to maintain their positions on the parapet. For almost twenty-four hours, without food or rest, the opposing infantry fired through every opening in the parapet, raised rifles and fired down over the parapet, and, in the case of the Federals, who could afford such extravagance, threw bayoneted guns spearlike down on the heads of the Confederates. The Federal troops enfiladed the Confederate positions on the opposite side of the entrenchments, but traverses made it possible for the Confederates to remain in their positions. Federal artillery and, for the first time in the campaign, mortars took their toll. Trees twenty-two inches in diameter were felled by the musketry fire.[73] "The dead were so numerous that they filled the ditch and had to be piled behind it. The survivors waded in mud and gore, stumbling over the mangled bodies of their comrades."[74] The greatly outnumbered defenders held. By midnight, the line at the gorge was ready, and Lee gave orders gradually to fall back. Just before dawn, the last Confederate soldiers passed behind the new line, bringing to an end perhaps the grimmest spectacle of trench warfare in the Civil War.[75]

Total Union losses were 6,800 men; those of the Confederates, though the records are unavailable, probably about 10,000 men.[76] Despite these heavy casualty figures, it is well to notice that the percentages are generally lower than in the battles of late 1862 and 1863, a fact no doubt attributable to the greater respect accorded field fortification and the increasing reluctance to resort to the frontal assault. The Wilderness and Spotsylvania indicated, however, that despite the cost, the frontal assault, though subdued, was not dead.

Heavy rains brought a halt to major offensive operations from May 12 through 19.[77] An attempted Federal assault on the 18th was easily broken up.[78] On May 19, Lee gave orders to advance as close to the enemy as possible without bringing on an engagement, and then entrench. On the 21st, the Confederates threw up a second line of advanced works.[79] Grant was finally convinced of the futility of further attacks. He shifted his supply base to Port Royal on the Rappahannock, and on May 21 began another attempt to turn Lee's flank, this time by way of Hanover Junction on the south bank of the North Anna. But again Lee anticipated the Federal route of march, and again he won the race.[80] When Grant arrived on the North Anna, he found Lee blocking his way.

Lee again failed to entrench his line, constructing only rudimentary breastworks to protect bridgeheads. Henderson suggests that Lee's omission was probably due to his belief that the enemy would not cross at this point.[81] In the light of past experience, it hardly seemed worthwhile for Lee to risk miscalculating Grant's intentions. Freeman's speculation is more reasonable, namely, that Lee realized that his positions close to the river were indefensible. They were dominated by the high ground on the other side of the river, and the water level was too low to stop a Federal crossing at any point Grant might choose.[82] This explanation, of course, leaves open the question of why Lee did not take up a more favorable position and entrench it immediately, or at least entrench his present position to protect it against flanking maneuvers. As the situation stood, if the Army of the Potomac forced a crossing, which Lee admitted he could not prevent,[83] Lee's army would have to scramble frantically to improvise entrenchments on the spot. Or was Lee again taking a calculated risk to decoy the enemy into an attack where he believed he could establish a defensive advantage?

When a large Federal force began to concentrate opposite one of the bridgeheads, Confederate horse artillery and supporting cavalry in the vicinity, acting on their own initiative, quickly improvised light breastworks of fence rails.[84] That turned out to be a feint. General Warren, meanwhile, pushed across the river on Lee's right. Lee did not entrench to await the attack, but rather sent Hill's corps into the thick woods to meet the Federal advance. The Confederate attack was a failure, largely because of a typical breakdown in coordination, arising from confusion in the dense woods and probably facilitated by poor leadership on the part of Hill and Wilcox. Warren's corps quickly entrenched.[85]

Following this setback on the 23d, Lee drew up and fortified an impressive defensive line. Near its center, he controlled heights from which his artillery covered the river. To protect his flanks, he centered his line on these heights. Half of his line ran to the right and terminated in swampy ground to the southeast. He drew back the left half and anchored it on Little River. He thus presented the Federal army with an inverted V safely secured on both flanks. Lee could easily communicate from one wing to the other, while Grant would have to fight with both wings separated.[86]

Grant made a futile attempt to cross the river at the center of the Confederate line in order to connect his right and left.[87] Deciding that the terrain made a turning movement against Lee's North Anna positions impossible, Grant was left with the alternative of seeking a tactical solution through frontal assaults. And the Confederate entrenchments grew stronger by the minute. But the Wilderness and Spotsylvania had at least temporarily sickened Grant of this type of warfare. "To make a direct attack from either wing," he exclaimed, "would cause a slaughter of our men that even success would not justify."[88]

Once again, Grant moved the Army of the Potomac in an attempt to get between Lee and Richmond. Lee, in familiar campaigning country, moved across the Federal line of march and took up defensive positions on a commanding ridge between Topotomy and Beaver Dam creeks, a position he knew well from the Peninsula campaign. Again Grant refused to engage, shifting once more to Lee's right. This time his destination was Cold Harbor and the territory of the Seven Days' Battles. After an unsuccessful assault on the Union lines in an attempt to check this movement, Lee again moved to block the way to Richmond.

Grant was frustrating Lee's attempt to force him to give battle against entrenched defensive positions, as Lee was frustrating Grant's attempt to win by maneuver. Lee, however, was failing to prevent Grant's drawing the string tighter and tighter on both the Army of Northern Virginia and the Confederate capital. There was to be one last encounter before Grant forced the Confederates into their last line of defense. The Battle of Cold Harbor, lasting from May 31 to June 3, showed that both armies had learned their lessons in field fortification to near-perfection. The two armies now instantly entrenched whenever they stopped. When troops changed positions, their entrenchments invariably followed.

An attempt to catch and to fold up a wing of Grant's army on its march to Cold Harbor failed for several reasons. A portion of the Confederate assault force got lost in the woods owing to a guide's error. There was a breakdown in coordination because of inferior tactical communications, poor staff work, and inadequate command procedures. Green troops, general malnutrition, war weariness among veterans, and the construction of strong entrenchments by the assailed Union troops completed the setting for failure.[89] Unsuccessful in his attempt to catch Grant outside his entrenchments, Lee strengthened and extended his fortifications for a defensive stand along a nine-mile front,[90] which he necessarily overextended to cover the approaches to Richmond.[91]

Grant, seemingly forgetful of the lessons of the recent past and the wisdom of his recently expressed desire not to have his troops slaughtered on the enemy's entrenchment on the North Anna, ordered a general attack along the Confederate line for June 3. The assault succeeded at first in capturing some of the Confederate entrenchments, but Lee's troops quickly restored the line.[92] Though the Confederates were greatly outnumbered by a better-armed and physically more fit army, the combination of rifled infantry weapons, well-placed artillery, and strong field fortifications brought them their most decisive triumph of the 1864 campaign, as well as one of the easiest victories of the war. The planned major assaults were broken up within eight minutes of their commencement.[93] Further assaults were unable even to approach the Confederate defenses under the withering fire from rifles and artillery. Grant gave up the offensive about 1:00 P.M., eight and a half hours after the first attacks. Lee had lost only between 1,200 and 1,500 men along the six miles of his front. Grant's casualties totaled about 12,000 men.[94]

In their setback, the Union troops put on one of the most impressive displays of hasty entrenchment of the war. After their repulse, the troops in the first assault wave dug in positions close against the Confederate line, at some places within fifty yards. "A singular thing about the whole attack," observed Colonel Theodore Lyman, Meade's aide-de-camp, "— was, that our men when the fire was too hot for them to advance and the works too strong, did not retreat—but lay down where some ridge offered a little cover, and there stayed, at a distance from the enemy varying from forty to perhaps 250 yards. When it was found that the lines could not be carried, General Meade issued orders to hold the advanced positions, all along, and to entrench."[95] There were too few tools to allow everybody to entrench with the desired speed, and many, to quote the commander of one of the brigades involved, "under a heavy fire . . . entrenched using bayonets, tin cups, and plates. . . ." During the night of June 3, the Federals strengthened their line close against the Confederate entrenchments and made embrasures for the artillery to be brought up. Once again, Federal commanders ordered multiple lines of works. After its unsuccessful assault on the 3d, Hancock entrenched his corps in four successive lines while under heavy fire.[96]

One dramatic and novel development to indicate the dimensions that trench warfare had assumed was the Federal use of zigzag entrenched approaches, a practice not previously employed by the eastern armies in field operations. Prior use had been reserved in accordance with doctrine for siege operations. The Federal troops began to dig their approaches immediately following their repulse on the 3d, and continued them through the remainder of the Cold Harbor campaign. On the night of the 3d, Colonel Theodore Lyman observed that

all the entrenching tools were ordered up and the lines were strengthened, and saps run out, so as to bring them still closer to the opposing ones. And there the two armies slept, almost within an easy stone-throw of each other; and the separating space ploughed by common shot and clotted with the dead bodies that neither side dared to bury! I think nothing can give a greater idea of deathless tenacity of purpose, than the picture of these two hosts after a bloody and nearly continuous struggle of thirty days, lying down to sleep with their heads almost on each other's throats! Possibly it has no parallel in history. So ended the great attack at Cool Arbor.[97]

Unknown to Lyman, the same tactical use of entrenchment to hold ground taken in unsuccessful assaults was occurring independently in Sherman's army in the West.

Amid these developments, Grant made an enigmatic statement. On June 5 he pronounced that "the feeling—now seems to be that the rebels can protect themselves only by strong entrenchments, while our army is not only confident of protecting itself without entrenchments, but that it can beat and drive the enemy whenever and wherever he can be found without this protection."[98] One wonders what could have induced Grant to utter such nonsense in the midst of the most impressive display of hasty entrenchment of the war. One is left to ponder whether he fully appreciated the tactical implications of developments of which he was a central figure. Grant's pragmatically motivated actions at the time of this strange pronouncement were out of necessity contrary to its sentiments.[99] Thus, although the use of field fortifications was growing daily more extensive, the tactical thought of the Union general in chief frequently lagged not only behind the reality of the changed character of warfare, but also behind his own actions.

The outlook Grant expressed could account, at least in part, for his ill-advised Cold Harbor offensive, as well as for earlier costly attempts to overrun Confederate entrenchments. But then we have to account for his rejection of an attack on Lee's entrenchments on the North Anna because such an attack "would cause a slaughter of our men that even success would not justify."[100] One plausible interpretation is that Grant did not have a systematic tactical outlook, but rather acted according to an appraisal of each situation as it arose, blending an erratic mixture of common sense about the new conditions of warfare with a predisposition to traditional tactics. Reinforcing this predisposition was a predisposition arguably to the warrior's test of battle. Out of this mix of motives came Grant's strategy of attrition.

Whatever his motives, Grant probably acted independently of Meade. Meade's aide-de-camp, Colonel Theodore Lyman, claimed that Grant did not seek the advice of others, including Meade, on principles of war or anything else connected with his command. According to Lyman,

"Grant . . . directs all and his subordinates are only responsible as executive officers having more or less important functions." Meade captured his own role in relation to Grant in a letter to his wife, May 19, 1864: "Coppee [the military critic] in his Army Magazine says, 'the Army of the Potomac, directed by Grant, commanded by Meade, and led by Hancock, Sedgwick and Warren which is quite good distinction, and about hits the nail on the head.' "

Meade, who previously had shown ambivalence himself on the merits of the frontal assault, indicated that he was in conflict with Grant over his use of frontal assaults at Spotsylvania and Cold Harbor. In a letter June 5, 1864, Meade indulges in some self-justification for his own past performance while stating his position at this stage of the war:

> The results of this campaign are the clearest indications I could wish of my sound judgement, both at Williamsport and Mine Run. In every instance that we have attacked the enemy in an entrenched position, we have failed, except in the case of Hancock's attack at Spotsylvania which was a surprise discreditable to the enemy. So, likewise, whenever the enemy has attacked us in position, he has been repulsed. I think Grant has had his eyes opened, and is willing to admit now that Virginia and Lee's army is not Tennessee and Bragg's army. Whenever the people will ever realize this fact remains to be seen.

Meade would justify his June 18 assault on the Petersburg lines on the grounds that "I had positive information the enemy had not occupied more than twelve hours and that no digging had been done on the lines prior to the occupation."[101]

The Battle of Cold Harbor was followed by over a week of skirmishing and sharpshooting before the onset of a side effect of trench warfare—large-scale fraternization. After a month of fighting and living in the trenches, the veterans of the two armies broke the stress, hardship, and monotony of their existence by arranging informal truces to exchange news, political views, newspapers, and small valuables, to share the common bond of a life that increasingly separated them from the rest of the world.[102]

After thirteen days at close quarters in the Cold Harbor trenches, Grant slipped away undetected to move once again to the left, shifting his base of supplies to City Point on the James. His destination was the southern approaches to Petersburg, over fifty miles and five days away. Grant relieved the logistical burden of the land movement by transporting the advance corps by water from Wilcox Landing on the north bank of the James River to the southern approaches to Petersburg. The

Union troops entrenched a strong bridgehead on the James to protect the army's crossing.[103]

Lee, not knowing whether Grant intended to take his troops south of the James, could not move. On June 17, his intelligence finally confirmed that Grant's entire army was advancing against Petersburg. Lee quickly moved to reinforce Beauregard, who was holding off the first two Federal corps of the Army of the Potomac to arrive before the Petersburg defenses. With the detachment of General Early to the Shenandoah Valley the very day Grant moved from his Cold Harbor defenses, Lee now had only about 41,000 effective troops with which to defend Petersburg and Richmond.[104] After an initial inconsistency, tactical evolution proceeded on its former course. In the first actions against Petersburg's outer works, some Federal units failed to entrench prior to making their first attacks, despite the fact that most had time, some all night. After this momentary letdown, all invariably entrenched before their second assaults, even when successful in the first, and they always dug in thereafter.[105]

The actions of the 3rd Division of the II Corps of the Army of the Potomac were typical. This division had thrown up earthworks immediately upon taking up position at Wilcox Landing before moving south of the James. When it took up position before the outer defenses of Petersburg, however, it did not entrench, even though it held positions from midnight until dawn. The next day, June 16, the 3rd Division drove the enemy from his works, and quickly dug in preparatory to an attack. The defenders drove back the division's attack, inflicting heavy losses. The 3rd Division was relieved on the 20th and took up new positions, which it quickly entrenched. When the Confederates turned the division's flank, it fell back to its prior line of works. Later it advanced again to find the enemy had withdrawn, and subsequently reoccupied its previously abandoned line of works. The 3rd Division did not move again until July 1, when it was transferred to a new position, which it quickly entrenched.[106]

Union entrenchments during these early operations against the Confederates' first line were constructed on lines laid out by engineering officers who accompanied the troops.[107] When it became apparent that he could not hold his overextended first line of defense, Beauregard had his chief engineer, Colonel D. B. Harris, lay out a shorter line. It was so close to Petersburg that the enemy could bombard the city, an unfortunate but necessary sacrifice. The line that Lee would have to hold to defend Petersburg and Richmond was twenty-six miles in length, well located on the best possible ground. The Confederates extended their lines into formidable systems of earthworks. Grant considered the enemy's earthworks "as strong as they can be made." The Confederate line was indented, affording mutual flanking. The ground was highly favorable to retrenchment, and abatis, palisades, and other obstructions fronted the earthworks.[108]

While under constant fire from artillery and sharpshooters, the Union troops threw up equally formidable entrenchments. Similarly, they featured strong redoubts and redans connected by curtains of rifle trenches. A second line of retrenchment covered threatened points. Artillery skillfully covered the open ground between the opposing lines. Although the artillerists seldom got the range of the enemy's works, sharpshooters made the slightest exposure fatal. Mortars, which the Federals used from the beginning, and the Confederates from June 24, added to the discomfort.[109] Confirming his policy against attacking strong entrenched positions, Lee wrote to President Davis on June 21 that Grant "is so situated that I cannot attack him."[110] But on June 24, given an advantage where Confederate artillery enfiladed a section of the Union line, Lee did attack. Because of a misunderstanding between the divisions involved as to their role in the offensive, the Confederate main line failed to support the skirmish line—which was successful in its assault—and the offensive failed.[111] Poor staff work and inadequate command procedures again had taken their toll.

Circumstances were making it difficult for Lee to avoid the tactical offense. For reasons already familiar, the Confederate army was in poor physical shape. Any major interruption in the flow of provisions over the four railroads that supplied Lee would leave him with three alternatives short of surrender: to starve in the trenches; to attempt to retreat to Richmond—which he considered tantamount to defeat; or to risk attacking Grant's entrenchments. When Union cavalry in early June put two of the four railroads over which Lee was being supplied out of commission for two weeks, Lee, on June 26, wrote to President Davis that "I fear the . . . difficulty [of procuring supplies] will oblige me to attack General Grant in his entrenchments, which I should not hesitate to do but for the loss it will inevitably entail." He added that "a want of success would in my opinion be almost fatal, and this causes me to hesitate in the hope that some relief might be procured without running such great hazard."[112] Thus, although the incentive to attack grew greater, Lee's appreciation of the risks caused him to wait, in the hope that some fortuitous development would make it not necessary.

Grant and Meade were as reluctant as Lee to challenge the entrenched defense. There was some evidence of war weariness and low morale among the Union troops. The recent loss of 8,000 men from a total of 64,000 engaged in the fighting from June 15 through 18 had taken its psychological toll. When the June 18 assault failed, Grant ordered that no more be made. The Army of the Potomac once again reverted to maneuver rather than have a repeat of Cold Harbor.[113]

This time Grant did not have a forward base of supplies from which to attempt to move across Lee's lines of communications. He ordered cavalry raids to tear up the enemy's railroad lines. Meanwhile, he extended his entrenchments toward the Appomattox River in an attempt to cut Lee's rail communications south of the James. This envelopment required a thinning of the existing line, which would have to hold any attempted Confederate breakout. Grant suggested to Meade that he meet this threat by manning the existing line with a small force. At the same time, he suggested that Meade hold back large reserves from each corps to check any assault on the existing front. Alternately, the reserve could support the movement to envelop Lee's lines. If Lee weakened his front to meet this Union maneuver on his right to the extent where an assault on the Confederate lines was feasible, Grant advised Meade to attack.[114]

The Federal offensive stumbled over several obstacles to strategic mobility. The cavalry raids did temporarily disrupt three of the four railroads over which Lee was supplied, two of them for over two weeks.[115] But enough got through to Lee to discourage either the evacuation of Petersburg or Lee's taking the tactical offensive.[116] Lee was temporarily reprieved when a number of developments combined to undermine the mobility of Grant's army. The cavalry was hampered by insufficient forage to live off the land. Lee also took advantage of his interior lines to send forces to interfere with Federal cavalry operations. The Union cavalry offensive collapsed when the cavalry so exhausted its horse supply that it was incapacitated for almost three weeks of July while the Quartermaster Department replaced its losses.[117]

Grant's attempt to cut Lee's communications by extending the Union trenches to the Appomattox River also collapsed. Difficult topography, poor staff work, inadequate command procedures, the technical limitations of tactical communications, and unclear orders again proved too great a burden. Evidence also suggests that low morale and war weariness affected marching. The movements were slow, and a breakdown in coordination left a gap between Warren's and Hancock's corps.[118] Lee again exploited his interior lines to entrench a force across Grant's path of maneuver. The Confederates took advantage of the gap in the Union line between Warren and Hancock to turn their positions. They badly mauled the Union troops, forcing them back a considerable distance before they managed to reestablish their lines. The Confederates' task was made easier when the fatigued and demoralized Federal infantry collapsed. Whole brigades and regiments from Hancock's celebrated corps, with an offensive record second to none in the Union army, abandoned their lines without firing a shot. Several regiments surrendered without resistance.[119] Grant abandoned hope of early success in extending his line to the Appomattox,[120] although he did not abandon this plan as central to his strategy. In the immediate future, however, the army needed rest. The Confederates, meanwhile, busily extended their entrenchments to parallel Grant's efforts to envelop them.

There was one untried strategic alternative, but Meade and Grant both rejected it. In preference to weakening the defensive line by extending the Union entrenchments, General Warren suggested that the Army of the Potomac abandon its present lines and move with about six days' supplies across the Weldon and Southside railroads, thus forcing Lee to come out of his defenses to attack. If Lee should cut its communications, the Union army could return to its supply base. Meade raised the objection that Lee might entrench himself across their communications, and that reduced supplies might prevent them from undertaking the turning maneuvers necessary to reestablish them. Grant dismissed the plan as impracticable almost without comment.[121] The implication was strong that any risk in strategic maneuver had been displaced by the relative security of attrition.

With the collapse of strategic maneuver, attention turned to the possibility of a breakthrough on the Confederate front.[122] The Federal maneuvers, though unsuccessful, had forced Lee to weaken his line to man the necessary extension parallel to the Union entrenchments. Neither Grant nor Meade, however, thought the enemy's lines were weak enough to attack. On July 4, both rejected a detailed plan presented by the chief engineer of the Union armies, General Barnard, which called for a massed frontal assault against a redoubt on Warren's front that was considered to be a key to rolling up Lee's Petersburg lines.[123]

But Meade and Grant were showing interest in mining activity on Burnside's front.[124] Late in June, Meade had given half-hearted and rather disinterested consent to a plan to run a mine beneath the Confederate line over 500 yards away.[125] As static stalemate set in, both Grant and Meade showed increasing interest in the scheme. On July 3, Meade asked Major James C. Duane, chief engineer of the Army of the Potomac, and General Henry Hunt, chief of artillery and director of siege operations at Petersburg, for their opinions on the feasibility of an assault by the corps of Burnside and Warren.

Duane and Hunt advised that the enemy's entrenchments were so strong and the ground so obstructed with abatis, stakes, and entanglements as to render an assault impracticable. They recommended that any attempt to take the Confederate line should be by regular siege approaches, but warned that "the siege will be a long one, inasmuch as soon as one line of works is carried another equally strong will be found behind it, and this will continue until the ridge is attained which looks into the town."[126] But Meade and Grant had decided that the mine being run from Burnside's front presented a feasible chance to break the tactical stalemate and roll up the Petersburg defenses.[127] They consequently ordered Duane and Hunt to draw up a plan of tactical operation against the Confederate works opposite Burnside's and Warren's fronts.

The mining scheme was an example of American technical ingenuity almost worthy of the challenge that the weapons revolution and fortification developments presented to the attack. Fitting to the proven inventiveness of the Union citizen soldier, the original response came from the 48th Pennsylvania Volunteers, a regiment composed chiefly of miners from Schuylkill County, Pennsylvania, and commanded by a volunteer officer who in civilian life had been a mining engineer,[128] an indication of the abundance of skilled labor available in the volunteer forces. It was labor, moreover, with a technological bent suitable for adaption to the tactical transition taking place under the impact of the revolution in weaponry. The plan, first suggested by privates and noncommissioned officers in the regiment, was to run a mine under the enemy line over 500 yards away, an unprecedented feat that most considered impossible because of the ventilation problems involved.[129] The excavation took just under a month, and was completed on July 23. It was probably the most impressive mining feat in the history of war to that time.

But in the detailed plan they drew up, Duane and Hunt were pessimistic about the probable results of successfully exploding the mine. They doubted whether the intended assault through the gap left in the enemy's line would be sufficient to overcome "the advantages of position on the part of the enemy." They believed that retrenched positions would prevent the assault from achieving its hoped-for objective, namely, the capture of the hill behind the main works and the subsequent turning of the Petersburg lines. Duane and Hunt thought the most that could be expected was a strong offensive lodgment after being checked at the enemy's retrenchments. They expected heavy losses. Siege operations, they recommended, could then be continued against successive lines of Confederate works until the crest was gained.[130]

By this time, the new tactical conditions brought about by the rifled musket and the matching skill in field fortification construction raised questions about the value even of siege operations. A major in the Corps of Engineers attached to the Army of the Potomac skillfully summarized developments in field fortification when, at the time the plan was being formulated, he observed that "the new era in field-works had so changed their character as in fact to render them almost as strong as permanent ones, and the facility with which successive lines can be constructed (so well proven throughout the whole campaign just terminated) renders it almost useless to attempt a regular siege."[131] Each line overrun merely led to the next hastily constructed line thrown up by well-practiced troops by now conditioned to instant entrenchment. The same officer pointed out that the sharpshooter had so perfected his art that he could take a heavy toll during the slow operations of a siege.[132]

On July 9, Meade, readying for an attack when the mine exploded, ordered siege approaches begun along Burnside's and Warren's fronts.[133] On July 23 the mine was ready. Preparations for the attack were rushed to completion. At dawn on the morning of July 30, the explosion of four tons of dynamite swallowed up most of a South Carolina regiment, and blew a hole in the Confederate line approximately 200 feet long and 50 feet wide. The grim spectacle was worthy of World War I, as were the results of the following assaults.

Although the Confederate lines at this point were only lightly held,[134] the defenders brutally beat back the Union assault. Their lines caught the Union attack with enfilading infantry fire from lines of retrenchment, from the traverses that led from the first line to the second, from both sides of the broken Confederate line, which closed to fill the gap, and from artillery and mortars that moved up and poured accurate fire into the breach. After they had checked the attack, the Confederate troops ran an earthwork around the edge of the pit to restore the line. The Federals could not even achieve their minimum objective of a lodgment from which to extend the offensive by siege approaches.[135] In addition to the defensive obstacles to success, there was a considerable delay in attempting to exploit the gap, and the assault never really got organized. Evidence suggests that the breakdown of the offensive was caused by a lack of coordination owing to inadequate staff work and procedures, poor leadership, green troops, and pushing too many troops into the crater with the difficulty of getting them out.[136]

Grant and Meade abandoned further assaults along the Petersburg front. They returned to the attempt to extend their lines to the Appomattox before winter rains made the roads impassable and forced them into winter quarters. General Warren succeeded in cutting the Weldon Railroad, but Lee retained its use by running a wagon train that connected with the railroad at a more distant point. Lee's cavalry beat back attempts to cut the Southside Railroad and the Weldon Railroad farther down the line. Grant slowly extended his lines toward the Appomattox, stretching Lee's lines thinner and thinner. It was further testimony to the ascendancy of positional warfare that Lee's enfeebled army had the satisfaction of seeing the enemy go into winter quarters without having achieved his objective.

The prospect of a winter in the trenches, on the other hand, was depressing. Although Lee's troops were temporarily safe from Union encirclement, his logistical problems were growing continually more desperate. The Army of Northern Virginia depended on daily shipments over a physically collapsing transportation system, and Lee was hindered by a supply system with the already noted limitations. To make matters worse, Johnston and Lee were now drawing provisions from the same forage area. Ordnance supply was equally hard-pressed. Percussion caps were so scarce that front-line Confederate troops were restricted to 18 rounds per man. By contrast, Federal skirmishers were under orders to fire 100 rounds every twenty-four hours.[137] A lack of soap made living conditions all the worse.[138]

The long months in the trenches under subhuman conditions and without leave became increasingly difficult to bear. The damp winter cold of the Virginia Peninsula added to hunger and a growing belief among the troops that the Confederate cause was hopeless. Discipline began to collapse, and there were large-scale desertions.[139] Fraternization and informal truces to eliminate sharpshooting became increasingly common. In November, the Confederate troops began to dig caves in the rear of the trenches to protect themselves from the cold and from mortars.[140] From December to February, there was no significant action on the Petersburg-Richmond front, the monotony and misery of life in the trenches broken only by the whine of sharpshooters' bullets and the explosion of mortars.

The Confederate logistical plight worsened. On January 15 Fort Fisher fell, closing Wilmington, North Carolina, the Confederacy's last port. Desertions were reducing Lee's numbers to where he was finding it difficult to man his overextended lines. Sherman, meanwhile, moved closer to a junction with Grant. In mid-March, Lee, in response to strategic necessity, reluctantly launched a tactical offensive.[141] His point of attack was a redoubt called Fort Stedman and its retrenched redoubts. The plan was to break and turn the Federal line: "so that if I could not cause their abandonment, General Grant would at least be obliged so to curtain his lines, that upon the approach of General Sherman I might be able to hold our position with a portion of the troops, and with a select body unite with General Johnston and give him battle."[142] But the Federal defenses proved too strong. The attack failed with heavy casualties. The exhausted and depleted Army of Northern Virginia was on the verge of collapse. With the alternative of waiting for Sherman to join Grant or attempting a withdrawal to join Johnston, Lee made the only possible decision: he prepared to evacuate Petersburg and attempt to join Johnston. His defensive strategy had finally broken down under logistical and manpower deficiencies.

Grant moved quickly to cut the Danville and Southside railroads to prevent the juncture of Lee and Johnston, and to force Lee to abandon any material he might otherwise save and take with him.[143] Lee sent a force of about 6,000 men to check the Union maneuver, but it was too small and was overrun. Lee manned his main line largely with green, poorly trained local defense troops to cover the withdrawal of his army.[144] The line was paper-thin. On April 1 there was an average of about 750 men for every mile of the Confederate line, or about 1 for every two and a half yards, with no second line and no reserve.[145] On April 1 the Confederate defensive line finally gave way, and the defenders fell back into the inner works of Petersburg. During the night, the inner line was stabilized, as the tactical defensive temporarily reasserted itself along this shortened line manned by veteran troops. Leaving about 16,000 men to cover his withdrawal, Lee the next night evacuated Petersburg, moving along the Richmond and Danville Railroad with about 12,000 infantry, the remaining troops to follow.

The nearest point where Lee could meet Johnston was 107 miles away, while Grant's route of interception to that point was only 88 miles. The positions of the two armies in the 1864 maneuver were thus reversed. Lee hoped to compensate with his one-day head start. But the men and horses of the Army of Northern Virginia were in no shape for such a march, by far the longest movement attempted since the beginning of the 1864–1865 campaign. Lee's supply situation collapsed completely after his first day's march. The stores upon which he was depending had not been collected at Amelia Court House, which he reached the first night. Lee had to sacrifice his head start and break up his supply train to send out foraging parties. They came back almost empty-handed. The countryside had been stripped clean. The Army of Northern Virginia now quickly began to disintegrate. The march slowed, as animals and men dropped from hunger. Many deserted. General Ewell's corps had started on April 3 with 6,000 men. By the 6th it had fewer than 3,000. Enemy cavalry captured more and more of what remained of the already stripped-down supply train. Lee was unable to pull away from the pursuing Federal army, and rear-guard attacks ate up most of what remained of his army. When Grant finally blocked the route of retreat, Lee surrendered.[146]

From the day almost a year before when they had first clashed in the Wilderness, the two armies had established the brutal reality of the new era of entrenched positional warfare. In this last, desperate, year-long campaign, Lee, by keeping Grant bottled up in the limited area between Washington and the James, had shown that an army fighting on interior lines, even under nearly overwhelming conditions of deprivation and against vastly superior numbers, could sustain a prolonged existence by the use of field fortification and defensive maneuver. Until its logistical base completely collapsed, the Army of Northern Virginia had successfully exploited the entrenched defense and defensive maneuver on interior lines. In the process, from the Wilderness through Cold Harbor, it had inflicted 64,000 casualties on the enemy,[147] a number equal to the largest size the Army of Northern Virginia attained during the year. In its defensive stand of almost eight months before Petersburg and Richmond, it inflicted approximately 50,000 more casualties, while itself suffering approximately one-third that number. In defeat and in victory, the two armies revealed the changed conditions of warfare as they affected tactical and strategic mobility, providing military thought with a great deal to digest as it sought to avoid the specter of endless trench warfare.

11

Organization, Maneuver, and the Strategy of Exhaustion

To Atlanta and Beyond

Grant, in consultation with Sherman, began to mix a strategy of penetration with a more ambitious raiding strategy for the 1864 campaign. In addition to his advice to Halleck to use the Army of the Potomac for a winter foray into North Carolina, he and Sherman planned Sherman's spectacular raid on Meridian, Mississippi. With the intention of destroying Confederate communications and resources without occupying territory, and with the option of retreating in any direction if confronted, Sherman, in February, moved an army of 20,000 men, mostly infantry, on a long, well-concealed march from Vicksburg to Meridian. Among the damage, his successful raid destroyed the only Confederate railroad connections between Mississippi and Alabama and Georgia. This left Mobile with only the Alabama River for communication to the interior. Sherman covered 110 miles direct distance, and probably between 150 and 175 miles actually traveled in reaching Meridian in eleven days—an average of 14 to 16 miles per day.

Several diversions, including a major cavalry raid into Mississippi from Memphis by General W. Sooy Smith, successfully shielded Sherman's objective. Joseph Johnston mistakenly assumed that Sherman's destination was Mobile and sent reinforcements for its defense. Sherman wrought his destruction on communications and resources unhindered by the enemy. A strategy of diversion and surprise based on the organizational ability to live off the land had received an impressive trial run.

Whether Grant and Sherman were to run the risk of a deep raid with Sherman's army of 100,000 as it organized to move from Chattanooga against Atlanta was another question. As the Union armies penetrated deeper into the South, the resources needed to occupy and hold the country were an increasing burden. Grant as general in chief began 1864 as cautious with Sherman's combined force, which included the armies of the Cumberland, Tennessee, and Ohio, as he was with the Army of the Potomac. He and Sherman devised a deliberate strategy of penetration to occupy Atlanta, a direct distance of approximately sixty-five miles, and actual distance traveled about ninety miles away. The offensive was planned as part of a two-pronged movement on the city, the other from Mobile. If successful, it would capture the logistical center of Atlanta while breaking every east-west railway in the Confederacy. Holding Joseph Johnston's army in place so he could not move troops to counter an intended raid with a small army from Mobile was also part of Grant and Sherman's thinking; as was the wish to hold Johnston from reinforcing Lee until the Army of the Potomac was secure south of Richmond.

Yet there is a question of whether Grant and Sherman were letting the growing advantages of numbers and resources weigh on the side of a conservative attitude toward the risks of maneuver in the West as in the East. Sherman and Grant were confident in their superior numbers. And they knew the land had good resources, though they were thinly distributed with respect to the foraging capacity of a Civil War army. While Johnston had to leave subsistence for his population, Sherman's rules of total warfare enabled him to live off what the Confederate army could not take from its own people, a predicament that later would draw frustrated comments from Johnston to Lee. Sherman also anticipated that if Johnston followed form, he would attempt to deny the Union army the opportunity to bleed him to death in tactical battles, instead drawing the enemy deeper and deeper into the South, biding his time while seeking to take advantage of the Union's extended lines deep in Confederate territory. Such a defensive strategy of withdrawal, Sherman realized, would give the Union army a certain freedom to forage and destroy Confederate resources.

Sherman prepared to take the offensive against Atlanta with a holding-turning strategy to keep Johnston on his front with George Thomas's

Army of the Cumberland, while he attempted to flank the Confederates with James McPherson's Army of the Tennessee and John Schofield's Army of the Ohio on his wings. He would live off the countryside supplemented by supplies from a mobile railroad constructed behind him as he moved by the Military Railroad Construction Corps. What he did not use, he would destroy or send back as war booty. The use of a railroad constructed to follow Sherman and give him the slow but steady mobility to penetrate and hold enemy territory was another vista on the changing nature of warfare. Having honed its skills from the Second Battle of Bull Run, where it had played a significant strategic role, the Military Railroad Construction Corps would have its finest hour during the Atlanta campaign, before proceeding on to further remarkable feats with the Army of the Potomac. This combination of railroad and animal-drawn field transportation reorganized to meet mid-nineteenth-century American needs for maneuver, and the offensive use of entrenched holding tactics to keep the enemy's army on his front while Sherman maneuvered against his flank en route to Atlanta provided one emerging face of modern warfare.

In an acrimonious debate over strategy in the West, Johnston prevailed in his opinion that the Confederacy should fight from a defensive stance because it did not have the capacity for the offense. Johnston first argued that the supply system could not provide the subsistence necessary for an offense. When pressed, he admitted that he could make do; but he shifted his argument for a defensive strategy to the inadequacy of his field transportation.[1]

Johnston asked for 1,000 more wagons. The inspector general of field transportation, Major Cole, largely substantiated Johnston's claims. He did question Johnston's preparations in fending off the problem. The field transportation standard of the Army of Tennessee, paralleling that of the Army of Northern Virginia, had been drastically reduced, from the approximately 35 wagons per 1,000 men set in August, 1863, to approximately 28 wagons per 1,000 men in the general order of September 24, 1863. A cut to the general supply train in late January, 1864, again slightly reduced the standard, to approximately 26 wagons per thousand. It is not clear what ratios were actually achieved, but Cole's agreement with Johnston's claims suggests that Johnston was some 1,000 wagons short of meeting the reduced standard of 26 wagons per 1,000 men. Considering that the supply organization was conventional, contrasted to the reforms of the Union army instituted in 1863, this standard even if realized was inadequate for offensive operations except at considerable cost to soldiers and animals.

The decreased field transportation standard accompanied reduced demands on the supply train, owing to the concurrent cut in supplies with fewer horses. Confederate army regulations on subsistence standards, after remaining set from 1861 to 1863 (except for a slight change in rations in 1862), were lowered in 1864. And Johnston, in February, 1864, reduced the standard of the Army of Tennessee still further. The formal supply standard was, under the circumstances, merely an organizational norm to be adjusted, almost invariably downward, to meet the deteriorating supply and transportation situation.

Inexplicably, Johnston sustained an extremely high baggage standard by comparison with reductions in the Army of Northern Virginia. In his general orders of January 28, 1864, Johnston set the baggage standard for general officers at 120 pounds, field officers at 100 pounds, captains at 50 pounds, and subalterns (lieutenants) at 30 pounds. These orders remained in effect for the Army of Tennessee until the end of the war. This compares with Lee's general order of April 20, 1863, which set the baggage standard at 80 pounds for general officers, 65 pounds for field officers, and 50 pounds for company officers. On April 5, 1864, Lee ordered a reduction to 60 pounds for general officers, 50 pounds for field officers, and 30 pounds for other officers. By comparison with both Johnston and Lee's shifting standards, army regulations, which remained unrevised through the war, called for 125 pounds for general officers, 100 pounds for field officers, eighty pounds for captains, and 80 pounds for subalterns.[2]

Johnston also considered his basic disadvantage in manpower. A projected Confederate army of 75,000 men was not realistic, with respect to either the number of troops that could be raised or the means to supply them. Johnston realized that he would be outnumbered about two to one by Sherman's forces. "The great numerical superiority of the Federal army made it expedient to risk battle only when position or some blunder on the part of the enemy might give us counterbalancing advantages," he concluded. Accordingly, Johnston

> determined to fall back slowly until circumstances should put the chances of battle in our favour, keeping so near the U.S. army as to prevent its sending reinforcements to Grant, and hoping, by taking advantage of position and opportunities, to reduce the odds against us by partial engagements. I also expected it to be materially reduced before the end of June by the expiration of the terms of service of many of the regiments which had not re-enlisted.[3]

Sherman's movement from Chattanooga to Atlanta displayed talent for experiment and practical improvisation informed by experience. At the same time it revealed, understandably, some apprehension and sometimes less-than-confident performance by Sherman and his talented chief quartermaster, Brigadier General L. C. Easton, around the supply and transportation system.[4] Despite Rosecrans's spectacular maneuvers with the 60,000-man Army of the Cumberland, with Easton as its quartermaster, and the experience of the Army of the Potomac, Sherman and Easton were obviously nervous about the logistics of moving a 100,000-man army in the face of such a respected practitioner of defensive strategy as Joseph Johnston. There is room for speculation as to whether they and Grant had the confidence at this time to seriously contemplate other than the cautious strategy they adopted.

Sherman certainly had an enormous field transportation system to begin his campaign. In addition to his mobile railroad, Easton reported that Sherman's army in the field on July 1, 1864, with 100,000 men, had 5,180 wagons,[5] approximately 52 wagons per 1,000 men.[6] Only Rosecrans's Army of the Cumberland, in the autumn of 1863, had previously reached so high a ratio. Sherman's animal standard, with 28,000 horses and 32,600 mules, also considerably exceeded the Union army average of approximately 1 animal for every 2 men from June, 1863, to June, 1864.[7] Sherman was, interestingly, close to John Moore's modern statistical analysis of Civil War field transportation needs for extended movements detached from a railhead or supply base.[8]

Sherman probably incorporated some features of a modified flying column into the organization of his field transportation and supply. Allowing for freelancing by individual field commanders, particularly in the West, Meigs was trying to develop a common doctrine. But Sherman had his men carry the conventional three days' supply, compared to the flying column, which loaded the soldiers with eight to twelve days' supply.

Even Grant in 1864 had his men carry six days' supply.[9] The availability of forage in Sherman's campaigning area, contrasted to the near-complete absence in Grant's, could have been a factor. Yet Sherman sacrificed a reduction of wagons when he put so little on the soldiers' backs. Perhaps he accepted the argument that prevailed in the East, that the troops lacked the discipline to carry a heavy load, especially in battle. By 1864, even Rufus Ingalls, a holdout in 1863 for flying column standards and the enforcement of discipline, succumbed, as noted, to the fact that the soldier in the Army of the Potomac had grown accustomed to so high a standard of living that he could never be disciplined to carry a heavy load.[10] Maybe Sherman had the same general problem. Or perhaps the increase in the wagon standard beyond the norm was

Sherman's cautious response to the number of wagons needed to make the logistical sweep to gather good but widely distributed forage in his campaigning area. After all, he had limited precedent upon which to draw for an army this size trying its best to live off the land. Grant's experience with the Army of the Potomac was of limited help, because Grant was campaigning in an area largely devoid of forage.[11] Perhaps Sherman weighed the experience of the Army of the Cumberland during its spectacular maneuvers in 1863 as the most valid criterion for the now-combined armies under his command. It is significant that he appointed the quartermaster who organized those movements, L. C. Easton, as quartermaster for his combined armies.

Sherman, of course, resolved part of the problem of detachment from his railhead by taking his railhead into the field. In a striking display of the organization of railroad resources to support field operations, the Military Railroad Construction Corps of the Quartermaster Department laid rail to accompany Sherman's movements and keep him linked with his Nashville supply base. At no time did the railroad fall more than four days behind the army. While dependent upon his rail link for periodic resupply, Sherman early indicated that his focus was on learning to live off the land as independent as possible of rail line or supply base. His organizational style was to load up with what he could not forage during periodic stops at the moving railhead, and then break loose for long runs, usually loaded with ten days' subsistence for the men, foraging the remainder of his needs from the land.[12]

Accompanying Sherman with the rail supply line proved a difficult organizational and administrative task, made more difficult by lively guerrilla activity. But the job got done amid the atmosphere of an ad hoc learning experience. There was a limited sense of the modern conception of staff organization to plan, organize, and integrate field command and supply procedures that had grown up in the East. The accumulated experience of the Union armies and Meigs's attempt to establish a coordinated logistical doctrine between high command, the Quartermaster Department, and operational planning no doubt played a role in the West. But the independence of the western armies within this process continued even into 1864 and was most evident in Sherman's logistical organization. Sherman's army gave a sense of needing to learn through its own experience somewhat removed from central direction and coordination.

Through preparations for the campaign, there was a sense of improvisation devoid of much staff coordination. This style seemed to suit Sherman. Easton was obviously uncomfortable; but a more modern conception of staff did not appear to be part of his thinking, either.

With respect to coordination with the Quartermaster Department, Meigs indicated that he felt Sherman and Easton were fighting their own private war.

There were administrative breakdowns. For instance, a considerable amount of grain was lost when it was shipped from Nashville to Chattanooga on platform cars without protection from the rain. Severe measures proved necessary to enforce what should have been routine procedure. Various problems forced Easton on August 16 to put the animals on half-rations of grain. Sherman's chief commissary, with only six full-day rations on hand, went to half-subsistence rations, a situation that was not alleviated until November 27, when the rivers rose enough to resume normal supply.

The growing distance of the army from Chattanooga caused the anticipated need to increase the number of cars and engines to deliver the same quantity of supplies. Unloading in the field rather than at a permanent depot was cumbersome and created organizational and administrative snags. The slow return of cars over a single-track railroad was a particular problem. Again reflecting the lack of staff coordination between the parts of the supply system, the Chattanooga and Nashville ends of the route showed little understanding of difficulties at the other end of the line. "As the army advanced," noted Easton, in emphasizing the enormity of the task, "the road had to be rebuilt, water-tanks to be constructed, and wood cut. The depot had to be established nearer the army, side tracks to be constructed, and whatever accumulation there was at the last depot had to be brought forward, and orders were frequently given to bring stores from the depot up to our very lines by rail, and to take back the sick and wounded."

Easton's chronicle of detail emphasized the administrative and organizational bottlenecks of railroad operation. "The commanding general would sometimes order ten days' subsistence and grain brought up immediately to fill the wagons. In such cases, we would have to take some of the cars that were usually kept between Nashville and Chattanooga. Some trains never returned to the North at all, as they were captured and burned by the enemy. They tore up the tracks and fired upon trains very frequently." Part of the problem, he contended, was an inadequate supply of cars. Easton also complained of the organizational problem created when the secretary of war, on October 19, 1863, forbade an army to interfere with the running of trains. "Yet their movements when near the front," maintained Easton, "were so frequently dependent upon those of the army that I found it necessary to telegraph frequently on this subject, and the commanding general made me the medium of most of his instructions to the superintendent and to the construction corps."

Sherman's practice of giving Easton his full plan of operations, and his appointment of Easton as a staff officer with full authority to co-ordinate the parts of the supply organization and link them with the operational planning, was, on the other hand, an important gesture toward a modern staff organization. But there is no evidence that Easton continued this structure down the line. Rather, he seemed reluctant to delegate the authority Sherman vested in him, running everywhere to do the job himself. Reports suggest that Sherman may have encouraged this, he himself shrinking from a broad delegation of authority. Again, the problem was the pull of traditional structures, perhaps accentuated by personality.

More troubles arose with the army at rest in Atlanta and unable to meet its needs by foraging. The railroad from Chattanooga couldn't do the job because raids and damage slowed down supply. Sherman or-dered Easton personally to supervise repairs. In the meantime, Easton collected all the teams that could be spared at Chattanooga to move grain between the damaged sections. The repairs completed, the ad-ministration of the railroad ran into other difficulties in preparing Sher-man for the march to the coast. As Sherman stripped down his army, he ordered everything not needed back to Chattanooga. At the same time, he returned a corps to Nashville by train, thus occupying a large part of the transportation. To compound Sherman's contribution to the confusion, either poor administration or a mixup owing to inade-quate staff procedures fouled up supply at the Atlanta end. There were delays in sending back both the sick and wounded and the enormous accumulations at the various depots along the way. Collusion by railroad employees complicated the problem of keeping private goods off cars. But by November 11, Sherman finally was resupplied and ready to begin his march to the sea.[13]

The problem of dealing with the railroads, owing in part to their being beyond his control, was perhaps one factor that encouraged Sher-man eventually to dispense with the service of his mobile railroad supply line. During Sherman's later march from Atlanta to the coast, Meigs originally ordered the Military Railroad Construction Corps to meet him where he emerged. But "as the army moved without depending upon railroad communications, destroying instead of repairing railroads in the march," to quote the slightly perplexed Meigs, he transferred the Construction Corps elsewhere. Meigs seems to have been left out of Sherman's logistical thinking, to say nothing of his plan of campaign.[14]

Sherman's advance to Atlanta was painfully slow. The long move from Chattanooga had nevertheless given him time to experiment and get used to the organizational problems of field supply and transportation for an army of 100,000 men. By the time he reached Atlanta, Sherman probably had acquired a confidence, perhaps lacking when he left Chattanooga, that his army could live off the land if it reverted to a raiding strategy.

Sherman's raid to the sea grew out of circumstances rather than planning. Grant had intended Sherman to link up with Union forces from Mobile to sever the eastern Confederacy from the resources of Alabama and Mississippi. But the collapse of that campaign and a daring counterthrust following the fall of Atlanta by Hood, who had replaced Johnston, led Grant and Sherman to take advantage of their opportunities. When Hood left Sherman's front, Grant persuaded Sherman to pick up his tail and head for the coast, leaving Hood's army behind. Part of the Army of the Cumberland and the Army of the Ohio fell back on interior lines to pursue a defensive strategy against Hood as he wore down his already depleted army in an offensive campaign.

Sherman initially was reluctant to attempt the raid because the Confederates still held Savannah, where he planned to come to the sea for supply. But Grant persuaded him with a plan to capture both Savannah and Wilmington, leaving the Confederates to guess where he was going. Sherman was eager to change his operational strategy.

> Our former labours in North Georgia had demonstrated the truth that no large army, carrying with it the necessary stores and baggage, can overtake and capture an inferior force of the enemy in his own country. Therefore, no alternative was left me but the one I adopted—namely, to divide my forces, and with the one part act offensively against the enemy's resources, while with the other, I should act defensively and invite the enemy to attack, risking the chances of battle.[15]

The raid was to be the vehicle to restore mobility through the principles of diversion, dispersion, and surprise. By October, when Sherman was convinced that Hood had abandoned the force before Atlanta and was heading for his communication link in Alabama on the Blue Mountain Railway, he decided it was feasible to begin his raid without possession of Savannah. "My first objective," stated Sherman, "was—to place my army in the very heart of Georgia, interposing between Macon and Augusta, and obliging the enemy to divide his forces to defend not only those points, but Millen, Savannah, and Charleston."[16]

Sherman would march with approximately 65,000 men for his self-contained raid to Savannah. This included one cavalry division of 5,000 troopers and a reduced artillery contingent of one gun per 1,000 infantry. He reduced his train to approximately 14,500 horses, 19,500 mules, and 2,500 wagons, 1,300 of which were for subsistence and forage. The army carried 5,500 head of cattle on the hoof. Sherman had constantly practiced foraging procedures with his army while at rest in Atlanta.[17] The lowering of the wagon standard from approximately fifty-two to forty wagons per thousand stands out in particular. One is left to speculate on whether Sherman and Easton considered this an absolute reduction, or whether they discovered, through the experience of the march to Atlanta, that a decrease in the size of the army from 100,000 to 65,000 men allowed far more than a proportionate reduction in the transportation system necessary to forage an army's needs.

Sherman loaded his supply train for the movement to Savannah with twenty days' bread, forty days' sugar and coffee, a double allowance of salt for forty days, and three days' forage in grain; he took forty days' supply of beef cattle, more than 5,000 head, on the hoof. Each man carried three days' rations in haversacks. "All were instrumented," noted Sherman, "by a judicious system of foraging, to maintain this order of things as long as possible, living chiefly, if not solely, upon the country, which I knew to abound in corn, sweet potatoes, and meats." The countryside also supplied enough animals to replace most of his army's losses. Sherman did not move into his foraging territory on speculation as to available resources; he had the census statistics showing the produce of every county through which he planned to pass.[18]

For his march to Savannah, Sherman organized his army for foraging in a way made possible in part by the absence of a serious enemy challenge. He spread his troops into four or more columns, fifteen or twenty miles apart. Each column was responsible for its own supply. Foragers covered the intervals "within call and supporting distance of the infantry." Cavalry maintained communications between the columns. The infantry columns marched beside the trains, which provided easy access to the foraged supplies while on the march. Even without serious resistance from an enemy army, the basic organizational problems were immense. But as Sherman noted at the time, "my army has by time and attention acquired too much personal experience and adhesion to disintegrate by foraging or its incident disorganizing tendency."[19]

This organization for foraging forced Sherman to do what a serious enemy challenge would have prevented, namely, to divide his field command by column, retaining command of only one column himself. Sherman gave up on signals communication in offensive operations because of the flat, heavily wooded countryside and the consistent movement of the army. He used signals personnel as staff scouts and couriers and, in particular, to supply information on roads. Close communication between the columns was impossible; but that was a necessary sacrifice for logistical survival.[20]

Sherman's spread-out columns cleared a 60-mile swath from Atlanta to Savannah of all resources. In the process, the invading army severed Confederate railroad connections eastward and westward for over 100 miles. Sherman calculated his impact on the enemy as he concurrently calculated his ability to live off the land. He estimated the cost to the state of Georgia at $100 million, $20 million accruing to the Union, "the remainder simple waste and destruction."[21]

Sherman's army was first resupplied with grain at King's Bridge on the Ogeechie River on December 18. The animals had subsisted on the country twenty-nine days during the march to the coast. They foraged at least 11 million pounds of fodder and hay—plus what the beef cattle consumed. Animals deteriorating from inadequate feed while at rest at Atlanta were in far better shape, according to Easton, when they arrived at Savannah.[22] Losses were heavy when the march began. Animals that survived the early going improved daily and were supplemented by the capture of a superior quality of mule.[23]

Easton was working out an imaginative logistical organization, consolidating observations of ad hoc experiments into a working, if not formal, doctrine for foraging. Out of practical necessity, logistics was organized around the corps, with no attempt to establish centralized staff procedures.

> The management of trains differed somewhat in each corps but I think the best arrangement was where the train of the corps followed immediately after its troops with a strong rear guard, in the following order: First, corps headquarters baggage wagons; second, division headquarters baggage wagons; third, brigade headquarters baggage wagons; fourth, regimental headquarters baggage wagons; fifth, empty wagons to be loaded with forage and other supplies taken from the country, and the proper details for loading them; sixth, ammunition train; seventh, ambulance train; eighth, general supply train. As the empty wagons reached points where forage and other supplies could be obtained, a sufficient number were turned out of the road to take all at the designated place, and so on during the day, until all the empty wagons were loaded. The empty wagons would be loaded by the time the rear of the general supply train came up to them, and they would fall into their proper place in the rear of the general supply train without retarding the march. This arrangement worked well, and is probably as good as any that could be made. As a general thing, the wagons were required

to go but a short distance from the line of march to obtain supplies, there being sufficient nearby. The march proceeded most successfully, there being little resistance from the enemy, and an abundance of food for men and animals being found everywhere until we took position before Savannah.[24]

Traveling over roads "whose condition," to quote one corps commander, "beggars all description," Sherman arrived at Savannah, having lived off the land for twenty-nine days, with more animals, approximately 35,000, and more wagons, approximately 2,700, than when he had left Atlanta.[25] He had marched somewhere between 350 and 550 miles actual distance, varying more or less with the distance covered by particular units. He had averaged between 12 and 15 miles per day.[26]

The problem of being at rest returned when Sherman emerged before the Savannah defenses. He had to remain stationary and suffered a brief shortage of forage while obstructed channels were opened to permit the approach of the supply fleet from Port Royal.[27] Meigs, very much in the dark as to Sherman's logistical organization and somewhat wary of his audacity, expressed concern to Sherman a week before he occupied Savannah that the supply system would not be able to provide sufficient forage if his army rested on the coast. Meigs urged that he move, continuing to feed off the land. He was especially concerned about the shortage of hay, the only item not available in adequate supply. Meigs expressed concern that Sherman strip himself of all horses and mules not absolutely necessary and send them away from the army to forage off the land.[28]

This advice, and the lack of communication that made it necessary, were reflected in the lack of staff coordination between Meigs and Sherman—even allowing for the exceptional circumstances of Sherman's detachment from base. Meigs certainly told Sherman nothing he didn't already know. Sherman reassured Meigs that all was well; he was most aware of the problem of being at rest. He reported his transportation to be in excellent shape; the animals were eating rice straw, which alleviated the shortage of long forage owing to the lack of hay. Sherman informed Meigs that he could continue to supply the army off the land with all the animals that it needed for the forthcoming operation. He requested only that Meigs sustain a small shipment of hay and the allotted grain. His army needed no additional animals or transportation other than a reserve of some 400 or 500 artillery horses, which were not available in sufficient size and weight in the countryside. As a final reassurance, Sherman told Meigs that he intended to keep his artillery to a minimum and to dismount the cavalry if it couldn't remount itself off the land.[29]

Sherman's strategy for the Carolinas campaign was to disguise the destination of his moves so that the enemy could not concentrate and interfere with his foraging and destruction of Confederate resources. He called for Admiral David Dixon Porter, commanding the North Atlantic Blockading Squadron, to "so maneuver as to hold a large portion of the enemy to the seacoast whilst I ravage the interior, and when I do make my appearance, we will make short work of them all." He asked Porter for "two or more points along the coast where I can communicate with you, and where I should have some spare ammunition and provisions in reserve."[30] The Quartermaster Department set up alternate supply depots at Hilton Head, Pensacola, and Port Royal to meet Sherman wherever he might come to the coast. From these bases, the department was to implement Sherman's orders to forward supplies to wherever his army appeared.[31]

The problem of resupplying Sherman's logistical monster while at rest in Savannah delayed departure. Consumption then became an increasing problem. Supplies were belatedly transferred from Pensacola to Savannah, most not arriving in time to be used. Shipments from the North also were slow to arrive. Forage resupply was especially slow. Sherman's army did not get its daily needs until January 10, almost three weeks after Savannah's occupation on December 21. The animals had one very bad week when they subsisted on rice straw in the vicinity. Though a good short-term substitute as long forage, it needed to be supplemented by hay to sustain the animals for any length of time.[32] The insatiable appetite of Sherman's army at rest devoured all around it. Eating a store of sixty days' rations for 70,000 men, the army had to go to daily supply.[33]

By January 15, Sherman's army was sufficiently resupplied to move. But the left and right wings encountered a problem created by the overflowing of the low country by heavy rains. The right wing couldn't depart until January 29, the left wing until February 1. They sat consuming provisions while the supply system attempted to reach them by light draft steamers. On departure, they were somewhat short of full supply. The only serious shortage was a lack of axle grease, a dilemma Easton partially remedied by confiscating tar from the Savannah Gas Company and mixing it with flour to produce, he noted, "a suitable substitute."[34] Sherman marched with 65,000 men. He cut another 4,000 animals by reducing still further his cavalry and artillery.[35] He had approximately 35,000 animals and 2,700 wagons, a slight increase over his standard for the march to Savannah.[36]

Sherman, who joined his army in the field on January 22, had Easton prepare resupply depots wherever he might come to the coast. He gave

Easton Georgetown, Wilmington, Morehead City, and possibly Charleston as potential destinations. Easton inspected the designated harbors and had the bulk of the vessels that were sitting laden with supplies at Hilton Head in the Savannah River sent to Morehead City. Some vessels containing forage and subsistence were left at Hilton Head; some were sent into the Cape Fear River so as to be prepared for the possibility of the army's coming to the coast at Charleston, Georgetown, or Wilmington.

Easton, however, confident of Sherman's ability to reach Goldsboro, began preparations for a depot at Morehead City. He built the depot and the wharfs from scratch. Easton got General Schofield to supply 1,500 men for working parties and guards; he bought the few thousand feet of lumber available and brought timber from Savannah to set up a sawmill; he got carpenters, mechanics, and laborers—and a supply of felt roofing—from New York and Washington. "The railroad being entirely occupied in forwarding rails and other materials used by the construction corps, I shipped large quantities of stores to New Berne in light draft steamers through Hatteras Inlet and Pimlico Sound . . . , and thence up the Neuse River to the bridge opposite Kinston."[37]

Joseph Johnston, meanwhile, was suffering the agony of an organizational perfectionist in an imperfect world. With a disposition to over-organization, Johnston put together a large staff system and personally attended to everything from logistics, to artillery tactics, to the details of entrenchment, to the whiskey ration.[38] Advocates of an offensive strategy criticized Johnston for his obsession with organization at the cost of fighting. On July 17 they finally succeeded in replacing him with General John B. Hood. Hood's address to the army was an extraordinary romantic throwback to an era that existing reality had left behind:

> Soldiers: Experience has proved to you that safety in time of battle consists in getting into close quarters with your enemy. Guns and colours are the only unerring indications of victory. The valour of troops is easily estimated, too, by the number of these secured. If your enemy be allowed to continue the operation of flanking you out of position, our cause is in peril. Your recent brilliant success proves the ability to prevent it. You have but to will it, and God will grant us the victory your commander and country so confidently expect.

Hood accompanied his stinging critique of Johnston's strategic and tactical principles by dismantling, in his first order upon succeeding to command, the staff Johnston had assembled to administer the details of army organization.[39]

Hood, however, quickly found himself preoccupied with the organizational realities, particularly in field transportation and supply, that his romantic élan had blurred. He reduced the wagon standard as he, like Johnston, encountered the problem of living off his own people.[40] Hood was greatly concerned about his troops' plundering the population. His field orders reduced but did not end the problem. There are continuing reports of incidents and of Hood's concern.[41] Of greater concern was the deterioration of field transportation that made it impossible to forage the thinly settled countryside or to carry adequate supplies if available. In a general order of August 9, Hood reduced the transportation standard to approximately nineteen wagons per 1,000 men. He added to the standard slightly on August 14 and again on August 20, but on November 3 he reduced it to approximately sixteen wagons per 1,000 men.[42]

Hood's two-month campaign against Sherman's communications after Sherman captured Atlanta was remarkable. To move an army that at the beginning numbered 40,000 men with such limited field transportation was a desperate gamble in the art of living off the land. Hood's intention was to place his army on Sherman's communications and draw supplies from the West Point and Montgomery Railroad. He would then move to his other line of supply on the railroad from Blue Mountain to Selma. As Hattaway and Jones observe, Hood's raid was in the growing tradition of Lee's at Antietam, Bragg's Kentucky raid, and Rosecrans's Tullahoma and Chattanooga maneuvers. As they further observe, by establishing communications with the Blue Mountain Railroad, Hood had the capacity to remain in the country and turn his raid into a penetration reminiscent of McClellan's position on the Peninsula and Grant's below Vicksburg.[43]

The flaw in the strategy was that the removal of Hood from his front allowed Sherman a relatively unobstructed passage for his raid to Savannah. It was when Grant and Sherman saw that Hood was not returning but was making for the Federal communication link on the Blue Mountain Railroad that Sherman moved. Hood, meanwhile, seriously weakened his army in futile assaults against the defensive positions of Schofield's army of 32,000 men at Franklin, Tennessee. The Confederate offensive came to an end at Nashville when the combined forces of Thomas and Schofield defeated Hood's outnumbered and weary army—the last army with the strength to retard Sherman's advance.

Following Hood's desperate and self-destructive resort to an offensive strategy, Joseph Johnston would finally return on February 23 to play out to the end the strategy that he had begun. When Lee, on February 25, ordered Johnston to concentrate all available forces against

Sherman, Johnston stuck to his original position. He rejected Lee's order on the grounds that the troops available were not adequate to the task. On March 11, Johnston reiterated this strategy. He told Lee that he would not fight Sherman's concentrated army. Only if he could find the enemy's forces divided would he attack.[44]

Johnston resumed command of an army of approximately 25,000 men. Half were without adequate transportation to move away from the railroad. Many South Carolina militia and reserves, Johnston knew, would not stay with the army beyond South Carolina. He subsequently decided that his best strategy would be to keep moving to prevent the enemy from concentrating against his shrinking numbers. When Bragg's small force joined Johnston on March 18, the combined strength of their infantry was only 18,000 men. Desertions were heavy. By March 31, infantry numbered only 16,000 men plus 5,000 cavalry. On April 17, strength was down to 15,000 men.

"The Federal army," observed Johnston, "is within the triangle formed by the three bodies of our infantry. It can therefore prevent their concentration or compel them to unite in its rear by keeping on its way without loss of time." Johnston complained to Lee that he did not know how he could follow orders to "remove or destroy all kinds of supplies on the enemy's route." Putting his finger on the great irony that made Sherman's foraging and logistical attrition possible, while leaving the Confederate army logistically impoverished, Johnston complained: "We are compelled to leave in the houses of the inhabitants the food necessary for their subsistence, but the U.S. officers feel no such obligations." Involuntary impressment of animals was rejected by the Confederate Congress, and the Quartermaster Department lacked the funds to buy what they could not impress. The logistical circle closed to strangle Johnston's army.[45]

While Easton exploited the sea and rivers, Sherman, pushing the dwindling Confederate forces before him, devastated the land and lived off his takings. His raid effectively had turned into a penetration. He demonstrated that he could dominate Georgia and the Carolinas, while the Confederacy could not challenge his army directly or threaten his logistics. On March 23, almost two months after he had left Savannah, Sherman emerged at Goldsboro, North Carolina. He had traveled from 400 to 500 actual miles, varying with the units of his army, at an average of from 8 to 10 miles per day. For actual marching days, which averaged approximately forty-six per division, he averaged about 9 to 10 miles per day. The daily march ranged from 5 or 6 to 17 or 18 miles per day. Marches of 15 miles a day were common; marches from 16 to 18 miles infrequent; marches at the lower end of performance quite common.[46] Marching conditions were horrendous, with heavy rains adding to difficulties worse than those on the march to Savannah. Some idea of the routine necessary to support the troops and their logistical weight is gathered from the itinerary of one division for the month of March alone. While marching 188 miles, the division corduroyed 10,208 yards of road and 150,787 yards of side road for infantry.[47]

Sherman's troops arrived literally in threads, their clothing worn out because, to quote Sherman, "we have been in water half the time since leaving Savannah." The army, though out of flour, bread, sugar, and coffee, had everything else but clothes in abundance. But field transportation came through unscathed. "We have not lost a wagon," Sherman reported, "and our animals are in good condition."[48] Nevertheless, Sherman did reorganize his logistics in an area where flexibility was leading to disorder. He evidently had decided, from the experience of the Carolinas campaign, that he needed tighter organizational and command procedures for foraging. He consequently ordered that all foraging be done by regiments or brigades with officers present. Corps or division commanders were to detail the units. The engineer regiment and other detachments could send details, but never fewer than two companies with their officers. The latter were ordered when practicable to attach themselves to regular detailed foraging regiments or brigades. Officers in charge of foraging were ordered always to have written authority. The division commander was to make special provision for his artillery by attaching its foraging details to a regular party.[49]

The change from Easton's report of earlier foraging practice is significant. It called first for a closer subordination of foraging to regular units, contrasted to more independent foraging columns operating out of the train. Second, foraging was made subject to tight, hierarchical command procedures from corps and divisional through regimental, brigade, and company levels. The latter reform replaced an improvised command structure for foraging parties that may have separated the activities of line organization from the trains. In part the reorganization was an attempt to keep the lawless independent activities of the "bummers," who had emerged during the march to Atlanta, under control. But the principal motive seems to have been an interest in tighter organization for its own sake.

Sherman's field order also reduced animal standards. When the commands of Generals Schofield and Alfred Terry joined Sherman at Goldsboro, they brought his total strength to 95,000 men. Yet, the army had only 23,000 mules and 10,500 horses, approximately the same number as when it had left Savannah with only 65,000 men. This was a reduction from a standard of about 2 to about 3 men per animal.

While Easton built the animal supply back up, his last figure on wagons is approximately 3,100, compared to the 2,500 wagons on the march to Savannah. This was a new standard for Sherman, down to 33 from 40 wagons per thousand.[50] And, as noted, a larger army required more than a proportional increase in wagons for a comparable foraging area. The fact that an adequate supply of everything was coming in from the North did reduce foraging needs—which leaves one to speculate whether Sherman had decided from the Carolinas campaign that his field supply and transportation could be trimmed, or whether the security of no opposition was the deciding factor. But Sherman indicated that he realized from experience that, even without opposition, supply was a problem, and that he had to move and forage to resolve it.[51]

There continued to be foul-ups caused by inadequate staff procedures. There was a mistake, for example, in sending locomotives and cars of 5-foot gauge for the 4-foot, 8½-inch gauge available. Easton consequently had only sixty cars and four engines, which he tightly regulated for supply use. As Sherman put it: "Judicious and efficient use did the job." Though sometimes weak on staff procedures, Sherman's army was strong on making the best of a chaotic situation.

But generally, resupply went well. Easton also had provisions shipped by way of Hatteras Inlet. He sent vessels under sail with grain to Hatteras Inlet, then by steamer to New Berne. From there they went by river steamer and a few barges to Kinston and Neuse River Bridge to connect with Sherman's supply train. Easton had the army resupplied and ready to go in the remarkable time of sixteen days. On April 10, Sherman was ready to move once again. He occupied Raleigh on April 13. Receiving news of Lee's capitulation, Joseph Johnston surrendered on April 14.[52] Sherman's army routinely prepared for its last move. The Military Railroad Construction Corps completed the line to Raleigh on April 18. They captured more cars and engines, for a total of 120 cars with enough engines to move them. When Sherman's army marched on April 30, it left the cavalry and two corps, reducing its bulk from an effective strength on April 18 of 103,000 men. The army arrived at Manchester, Virginia, and refilled its wagons on May 8, 9, and 10. It continued on to Alexandria, marching out of the war in the logistical style with which Sherman had fought.[53] Sherman left a heritage of successful experimentation in logistical organization for the strategic offensive in mid-nineteenth-century warfare; a heritage at the historical roots of modern warfare.

As the new technology of modern warfare brought tactical stalemate, Sherman, with Grant's active involvement, gave the most spectacular display of the growing search for an alternative through strategic maneuver. In a spirit that revived the ghost of the French Revolutionary reformer Bourcet, Sherman and Grant exploited diversion, dispersion, and surprise to pursue successfully a modern total-war strategy of exhaustion against the enemy's resources, communications, and will. The vehicle that made it possible was the Union development of field transportation and supply organization. While World War I would express the side of emerging modern warfare that drifted toward positional stalemate and trench warfare, Sherman's example would inform such influential strategists of mobility and maneuver for the World War II generation as his British biographer, B. H. Liddell Hart. The German armies of World War II, which learned so much about mobility and maneuver from Liddell Hart and which, except for the panzer and other elite motorized units, moved with horse-drawn transportation, were the descendants of Sherman's army marching through Georgia and the Carolinas.[54]

TACTICS

The fighting from Chattanooga to Bentonville consolidated the pattern of trench warfare that had emerged by the end of 1863. The most significant development was Sherman's habitual use of offensive entrenchments in assault tactics, which he introduced in 1863. The Army of the Potomac began the same regular practice with the Battle of Cold Harbor. Sherman continued to show a distinct aversion to the frontal assault. But in his strategy of holding the enemy on his front while he maneuvered and scoured the countryside, he developed aggressive holding tactics. He routinely advanced in a heavy skirmish line closer and closer to the enemy's entrenched defensive positions, covering each stage of the advance by fortification until he held the enemy only a few hundred yards from his entrenched lines.

Sherman's most spectacular offensive entrenchment was during his one major assault in the final two years of the war. His explanation in the immediate aftermath of this, by his admission, "disastrous" attack during the Battle of Kennesaw Mountain in mid-June, 1864, also revealed the balance between his cautious and aggressive tendencies. On the one hand, Sherman held the frontal assault in reserve; on the other, he feared that passive defensive tactics would have a dangerous effect on the attitude of his officers. Sherman stated that he had attacked Johnston's strongly entrenched positions because both Johnston and his own officers expected him not to attack, but to attempt a turning movement. Sherman decided to convince both that "an army to be efficient must not settle down to a single mode of offense, but must be prepared to execute any plan which promises success. I wanted, therefore, for moral effect to make a successful assault against the enemy behind his breast-works, and resolved to attempt it at that point where success would give the largest fruits of victory." Even while accepting full responsibility for what he acknowledged was a disaster costing in excess of 3,000 casualties with little loss to the enemy, Sherman claimed that the assault nevertheless "produced good fruits, as it demonstrated to General Johnston that I would assault and that boldly."[55] But Sherman was continuing to develop a more basic balance between offensive and defensive tactics. Despite his slaughter on the Confederate fortifications, he did not retreat. He entrenched his failed attack and "held ground so close to the enemy's parapets that he could not show a hand above them."[56] These tactics extended the pattern Sherman had set in the action leading to the battle, during which he slowly advanced by skirmish line from one entrenched position to another, closer and closer to Johnston's entrenchments.[57]

The tactical approach to the Confederate works protecting Atlanta may have introduced one more innovation. Sherman rejected a siege. Instead, he approached in skirmish line increasingly closer to the enemy works. The line protected itself by digging individual rifle pits. Working parties then joined the chain of pits into an ordinary rifle trench, which thereafter they strengthened. By this means, Sherman pushed his infantry to within 200 yards of the enemy's entrenchments.[58] The special attention given to this digging of rifle pits and joining them into trenches by Sherman's tactically observant chief engineer, Captain Orlando Poe, suggests that this innovation was meant to hold the enemy in place rather than overrun him with frontal assaults.[59]

When necessary, Sherman would go over the top. He did so in his successful attack on the undermanned Fort McAlister in the Savannah defenses, an attack necessary to clear the way for supplies from the Union fleet.[60] Otherwise, tactics at Savannah followed the pattern of Atlanta. Sherman's troups connected rifle pits, which they pushed to within 150 to 200 yards of the enemy defenses.[61] Sherman also used a novel balance of radical skirmish order and line and column. He moved his troops into entrenched positions deployed as skirmishers. But when he attacked, he did so in column or successive lines. At Kennesaw Mountain he deployed one of his three attacking divisions in column, with the other two in successive lines. They attacked on a very narrow front with great depth, owing to the regiments being under strength and the number of regiments per brigade consequently increased.[62] Sherman repeated this attack pattern on the few subsequent occasions where he launched open assaults.[63]

Sherman's formal deployment in open assault was probably motivated by considerations of discipline and tactical control. He was aware that the loose order of the skirmish line reduced both. But citing terrain, the rifled musket, and the organizational advantage for the independent and hard-to-discipline citizen soldier, he used the heavy skirmish line more extensively in 1864–65 than any other Civil War commander. In his integration of traditional with innovational forms, Sherman reached a practical synthesis for his cautious yet aggressive tactical outlook under changing conditions of warfare.[64] When Sherman changed his strategy to emphasize the destruction of Johnston's army near Raleigh—in response to Lee's being bottled up and near defeat at Petersburg—his tactics remained the same. In the Battle of Bentonville, a heavy skirmish line entrenched positions gained, forming at least two and as many as four lines of offensive entrenchments along the entire front.[65]

The increasing scale of entrenchment was evident on the march through the South. There is evidence that Sherman began using as many as four lines of works during the Carolinas campaign.[66] During the fighting before Atlanta, after a bad experience with Hardee's corps, Union troops began to entrench the rear as well as the front of their lines.[67] The role played by troops and the correspondingly decreasing role by engineers in laying out the line of entrenchment reflected the development of routine expertise. The reports of Sherman and his chief engineer, Poe, suggested that the engineers selected the line and directed entrenchment on the march to Atlanta.[68] But thereafter the troops routinely performed this function. "The constant practice of our troops has made them tolerably good judges of what constitutes a good defensive line, and lightened the labours of the engineer staff very materially," observed Poe. "I was frequently surprised by the admirable location of rifle trenches and the ingenious means adopted to put themselves under cover."

Poe admired one particularly clever engineering innovation by the troops: the "head-log." Invented to cope with the deadly accuracy of sharpshooters, the head-log, observed Poe, was a

> stout log, of hard wood if possible, which is cut as long as possible and laid upon blocks placed on the superior slope for a foot or two outside the interior crest. The blocks supporting the 'head-log' raise it sufficiently from the parapet to allow the musket to pass through underneath it and steady aim to be taken, while the log covers the head from the enemy's fire. Frequently, the blocks are replaced by skids, which rest on

the ground in rear of the trench, so that if the 'head-log' is knocked off the parapet by artillery fire, it rolls along these skids to the rear without injuring anybody. I examined many miles of these 'head-logs' without finding any indication that their use had been otherwise than advantageous.[69]

The independence of the soldiers grew in part from the ad hoc nature of engineering organization. Yet even with the comparatively well-organized and adequately staffed engineering structure of the Army of the Potomac, as noted, the troops began to select the line and entrench independently by Cold Harbor.

Sherman nevertheless lacked the organization to do what was reasonably necessary. As noted, the first regular engineering regiment did not join the Army of the Tennessee until August 31, 1864.[70] The Army of the Cumberland had an engineer officer detailed from the ranks for each corps, each division, and nearly every brigade. Not until May did it get a regular engineer officer. Previously the chief engineer was a captain originally commissioned in engineering who was detailed from the line for temporary duty. He, in turn, was given permission to organize a volunteer regiment. With the enormous responsibilities this improvised engineering organization assumed during Sherman's 1864–65 campaign, it is understandable that they let the line officers and troops take over entrenchment activity when and where they proved competent.[71]

The infantry war absorbed the cavalry and artillery. Terrain was, of course, part of the reason. But technologically, the infantry continued to assert its tactical dominance. McClellan started the war with four guns per 1,000 men. Sherman reduced his standard from three to two guns per 1,000 men when he started for Atlanta. He left his reserve artillery behind. He had no horse artillery but did organize lightly equipped mounted batteries to accompany the cavalry. There was no siege train. He had some success with the 4½-inch rifled gun using Shenkl projectiles, but the twelve-pounder Napoleon was the mainstay with Sherman's army as elsewhere. Artillery was now established primarily as a defensive weapon in an army that was on the tactical offense.[72]

Union, like Confederate, cavalry and mounted infantry continued to fight for the most part dismounted as skirmishers. They routinely constructed fortifications. There were some anomalous incidents. Brigadier General Judson Kilpatrick, Sherman's cavalry commander, occasionally lapsed back into the cavalry manuals. Near Waynesboro on December 2, 1864, with dismounted skirmishers in front, Kilpatrick attacked Wheeler's dismounted and entrenched Confederate cavalry with

columns of four by battalion—and he was successful. On another occasion, he attacked in line with skirmishers in front. Union cavalry made
a saber charge in pursuit of a retreating enemy near Lovejoy's Station
on November 16, 1864.[73] It is to be remembered that the same Judson
Kilpatrick had earlier in the war ordered a brigade to make a mounted
charge with one-third losses against a position protected by a stone wall.
One can only surmise that Sherman would have been more comfortable
with the tactics of Kilpatrick's innovative tactical opponent, General
Wheeler. But for the most part, Kilpatrick, like Wheeler, fought dismounted in skirmish lines using field fortifications.[74]

The predictability of skilled entrenchment characterized Joseph Johnston's tactics on the strategic defensive.[75] His troops constructed as
many as three lines of field works.[76] Johnston, in his typical meticulous
manner, attended to both the general organization and detail of entrenchment. The engineer officers of each corps were in charge of
entrenchment. They selected the lines and placed each corps in position.[77] Johnston's attention to particulars included elaborate instructions at the beginning of the campaign on the use of entrenching tools,
as well as their transportation and care.[78] He also issued a circular that
detailed the strengthening of redoubts while in the field.[79] Johnston's
attention extended to artillery organization. On April 4, 1864, he issued
specific orders reorganizing the system of evolutions for batteries of
light artillery.[80] The stream of tactical orders suggests that Johnston
either had the disposition of a drill master or believed that constant
attention to tactical detail was the way to maintain discipline—or both.

Hood's brief command led to costly offensive tactics for an already
depleted army.[81] But Hood was an anomaly. Perhaps the most offensively minded commander on either side, he had launched assaults as
a subordinate commander at Gaines Mill, Antietam, and Gettysburg.
As an independent field commander, he had taken the tactical offense
on every occasion possible until Nashville, on which occasion his troops
were too exhausted to take the offensive. In his memoirs, Hood argued
that Johnston's use of the tactical defense had ruined the Army of
Tennessee. Hood was perhaps the most uncompromising advocate of
the orthodox view that entrenchments weakened morale and made troops
cautious.[82] The troops did not like his philosophy, and the large-scale
fraternization even amid the brutality of Hood's tactical style suggested
how warfare had passed by his military world view.[83]

The Confederate cavalry perhaps best displayed the growing intensity of trench warfare. Continuing the pattern he had set in the West
by the end of 1863, Wheeler continued to fight his cavalry in dismounted

skirmish order using field fortification, whether skirmishing independently or in the line. As early as the Atlanta campaign, Wheeler fought his cavalry from behind as many as three successive lines of barricades. In his last major action of the war, he dramatically displayed how cavalry had become tactically integrated with infantry. At Bentonville, while fighting his cavalry dismounted, first on the right, then moving mounted to the left flank, Wheeler constructed a line of breastworks 1,200 yards long. It is fitting to the changing nature of warfare that some of the most vivid description of trench warfare is found in Wheeler's report of cavalry action as fighting came to an end at Bentonville.[84]

Notes

1. Theory, Doctrine, and the Tactical Maze

1. E. M. Lloyd, *A Review of the History of Infantry* (New York: Longman, Green and Co., 1908), p. 214. For the lively debate on Jomini, see B. H. Liddell Hart, *The Ghost of Napoleon* (New Haven: Yale University Press, 1935); Crane Brinton, Gordon Craig, and Felix Gilbert, "Jomini," in Edward Meade Earl, ed., *Makers of Modern Strategy* (Princeton: Princeton University Press, 1960); John R. Elting, "Jomini: Disciple of Napoleon?" *Military Affairs* 28 (Spring, 1964): 17–26; Edward Hagerman, "From Jomini to Dennis Hart Mahan: The Evolution of Trench Warfare and the American Civil War," *Civil War History* 13 (September, 1967): 197–220. Archer Jones, "Jomini and the Strategy of the American Civil War: A Reinterpretation," *Military Affairs* 34 (December, 1970): 127–131; James W. Pohl, "The Influence of Antoine Henri Jomini on Winfield Scott's Campaign in the Mexican War," *Southwestern Historical Quarterly* 77 (1973): 85–110; Joseph L. Harsh, "Battlesword and Rapier: Clausewitz, Jomini, and the American Civil War," *Military Affairs* 38 (December, 1974): 133–138; T. Harry Williams, "The Return of Jomini: Some Thoughts on Recent Civil War Writing," *Military Affairs* 39 (December, 1975): 204–206; Michael Howard, "Jomini and the Classical Tradition in Military Thought," in Michael Howard, ed., *The Theory and Practice of War* (Bloomington and London: Indiana University Press, 1965); Herman Hattaway and Archer Jones, *How the North Won* (Urbana, Chicago, London: University of Illinois Press, 1983), pp. 20–24, nn. 7–9; see also John T. Alger, *Antoine Henri Jomini: A Bibliographic Survey* (West Point: United States Military Academy, 1975). For the development of the Revolutionary tradition in military thought, see Robert S. Quimby's brilliant *The Background of Napoleonic Warfare: The Theory of Military Tactics in Eighteenth Century France* (New York: Columbia University Press, 1957). See also David G. Chandler, *The Campaigns of Napoleon* (New York: Macmillan, 1966).

2. Antoine Henri Jomini, *Summary of the Art of War*, translated by Captain G. H. Mendell and Captain W. P. Craighill (Philadelphia: J. B. Lippincott and Co., 1863), pp. 207, 212, 214. See also pp. 188, 197, 201–202, 204. This work, Jomini's most influential, was first published in English in 1854.

3. For some particularly vivid expressions of Jomini's ambivalence on the tactical defense versus the offense, see *Summary of the Art of War*, pp. 72–74, 298.

4. Francois Gay de Vernon, *A Treatise on the Science of War and Fortification*, 2 vols., translated for use at the U.S. Military Academy by John Michael O'Connor (New York: J. Seymour, 1817), vol. 1, pp. 194–196. See also pp. 241–242.

5. Sidney Forman, *West Point: A History of the United States Military Academy* (New York: Columbia University Press, 1956), pp. 57, 74–90. For the class rank and background of Civil War commanders, see Mark Boatner III, *The Civil War Dictionary* (New York: David McKay Co., 1961). Top-ranking graduates could choose their branch of service. The elite status of the Corps of Engineers and the social prestige of the engineering profession in American society assured

that few who had the choice would choose another branch. For a case study and explanation of a notable exception, see B. H. Liddell Hart, *Sherman* (New York: Dodd, Meade and Company, 1930).

6. A major deficiency in the military engineering curriculum was the lack of any practical training in surveying.

7. For the details of the West Point curriculum and Mahan's courses in particular, see George Peterson Winton, Jr., "Ante-bellum Military Instruction of West Point Officers and Its Influence upon Confederate Military Organization and Operations" (Ph.D. diss., University of South Carolina, 1972), especially pp. 24–25, 77–78, 234; James L. Morrison, Jr., "The U.S. Military Academy, 1833–1866" (Ph.D. diss., Columbia University, 1970), pp. 159–167, 214–216.

8. Thomas F. Griess, "Dennis Hart Mahan: West Point Professor and Advocate of Professionalism, 1830–1871" (Ph.D. diss., Duke University, 1969), pp. 236–237.

9. Charles King, *The True U. S. Grant* (Philadelphia: J. B. Lippincott Co., 1932), pp. 52–53.

10. Frederick Augustus Mahan, "Professor Dennis Hart Mahan," *Professional Memoirs of Corps of Engineers, U.S. Army and Engineer Department-at-Large* (Washington, D.C., 1917), pp. 73–74.

11. For further testimony from Civil War soldiers affirming his influence on professional soldiers and volunteers alike, see Perry David Jamieson, "The Development of Civil War Tactics" (Ph.D. diss. Wayne State University, 1979), p. 35. Hereafter referred to as "Tactics." See also Thomas Vernon Moseley, "Evolution of the American Civil War Infantry Tactics" (Ph.D. diss., University of North Carolina, 1967), p. 58. Hereafter referred to as "Tactics."

12. Mahan expresses these motives behind his thought in his preface to *A Complete Treatise on Field Fortification* (New York: Wiley and Long, 1836). Hereafter referred to as *Field Fortification*.

13. Dennis Hart Mahan, *An Elementary Treatise on Advanced-Guard, Out-Post, and Detachment Service of Troops* (New York: Wiley and Putnam, 1847), pp. 30–31. Hereafter referred to as *Out-Post*. This is a different book from the lithographed textbook of the same title. I make reference only to the former, though a small amount of information on offensive tactics that I have taken from Jamieson, "Tactics," the author derived from the latter. Mahan's analysis of Napoleon's tactics probably came from Jomini.

14. Mahan, *Field Fortification*, p. 14.

15. For the details of the use of skirmishers in relation to the line, see Moseley, "Tactics," p. 320.

16. Mahan, *Field Fortification*, p. xix; Moseley, "Tactics," p. 319.

17. Mahan, *Field Fortification*, pp. 93, 95; Mahan, *Out-Post*, pp. 34, 54–55, 144, 147; Jamieson, "Tactics," pp. 31–34. Mahan extended into a tactical system observations made by Heinrich von Bulow and a British theorist, Colonel George Gauler. As early as 1837, they observed that the rifled musket would result in the increased use of skirmishers in combination with loose order (Moseley, "Tactics," pp. 8–9).

18. For a slightly different reading of Mahan's tactical thought in this respect, see Jamieson, "Tactics," pp. 31–34.

19. The distinction between temporary field fortifications and permanent fortifications is that field fortification comprises "all the daily or momentary works executed in the progress of an army to favour its operation," while

permanent fortification "comprehends all kinds of solid and permanent works used in the construction of strong places, forts, and permanent post." Apart from the above, the principal differences are in size and sophistication of construction. The construction of permanent fortifications requires more time and greater mathematical and engineering skill. Permanent fortifications have a rampart beneath the parapet. Also, masonry walls still used in permanent works are absent in field works. Except for the rampart and masonry wall, the least complex permanent fortification is similar in profile and engineering sophistication to the most complex temporary field works. For an analysis of the various categories of field fortifications ranging from "lines" or "complex entrenchments" to "hasty entrenchments" as presented in American military doctrine, including details of construction and when and where to employ them, see, particularly, Mahan, *Field Fortification*, pp. 9-10, 14-19, 67-68, 75, 106-141; Mahan, *Out-Post*, pp. 90-91, 128-129, 145, 157, 159-160; Gay de Vernon, *Fortification*, pp. 258-259.

20. Gay de Vernon, *Fortification*, vol. 1, pp. 258-259; Mahan, *Field Fortification*, p. 9.

21. Mahan, *Field Fortification*, p. 19.

22. In lines with interval, lunettes or square redouts conventionally were used (ibid., p. 112).

23. Ibid., p. 106.

24. Ibid., pp. 112-113.

25. Ibid., pp. 9-10.

26. Ibid., pp. 111-115.

27. Ibid., pp. 14-15.

28. Ibid., pp. 16-17.

29. Mahan, *Out-Post*, p. 145.

30. Mahan, *Field Fortification*, pp. 112-113.

31. Mahan, *Out-Post*, pp. 128-129.

32. Ibid., pp. 90-91.

33. "Detachments consist of small bodies of troops, composed of one or several arms to which are entrusted some missions, connected with the operations of the main body, but for the most part, performed beyond the sphere of its support" (ibid., p. 117). Mahan stated that in any position taken up for a detachment, cover should be provided for infantry, artillery, and cavalry (ibid., pp. 128-129).

34. Ibid., pp. 117, 128-130. Of considerable significance is Mahan's provision for the entrenchment of the advanced-guard so that "its means of resistance, *whether acting offensively or otherwise,* may be greatly augmented." An advanced-guard is "any body of troops placed between the main force and the presumed direction of the enemy." Though "detached from the main force," it "always acts with reference to it." Tactical doctrine relating to the advanced-guard is particularly significant since that body contains between a third and a fifth of the total force of an army (ibid., pp. 83-84).

35. Ibid., p. 75.

36. Mahan, *Field Fortification*, pp. 67-68.

37. Mahan, *Out-Post*, pp. 157, 159-160.

38. Mahan, *Field Fortification*, p. 141.

39. Ibid., pp. 118-141.

40. For variations on the theme of Mahan's military ideas, see Grady McWhiney

and Perry D. Jamieson, *Attack and Die: Civil War Military Tactics and the Southern Heritage* (University, Ala.: University of Alabama Press, 1982); chap. 2, pp. 28–40. Hereafter referred to as *Attack and Die*; Stephen E. Ambrose, *Duty, Honor, Country: A History of West Point* (Baltimore: Johns Hopkins University Press, 1966); Winton, "Ante-bellum Military Instruction." See also Jamieson, "Tactics."

41. Halleck's lengthy bibliography of recommended works is a useful guide to what was being read at the time in American military circles. Halleck, *Elements of Military Art and Science* (New York: D. Appleton and Co., 1846).

42. Ibid., pp. 148–149, 73–74; Jones, "Jomini and the Strategy of the American Civil War," p. 9; Ambrose, *Duty, Honor, Country*, pp. 101–102; Hattaway and Jones, *How the North Won*, pp. 46–47.

43. James St. Clair Morton, one of the more perceptive American military writers of the post-Jominian generation, made the point that American troops in the Mexican War, including the volunteers, were sufficiently well-drilled to meet the standards of European troops (Morton, *Memoir on American Fortification* [Washington: William A. Harris, 1859], p. 70). The Seminole campaigns and the policing of Indians in the West do not appear to have influenced doctrine for regulars. Whether they influenced partisan warfare is a question worth exploring. Several general histories of the Mexican War in English have followed Otis Singletary's 1960 study *The Mexican War* (Chicago: University of Chicago Press). See Alfred Hoyt Bill, *Rehearsal for Conflict: The War with Mexico, 1846–1848* (New York: Cooper Square, 1969); Rowell S. Ripley, *The War with Mexico* (New York: D. Franklin, 1970); Karl Jack Bauer, *The Mexican War, 1846–1848* (New York: Macmillan, 1974); John Edward Weems, *To Conquer a Peace: The War between the United States and Mexico* (Garden City, N.Y.: Doubleday, 1974); Milton Meltzer, *Bound for the Rio Grande: The Mexican Struggle, 1845–1850* (New York: Knopf, 1974). See also James Norman Schmidt, *The Young Generals* (New York: Putnam, 1968).

44. For lessons learned in the Mexican War respectful of entrenched holding-turning maneuvers as the preferred alternative to the frontal assault, see Richard Allan McCoun, "George Brinton McClellan, from West Point to the Peninsula: The Education of a Soldier and the Conduct of the War" (Master's thesis, California State College, Fullerton, 1973), pp. 6, 10–11, 15–16, 54–98. Hereafter referred to as "McClellan." For emphasis upon the offensive lessons of the War, see Jamieson, "Tactics," pp. 10–11, 15–16; McWhiney and Jamieson, *Attack and Die*, pp. 153–169; Grady McWhiney, *Southerners and Other Americans* (New York: Basic Books, 1973), pp. 61–71; Grady McWhiney, *Braxton Bragg and Confederate Defeat* (New York: Columbia University Press, 1969) pp. 72–73, 89, 227, 271. For a detailed analysis of Mexican War tactics in the context of antebellum tactical thought and organization, see McWhiney and Jamieson, *Attack and Die*, pp. 27–40. For the influence of Antoine Henri Jomini on Winfield Scott's campaign in the Mexican War, see Pohl, "The Influence of Antoine Henry Jomini on Winfield Scott's campaign in the Mexican War."

For memoirs of officers from the Mexican War, see *General Scott and His Staff* (Freeport, N.Y.: Books for Libraries Press, 1970); George B. McClellan, *The Mexican War Diary of George B. McClellan*, edited by William Starr Myers (New York: Da Capo Press, 1972). For "personality and culture" as a factor balancing experience in the determination of tactical preference, the most useful hypotheses are Michael C. C. Adams, *Our Masters the Rebels: A Speculation on Union Military Failure in the East, 1861–1865* (Cambridge: Harvard University

Press, 1978); Thomas Connelly, *The Marble Man: Robert E. Lee and His Image in American Society* (New York: Knopf, 1977); McWhiney and Jamieson, *Attack and Die*, chap. 12, "The Rebels Are Barbarians," pp. 170–191. For my comments on Adams and Connelly, see Edward Hagerman, "Looking for the American Civil War: War, Myth, and Culture," *Armed Forces and Society* 9 (Winter, 1983): 341–347.

45. Bernard and Fawn Brodie, *From Crossbow to H-Bomb* (New York: Dell, 1962), pp. 131–132.

46. J. K. Mahon, "Civil War Infantry Assault Tactics," *Military Affairs* 25 (Summer, 1961): 57; Brodie, *From Crossbow to H-Bomb*, p. 132.

47. Lloyd, *History of Infantry*, pp. 236–237. A survey of ordnance development in the Continental armies is to be found in the report of Major Mordecai, the ordnance expert on the military commission sent to Europe in 1855–1856. 36th Congress, 1st Session, Senate Executive Document, no. 60, 1860.

48. Claud J. K. Fuller, *The Rifled Musket* (Harrisburg, Pa.: Stackpole Co., 1958). Mahon, "Civil War Infantry Assault Tactics," pp. 58–59. See also Allan Nevins, *The War for the Union*, 2 vols. (New York: Charles Scribner's Sons, 1959–60), vol. 1, pp. 342–369; Jack Coggins, *Arms and Equipment of the Civil War* (Garden City, N.Y.: Doubleday and Co., 1962); Steven Ross, *From Flintlock to Rifle: Infantry Tactics, 1740–1866* (Rutherford and London: Fairleigh Dickinson University Press and Associated University Presses, 1979), chap. 5.

49. Lloyd, *History of Infantry*, pp. 236–241.

50. Jomini's article is included as the second appendix to the 1863 edition of Jomini's *Summary of the Art of War*, translated by Mendell and Craighill.

51. Ibid., pp. 347, 355, 359–360. The military history of the Crimean War has attracted considerable attention over the past two decades. In addition to works in Russian, in English there are A. Barker, *The Vainglorious War, 1854–56* (London: Weidenfeld and Nicholson, 1970); R. L. V. Ffrench Blake, *The Crimean War* (London: L. Cooper, 1971); G. A. Embleton, *The Crimean War, 1853–56* (London: Almark Publishing Co., 1975); Denis Judd, *The Crimean War, 1853–56* (London: Hart-Davis, MacGibbon, 1975); John Shelton Curtiss, *Russia's Crimean War* (Durham, N.C.: Duke University Press, 1979). See also Rene Guillemin, *La Guerre de Crimee* (Paris: Éditions France-Empire, 1981).

52. Jay Luvaas, *The Military Legacy of the Civil War* (Chicago: University of Chicago Press, 1959), p. 3.

53. Lloyd, *History of Infantry*, pp. 241–244. There is need for a military history in English of the War of Italian Independence.

54. Ironically, Butterfield led the V Corps, Army of the Potomac, in the most dramatic example of the failure of frontal assault tactics against an entrenched enemy in the Civil War, the assault against Marye's Heights in the Battle of Fredericksburg. What is more ironic, his Fredericksburg attack followed upon the publication of his ideas in the same year.

55. Jamieson, "Tactics," pp. 26, 50–53; Moseley, "Tactics," pp. 277–332.

56. Unrevised editions appeared in 1857, 1860, and 1861.

57. Moseley, "Tactics," pp. 263–276. For complementary material on the tactical ideas of Scott, Hardee, and Casey, see Jamieson, "Tactics"; McWhiney and Jamieson, *Attack and Die*, pp. 48–56; Winton, "Ante-bellum Military Instruction." For details of general tactical instruction at West Point, see ibid., pp. 56–87.

58. The material on cavalry tactics comes largely from Jamieson, "Tactics,"

pp. 60–67. See also McWhiney and Jamieson, *Attack and Die*, pp. 62–67. For the history of early cavalry development in the Civil War, see Thomas F. Thiele, "The Evolution of Cavalry in the American Civil War, 1861–1863" (Ph.D. diss., University of Michigan, 1951). The Mexican War also provided some selective support for the cavalry charge from events during the battles of Churubusco and Reseaca de la Palma.

59. The material on artillery tactics is largely drawn from Jamieson, "Tactics," pp. 54–61; and Vardell E. Nesmith, Jr., "Field Artillery Doctrine, 1861–1905" (Ph.D. diss., Duke University, 1977), hereafter referred to as "Artillery." For details of Davis's deemphasis of field artillery, see Henry J. Hunt, "Artillery," *Papers of the Military Historical Society of Massachusetts* (Boston, 1913), vol. 10, p. 11. See also McWhiney and Jamieson, *Attack and Die*, pp. 59–62, 67–68.

60. For antebellum signals development, see Paul Joseph Scheips, "Albert James Myer, Founder of the Army Signal Corps: A Biographical Study" (Ph.D. diss., American University, 1965). Hereafter referred to as "Myer."

61. Morton, *Memoir on American Fortification*, pp. 37–38.

62. U.S. Senate, *Report of the Secretary of War Communicating the Report of Captain George McClellan*, one of the officers sent to the Seat of War in Europe in 1855 and 1856. Senate Executive Document, no. 1, 35th Congress, Special Session, 1859, pp. 16, 22.

63. Ibid., p. 7.

64. Morton, *Memoir on American Fortification*, pp. 3, 70–71.

65. Ibid., p. 42.

66. Mahan, *A Summary of the Course of Permanent Fortification and the Attack and Defense of Permanent Works* (Richmond: West and Johnston, 1863), pp. 229–230. The text of this book suggests that it was written before the war.

67. Jomini, *Summary of the Art of War*, p. 44.

68. On military organization during the "intellectual renaissance" of the U.S. Army, see William B. Skelton, "The United States Army, 1829–1837: An Institutional History" (Ph.D. diss., Northwestern University, 1968); "Professionalization in the U.S. Army Officer Corps during the Age of Jackson," *Armed Forces and Society* 1 (August, 1975): 443–471; "The Commanding General and the Problem of Command in the United States Army, 1821–1841," *Military Affairs* 34 (December, 1970): 117–122.

2. Tactical and Strategic Organization

1. In 1857, McClellan accepted the post of chief engineer of the Illinois Central Railroad. In 1858 he became its vice-president. In 1860 he accepted the presidency of the Eastern Division of the Ohio and Mississippi Railroad. For the emergence of military professionalism in the period that shaped McClellan's world view, including the ambivalent debate within the professional officer corps over whether it was the responsibility of the professional soldier to play alternate social roles within the preindustrial community tradition or to restrict himself to modern functional definitions of military roles, see Skelton, "The United States Army, 1821–1837," and "Professionalization in the U.S. Army Officers Corps during the Age of Jackson"; Charles F. O'Connell, "The United States Army and the Origins of Modern Management, 1818–1860" (Ph.D. diss., Ohio State University, 1982). For the civilian context of the conflict between identification as a professional military officer and identification with the civilian

profession of civil engineering, see Daniel H. Calhoun, *The American Civil Engineer: Origins and Conflict* (Cambridge, Mass.: Technology Press, Massachusetts Institute of Technology; distributed by Harvard University Press, 1960). For the civilian atmosphere that might persuade a professional officer to opt for a civilian identification, see Charles Robert Kemble, *The Image of the Army Officer in America: Background for Current Views* (Westport, Conn.: Greenwood Press, 1973).

For major contributions to more traditional views of McClellan's motives, and those of other commanders of the Army of the Potomac, see Warren W. Hassler, Jr., *George B. McClellan, Shield of the Union* (Baton Rouge: Louisiana State University Press, 1957); Warren W. Hassler, Jr., *Commanders of the Army of the Potomac* (Baton Rouge: Louisiana State University Press, 1962); Kenneth P. Williams, *Lincoln Finds a General*, 5 vols. (New York: Macmillan, 1949–58); T. Harry Williams, *Lincoln and His Generals* (New York: Knopf, 1952). See also Ludwell Johnson's fiesty essay "Civil War Military History: A Few Revisions in Need of Revision," *Civil War History* 17 (1971): 115–130. For a contemporary view of formal strategic motives, see Hattaway and Jones, *How the North Won*, and their follow-up study on Confederate strategy not yet published when this study was completed.

An interesting speculation on how McClellan's cultural background and his consequent social and political world view influenced his military performance, and that of the eastern command elite in general, is Adams, *Our Masters the Rebels*. For my comments on Adams's thesis, see "Looking for the American Civil War: War, Myth, and Culture." For the broader social and intellectual context that relates to Adams's analysis of the eastern command elite, see George Fredrickson, *The Inner Civil War: Northern Intellectuals and the Crisis of the Union* (New York and Evanston: Harper and Row, 1965). See especially the chapter on the U.S. Sanitary Commission as a potentially subversive cover for the reorganization of power in the Union government by conservative elite interests. McClellan was viewed as a potential instrument for their plans, though there is no evidence he supported them. For a good summary of the debate and literature calling for an appraisal of cultural, social, psychological, and historical change in the friction or fog of what motivated Civil War field commanders, including McClellan, as well as rank and file, see Marvin Cain, "A 'Face of Battle' Needed: An Assessment of Motives and Men in Civil War Historiography," *Civil War History* 28 (1982): 5–28. See also Joseph L. Harsh, "On the McClellan-Go-Round," *Civil War History* 17 (1971): 115–130. There are interesting insights into McClellan's strategic outlook in friction with institutional factors while he was general in chief in Rowena Reed, *Combined Operations in the Civil War* (Annapolis: Naval Institute Press, 1978). This is a pathbreaking study on combined land and water operations at a transitional stage in modern field command.

Valuable studies of McClellan's organizational perspectives are: Jen-Hwa Lee, "The Organization and Administration of the Army of the Potomac under George B. McClellan" (Ph.D. diss., University of Maryland, 1960), hereafter referred to as "McClellan"; McCoun, "McClellan"; David Lawrence Valuska, "The Staff Organization of the Army of the Potomac under General McClellan" (Master's thesis, Louisiana State University, 1966), hereafter referred to as "McClellan."

2. For McClellan's recommendations on staff procedures, see George B. McClellan Papers, ser. A, vol. 11, Library of Congress. For the detailed technical

nature of McClellan's European observation, see his notebooks, ibid., ser. A, vol. 11. For McClellan's participation in the Napoleon Club, see McCoun, "McClellan," pp. 99–104.

3. *The War of the Rebellion: A Compilation of the Official Records of the Union and Confederate Armies*, 128 vols. (Government Printing Office, 1880–1901), ser.4, I, 1024. Hereafter referred to as *OR*.

4. Skelton, "The United States Army, 1821–1837," pp. 391–405; E. G. Campbell, "Railroads in National Defense, 1828–1848," *Mississippi Valley Historical Review* 27 (1940); see also Forest G. Hill, *Roads, Rails, and Waterways: The Army Engineers and Early Transportation* (Norman: University of Oklahoma Press, 1957).

5. O'Connell, "The United States Army and the Origins of Modern Management," sees a significant transfer of organizational models from the army to railroad management. Alfred D. Chandler, Jr., and Stephen Salzburg, in "The Railroads: Innovation in Modern Business Administration," in Bruce Mazlish, ed., *The Railroad and the Space Program: An Exercise in Historical Analogy* (Cambridge, Mass.: MIT Press, 1965), see little influence other than the contribution of Academy-educated analytical minds who worked out railroad problems as railroad problems. I draw my conclusions about the limited organizational world view of the antebellum army and railroad organization from data in O'Connell's study that the author seems to interpret somewhat differently, though the difference may be more of definition with respect to the nature of modern bureaucratic organization than of content as to what happened. On the emergence of professional management in the antebellum railroad industry, see also Alfred D. Chandler, Jr., *Henry Varnum Poor: Business Editor, Analyst, and Reformer* (Cambridge, Mass.: Harvard University Press, 1962), and Alfred Chandler, Jr., *The Invisible Hand: The Managerial Revolution in American Business* (Cambridge, Mass.: Belknap Press of Harvard University Press, 1977).

6. *OR*, ser. 1, II, 199, 202, 205–206. McClellan also repeated the qualified support of volunteers that he derived from the Mexican War: "The conduct of the volunteers was unexceptionable—all they require to make them good and reliable soldiers is a little more drill and discipline" (ibid., pp. 207–208). Rosecrans, who graduated fifth in his 1842 West Point class of fifty-six, was also an instructor at West Point and worked as a civilian engineer and architect.

7. Ibid., pp. 302, 332, 334–335, 374.

8. *OR*, ser. 3, III, 975. Rosecrans followed up this experience by using the telegraph again in September, 1861 (ibid.).

9. For the conflict between social and political attitudes and military discipline and training, see Fred Albert Shannon, *The Organization and Administration of the Union Army, 1861–1865*, 2 vols. (Cleveland: Arthur H. Clark Co., 1928), "The States-Rights Principle Applied to the Army," vol. 1, pp. 15–53; "The Evolution of Discipline," vol. 1, pp. 151–195; Allan Nevins, *The War for the Union: The Improvised War, 1861–1862* (New York: Charles Scribner's Sons, 1959–1960), chap. 9, "The Greenhorn Armies," vol. 1, pp. 163–180; Francois Ferdinand Phillipe Louis Marie d'Orleans, Prince de Joinville, *The Army of the Potomac: Its Organization, Its Commander, and Its Campaign*, translated from the French by William Henry Hurlbert (New York: A. D. F. Randolph, 1862), pp. 14–16; Philippe Regis Denis de Keredern, Comte de Trobriand, *Four Years with the Army of the Potomac*, translated from the French by George K. Dauchy (Ticknor and Co., 1889), pp. 63, 89, 119, 125; Augustus Louis Chetlain, *Recollections of Seventy Years* (Galena: Gazette Publishing Co., 1899); Louis Philippe Albert d'Orleans,

Comte de Paris, *History of the Civil War in America*, translated from the French by L. F. Fasistro, edited by Henry Coppee (Philadelphia, 1875–1888), vol. 1, pp. 176–177; T. W. Higginson, "Regular and Volunteer Officers," *Atlantic Monthly* 14 (September, 1864): 348–357; C. C. Buell and R. U. Johnson, eds., *Battles and Leaders of the Civil War*, 4 vols. (New York: Century Co., 1884–1888), vol. 1, pp. 267–271, hereafter referred to as *B & L*; George B. McClellan, *McClellan's Own Story* (New York: Charles L. Webster and Co., 1887), pp. 97, 100, 385. Hereafter referred to as *Own Story*. Studies of McClellan's early organizational behavior are the previously referred-to studies by Jen-Hwa Lee, McCoun, and Valuska.

10. McClellan, *Own Story*, p. 120.

11. For the early distribution of engineering officers, see chapter nine.

12. For McClellan's problems and the related details of engineering organization, see *OR*, ser. 1, V, 25, 895, 908; ibid., ser. 3, I, 397, 401–402; ibid., II, 279–280, 762–763; ibid., III, 963; ibid., V, 162; ibid., ser. 4, II, 259, also ibid., ser. 1, X, 11, 65, 678, 699. For McClellan's plans to carry an adequate supply of entrenching tools, see ibid., p. 12.

For a delightfully biased contemporary chronicle of reservations about the Corps of Engineers as a defensive-minded elite that should be discouraged from entrenchment activity, see John J. Lenney, *Caste System in the American Army: A Study of the Corps of Engineers and Their West Point System* (New York: Greenberg, 1949). Gideon Welles's running commentary on this theme in his *Diary* represents a point of view from a significant presidential advisor. General Richard Taylor, the distinguished, intelligent amateur soldier who rose to be a lieutenant general in the Confederate army, took this prejudice to the extreme of trying to make a case against Lee in support of his contention that the Corps of Engineers left American officers unfit for command, particularly in offensive warfare (Richard Taylor, *Destruction and Reconstruction*, edited by Charles P. Roland [Waltham, Mass.: Blaisdell Publishing Co., 1968], pp. 90–92). There was a tactical attitude that reappeared within military culture and among politicians that entrenchment encouraged undue caution and destroyed the discipline, hence offensive initiative and ability, of green troops. For some political variations on this theme, see T. Harry Williams, "The Attack upon West Point during the Civil War," *Mississippi Valley Historical Review* 25 (March, 1939).

13. Jamieson, "Tactics," pp. 55–56; Arthur L. Wagner, *Organization and Tactics*, 2d ed. (London: W. H. Allan and Co., 1894).

14. Nesmith, "Artillery," p. 27.

15. For signals development in the Union Army, see Scheips, "Myer"; Scheips, "Union Signal Communications: Innovation and Conflict." See also George Raynor Thompson, "Civil War Signals," *Military Affairs* 18 (Winter, 1954): 188–201; J. Willard Brown, *The Signal Corps, U.S.A. in the War of the Rebellion* (Boston: U.S. Veterans Signal Corps Association, 1896). Brown drew heavily from Myer's unpublished "Report of the Operations and Duties of the Signal Department of the Army, 1860–1865"; Max L. Marshall, ed., *The Story of the U.S. Army Signal Corps* (New York: Franklin Watts, 1965); Lester L. Swift, "The Recollections of a Signal Officer, *Civil War History* 9 (1963): 36–55; William R. Plum, *The Military Telegraph during the Civil War in the United States*, 2 vols. (Chicago: Jansen, McClury and Co., 1882). Hereafter referred to as *Military Telegraph*. For the organization and procedure of the courier service in both the Union and Confederate armies—the alternative to signals—see the various editions of the *United States Army Regulations*. See also John Alan English, "Confederate Field Communications" (Master's thesis, Duke University, 1964).

16. For the history of nineteenth-century experiments in military signals, see Scheips, "Myer," pp. 355–356; Plum, *Military Telegraph*, vol. 1, pp. 24–26, 28–29, 62–63, 73–76.

17. *OR*, ser. 3, IV, 818–841. The West Point course in signaling while it existed included instruction in drill and management, signal parties, theory and practice of aerial and electric telegraphy, and practice with the field line.

18. *OR*, ser. 4, I, 672.

19. *OR*, ser. 3, I, 12.

20. Ibid., II, 544, 654–655, 671–672, 797–798. For the application of modern standards of animal nutrition, see John G. Moore, "Mobility and Strategy in the Civil War," *Military Affairs* 24 (Summer, 1960): 71.

21. For the statistical analysis, see Moore, ibid. Moore gives nine pounds as army regulation. Quartermaster records indicate that ten pounds was the usual allotment for mules.

22. For Meigs's early advocacy of the Napoleonic standard on October 9, 1862, see *OR*, ser. 3, II, 655. See Moore's mathematical analysis of the escalating increase in wagon, hence animal, requirements with the increased radius of the area needed for foraging in the context of comparative needs in Napoleonic France and the Civil War campaigning areas (Moore, "Mobility and Strategy in the Civil War"). For comparative Civil War and Napoleonic ration standards, see Hattaway and Jones, *How the North Won*, p. 141.

23. McClellan, *Own Story*, pp. 198–199. For a general survey of quartermaster and subsistence organization during the Civil War, see Erna Risch, *Quartermaster Support of the Army: A History of the Corps, 1775–1939* (Washington: Quartermaster Historian's Office, Office of the Quartermaster General, 1962). For a general history of logistics, see Martin Van Creveld, *Supplying War: Logistics from Wallenstein to Patton* (Cambridge, London, New York, Melbourne: Cambridge University Press, 1977).

24. Records of the Office of the Quartermaster General, Record Group 92, *U.S. War Department Collection of Union Records*, entry 1317. See especially the report of July 30, 1862, National Archives of the United States. Hereafter referred to as *NA*, RG 92. James Huston, *The Sinews of War: Army Logistics, 1775–1953* (Washington, D.C.: Office of the Chief of Military History, United States Army, 1966), p. 222; Moore, "Mobility and Strategy in the Civil War."

25. Risch, *Quartermaster Support of the Army*, pp. 420–423.

26. *OR*, ser. 3, II, 786–814; ibid., ser. 1, XI, pt. 1, 164–177; 221; ibid., XIX, pt. 1, 8–24, 74–82, 13, 18; McClellan, *Own Story*, p. 256.

27. *OR*, ser. 3, II, 794; Daniel H. Hill, "McClellan's Change of Base and Malvern Hill," *B & L*, vol. 2, p. 394. For studies of Meigs and the Quartermaster Department under his direction, see Russell F. Weigley, *Quartermaster General of the Union Army: A Biography of M. C. Meigs* (New York: Columbia University Press, 1959), and Sherrad E. East, "Montgomery C. Meigs and the Quartermaster Department," *Military Affairs* 26 (1962).

28. *OR*, ser. 3, II, 8, 11, 13, 16–17, 19; McClellan, *Own Story*, p. 125.

29. *OR*, ser. 1, XI, pt. 1, 20, 22; English, "Confederate Field Communications," pp. 99–100.

30. *OR*, ser. 1, XI, pt. 1, 7, 10, 21, 51.

31. The breakdown of weapons in American arsenals at the outbreak of war was as follows: 500,000 flintlock muskets altered to percussion and the 1842 model percussion musket; 42,000 .54-caliber rifled muskets; 35,000 .58-caliber

rifled muskets; 12,500 .58-caliber muzzleloading rifles, model 1855 (a separate weapon from the 1855 model rifled musket. This weapon was heavier and shorter in barrel and stock). Of these rifles and muskets, 119,000 fell into the hands of the Confederacy (Letter from Col. Craig of the Ordnance Department to Hon. J. Holt, Secretary of War, January 21, 1861. Reproduced in Fuller, *The Rifled Musket*, p. 2). For details of the infantry weapons introduced in the 1855 changeover to rifled shoulder arms, see ibid., pp. 10–11.

32. For tactical details of the siege, see the report of Gen. J. G. B. Barnard, Chief Engineer of the Army of the Potomac (*OR*, ser. 1, XI, pt. 1, 17–18).

33. For tactical details of the fighting, see especially ibid., pp. 853, 869, 895, 899–900. See also Shirley M. Gibbs, "Lee's Command Procedures" (Master's thesis, Duke University, 1962); McClellan, *Own Story*, p. 377.

34. *OR*, ser. 1, XI, pt. 1, 344.

35. For McClellan's sense of his predicament in the preceding events as expressed in the official records, see ibid., pp. 48–52, 59–60; ibid., pt. 3, 164.

36. For the following section on McClellan's staff and command procedures on the Peninsula, I am heavily indebted to Jen-Hwa Lee, "McClellan." For the statistics on McClellan's wagon losses during the retreat to the James as well as other supporting material on his logistics, see *OR*, ser. 3, II, 798; ibid., ser. 1, XI, pt. 1, 48–52, 59–60; ibid., pt. 3, 164.

37. For McClellan's praise of the Signal Corps, see *OR*, ser. 1, V, 31. For Lowe's balloons, see his report on the history of balloons from the beginning of the war through his departure after Chancellorsville (*OR*, ser. 3, III, 252–319). See also Professor T. S. C. Lowe, "The Balloons with the Army of the Potomac," Francis Trevelyan Miller, *The Photographic History of the Civil War*, 10 vols., edited by Henry Steele Commager (New York: Yuseloff, 1957), vol. 8, pp. 370–380, and "Observation Balloons in the Battle of Fair Oaks," *Review of Reviews* 43 (1911): 186–190. For the history of Civil War balloons, see F. Stansbury Haydon, *Aeronautics in the Union and Confederate Armies* (Baltimore: Johns Hopkins Press, 1941), and J. David Squires, "Aeronautics in the Civil War," *American Historical Review* 42 (1937): 652–669. See also Russell J. Parkinson, "Politics, Patents, and Planes: Military Aeronautics in the United States, 1863–1907" (Ph.D. diss., Duke University, 1963). See especially pp. 8–12. The quotation is from p. 12. The Confederates attempted to develop balloons, and did put a cotton balloon in the air that made three flights and a silk balloon that was captured after a week of service. Problems of priority and supply discouraged further efforts.

38. Rufus Ingalls used fugitive slaves to construct entrenchments during the siege operations on the Peninsula and the entrenched withdrawal to the James. Northerners tended to break down under the heat and humidity of the Peninsula. Ingalls also impressed fugitive slaves as teamsters. He incorporated over 2,000 of the slaves into the organization of the Army of the Potomac, keeping them with the army after the Peninsula campaign (*OR*, ser. 1, XI, pt. 1, 164–177). This labor foraging was a novel innovation.

39. The Confederate success at Gaines Mill was a special case. The Confederates were actually repulsed at the Federal entrenchments when the Federal cavalry, moving to assault the retreating enemy infantry, charged between the Federal artillery and Federal infantry on the left flank. The heavy infantry fire and cannonading threw the horses into confusion, and the bewildered animals turned about and dashed through the Union batteries. The Union cavalry was

operating in this vicinity contrary to orders, and the Federal gunners, convinced that they were being charged by the enemy, scattered. The Confederate infantry took advantage of the opportunity and, for one of only two times during the Seven Days, successfully breached the Union lines (*OR*, ser. 1, XI, pt. 2, 225–226). The Confederates also breached a flank of the Union line at Frazier's Farm by sheer weight of numbers—three to one in hand-to-hand combat, but McClellan quickly reestablished the line with reserves (ibid., p. 391).

40. For the details of tactics in the Seven Days' Battles, see ibid., pt. 1, 869, 899–900; ibid., pt. 2, 24, 50–51, 222–226, 384–397, 391, 489–497, 565, 836. On the breakdown of Confederate tactical communications, see English, "Confederate Field Communications," pp. 48–59.

41. *OR*, ser. 1, XI, pt. 2, 565, 836.

42. Ibid., p. 54. About the only solace Federal advocates of the frontal assault received during the Peninsula campaign was General Winfield Scott Hancock's successful bayonet attack at Williamsburg, when the Confederate line broke before being engaged, and a Federal bayonet attack at Frazier's Farm (Jamieson, "Tactics," pp. 83–85). For the rare instances of bayonets playing a role in battle, see John Buechler, "Give 'em the Bayonet—A Note on Civil War Mythology," *Civil War History* 7 (1961): 128–132.

43. Jamieson, "Tactics," p. 146.

44. *OR*, ser. 1, XIX, pt. 1, 80–81.

45. Ibid., p. 80.

46. For the data on artillery and cavalry tactics at Antietam, I am heavily indebted to Jamieson, "Tactics," pp. 83–85, 91–93, 146–147, 162, 171–172. For the Delafield Commission report of McClellan, see Senate Executive Document, no. 1, 35th Congress, Special Session, 1859. For Delafield's report, see Senate Executive Document, no. 59, 36th Congress, 1st Session, 1860. For the report of the third member of the commission, Alfred Mordecai, see Senate Executive Document, no. 60, 36th Congress, 1st Session, 1860. For a recent study of the Battle of Antietam, see Stephen Sears, *Landscape Turned Red* (New Haven: Ticknor and Fields, 1983).

47. *OR*, ser. 1, XIX, pt. 1, 67.

48. Comte de Paris, *History of the Civil War in America*, vol. 1, p. 265.

49. *OR*, ser. 1, XIX, pt. 1, 78.

50. Scheips, "Myer," p. 452.

51. McClellan, *Own Story*, pp. 130–131, 198–199; *OR*, ser. 3, II, 371–373, 738; ibid., III, 43; ibid., ser. 1, XIX, pt. 1, 23–24.

52. In his reports, McClellan estimated his strength for the Maryland campaign to be 122,000 aggregate present. Meigs estimated the effective strength of the army at 130,000. Meigs worked out detailed wagon statistics of twenty-nine wagons per 1,000 men, which, adjusted to McClellan's estimate of his numbers, increases to thirty-one wagons per 1,000 men. The problem in wagon supply appears to have been caused by the problem of replacing losses suffered during the retreat to the James (*OR*, ser. 1, XIX, pt. 1, 95–96). For McClellan's and Meigs's dialogue on field transportation and supply needs in the aftermath of Antietam and preparations to advance against Lee, see ibid., ser. 3, II, 671–672, 797–798. For the development of an order of march and the staff system to implement it, see Risch, *Quartermaster Support of the Army*, pp. 425–426.

53. Ibid., XI, pt. 3, 365.

54. Ibid., ser. 3, II, 544, 671–672.

55. Ibid., 671–672.

56. Ibid., ser. 1, XIX, pt. 1, 11; ibid., ser. 3, II, 798. The extra duty personnel of the Army of the Potomac numbered approximately one-sixth the total strength of the army (McClellan, *Own Story*, p. 76).

57. *OR*, ser. 3, II, 654–655.

58. Ibid., p. 797. For details of the field transportation of the Army of the Potomac from the Peninsula to Antietam, see ibid., pp. 798–800.

59. Ibid., ser. 1, XIX, pt. 1, 80.

60. The statistical analysis is taken from Moore, "Mobility and Strategy in the Civil War." For the following table, see ibid., p. 76.

61. Moore quotes nine pounds as army regulation and uses that figure in his calculation. Quartermaster reports indicate the standard actually used was ten pounds.

62. Moore, "Mobility and Strategy in the Civil War," p. 76. For Moore's rationale for his steady states, see ibid., p. 71.

63. *OR*, ser. 1, XIX, pt. 1, 96.

64. Ibid., XXI, 146.

65. Calculated from quartermaster reports (ibid., XXV, pt. 2, 547–562).

66. Ibid., XIX, pt. 1, 8–24, 74–82.

67. Ibid., pp. 13, 18.

68. Ibid., XXI, 147.

69. Risch, *Quartermaster Support of the Army*, pp. 425–426.

70. *OR*, ser. 1, XIX, pt. 1, 96; ibid., XXI, 145–151. See also the fiscal year report ending June 30, 1863, ibid., XIX, pt. 1, 99–106.

71. In my strategic observations, here and elsewhere, I owe a considerable debt to Hattaway and Jones, *How the North Won*. This manuscript was completed prior to the publication of their sequel volume on the Confederacy. Though the focus of this study is the analysis of theory, doctrine, and practice relevant to tactical and strategic organization, I have attempted to relate these organizational developments in a general way to concepts of general strategy and what is alternately called grand tactics or minor, field, or battle strategy. I am disposed to use the latter term. From my own limited research in relation to writings on strategies, I find myself generally in agreement with the analysis of Hattaway and Jones with respect to the "formal" study of strategy in relation to available theory and doctrine—again with due respect for other motives in the friction of strategic decision making. An exception is my conclusion that Grant, in addition to his strategies of maneuver in the West as general in chief through 1864–1865, concurrently pursued a strategy of attrition against Lee's Army of Northern Virginia.

3. More Reorganization

1. *OR*, ser. 1, XXV, pt. 2, 544, 547–562.

2. Ibid., pp. 547–562. In May, 1863, Ingalls expressed puzzlement about the cause of the unusually high loss of horses when there is "no complaint of extraordinary marches or want of forage" (ibid., p. 547). This lends support to speculation that the inadequate nutritional standard for horses indicated by John Moore was the mysterious cause of the heavy losses.

3. A mule's average load was approximately 200 pounds. The average load of a wagon was 2,500 pounds (calculated from reports of corps quartermasters, ibid., pp. 547–562).

4. Ibid., XXVII, pt. 3, 88–89.

5. Ibid., pt. 2, 489–491.

6. Ibid.

7. Ibid., p. 487.

8. Ibid., p. 488.

9. The board recommended ten days' rations of biscuit, coffee, and sugar, rice, and desiccated vegetables. They found that they could not eliminate meat from the diet, and recommended five days' rations of bacon as absolutely necessary (ibid.).

10. Ibid., pp. 487–499. Problems in the excesses and disorganizations of field transportation were of sufficient prominence to produce a published tract from even the quartermaster of a volunteer regiment, the 119th New York Volunteers. He made recommendations based upon usage and his observation of command problems in the wagon trains. His reorganization, he argued, would so reduce the train as to add six miles daily to an average five-day march, in summer increasing the distance traveled from fourteen to seventeen miles and in winter from ten to fifteen miles. The same addition of six miles would apply to three-day forced marches from twenty to twenty-two miles per day (N. S. Dodge, *Hints on Army Transportation* [Albany: Charles van Benthuysen, 1863]). Meigs ordered this tract circulated throughout the Union armies.

11. For entrenching tools, see tables, *OR*, ser. 1, XXVII, pt. 2, 558–559.

12. Ibid., pp. 203–204, 485–491, 544–563; for Ingalls's optimistic summary of the campaign, see ibid., XXVII, pt. 1, 221.

13. Ibid., XXV, pt. 2, 546. For the details of why the pack trains proved unfeasible, see ibid.

14. Ibid., XXVII, pt. 3, 416–417, 473.

15. Ibid., pp. 213, 230–231, 275.

16. Ibid., pt. 1, 221–224. For a supplementary description of the details of how the trains followed the columns, parked behind the lines, and ran material to the front as needed, see the report of Lt. Col. C. W. Tolles, chief quartermaster, XI Corps, Army of the Potomac, for the Chancellorsville campaign (ibid., XXV, pt. 2, 553–555).

17. Ibid., pt. 1, 84; ibid., pt. 2, 311; ibid., pt. 3, 543, 568, 569, 590.

18. Ibid., XXIX, pt. 2, 14–15, 86–87; ibid., XXV, pt. 2, 487–489.

19. Ibid., XXV, pt. 2, 191–192, 195–196, 200–202, 206–208, 251, 262–263, 277; ibid., XXIX, pt. 1, 227–229.

20. Ibid., XXV, pt. 2, pp. 758, 794, 830–832; ibid., pt. 1, 408–411, 426–428, 445, 611, 622–625.

21. Ibid., pt. 1, 611; ibid., pt. 2, 830–832; ibid., XXIX, pt. 1, 227–229.

22. My analysis of staff integration in logistics down through operational planning extends a theme developed by Hattaway and Jones, *How the North Won*, p. 138.

23. *OR*, ser. 1, XXI, 61–87, 148–151, 546; ibid., ser. III, 293–294.

25. *OR*, ser. 1, XXI, 87–89.

26. Ibid., 87–89, 106–107, 552, 578–579, 630, 643, 645, 663, 675, 676; English, "Confederate Field Communications," pp. 106, 111; G. F. R. Henderson, *The Civil War: A Soldier's View*, edited by Jay Luvaas (Chicago: University of Chicago Press, 1958), pp. 42–57; James Longstreet, *From Manassas to Appomattox* (Philadelphia: Lippincott, 1896), p. 300.

27. *OR*, ser. 1, XXI, 151–167; English, "Confederate Field Communications,"

pp. 109–110; Scheips, "Myer," pp. 452–453. Myer attempted to exploit the success of his field telegraph. On Christmas Day, 1862, he put his experts to work "on a plan for a very light and small train to be run by hand, and to be used in battle only" (ibid.).

28. OR, ser. 1, XXI, 47, 91–94, 450, 453, 576, 581–584, 589; ibid., ser. 3, III, 293–294; Southern Historical Society Papers, vol. 10, p. 457; G. W. Redway, Fredericksburg: A Study in War (London: Allen and Unwin, 1906), p. 154; English, "Confederate Field Communications," p. 113.

29. OR, ser. 1, XXV, pt. 1, 218–220; ibid., pt. 2, 323, 326, 333, 336; ibid., ser. 3, III, 313, 959; Plum, Military Telegraph, vol. 2, p. 89; Thompson, "Civil War Signals," p. 198; English, "Confederate Field Communications," pp. 118, 120, 122–123.

30. OR, ser. 1, XXV, pt. 1, 194; ibid., pt. 2, 292; ibid, ser. 3, III, 294, 310–318; English, "Confederate Field Communications," pp. 116–117, 122–123.

31. OR, ser. 1, XXV, pt. 1, 198–199, ibid., pt. 2, 324–326; ibid., ser. 3, III, 313.

32. The opinion of Douglas S. Freeman, Lee's Lieutenants: A Study in Command, 3 vols. (New York: Charles Scribner's Sons, 1942–44), vol. 2, p. 645.

33. For Sedgwick's offensive, see OR, ser. 1, pt. 1, 220–222, 228–229; ibid., pt. 2, 384–385; English, "Confederate Field Communications," pp. 120–123; Brown, Signal Corps, U.S.A., pp. 350–355.

34. OR, ser. 3, III, 960.

35. OR, ser. 1, XXVII, pt. 3, 416–417; ibid., pt. 1, 212.

36. OR, ser. 3, IV, 820–922; Scheips, "Myer," pp. 584, 586, 587, 821, 822. By the end of October, 1863, thirty Signal Corps telegraph trains were in service in the Union army. Seventeen went to the field after May 1, 1863 (ibid., p. 559). For testimonials from corps and divisional commanders of the Army of the Potomac on the value of the Signal Corps' portable train with recommendations for its continuation, see OR, ser. 3, IV, 839–884.

37. The Signal Corps was not officially excluded from telegraph field communication until November 10, 1863 (OR, ser. 3, IV, 821); OR, ser. 1, XXVII, pt. 1, 220–203; Plum, Military Telegraph, vol. 2, p. 122; Thompson, "Civil War Signals," p. 197; English, "Confederate Field Communications," pp. 133–134; B & L, vol. 3, p. 358.

38. Unofficial letter, May 5, 1862, McClellan, Own Story, p. 245.

39. E.g., OR, ser. 1, XXI, 219, 222, 227, 291, 350, 633, 646.

40. Ibid., 106–107, 576, 581, 583–584, 589; Southern Historical Society Papers, vol. 10, p. 457.

41. OR, ser. 1, XXX, 95, 571.

42. Ibid., pp. 634, 666.

43. OR, ser. 1, XXV, pt. 1, 198–199; ibid., pt. 2, 324–326; ibid., ser. 3, III, 313; Freeman, Lee, vol. 3, p. 518.

44. Alexander, Memoirs, pp. 325, 327–328. The entrenching tools, except for those carried by the pioneer troops, were carried in the reserve trains of the corps. There were seven wagons of entrenching tools, each wagon weighing 2,400 pounds (OR, ser. 1, XXV, pt. 2, 559).

45. OR, ser. 1, XXV, pt. 1, 1012.

46. Alexander, Memoirs, p. 325.

47. Atlas, vol. 1, pl. XLI.

48. Alexander, Memoirs, p. 34.

49. Figures calculated from the *Official Records* by Alexander (ibid., pp. 359–362).

50. Jamieson, "Tactics," pp. 99–110.

51. *OR*, ser. 1, XXV, pt. 1, 220, 229; *Atlas*, vol. 1, pl. XII.

52. Alexander, *Memoirs*, pp. 357–358; *Atlas*, vol. 1, pl. XLI.

53. USMA 1850 (2/44); Topographical Engineers.

54. Hooker initially had rejected the recommendation of his chief of artillery, Henry Hunt, to organize the artillery into a single corps. Hooker preferred to retain the traditional dispersal among divisions. The enmity between the two men was such that Hooker curtailed Hunt's authority. He restored Hunt to full authority and reorganized the artillery after its poor performance at Chancellorsville in Hunt's absence (*OR* ser. 1, XXV, pt. 2, 471–472); L. Van Loan Naisawald, *Grape and Cannister: The Story of the Field Artillery of the Army of the Potomac, 1861–1865* (New York: Oxford University Press, 1960), pp. 329–332. For Hunt's biography, see Edward G. Longacre, *A Biography of Henry J. Hunt, Commander of Artillery, Army of the Potomac* (South Brunswick, N.J.: A. S. Barnes, 1977).

55. *OR*, ser. 1, XXIX, pt. 1, 835, 896; *B & L*, vol. 3, pp. 302–303.

56. *OR*, ser. 1, XXVII, pt. 2, 72, 298, 358–359, 411–413, 417, 444–448, 470, 556, 666; ibid., pt. 1, 199–220, 319, 446; W. H. Taylor, *Four Years With General Lee* (New York: D. Appleton and Co., 1877), pp. 99, 101, 103–110; Charles Marshall, *An Aide-de-Camp of Lee* (Boston: Little, Brown and Co., 1927), p. 323; Alexander, *Memoirs*, pp. 393–413; A. L. Long, *Memoirs of Robert E. Lee* (New York, Philadelphia, and Washington: J. M. Stoddart and Co., 1887), p. 294; *B & L*, vol. 3, pp. 312–313, 327. For maps of entrenchments at Gettysburg, see *Atlas*, vol. 1, pl. XL (2).

57. *OR*, ser. 1, XXVII, pt. 2, 72–73; *B & L*, vol. 3, pp. 313–314.

58. *B & L*, vol. 3, p. 315. Italics inserted.

59. Livermore, *Numbers and Losses*, p. 103.

60. Jamieson, "Tactics," pp. 141, 147–148, 152, 162–166, 173; Nesmith, "Artillery," pp. 35–38.

61. *OR*, ser. 1, XXIX, pt. 1, 81–94, 105–107; ibid., pt. 2, 206–208, 251, 252–263, 277.

62. Ibid., pt. 1, 426–428, 592, 622–625; Early, *War between the States*, p. 316.

63. Ibid., p. 611; ibid., pt. 2, 830–832; Taylor, *Lee*, p. 119.

64. *OR*, ser. 1, XXIX, pt. 1, 611, 834; ibid., pt. 2, 830–832; Taylor, *Lee*, pp. 120–121; Arthur L. Wagner, "Hasty Entrenchment in the War of Secession," *Papers of the Military Historical Society of Massachusetts*, 14 vols. (Boston: Houghton Mifflin and Co., 1895–1918), vol. 13 (1913), p. 140.

65. *OR*, ser. 1, XXIX, pt. 1, 698, 829, 835, 896.

4. Élan and Organization

1. Richard Peter Weinert, Jr., "The Confederate Regular Army: 1861–1865" (Master's thesis, American University, 1964), p. 10. An interesting speculation on the impact of the tribal Celtic warrior tradition of the South on Confederate military culture, particularly with respect to its sense of élan, is McWhiney and Jamieson, *Attack and Die*.

2. Winton, "Ante-bellum Military Instruction," pp. 156–157.

3. A useful general survey of problems of Confederate command organization is Frank E. Vandiver, *Rebel Brass: The Confederate Command System* (Baton Rouge: Louisiana State University Press, 1956).

For the historical debate on Confederate strategic decision making pertinent to the following synopsis, see Johnson, "Civil War Military History." This essay is a useful if somewhat combative introduction to some of the issues and historians of Confederate strategy as defined prior to the 1970s. Johnson covers work by T. Harry Williams, Thomas Connelly, Albert Castel, Frank E. Vandiver, Douglas S. Freeman, and Charles P. Roland. For an additional perspective, see Louis H. Manarin, "Lee in Command: Strategical and Tactical Policies" (Ph.D. diss., Duke University, 1964). Valuable contributions to the subsequent debate are Thomas L. Connelly and Archer Jones, *The Politics of Command: Factions and Ideas in Confederate Strategy* (Baton Rouge: Louisiana State University Press, 1973); Richard M. McMurray, "The Atlanta Campaign of 1864: A New Look," *Civil War History* 22 (1976): 5–15; Richard M. McMurray, *John Bell Hood and the War of Southern Independence* (Lexington, Ky.: University of Kentucky Press, 1982). With reference to Hood and Confederate strategy, see also Vandiver's earlier "General Hood as Logistician," *Military Affairs* 16 (1952): 1–11. See also Herman Hattaway and Archer Jones, *How the South Lost*, unpublished at the time this manuscript was completed. There is valuable material on Confederate strategic thinking in Hattaway and Jones, *How the North Won*. For the South as for the North, Cain, "A 'Face of Battle' Needed," is a useful summary article on the factors of politics, personality, culture, and morale as strategic considerations to weigh in the friction of war.

4. *OR*, ser. 1, LI, pt. 2, 150; E. P. Alexander, *Military Memoirs of a Confederate* (New York: Charles Scribner's Sons, 1908), p. 14, hereafter referred to as *Memoirs*; E. H. Cummins, "The Signal Corps in the Confederate Army," SHSP 16 (1888): 93.

5. *OR*, ser. 3, IV, 820; ibid., ser. 1, XLII, pt. 2, 868; Scheips, "Myer," pp. 351–352, 595. I am indebted to David Gaddy for leading me through the difficult reconstruction of the story of Confederate signals organization and for sharing material and ideas that he has accumulated toward a history of Confederate signals. There is a paucity of published material on the subject. Valuable information is to be found in David W. Gaddy, "William Norris and the Confederate Signal and Secret Service," *Maryland Historical Magazine* 70 (Summer, 1975): 167–188. Cummins; "The Signal Corps in the Confederate Army"; David J. Marshall, "The Confederate Army's Signal Corps," in Max L. Marshall, ed., *The Story of the U.S. Army Signal Corps* (New York: Franklin Watts, 1965), pp. 63–75; J. Cutter Andrews, "The Southern Telegraph Company, 1861–1865: A Chapter in the History of Wartime Communications," *Journal of Southern History* 30 (August, 1964): 319–344; Plum, *Military Telegraph*.

6. For elaboration on the Confederate cipher and its vulnerability, see Plum, *Military Telegraph*, vol. 1, pp. 35–40.

7. For the Celtic temperament thesis, see McWhiney and Jamieson, *Attack and Die*.

8. Plum, *Military Telegraph*, vol. 1, pp. 134–136. See also pp. 116–121.

9. Ibid., pp. 136–141.

10. Ibid., p. 147.

11. Correspondence with David Gaddy based on his unpublished research on Confederate signals development. With regard to the relationship between the Signal Corps and the telegraph, Gaddy speculates: "I imagine these circumstances: staff officer (possibly signal) takes telegram to local telegraph office, pays (or "charges it" with a voucher), and the process is reversed on the receiving

end; similarly, the CS Military Telegraph (but without paying? not sure). There is some evidence of the signal officer demanding that the telegraph office be kept open for government business, virtually commandeering it." Gaddy further notes evidence of a constraining order to cut down on the use of telegraph because of the costs. An interesting ad hoc use of telegraphers was the employment by cavalry commanders of volunteer or semiofficial telegraphers who performed whatever services they could improvise. Some became quite famous as wiretappers.

12. *OR*, ser. 1, II, 328–333, 500; Brown, *Signal Corps, U.S.A.*, p. 44.

13. Report to President Jefferson Davis on the Battle of Manassas and General Orders, no. 41, July 17, 1861. Quoted in P. G. T. Beauregard, *A Commentary on the Campaign and Battle of Manassas, of July 1861* (New York: G. P. Putnam's Sons, 1891), pp. 141–142, 154. See also p. 85. For Beauregard's position on his controversial career filtered through his aide, see Alfred Roman's prejudiced *The Military Operations of General Beauregard in the War between the States, 1861 to 1865, Including a brief Personal Sketch and a Narrative of His Services in the War with Mexico, 1846–1848* (New York: Harper, 1983). See also T. Harry Williams, *P. G. T. Beauregard: Napoleon in Gray* (Baton Rouge: Louisiana State University Press, 1954).

14. *OR*, ser. 1, II, 303; William C. Davis, *Battle at Bull Run* (New York: Doubleday, 1977), p. 61. This study is quite good on the organizational as well as general detail of the Bull Run campaign. For an analysis of Beauregard's *Principles and Maxims of the Art of War*, see Hattaway and Jones, *How the North Won*, pp. 13–14. Beauregard's 1863 treatise is reprinted in Beauregard, *Commentary on the Campaign of Manassas*. Hattaway and Jones observe that Beauregard plagiarized part of his principles from a British interpreter of Jomini, P. L. MacDougall, *The Theory of War* (London, 1958).

15. *OR*, ser. 1, V, 777. Johnston's account of his Civil War experience is the valuable *Narrative of Military Operations* (Bloomington: Indiana University Press, 1959). For a defense of Johnston's defensive cast of mind, see Gilbert E. Govan and James W. Livingood, *A Different Valor: The Story of General Joseph E. Johnston, CSA* (New York: Bobbs-Merrill, 1956).

16. Richard D. Goff, "Logistics and Supply Problems of the Confederacy" (Ph.D. diss., Duke University, 1963), pp. 40–55; published as *Confederate Supply* (Durham: Duke University Press, 1969). The dissertation has a sense of process lost in the drastic condensation for publication. The dissertation is referred to hereafter as "Logistics," the book as *Supply*. See also Winnifred P. Minter, "Confederate Military Supply," *Social Science* 34 (1959): 163–171, and June I. Gow, "Theory and Practice in Confederate Military Administration," *Military Affairs* 21 (1975): 118–123.

17. *OR*, ser. 1, XII, pt. 3, 896–891; ibid., XI, pt. 1, 939–940; Joseph Johnston, "From Manassas to Seven Pines," *B & L*, vol. 2, p. 212; *Narrative of Military Operations*, pp. 307, 343.

18. *OR*, ser. 1, XI, pt. 1, 853; Gibbs, "Lee's Command Procedures," pp. 32–33; McClellan, *Own Story*, p. 377.

19. Long, *Memoirs of Robert E. Lee*, pp. 168–169.

20. Clifford Dowdey and Louis H. Manarin, eds., *The Wartime Papers of Robert E. Lee* (Boston: Little Brown, 1961). Hereafter referred to as Lee, *Papers*, pp. 182–183.

21. Ibid., p. 184. For Lee's Celtic warrior élan, see McWhiney and Jamieson, *Attack and Die*.

22. Ibid., pp. 201, 203.

23. Ibid., p. 200.

24. For the deficiencies of Lee's staff and command procedures and the subsequent breakdown in tactical and strategic communications, see English, "Confederate Field Communications," and Gibbs, "Lee's Command Procedures." For Lee's reservations about attacking McClellan's entrenchments with green troops and his advocacy of a holding-turning action reminiscent of Scott's Mexican War operations, see Douglas S. Freeman, ed., *Lee's Dispatches*, new edition with additional dispatches and foreword by Grady McWhiney (New York: G. P. Putnam and Sons, 1957), pp. 5–10. Lee, interestingly, praised McClellan's entrenching activity while complaining of the laxness of Southerners in fortification work (ibid). Lee's subsequent failure to entrench in the course of field operations constitutes something of a contradiction to his early thought on the role of field fortifications. Some interesting material on Lee's tactical and strategic thought is to be found in Manarin, "Lee in Command."

25. For the official accounts of assault tactics, battlefield entrenchment, the failure of Lee's staff, and command procedures that led to direct tactical confrontation at Mechanicsville and in the Seven Days' Battles, see *OR*, ser. 1, XI, pt. 1, 869, 899–900; ibid., pt. 2, 24, 50–51, 222–226, 384–387, 391, 489–497, 565, 836; see also English, "Confederate Field Communications," pp. 48–50.

26. English, "Confederate Field Communications," p. 49.

27. G. F. R. Henderson, *The Science of War* (New York: Longmans, Green, and Co., 1933), p. 219.

28. Hattaway and Jones, *How the North Won*, pp. 220–221. Hattaway and Jones make an interesting observation on Lee's terminology and its meaning with respect to such objectives as "destroy," "strike a blow," "break up his position," "attack," "crush," and "suppress" (ibid., n. 35, p. 235).

29. *OR*, ser. 1, XI, pt. 3, 648; Douglas S. Freeman, *R. E. Lee: A Biography*, 4 vols. (New York: Charles Scribner's Sons, 1934–1935), vol. 2, p. 477; English, "Confederate Field Communications," pp. 59–60.

30. English, "Confederate Field Communications," p. 47; R. L. Dabney, *Life and Campaigns of Lieutenant General Thomas J. Jackson* (New York: Blelock and Co., 1880), p. 367. For a typical incident, in which Jackson ran somewhat roughshod over the sensibility of A. P. Hill by appointing a staff officer to Hill's division to ensure that Hill obeyed orders, see Frank E. Vandiver, *Mighty Stonewall* (New York: McGraw Hill, 1957), p. 348.

31. English, "Confederate Field Communications," pp. 46–47, 67–68; Freeman, *Lee's Lieutenants*, vol. 2, p. 90; *B & L*, vol. 2, p. 50; ibid., vol. 3, p. 642.

32. English, "Confederate Field Communications," pp. 43–44.

33. Ibid., p. 46.

34. *OR*, ser. 1, XII, pt. 3, 925–926; Hattaway and Jones, *How the North Won*, pp. 222–224.

35. English, "Confederate Field Communications," pp. 61–73; *OR*, ser. 1, XII, pt. 1, 169; ibid., pt. 2, 5–6, 28–29, 32, 37, 39, 65–67, 70–72, 176, 178–179, 181–185, 523–524, 552, 554, 557–558, 562, 568, 641–648, 650, 656, 670, 710, 725–739; ibid., pt. 3, 435, 652–655, 669, 715, 918–919, 928–929, 931, 940–942, 957–958.

36. *OR*, ser. 1, XII, pt. 2, 14–15, 157, 268; English, "Confederate Field Communications," pp. 63–72; Sir James Edmonds and W. B. Wood, *A History of the Civil War in the United States* (New York: Putnam's Sons, 1905), pp. 109–111; Hattaway and Jones, *How the North Won*, pp. 225–236.

37. One of Lee's first concerns, expressed in a letter April 27, 1861, just after assuming field command, was with securing sufficient field transportation to move from his railhead and take the field (*OR*, ser. 1, II, 784–785). For increasing supply and transportation concerns during this campaign, see *OR*, ser. 4, II, 47–48, 65–66, 299, 417; ibid., ser. 1, XIX, pt. 1, 156; ibid., pt. 2, 590, 709, 716; ibid., XXI, 1016; Goff, "Logistics," pp. 131, 134–142; Goff, *Supply*, pp. 73–75; Charles W. Ramsdell, "General Robert E. Lee's Horse Supply, 1862–1865," *American Historical Review* 35 (July, 1930): 758–759, hereafter referred to as "Lee's Horse Supply."

38. *OR*, ser. 1, XIX, pt. 2, 590–591; ibid., pt. 1, 145; Hattaway and Jones, *How the North Won*, pp. 232–233, 240. For the details of the Maryland campaign, though the study is not interested in organizational perspectives, see James Murfin, *The Gleam of Bayonets: The Battle of Antietam and Robert E. Lee's Maryland Campaign, September,* 1862 (Baton Rouge: Louisiana State University Press, 1982).

39. *OR*, ser. 1, XIX, pt. 1, 140, 145, 147–148, 839, 914, 955, 1021–1022; ibid., pt. 2, 603–604; Transportation, Subsistence, Special, General, and Field Orders and Circulars for Geographical and Higher Mobile Commands, Confederate State Armies, Record Group 104, *U.S. War Department Collection of Confederate Records*, entry 4. National Archives of the United States. Hereafter referred to as *NA*, RG 109; English, "Confederate Field Communications," pp. 73–84.

40. *OR*, ser. 1, XIX, pt. 2, 590; ibid., pt. 1, 143–151; ibid., LI, pt. 2, 616–619; *NA*, RG 109, chap. 2, vol. 82½, pp. 20–21.

41. *OR*, ser. 1, XIX, pt. 1, 54, 424.

42. Ibid., pp. 156, 327; *Atlas*, vol. 1, pl. XXXVIII (1).

43. *OR*, ser. 4, II, 47–48, 65–66, 299; *OR*, ser. 1, XIX, pt. 1, 156; ibid., pt. 2, 590; Goff, "Logistics," pp. 131, 134–142.

44. *OR*, ser. 1, XIX, pt. 1, 143, 151.

45. Goff, "Logistics," pp. 142–168, 184–191.

46. Ibid., pp. 92–106.

47. *OR*, ser. 4, I, 767: Goff, "Logistics," pp. 67–68.

48. Goff, "Logistics," pp. 200–217, 252–253.

49. Ibid., p. 60.

50. *OR*, ser. 1, XIX, pt. 2, 709, 716; ibid., XXI, 1016; ibid., ser. 4, II, 417; Ramsdell, "Lee's Horse Supply," pp. 758–759; Goff, *Supply*, pp. 73–75.

51. Goff, "Logistics," p. 112.

52. Ibid., p 133.

53. Ibid., pp. 131, 156–160.

54. *OR*, ser. 1, XXI, 546; *NA*, RG 109, chap. 2, vol. 82½, 48–49.

55. G. Moxley Sorrel, *Recollections of a Confederate Staff Officer* (New York: Neale Publishing Co., 1905), p. 132. As Jay Luvaas notes in his unpublished essay "Looking for the Civil War," Freeman's explanation that Lee did not construct elaborate entrenchments so as not to discourage an attack on naturally strong positions is speculation (Freeman, *Lee*, vol. 2, pp. 441–442).

56. *OR*, ser. 1, XXI, 630–635.

57. Heros von Borcke, *Memoirs of the Confederate War for Independence*, 2 vols. (New York: Peter Smith, 1938), vol. 2, p. 44.

58. For the portrayals of Jackson and Lee as temperamentally disposed to aggressive offensive war, see Vandiver, *Mighty Stonewall*, pp. 19–44, and Connelly, *The Marble Man*. At the First Battle of Bull Run, Jackson made a successful, though very costly, bayonet charge (Vandiver, *Mighty Stonewall*, p. 163). For my attempt to modify Connelly's thesis, see "Looking For the American Civil War."

59. *OR*, ser. 1, XXI, 569.
60. Ibid., pp. 583–584.
61. Alexander, *Memoirs*, p. 307; Freeman, *Lee*, vol. 2, pp. 443, 453.
62. *OR*, ser. 1, II, pt. 1, 173.
63. Longstreet, *From Manassas to Appomattox*, p. 316.
64. Quoted by von Borcke, *Memoirs of the Confederate War for Independence*, vol. 2, p. 132.
65. *OR*, ser. 1, XXI, 634, 666; Jubal A. Early, *Autobiographical Sketch and Narrative of the War between the States* (Philadelphia: J. B. Lippincott, 1912), pp. 177–178. Hereafter referred to as *War between the States*.
66. *OR*, ser. 1, XXI, 1095–1096.
67. Vandiver, *Mighty Stonewall*, pp. 134–135.
68. Ibid., XXV, pt. 1, 796.
69. Ibid., pp. 194–198.

5. Intimations of Modern Warfare

1. Freeman and McWhiney, eds., *Lee's Dispatches*, Lee to Davis, February 24, 1863, pp. 73–75; Ramsdell, "Lee's Horse Supply," pp. 760–761.
2. Goff, "Logistics," p. 187; Frank E. Vandiver, *Ploughshares into Swords: Josiah Gorgas and Confederate Ordnance* (Austin: University of Texas Press, 1952), pp. 164–165.
3. *OR*, ser. 1, XXV, pt. 2, 730.
4. Goff, "Logistics," pp. 72–83, 160–161.
5. The first record of Confederate field transportation standards begins in 1863. The following references to general orders, unless otherwise indicated, are from *NA*, RG 109, chap. 5, vol. 154½. This document contains the transportation standards set for the Army of North Virginia from April, 1863, to April, 1864, and for the Army of Tennessee from August, 1863, to November, 1864.
6. In addition to the detailed standards set forth in *NA*, RG 109, chap. 5, vol. 154½, see *OR*, ser. 1, XXV, pt. 2, 659, 739–740. There is no record of the previous standard against which Lee made the reduction of April 20, 1863.

The order of April 20, 1863 set a standard that included: one wagon per 100 men present; one wagon for ordnance per regiment, which calculates at approximately one per 500 men in accordance with the reduced size of regiments varying from 375 to 500 men; one wagon per 375 men for the reserve ordnance train; one ambulance wagon per 300 men. This adds up to a total of approximately thirty-four wagons per 1,000 men including the reserve train.

The reserve ordnance train and ambulance allotments are not noted in the general order of April 20, whereas they are in later orders. I am speculating on a standard based on orders later in 1863. I am also speculating that the one reference to a reserve train that does not designate it to be an ordnance train in fact refers to the reserve ordnance train, since all other reference to the reserve is to the ordnance train.

The general orders are frustrating with respect to the random inclusion of various categories from one order to the next. Since the categories do not disappear, one possible explanation is that orders deliberately or accidentally left out areas that were not a source of problems at the time, including them again when problems occurred. Another explanation, of course, is a sloppy compilation of general orders.

7. Increasingly, the Army of Northern Virginia reduced its headquarters standard below that of the Army of Tennessee.

8. The standard of the Army of Tennessee will be developed in the analysis of the western theater.

9. The following section on baggage, subsistence, and forage standards, unless otherwise noted, is based on *Army Regulations, CSA* (Richmond: West and Johnston, 1861); *Regulations, CSA* (Richmond: J. W. Randolph, 1862); *Regulations, CSA* (Richmond: J. W. Randolph, 1863); *Regulations for the CSA and for the Quartermaster's and Pay Departments* (New Orleans: Bloomfield and Steel, 1861); *Regulations for the CSA for the Quartermaster's Department and Pay Branch Thereof* (Richmond: Ritchie and Dunnavent, 1862); *The Quartermaster's Guide: Being a Compilation of Army Regulations from the Army Regulations and Other Sources* (Richmond: West and Johnston, 1862).

10. The decline in coffee, soup, and candle standards is calculated from weekly accounts of hospital rations from November 8, 1861, to April 25, 1862. These accounts stated explicitly that the reductions were in accordance with reductions to the troops. These are the only statistics that I have found on adapting standards to day-to-day realities of supply (Virginia Historical Society, Richmond, papers of Herbert Augustine Clairburne, Section 44, Subsistence Department papers). Subsistence and forage standards are otherwise available only in army regulations. If they were formally revised to adapt to Civil War realities, the evidence seems to have disappeared. The slim evidence available suggests sporadic ad hoc adjustments to circumstances.

11. Goff, "Logistics," pp. 184–186.

12. *OR*, ser. 4, II, 380, 530; Goff, "Logistics," pp. 188–192, 200–217.

13. Ibid., pp. 192–198, 217–238.

14. Ibid., pp. 247–250.

15. *OR*, ser. 1, XI, pt. 3, 613.

16. Ibid., XIX, pt. 1, 803–810; ibid., pt. 2, 660–662; Maury Klein, *Edward Porter Alexander* (Athens: University of Georgia Press, 1971), p. 58. Referred to hereafter as *Alexander*; Jennings Cooper Wise, *The Long Arm of Lee: The History of the Artillery of the Army of Northern Virginia* (New York: Oxford University Press), pp. 198–202, 257–259, 336, 344, 357–359.

17. For Alexander's career, See Klein, *Alexander*. Klein is less sympathetic than Wise, *The Long Arm of Lee*, to Pendleton's role in the history of Lee's artillery. Within a few years of the Civil War, the battalion system pioneered by Lee and shortly thereafter developed in the Army of the Potomac by General Hooker and the army's brilliant chief of artillery, Henry Hunt, would be adopted by Prussia, Austria, France, and Great Britain.

18. *OR*, ser. 1, XXV, pt. 2, 614–618; Nesmith, "Artillery," p. 37; Klein, *Alexander*, p. 59.

19. Fitzhugh Lee, *General Lee* (New York: D. Appleton and Co., 1894), p. 222; Alexander, *Memoirs*, p. 324.

20. *OR*, ser. 1, XXV, pt. 1, 850.

21. Fitzhugh Lee, *General Lee*, p. 22.

22. Ibid.; Alexander, *Memoirs*, p. 324.

23. Ibid., p. 34.

24. *OR*, ser. 1, XXV, pt. 1, 826.

25. *B & L*, vol. 3, p. 209; English, "Confederate Field Communications," p. 119.

26. Ibid., p. 120; Moseley, "Tactics," p. 35.

27. Jamieson, "Tactics," p. 171.

28. Alexander on the night of May achieved a rare instance of successful indirect fire, especially rare on the offensive. He used firing directions marked out earlier in the day to shell retreating Union troops (Klein, *Alexander*, p. 68).

29. Alexander, *Memoirs*, pp. 346–349. Alexander commanded Jackson's artillery during the turning movement (Jamieson, "Tactics," pp. 149–150).

30. Figures calculated from the *Official Records* by Alexander, *Memoirs*, pp. 359–362.

31. Klein, *Alexander*, p. 71.

32. Ramsdell, "Lee's Horse Supply," pp. 763–769.

33. Losses of 1,600 killed and 9,000 wounded out of an effective strength of 40,000 men *(OR*, ser. 1, XXV, pt. 1, 806–809; ibid., pt. 2, 782).

34. Ramsdell, "Lee's Horse Supply," pp. 763–769.

35. *OR*, ser. 4, II, 417.

36. *OR*, ser. 1, XXV, pt. 2, 141, 741; Goff, *Supply*, p. 73. Ramsdell observes that Lee's prognosis was correct; he would never again be supplied adequately (Ramsdell, "Lee's Horse Supply," p. 763).

37. *OR*, ser. 1, XXV, pt. 2, 709–749.

38. Ibid., XXXVII, pt. 3, 858.

39. Ibid., XXV, pt. 2, 820.

40. Ibid., pp. 814–846; ibid., XXVII, pt. 3, 930.

41. Ibid., XXVII, pt. 3, 868–869, 880–882.

42. Ibid., p. 896.

43. For the regulations Lee set for procuring supplies in the North, see General Orders, no. 72, June 21, 1863, ibid., pp. 912–913, 930–931. Meigs observed Lee's logistical organization in the field while walking Lee's route of march following the Battle of Gettysburg (ibid., XLVII, pt. 2, 512). See also Hattaway and Jones, *How the North Won*, pp. 400–401.

44. *OR*, ser. 1, XXVII, pt. 2, 298, 318, 631.

45. Ibid., p. 318.

46. *B & L*, vol. 3, p. 339.

47. Long, *Memoirs*, pp. 276–287; Marshall, *Aide-de-Camp of Lee*, pp. 232, 250; *NA* RG 109, chap. 2, vol. 90, pp. 89–90; *OR*, ser. 1, XXVII, pt. 2, 308, 318; Henderson, *The Science of War*, p. 290; Freeman, *Lee*, vol. 2, p. 82.

48. *OR*, ser. 1, XXVII, pt. 1, 199–220; Sorrel, *Recollections*, p. 157; *B & L*, vol. 3, p. 363. See Edwin B. Coddington, *The Gettysburg Campaign: A Study in Command* (New York: Charles Scribner's Sons, 1968). Coddington, though only incidentally interested in organizational structures for tactical and strategic command, is quite good on the resulting problems of coordination in command procedures in the Union and Confederate armies for the Gettysburg campaign. Coddington provides a judicious weighing of the circumstances surrounding Lee's motives in deciding upon a tactical assault rather than accepting Longstreet's argument for a turning maneuver.

49. *OR*, ser. 1, XXVII, pt. 2, 359, 411–413, 417.

50. Quoted by W. H. Taylor, *Four Years with General Lee* (New York: D. Appleton and Co., 1877), p. 101. Hereafter referred to as *Lee*. For a different phrasing by Lee of why he attacked, see *OR*, ser. 1, XXVII, pt. 2, 308.

51. *OR*, ser. 1, XXVII, pt. 2, 351.

52. Taylor, *Lee*, p. 101.

53. *B & L*, vol. 3, p. 358.

54. Alexander, *Memoirs*, pp. 393–413; Taylor, *Lee*, pp. 100–101, 103–110; Lee, p. 394; *B & L*, vol. 3, pp. 312–313, 358; Sorrel, *Recollections*, p. 157.

55. Nesmith, "Artillery," p. 37.

56. Jamieson, "Tactics," p. 150.

57. Ibid., pp. 150–151; Nesmith, "Artillery," pp. 37–38.

58. Alexander, *Memoirs*, p. 416.

59. *OR*, ser. 1, XXVII, pt. 2, 352.

60. *B & L*, vol. 3, pp. 373–374.

61. *OR*, ser. 1, XXVII, pt. 2, 353.

62. Moseley, "Tactics," p. 357.

63. Jamieson, "Tactics," pp. 173–174. The cavalry battle at Yellow Tavern, in May, 1864, was the only truly mounted engagement for Lee's cavalry (ibid.).

64. *OR*, ser. 1, XXIX, pt. 2, 355–356, 406, 625, 628, 661; Livermore, *Numbers and Losses*, p. 103; it will be remembered that Lee cut his supply lines with the South because of inadequate numbers to protect them and was living off the land. After Gettysburg, his capacity to open up supply routes was even more restricted.

65. *OR*, ser. 4, II, 615; Ramsdell, "Lee's Horse Supply," pp. 764, 766.

66. *OR*, ser. 1, XXIX, pt. 2, 681, 709; ibid., XXV, pt. 2, 28, 845–846.

67. Ibid., XXIX, pt. 2, 549.

68. Ramsdell, "Lee's Horse Supply," pp. 764–766.

69. Goff, *Supply*, p. 247.

70. *OR*, ser. 4, II, 914–915.

71. *OR*, ser. 1, XXIX, pt. 1, 445.

72. Ibid., pt. 2, 758.

73. Ibid., pt. 1, 408–411, 426–428, 622–625; ibid., pt. 2, 794; Early, *War between the States*, p. 316; Goff, "Logistics," pp. 390–392.

74. Taylor, *Lee*, p. 119.

75. *OR*, ser. 1, XXIX, pt. 1, 611; ibid., pt. 2, 830–832.

76. Goff, "Logistics," p. 397.

77. *OR*, ser. 1, XXIX, pt. 1, 407–408, 411.

6. Maneuver and Tactics

1. *Atlas*, vol. 1, pl. V (2).

2. Comte de Paris, *History of the Civil War in America*, vol. 1, pp. 480–481.

3. Ibid., pp. 479–480.

4. *Atlas*, vol. 1, pl. XI (1, 4–7); U. S. Grant, *Personal Memoirs* (New York: World Publishing Co., 1952), p. 147. Hereafter referred to as *Memoirs*.

5. *OR*, ser. 1, VII, 535, 946.

6. Ibid., p. 529.

7. An example of early discipline problems is strikingly portrayed in a description of General Sterling Price's Confederate Army of Missouri volunteers in the early stages of the war (*B & L*, vol. 1, pp. 267–271). Some of the more scathing and revealing comments on the citizen soldier and the discipline problems he created early in the war are to be found in the private correspondence of William T. Sherman. See M. De Wolfe Howe, ed., *Home Letters of General Sherman* (New York: Charles Scribner's Sons, 1909). Hereafter referred to as *Home Letters*. For a statistical breakdown of the distribution of West Point grad-

uates, see Winton, "Ante-bellum Military Instruction," pp. 156–157. The eastern armies of both sides had a higher proportion of West Point graduates at each level. The Confederates had a high proportion at the corps and division level; the Army of Northern Virginia had the heaviest concentration of any army at the corps and division level. For Grant's indifference to the military telegraph, which was not present at Donelson, though Plum maintained "there had been ample time for the erection of field telegraphs," see Plum, *Military Telegraph*, vol. 1, p. 174. Plum contends that Halleck, also slow to appreciate the Military Telegraph, ignored Stager during the Donelson campaign. This issue may, however, have been one of jurisdiction rather than indifference. Halleck attempted to take over direction of two military telegraph parties as they made their way toward Fort Donelson (ibid., p. 175). Plum also lumps Sherman among the unappreciative before Shiloh (ibid., p. 177).

8. *OR*, ser. 1, IV, 199; Grant, *Memoirs*, p. 171.

9. Letter to Stanton, February 3, 1862, McClellan, *Own Story*, p. 200. On McClellan as general in chief of combined operations, see Reed, *Combined Operations in the Civil War*.

10. E.g., *OR*, ser. 1, VII, 442–443, 445, 505, 520–521, 530, 931.

11. A good sense of these early problems is contained in Records of the United States Army Continental Consolidated Commands, 1821–1920, Record Group 393, pt. 1, entry 3552, 2 parts, *U.S. War Department Collection of Union Records*, National Archives of the United States. Hereafter referred to as *NA*, RG 393.

12. Ibid., pt. 2, p. 18.

13. *OR*, ser. 3, III, 1124.

14. *NA*, RG 92, entry 1318, vol. 1, pp. 41, 60, 210. These abstracts of reports of means of transportation do not separate serviceable and unserviceable animals. The return and inspection reports of the adjutant general's office (*NA*, RG 94), which provide statistics on serviceable animals, are not available for 1861–62.

A separate set of records, the unfiled trimonthly quartermaster returns, with statistics for serviceable animals, are available for 1861–62 and are of some help in building an informed speculation. But these records are mostly small unit returns, difficult to use, and difficult to interpret with reliability. They do suggest a somewhat erratic supply of unserviceable animals regardless of time and place, with units in the same army having varied records of performance. This is likely the result, in part, of fluctuating standards of animal care in the early stages of the war, especially serious with the unanticipated problem of the vulnerability of horses.

Of particular value for comparison with later sources from the adjutant general's office is the trimonthly return for the Army of the Mississippi under Rosecrans for August 15, 1862, an unusual instance in these records of a return for a complete army (*NA*, unfiled trimonthly quartermaster returns [Box 209, RP 1257/NA 2632]. The adjutant general's returns for 1863 suggest that the quartermasters could, with good foraging conditions, keep the problem of unserviceable animals under control. But in poor foraging conditions, especially while stationary, there were great problems.

In documented conditions for March, 1863, comparable to nondocumented conditions one year earlier, Rosecrans reported 25 percent of his animals unserviceable, including 50 percent of his cavalry horses. Presuming that his harness horses were in comparable shape to his cavalry horses, and based upon 1863 records for the durability of mules, I have used a rough working speculation of 40 percent unserviceable horses and 10 percent unserviceable mules to calculate the low end of transportation standards where poor foraging conditions prevailed in 1861–62, especially with a stationary army. This working hypothesis must be modified by the allowance, as mentioned, for somewhat erratic numbers of serviceable animals during the early stages of the war. Spring returns for western armies other than the Army of the Mississippi are unavailable or too incomplete to use for speculation on their transportation standards through June of 1862.

15. *NA*, RG 92, entry 1318, vol. 1, pp. 42, 46, 48, 172.

16. Ibid., pp. 41, 42, 48, 60–61, 64–65, 172, 210.

17. Ibid., pp. 55, 58–59, 61.

18. Ibid., p. 64. The rare column for wagon statistics, added to the previously mentioned August 26, 1862, return for the Army of the Mississippi, perhaps indicates the special concern Rosecrans and his quartermaster had for their transportation standard (*NA*, unfiled trimonthly quartermaster returns, Box 209, RP-12571/NA-2632).

19. *NA*, RG 1318, vol. 1, pp. 150–152, 183, 212, 263. Field transportation returns for the Army of the Tennessee and the Army of the Cumberland do not appear to be available for the summer of 1862.

20. Special Orders, no. 10, April 10, 1862, *NA*, RG 109, entries 97–98, n.p.

21. Ibid.

22. Ibid.

23. Ibid.

24. Ibid., entries 99–100, n.p.

25. Ibid., chap. 5, vol. 152, pp. 1–4. There are not sufficient data to determine Confederate transportation standards prior to 1863.

26. General Orders, no. 30, April 30, 1862; ibid., entries 97–98, n.p.; *Army Regulations, CSA* (Richmond: J. W. Randolph, 1862).

Per ration	Army of the Mississippi	Army Regulation
pork or bacon	10 oz.	¾ lb.
salt or fresh beef	1 lb.	1¼ lb.
flour or cornmeal	24 oz.	18 oz. flour or
or		1¼ lbs. cornmeal
cornbread	1 lb.	18 oz.

Per 100 rations		
beans and peas	8 qts.	8 qts.
rice	15 lbs.	10 lbs.
coffee	3 lbs.	6 lbs.
rye	3 lbs.	no provision
sugar	15 lbs.	12 lbs.
salt	no provision	2 qts.
molasses	1 qt.	no provision
vinegar	4 qts.	4 qts.
soap	4 lbs.	4 lbs.
sperm candles	1 lb.	1 lb.
or		
tallow	1½ lb.	1½ lb.

27. *OR*, ser. 1, VII, 548–549.

28. Ibid., p. 548.
29. Ibid., pp. 532–533.
30. Ibid., p. 549.
31. Ibid., p. 521.
32. Ibid., pp. 546–547.
33. Ibid., p. 555.
34. Ibid., pp. 75–76.
35. Ibid., pp. 76, 520–521, 530, 542, 555, 925.
36. The Confederates had the unusual advantage, at this stage of the war in the West, of a competent engineer to lay out the Mill Springs fortifications (ibid., pp. 102–105, 108, 542, 545; B & L, vol. 7, p. 387).
37. OR, ser. 1, VII, 87.
38. Ibid., pp. 87, 93–94. Italics are inserted.
39. OR, ser. 1, VII, 100.
40. Ibid., pp. 107–108.
41. Ibid., pp. 80–81, 101–102, 104; Plum, Military Telegraph, vol. 1, pp. 187–189.
42. Ibid, p. 568.
43. Ibid., pp. 931–932.
44. Ibid.
45. For Halleck's strategic thinking, as well as that of Buell and A. S. Johnston, see Hattaway and Jones, How the North Won, pp. 61–77.
46. OR, ser. I, VII, 195, 575, 579, 601, 674–675; Grant, Memoirs, pp. 154–155; John Y. Simon, ed., The Papers of Ulysses S. Grant (Carbondale, Ill.: Southern Illinois University Press, 1967), vol. 4, pp. 302–304, 326. Hereafter referred to as Grant, Papers. I have been unable to uncover statistics on transportation standards in the Army of the Tennessee prior to October, 1862. As noted, Plum maintained that Grant and Halleck were both slow to appreciate the Military Telegraph, which could have been in place for the Donelson campaign.
47. Grant, Memoirs, p. 153.
48. Ibid., p. 152.
49. OR, ser. 1, VII, 608; control of the Tennessee River with the fall of Fort Henry enabled the Federal forces to destroy the Danville Railroad bridge, cutting off the Confederate reinforcements and supplies for Donelson (ibid., p. 163); Grant, Papers, vol. 2, p. 204, n. 1.
50. Grant, Memoirs, p. 142.
51. Ibid., p. 140.
52. B & L, vol. 1, p. 355.
53. Grant, Memoirs, p. 155.
54. Ibid., pp. 156–157; Moseley, "Tactics," pp. 354–357.
55. Hattaway and Jones, How the North Won, p. 98. For a detailed critique of Confederate strategy along the first line of defense, see ibid., pp. 68–76.
56. Fort Donelson and Fort Henry had been the keys to the resource-rich Confederate perimeter in the West. With the loss of Nashville went most of the supply reserves collected for the 1862 campaigning year. The loss of the Lower Tennessee Valley cost the Confederacy their richest iron ore area and most of their major meat-producing regions. Richard Goff, the historian of Confederate supply, considers the fall of Forts Henry and Donelson to have been the greatest Confederate logistical disasters of the war (Goff, "Logistics," pp. 123–124, 126).
57. OR, ser. 1, VII, 915.
58. Ibid., X, pt. 2, 607; Atlas, vol. 1, pl. XIII (6); Comte de Paris, History of the Civil War in America, vol.2, p. 183.
59. OR., ser. 1, X, pt. 2, 387.

60. Ibid., pp. 77, 91–92. There are insufficient data to speculate on Buell's transportation standard or other logistical details of his march.

61. Ibid., pp. 384–387.

62. Ibid., p. 384.

63. Ibid., p. 51; Hattaway and Jones, *How the North Won*, p. 164.

64. Grant, *Memoirs*, p. 171. Italics are inserted.

65. Ibid., p. 186.

66. Grady McWhiney, "Ulysses S. Grant's Pre-Civil War Military Education," in *Southerners and Other Americans*, pp. 61–72. McWhiney has some interesting observations on Grant's military education.

67. W. T. Sherman, *Memoirs* (Bloomington: Indiana University Press, 1957), p. 229. For Mahan's views on Grant and Sherman as students, see Dennis Hart Mahan, "The Cadet Life of Grant and Sherman," *Army and Navy Journal* 3 (March 31, 1866): 507.

68. Jamieson, "Tactics," pp. 90–91.

69. Special Orders, no. 8, April 3, 1862, *NA*, RG 109, entries 97–98, n.p.

70. *OR*, ser. 1, X, pt. 1, 169, 527, 531, 599; Jamieson, "Tactics," p. 171.

71. *OR*, ser. 1, X, pt. 1, 146–147, 167–168, 245–248, 273–274, 276, 373–374, 527, 561, 609; Jamieson, "Tactics," p. 145. Interesting contemporary studies of the detail of the Battle of Shiloh, though not interested in doctrine or organization, are James Lee McDonough, *Shiloh: In Hell before Night* (Knoxville: University of Tennessee Press, 1977), and Wiley Sword, *Shiloh: Bloody April* (New York: William Morrow and Co., 1974).

72. English, "Confederate Field Communications," pp. 125–126.

73. *OR*, ser. 1, X, pt. 2, 54, 74–75. Strategic communication between the headquarters of the western armies of the Union was extensive (e.g., ibid., p. 11. See also *OR*, ser. 3, III, 969–980; ibid., IV, 841–868, 885).

74. *OR*, ser. 1, X, pt. 2, 73. Grant, once he came to terms with the Military Telegraph, was, according to Plum, as uncomfortable as Halleck with Stager's independent authority. Grant would attempt, unsuccessfully, to appoint a superintendent of telegraph lines in his department with authority over Stager (Plum, *Military Telegraph*, vol. 1, pp. 264–268).

75. *OR*, ser. 3, II, 162–163, 755; Brown, *Signal Corps*, pp. 457–466, 486.

76. *OR*, ser. 3, III, 949–953; Brown, ibid., 509–511.

77. *OR*, ser. 1, X, pt. 2, 103.

78. Grant, *Memoirs*, pp. 195–196.

79. *OR*, ser. 1, X, pt. 2, 201–202.

80. Ibid., pp. 478, 523, 544, 546, 547; Hattaway and Jones, *How the North Won*, p. 171. On Halleck, see Stephen Ambrose, *Halleck: Lincoln's Chief of Staff* (Baton Rouge: Louisiana State University Press, 1962).

7. The Emergence of Trench Warfare

1. *Atlas*, vol. 1, pl. XXXVI (2).

2. *OR*, ser. 1, XVI, pt. 2, 684–685, 694–695.

3. Ibid., X, pt. 2, 235.

4. Ibid., pp. 235, 286–287; ibid., XVI, pt. 2, 12, 15–16.

5. Ibid., XVI, pt. 1, 791, 1089; ibid., pt. 2, 701, 740–741, 749, 751–752, 760–761.

6. Ibid., pp. 234, 237, 241, 741; ibid., pt. 1, 1089.

7. *OR*, ser. 1, XVI, pt. 1, 9.

8. *NA*, RG 92, entry 1318, vol. 1, pp. 150–152, 183, 212, 263; ibid., RG 393, pt. 1, entry 3554, 2 parts, pt. 2, p. 18; *OR*, XVI, pt. 2, 3, 5; ibid., X, pt. 2, 235.

9. Ibid., pt. 2, 3, 5; ibid., X, pt. 2, 235.

10. Ibid.; General Orders, no. 1, May 8, 1862, *NA*, RG109, entries 98–99, n.p.; *OR*, ser. 1, XVI, pt. 2, 769; Comte de Paris, *History of the Civil War in America*, vol. 1, p. 376. Interesting material on Bragg's controversial field command is to be found in McWhiney, *Bragg*, and Thomas Connelly, *Army of the Heartland: The Army of Tennessee, 1861–1862* (Baton Rouge: Louisiana State University Press, 1967) and *Autumn of Glory: The Army of Tennessee, 1862–1865* (Baton Rouge: Louisiana State University Press, 1971).

11. *OR*, ser. 1, XVI, pt. 1, 722.

12. Ibid., pp. 1089–1090.

13. Ibid., p. 968; Goff, "Logistics," pp. 129–130.

14. *OR*, ser. 1, XVI, pt. 1, 1090; ibid., pt. 2, 876.

15. Ibid., pt. 1, 1090.

16. Ibid., pp. 722, 1090–1091; ibid., pt. 2, 722, 876; McWhiney, *Bragg*, pp. 287–288.

17. *OR*, ser. 1, XVI, pt. 1, 1023–1024; ibid., pt. 2, 552, 564.

18. *NA*, RG 92, entry 1318, vol. 1, pp. 150–156, 183, 212, 217, 219, 229, 263.

19. Ibid., pp. 55, 58–59, 61, 64.

20. *OR*, ser. 1, XVI, pt. 2, 876.

21. Ibid., pt. 1, 1090–1091.

22. Ibid.

23. Brown, *Signal Corps*, pp. 467–468; Plum, *Military Telegraph*, vol. 1, pp. 279–312.

24. *OR*, ser. 1, XVI, pt. 1, 1037, 1039–1041.

25. Ibid., pp. 1031–1040, 1042, 1050, 1057, 1087, 1092, 1112, 1133–1134; McWhiney, *Bragg*, pp. 312–320.

26. *OR*, ser. 1, XVI, pt. 1, 1093.

27. Ibid., pp. 1093–1094.

28. McWhiney, *Bragg*, pp. 72–73, 348.

29. *OR*, ser. 1, XVII, pt. 1, 65–66.

30. Calculated from Rosecrans's September statistics of 568 wagons for 23,000 men and the Army of Tennessee's October statistics of 762 wagons for 25,000 men. There was no surplus of animals, but the three-to-one ratio of mules to horses plus the reduced attrition rate for animals with the army in motion probably prevented a reduction of the wagon standard from unserviceable animals (*NA*, RG 92, entry 1318, vol. 1, pp. 65, 200, 254).

31. Ibid., pp. 65–68; Grant, *Memoirs*, p. 219.

32. *OR*, ser. 1, XVII, pt. 1, 378; Comte de Paris, *History of the Civil War in America*, vol. 2, pp. 409–410.

33. *OR*, ser. 1, XVII, pt. 1, 386.

34. Comte de Paris, *History of the Civil War in America*, vol. 2, pp. 409–410.

35. *OR*, ser. 1, XVII, pt. 1, 205–206, 251–261, 387.

36. Ibid., p. 384.

37. Ibid., pp. 158, 182.

38. Ibid., p. 163.

39. Ibid., p. 156.

40. Ibid., p. 164.

41. Ibid., p. 379.

42. Ibid., III, 185–193; *B & L*, vol. 1, pp. 307–314.

43. *OR*, ser. 1, XVII, pt. 1, 382–385.

44. Ibid., pp. 466–467, 471; *NA*, RG 92, entry 1318, vol. 1, pp. 201, 235. Grant moved with a considerable surplus of animals for the wagons available. The distribution of wagons to the army in the field is not available. The standard arrived at is speculation on the assumption that the whole army was stripped to the minimum to supply the army in the field, and that the surplus horses and mules were, in accordance with general practice, used as pack animals. A minimal attrition of animals in motion in the field is also assumed.

45. *OR*, ser. 1, XVII, pt. 1, 616; ibid., pt. 2, 361, 392, 479.

46. Ibid., pp. 369, 785.

47. E.g., ibid., pp. 366–367.

48. Ibid., p. 370; ibid., pt. 1, 47.

49. Ibid., pp. 470–475, 528–529, 616–617.

50. Ibid., pp. 621–623.

51. Ibid., pp. 618, 621–623. In the light of his future performance, it is to be noted that Sherman at this time was not equipping soldiers individually with spades. Entrenching equipment was carried in the divisional train (ibid., p. 618).

52. Ibid., pp. 469–470, 477–478, 496.

53. Ibid., pp. 607, 609, 613–614; Brown, *Signal Corps*, p. 598.

54. The Army of the Tennessee, with some 47,000 men in December, 1862, had a transportation standard of fewer than 13 wagons per 1,000 men. Grant had 900 wagons but animals for only some 650 wagons. And this did not allow for unserviceable animals, which, when local forage gave out, may have been high. Even a concentration of these wagons for Sherman's movement could not have brought Sherman near a standard of 20 wagons per 1,000 men (*NA*, RG 1318, vol. 1, p. 202).

55. *OR*, ser. 1, XVII, pt. 1, p. 602.

56. Ibid., pp. 606–610, 612, 640–643.

57. Ibid., pp. 608–609.

58. Ibid., pp. 61, 612.

59. Ibid., XX, pt. 1, 189.

60. Ibid., pp. 86, 88–92, 189, 201, 234; Brown, *Signal Corps*, p. 469. Brown observed that even had the topography been favorable to signals, the fact that Rosecrans and his division generals were constantly in motion would have worked against their effectiveness. This again emphasized the problems of using the existing state of signals technology and organization from other than static defensive positions. For Rosecrans's wagon standard, see *NA*, RG 92, entry 1318, vol. 1, pp. 203–205.

61. *OR*, ser. 1, XX, pt. 1, 192.

62. Ibid., p. 234; Brown, *Signal Corps*, p. 470.

63. *OR*, ser. 1, XX, pt. 1, 183.

64. Ibid., p. 185.

65. Ibid., p. 245; *Atlas*, vol. 1, pl. XXI (1).

66. E.g., *OR*, ser. 1, XX, pt. 1, 602, 869.

67. Ibid., 663.

68. Ibid., pp. 185, 192, 256–267, 566, 689, 868, 930, 932, 934; *Atlas*, vol. 1, pl. XXX (1); McWhiney, *Bragg*, p. 348.

69. *OR*, ser. 1, XX, pt. 1, 185, 192–193, 663–664.

70. Ibid., p. 193.
71. Ibid., pp. 193, 256.
72. Ibid., p. 665.
73. Jamieson, "Tactics," pp. 148–149.
74. *OR*, ser. 1, XX, pt. 1, 194–195.
75. Ibid.
76. Ibid., pp. 236–237, 239, 244, 248, 250, 256, 271, 277, 667.
77. Ibid., p. 783.
78. Ibid., pp. 246, 257, 667. Rosecrans also makes reference to the enemy's entrenchments (ibid., pp. 185, 196).
79. Ibid., p. 195.
80. Ibid., pp. 617–619, 624–625, 958–959.
81. Ibid., pp. 195–196.
82. Ibid., pp. 668–669.
83. Ibid., p. 228.
84. Ibid., pp. 195, 662.
85. Goff, "Logistics," p. 132.
86. *OR*, ser. 1, XX, pt. 1, 215, 674. A recent general study good on the detail of the winter campaign in Tennessee, though the author is not interested in doctrine or organization, is James Lee McDonough, *Stones River: Bloody Winter in Tennessee* (Knoxville: University of Tennessee Press, 1984).

8. Trench Warfare and Maneuver

1. *OR*, ser. 1, XXIV, pt. 1, 33, 48, 54, 58; Sherman, *Home Letters*, pp. 251–252, 258, 260, 263, 273. Data are not available to calculate the transportation standards of Grant and Sherman. But limited data shortly after Vicksburg suggest that the army had a standard of forty wagons per 1,000 men that may have been applied at the time of the Vicksburg campaign.
2. Brown, *Signal Corps*, pp. 510–511.
3. *OR*, ser. 3, III, 953, 959; Brown, *Signal Corps*, pp. 510–511. The Army of the Potomac had five field trains by comparison.
4. *OR*, ser. 1, XXIV, pt. 1, 41, 242. For the low priority that Confederate strategists put on Vicksburg and the consequences, see Hattaway and Jones, *How the North Won*, chap. 13. See especially p. 375.
5. Livermore, *Numbers and Losses*, pp. 99–100.
6. *OR*, ser. 1, XXIV, pt. 1, 54, 151–152; ibid., pt. 2, 69; *Atlas*, vol. 1, pl. XXVII (7).
7. *OR*, ser. 1, XXIV, pt. 1, 54, 152.
8. Ibid., pt. 2, 181, 330.
9. *OR*, ser. 1, XXIV, pt. 2, 169–170; Comte de Paris, *History of the Civil War in America*, vol. 3, p. 364.
10. *OR*, ser. 1, XXIV, pt. 1, 273; ibid., pt. 2, 330.
11. Ibid., pt. 1, 273.
12. Ibid.; Livermore, *Numbers and Losses*, p. 100. Numbers are effective strength.
13. Ibid., pt. 1, 273; ibid., pt. 2, 170, 330.
14. Ibid., pt. 2, 170.
15. Ibid., pt. 3, 334.
16. Moseley, "Tactics," p. 356.
17. *OR*, ser. 1, XXIV, pt. 3, 343–344; ibid., pt. 2, 170; Grant, *Memoirs*, p. 278.

18. *OR*, ser. 1, XXIV, pt. 2, 131.

19. Ibid., p. 170.

20. Ibid., p. 181.

21. Ibid., p. 170.

22. Ibid., pt. 1, 56–57, ibid., pt. 2, 170–171, 177.

23. Gabions are cylindrical baskets of various dimensions open at both ends, used to rivet the interior slopes of batteries and the cheeks of embrasures, and to form or reinforce the parapets of trenches.

24. Fascines are long cylindrical fagots, normally constructed of brushwood, used for supporting and reinforcing earthen parapets.

25. Sap rollers are two large gabions that sappers roll before them while digging trenches of approach.

26. *OR*, ser. 1, pt. 2, 176; Comte de Paris, *History of the Civil War in America*, vol. 3, p. 370.

27. *OR*, ser. 1, XXXIV, pt. 2, 171; Sherman, *Home Letters*, pp. 264, 266.

28. *OR*, ser. 1, XXXIV, pt. 2, 177.

29. Ibid., pp. 175–176.

30. Ibid., pp. 175, 181–182, 336.

31. A retrenchment is an inner defensible line, either constructed in the original design of a line or executed on the spur of the occasion, to cut off a breach or to protect a weak point of the line.

32. *OR*, ser. 1, XXXIV, pt. 2, 332.

33. Ibid., p. 333.

34. Ibid., pp. 333–334.

35. Ibid., pt. 1, 279–285. For a recent history of the siege of Vicksburg, see Richard Wheeler, *The Siege of Vicksburg* (New York: Crowell, 1978).

36. Ibid., p. 41; *Atlas*, vol. 1, pl. XXXVI (2); Comte de Paris, *History of the Civil War in America*, vol. 3, p. 378. *Circumvallation* is the military term for works that face outwards to protect against any attempt to lift a siege by direct attack from the rear or flanks.

37. *OR*, ser. 1, XXXIV, pt. 1, 41.

38. Ibid., p. 242.

39. Comte de Paris, *History of the Civil War in America*, vol. 3, p. 323.

40. John G. Barrett, *Sherman's March through the Carolinas* (Chapel Hill: University of North Carolina Press, 1956), pp. 14–17. On Sherman's philosophy of war, see also J. B. Walters, "Sherman and Total War" (Ph.D. diss., Vanderbilt, 1947); J. B. Walters, "General William T. Sherman and Total War," *Journal of Southern History* 14 (November, 1948): 447–480.

41. *OR*, ser. 1, XXIV, pt. 3, 475. Data are lacking on the details of Sherman's transportation standard, but limited available evidence suggests that the Army of the Tennessee probably had a standard of approximately forty wagons per 1,000 men (*NA*, RG 92, entry 1317).

42. *OR*, ser. 1, XXIV, pt. 2, 522.

43. Ibid., XXIV, pt. 2, 525.

44. Ibid., pp. 523–525, 534–535; ibid., *Atlas*, vol. 1, XXXVII(5).

45. *OR*, ser. 1, XXIV, pt. 2, 526.

46. Ibid., pp. 530–531.

47. Ibid., pp. 528–532.

48. Ibid., XXIII, pt. 1, 8–9; Hattaway and Jones, *How the North Won*, p. 387.

49. *OR*, ser. 1, XXIII, pt. 2, 281–282, 300–304, 320–321.

50. Ibid.

51. Rosecrans's army had 45,000 animals on August 8, 1863 (*OR*, ser. 1, XXII, pt. 2, 601). From the tone of the quartermaster reports, it can be assumed that this is the standard to which Rosecrans aspired and which he achieved for the Tullahoma campaign as well as for the subsequent maneuver to turn Bragg out of Chattanooga. Evidence of this is the fact that he had 43,000 animals, as noted, on March 23, before the attrition in horses drastically cut his numbers. The Union army as a whole had 11,000 wagons on July 31, 1863 (ibid., ser. 3, III, 1124–1125). The Army of the Potomac had 3,500 of these for the Gettysburg campaign. Allowing for wagons with other Union forces, which are impossible, it appears, to calculate with accuracy, a reasonable estimate is that Rosecrans probably had around 3,000 wagons. Incomplete and difficult-to-calculate field reports on transportation tend to confirm this estimate (*NA*, RG 94, entry 65, infantry and battery inspection reports on transportation, July through September; ibid., RG 92, entry 1317, monthly reports of the means of transportation of the quartermaster general's office for October and December, 1863. The infantry and battery inspection reports of the adjutant general's office are less than complete for the Army of the Cumberland, whereas the monthly reports of the means of transportation of the quartermaster general's office are complete. By correlating reports from the two sources when they overlap, one can calculate reasonable estimates of the probable totals from the incomplete inspection reports—when the latter are available).

The dramatically fluctuating ratio of horses to mules with the heavy attrition of horses and attempts, as noted, to replace them with mules, makes it difficult to estimate the ratio of horses to mules at the time of the two maneuvers. Hence, it is difficult to calculate with accuracy the number of animals left over for extras, for relief, and for pack trains, as six-mule and four-horse teams hauled the same load. The attrition rate for mules, as noted, was negligible.

If we make a hypothetical arithmetic breakdown of 2 mules to 1 horse and allow 35,000 animals for transportation, including artillery (excluding 10,000 cavalry horses), and if we generously allow that Rosecrans was rotating his vulnerable horses so that half hauled while half foraged, we get the following: Rosecrans hauled 1,500 wagons with 9,000 of his 23,000 mules, the other 1,500 with one-half of his 12,000 horses. This left 14,000 mules for a pack train. Using conversions noted earlier, 14,000 mules in a pack train is the equivalent of approximately 1,150 wagons. This gave Rosecrans the carrying capacity of approximately 4,150, wagons for a standard of 69 wagons per 1,000 men. The nature of the terrain—and the weather conditions for the Tullahoma campaign—made the less-than-popular mule trains particularly advantageous for Rosecrans's 1863 campaign, increasing the likelihood that they were used. As noted earlier, despite Rufus Ingalls's attempts to have them eliminated from the Army of the Potomac, Halleck insisted that mule trains be retained. The campaigning conditions and the presence of such a surplus of mules increased the likelihood that Rosecrans used a mule train.

Rosecrans did not maintain a wagon supply line for the Tullahoma campaign. Hence, he may have realized the standard of 69 wagons per 1,000 men. He did maintain a wagon supply line for his movement to turn Bragg out of Chattanooga. And it would have made increasing demands for wagons and animals as it grew longer and longer. By September 30, 1863, there was an increase of 1,300 wagons in the entire Union army from July 31 (*OR*, ser. 3, III, 1124–1125).

One presumes that most of these went to where the need was greatest, namely, to Rosecrans's supply line. With a standard of 50 wagons per 1,000 men, Rosecrans could have maintained a supply line of approximately 1,000 to 2,300 wagons. The former figure is without any of the additional wagons, the latter with all the additional wagons. The figure of 50 as a probable standard is based largely on the fact that this is the standard that Sherman established for his combined western armies, including the Army of the Cumberland, for the continuation of the campaign to penetrate to Atlanta in the spring. This assumption is based further on the speculation that Sherman probably accepted the 1863 experience—and the resulting transportation standard—from the Army of the Cumberland. Significant to this argument is the fact that Sherman selected the quartermaster of the Army of the Cumberland, L. C. Easton, as the chief quartermaster for his combined armies for 1864–65.

52. *OR*, ser. 1, XXIII, pt. 1, 9. Hattaway and Jones make an elaborate analysis of how the more serious ground moisture problem in the West made roads, especially in severe weather, a greater burden to mobility than in the East (Hattaway and Jones, *How the North Won*, pp. 151–152, fn. 28).

53. *OR*, ser. 3, IV, 879.

54. For the biography of Rosecrans, see William M. Lamers, *Edge of Glory: A Biography of General William S. Rosecrans* (New York: Harcourt Brace, 1961). See also Hattaway and Jones on Rosecrans, *How the North Won*.

55. *OR*, ser. 1, XXX, pt. 3, 818; ibid., pt. 2, 36–37.

56. Calculated from General Orders, no. 171, August 26, 1863, *NA*, RG 109, chap. V, vol. 54½.

57. Calculated from General Orders, no. 182, September 24, 1863, ibid.; For Longstreet's arrival without wagons, see *OR*, ser. 1, XXX, pt. 3, 818; ibid., pt. 2, 36–37.

58. Ibid., pt. 4, 551, 729–730.

59. Alexander, *Memoirs*, pp. 452–453; *OR*, ser. 1, XXX, pt. 1, 57.

60. Hattaway and Jones, *How the North Won*, pp. 448–450.

61. English, "Confederate Field Communications," pp. 127–128.

62. Alexander, *Memoirs*, p. 452.

63. *OR*, ser. 1, XXX, pt. 1, 57.

64. Ibid., pt. 2, 24.

65. Ibid., p. 393; *B & L*, vol. 3, p. 652.

66. *OR*, ser. 1, XXX, pt. 2, 33.

67. Alexander, *Memoirs*, p. 458; *OR*, ser. 1, XXX, pt. 2, 172.

68. *OR*, ser. 1, XXX, pt. 1, 705–706.

69. Ibid., pp. 38–39, 59–61; Alexander, *Memoirs*, pp. 460–462. For the biography of the general made famous by his stand at Chickamauga, see Freeman Cleaves, *Rock of Chickamauga: The Life of General George H. Thomas* (Westport, Conn.: Greenwood Press, 1974).

70. *OR*, ser. 1, XXX, pt. 1, 39; Alexander, *Memoirs*, pp. 461–462, 465. Total Federal casualties numbered just under 30 percent of the forces equipped and ready for duty (*OR*, ser. 1, XXX, pt. 1, 170). Alexander, from the *OR* and his own information, calculated Federal dead and wounded to be 21 percent of their total strength (*Memoirs*, p. 462).

71. *OR*, ser. 1, XXX, pt. 2, 22–24, 34–37. Richard Goff analyzes Bragg's motives on the double edge of tactical and logistical factors (*Supply*, pp. 190–191).

72. *OR*, ser. 1, XXX, pt. 1, 705–706.

73. Jamieson, "Tactics," pp. 98–99, 102.

74. Ibid., p. 152.

75. *OR*, ser. 1, XXX, pt. 1, 412–413, 446–447, 450, 452, 454, 456, 887–891, 896–897, 902–904, 920–923; ibid., pt. 2, 115, 117, 172–175, 187, 229, 287, 520–527, 525; ibid., XXXI, pt. 1, 545.

76. *OR*, ser. 1, XXX, pt. 3, 823; *Atlas*, vol. 1, pl. XLIX (2).

77. *OR*, ser. 1, XXX, pt. 3, 818.

78. Ibid., p. 823.

79. Grant, *Memoirs*, pp. 322–323.

80. *OR*, ser. 1, XXX, pt. 3, 823.

81. *Atlas*, vol. 1, pl. XLIX (2); *OR*, ser. 1, XXXI, pt. 2, 315–316.

82. E.g., *OR*, ser. 1, XXXI, pt. 2, p. 676; Alexander, *Memoirs*, p. 477; *OR*, ser. 1, XXX, pt. 3, 110–111, 922, 928–929, 947.

83. Ibid., ser. 3, IV, 879.

84. Ibid., ser. 1, XXX, pt. 1, 216–221; ibid., pt. 4, 208.

85. Ibid., XXXI, pt. 1, 752.

86. Ibid., pt. 2, 27, 29.

87. Ibid., p. 11.

88. Ibid., pt. 3, 89–91; Sherman, *Home Letters*, p. 277.

89. Monthly reports of the means of transportation, Army of the Tennessee, October and December, 1863, *NA*, RG 92, entry 1317.

90. *OR*, ser. 3, IV, 880. The detailed itinerary for the Carolinas campaign in 1865 suggests that the direct distance traveled was approximately three-quarters to three-fifths the actual distance marched, varying with the routes of different units (*OR*, ser. 1, XLVII, pt. 1, 76–165.) The speculative figure for Sherman's march assumes, perhaps dangerously, approximately the same factors affecting the distance traveled.

91. Ibid., ser. 3, IV, 887–888. Sherman early emphasized a disciplined order of march in which he called for close-order marching to "prevent even marching by side paths—to keep in ranks as on parade." He called for frequent rests and set a standard of two miles per hour (Order of March 16, 1862, *OR*, ser. 1, X, pt. 1, 26). Sherman also solved a recurring problem by impressing local citizens when army guides were not available (ibid.).

92. *OR*, ser. 1, XXXI, pt. 2, 29–30.

93. Ibid., p. 29.

94. Ibid., p. 31.

95. Ibid., pp. 24, 32–33, 41–42, 90; Grant, *Memoirs*, pp. 331–332.

96. *B & L*, vol. 3, pp. 112–113.

97. *OR*, ser. 1, XXXI, pt. 2, 33.

98. Ibid., p. 573. His artillery constructed "bombproofs" (ibid., p. 383).

99. Ibid., pp. 574, 748–749.

100. Ibid., pp. 316–317.

101. Ibid., pp. 31, 33; English, "Confederate Field Communications," p. 131.

102. For the Signal Corps, see *OR*, ser. 1, XXX, pt. 1, 241–243; ibid., XXXI, pt. 2, 100–102, 103, 107–108, 110, 596–598; ibid., ser. 3, III, 949; Brown, *Signal Corps*, pp. 474–485. Problems still remained. The December 28, 1863, report from the inspector of the signal detachment in the Army of the Cumberland complained of a lack of military procedure and a pattern of irregular, informal operations. He noted that this was part of the reason the Signal Corps was

having difficulties in gaining acceptance (*NA*, RG 393, pt. 1, entry 1137, pp. 17–18).

103. *OR*, ser. 1, XXXI, pt. 2, 750–751.
104. Ibid., p. 34.
105. Jamieson, "Tactics," pp. 113–114.
106. Alexander, *Memoirs*, p. 477; *OR*, ser. 1, XXXI, pt. 2, 676.
107. Alexander, *Memoirs*, pp. 477–478.
108. *OR*, ser. 1, XXXI, pt. 2, 79.
109. Livermore, *Numbers and Losses*, pp. 107–108.
110. The Union forces used artillery effectively in the line on offense, particularly on occasions when they secured positions that swept Confederate infantry entrenchments. Superior defensive dispositions to those at Chickamauga also allowed the Confederate artillery to take its toll on the Union assaults. It is difficult to determine when the attacking Union artillery was in advance of, in rear of, or in the infantry line. There is a general impression from the reports that the artillery was positioned where opportunity afforded. John Brannen, now in command of the artillery of the Army of the Cumberland, eventually would fight his artillery, on occasion, in the skirmish line (Jamieson, "Tactics," p. 153); but Chattanooga does not appear to have been one of those occasions.

Ordnance complaints from Brannen and some of his battery commanders were indicative of the technological problems that undermined the effectiveness of all artillery except the Napoleon when firing shot from entrenched defensive positions. Brannen rated various shells in use from unsatisfactory to useless. The principal problem was the quality of the timing fuses, but artillery officers also complained about the quality of powder as well as the defective design of the cap plunger on the ten- and twenty-pounder Parrots (*OR*, ser. 1, XXXI, pt. 2, 553–555, 558). Cavalry failed to play a role on the battlefield, though Sherman used both his cavalry and mounted infantry effectively in their strategic role of disrupting Confederate supply and telegraph lines, as well as for reconnaissance. In one instance, where Union cavalry attacking a supply train were attacked by Confederate infantry and artillery, the cavalry fought dismounted (ibid., pp. 561–568, 578).

111. *B & L*, vol. 3, pp. 731–732.
112. *OR*, ser. 1, XXIII, 28.
113. Ibid., pp. 176, 289.
114. Ibid., XXX, pt. 3, 291–293.
115. Brown, *Signal Corps*, p. 503.
116. *OR*, ser. 1, XXXI, pt. 1, 459.
117. Ibid., p. 306.
118. Ibid., pp. 306–307, 504; *Atlas*, pl. XLVIII (2), pl. CXI (5).
119. *OR*, ser. 1, XXXI, pt. 1, pp. 307, 459, 483.
120. Ibid., pp. 460, 484.
121. Ibid., pp. 460–461.
122. Ibid., pp. 478–480.
123. Ibid., pp. 460–461.
124. Ibid., pp. 439, 541–549.
125. Ibid., 406–420, 440–441, 542, 545.
126. Ibid., pt. 2, 25; ibid., pt. 3, 818.

9. Loss of Legitimacy

1. For the Washington defenses, constructed under the direction of the greatest military engineer of the Civil War era, John G. Barnard, see Benjamin

F. Cooling, *Symbol, Sword, and Shield: Defending Washington during The Civil War* (Hamden, Conn.: Archon Books, 1975). See also John G. Barnard, *A Report on the Defenses of Washington* (Washington, D.C.: Government Printing Office, 1871). For the merger of the Corps of Engineers and the Topographical Engineers, see *OR*, ser. 1, XXV, pt. 1, 194.

2. This chapter does not pretend to be a history of engineering organization during the Civil War. It is a limited accumulation of evidence in support of speculations about the decline of the engineers and their view of military professionalism during the Civil War.

3. *OR*, ser. 1, V, 25.

4. Ibid., XXIV, pt. 1, 56–57; ibid., pt. 2, 170–171, 176–177.

5. Ibid., ser. 4, II, 259.

6. Ibid., ser. 3, II, 762–763.

7. Hill, *Roads, Rails, and Waterways*. On the dispersion of engineers, see also Samuel R. Bright, Jr., "Confederate Coast Defense" (Ph.D. diss., Duke University, 1961).

8. *OR*, ser. 3, V, 162. For the problem of social roles for the Corps of Engineers, see Skelton, "The United States Army, 1821–1837."

9. *OR*, ser. 3, 11, 762–763.

10. *OR*, ser. 3, I, 397.

11. For the history of the Corps of Topographical Engineers, see Henry P. Beers, "A History of the U.S. Topographical Engineers, 1813–1863," *Military Engineer* 34 (1942): 287–291, 348–352.

12. *OR*, ser. 3, I, 401–402.

13. Ibid., II, 763.

14. *OR*, ser. 1, V, 895, 908. The engineer organization of the Army of the Potomac through Chancellorsville consisted of the Topographical Engineers, attached to headquarters staff, the regular Engineer Battalion, also attached to headquarters staff, and the volunteer engineer brigade, which by Chancellorsville numbered about 2,000 strong, under command of a regular engineer, holding the rank of brigadier general of volunteers (ibid., XXV, pt. 1, 194).

15. *OR*, ser. 3, II, 279–280.

16. Ibid., IV, 490–510.

17. Ibid., pp. 1223, 1254–1255.

18. *OR*, ser. 1, XXXVIII, pt. 1, 136.

19. For the improvised engineering organization in Sherman's army, see ibid., pp. 127–139. See especially p. 128.

20. Ibid., p. 793.

21. Ibid., ser. 4, II, 259–260.

22. *OR*, ser. 4, II, 47, 198, 259–261, 445–446.

23. *OR*, ser. 3, IV, 793; ibid., V, 162.

24. *OR*, ser. 4, III, 1084–1085.

25. Quoted from Gilmer's personal papers by Bright, "Confederate Coast Defense," p. 193.

26. *OR*, ser. 4, II, 260.

27. Ibid., p. 289.

28. Ibid., pp. 445–446.

29. Ibid., p. 289.

30. Ibid., p. 260.

31. For Sherman's attitude on the engineers, see U.S. Congress, House Re-

ports on Committees, Report no. 74. "Army Staff Reorganization," 42d Congress, 3d Session, 1873; See also Sherman, *Memoirs*. The Civil War also had a limited impact on European military thought (Luvaas, *The Military Legacy of the Civil War*). The lack of direct or immediate impact, and the fact that subsequent change learned little from history, does not diminish the historical place of the Civil War in the historical evolution of war.

10. Position and Attrition

1. *OR*, ser. 1, XXXIII, 1144.
2. Freeman, *Lee*, vol. 3, pp. 248–253.
3. *OR*, ser. 1, XXXIII, 1273.
4. *Lee's Dispatches*, pp. 166–167; *OR*, ser. 1, XXXIII, 1320–1321.
5. *OR*, ser. 1, XLVI, pt. 1, 11. For a balanced analysis of Grant's strategy that comes to a different conclusion on the issue of attrition, see Hattaway and Jones, *How the North Won*, chaps. 16–19.
6. *OR*, ser. 3, V, 243, 255–256.
7. Ibid., pp. 242–243. There were detailed alterations in the specifications of the six-mule wagon in the winter of 1864–65 (*NA*, RG 92, entry 225, Box no. 1193). Good data on the history of the development of the army wagon are to be found in ibid. The reports and correspondence pertinent to supply generally indicate that the Union supply bureaus were meeting the needs of the Army of the Potomac with promptness and efficiency, and that the supply of the army was efficiently organized and administered in the field, e.g., *OR*, ser. 1, XXXVI, pt. 2, 353–355, 482; ibid., XL, pt. 1, 37–39; ibid., pt. 2, 211; ibid., ser. 3, V, 242–243. The wisdom of the standard of supply and transportation that Grant permitted in the Army of the Potomac is another matter. For the detailed organization of his quartermaster department, see ibid., ser. 3, IV, 894–901.
8. *OR*, ser. 1, XXXVI, pt. 1, 354–355.
9. *OR*, ser. 3, V, 216; ibid., ser. 1, XLII, pt. 3, 703, 709.
10. Ibid., XLVI, pt. 2, 39–40, 82.
11. Ibid., XXXVI, pt. 2, 352–353, 482; ibid., pt. 1, 15.
12. Ibid., pt. 2, 560–561; ibid., pt. 1, 563–564, 598–599. Acquia Creek is a small tributary of the Potomac.
13. Ibid., pt. 2, 481.
14. Ibid., pt. 1, 3–4, 7, 9.
15. Ibid., p. 15.
16. Ibid., XL, pt. 1, 13.
17. Ibid., pp. 37–38.
18. Ibid., pp. 12–13.
19. Theodore Lyman, *Meade's Headquarters, 1863–1865: Letters of Col. Theodore Lyman from the Wilderness to Appomattox*, edited by George R. Agassiz (Boston: Atlantic Monthly Press, 1922), p. 159. Hereafter referred to as *Meade's Headquarters*. Lyman's correspondence is a valuable source of detail on tactical entrenchment by both the Army of the Potomac and the Army of Northern Virginia.
20. *OR*, XXXVI, pt. 2, 355.
21. Ibid., p. 352; ibid., pt. 1, 113.
22. Ibid., XXV, pt. 2, 547–562; ibid., ser. 3, IV, 888.
23. Ibid., ser. 1, XL, pt. 1, 41.
24. Ibid., XXXVI, pt. 2, 333.

25. For the preceding section on Meigs and Grant, see ibid., pp. 352, 355; ibid., pt. 1, 3; ibid., ser. 3, IV, 888; ibid., V, 242–243.

26. *OR*, ser. 1, XXV, pt. 2, 546.

27. Ibid., XL, pt. 1, 30. The new standard, in practice, was in place for the Union army, allowing for variations on the theme by Sherman, for the remainder of the war. For Meigs's acknowledgment that the average for the Union armies for the 1864 campaign was approximately 40 wagons per thousand, and for details on wagon purchases, subsistence, and forage for 1864, see *OR*, ser. 3, IV, 888; ibid., V, 232, 236–237, 243, 255–256.

28. *OR*, ser. 1, XLVI, pt. 1, 11. Grant, in keeping with his overall strategic view, expanded his statement to say: "I determined to use the greatest number of troops practicable against the armed force of the enemy preventing him from using the same force at different seasons against first one and then another of our armies, and the possibility of repose for refitting and—producing necessary supplies to carry on resistance" (ibid.).

29. There is extensive correspondence on the debate over the Horsford marching ration from the summer of 1864 through 1865 (*NA*, RG 92, entry 225, Box 416). For the canteen episode, see Horsford to Stanton, February 20, 1865, and Meigs to Stanton, March 20, 1865). For Butterfield's early plea for a concentrated ration, see *OR*, ser. 1, XXV, pt. 2, 487.

30. *OR*, ser. 1, XL, pt. 1, 38, 273–277.

31. Lee reduced the officers' baggage standard of 80 pounds for general officers, 65 pounds for field officers, and 50 pounds for company officers set by General Orders, no. 58, April 20, 1863, to 60 pounds for general officers, 50 pounds for field officers, and 30 pounds for other officers in General Orders, no. 27, April 5, 1864. But this amounted to a relatively insignificant reduction in total transportation. For the general, though incomplete, breakdown, and for the modifications of April 19 in General Orders, no. 32, see *NA*, RG 109, chap. 5, vol. 154½.

32. General Field Orders, no. 12, August 9, 1864, and General Orders, no. 27, November 3, 1864 (ibid.). There appears to be no record of field transportation and supply standards for 1865.

33. The formal standard for other subsistence items remained substantially unchanged (*Regulations, CSA* [Richmond; J. W. Randolph, 1864]).

34. Freeman, *Lee*, vol. 3, p. 241. For the role of religion as a motivating factor in the Confederate armies that compensated to a degree for organizational deficiencies in the friction of war, see Herman Norton, "Revivalism in the Confederate Armies," *Civil War History*, 6 (1960): 410–424; Robert Partin, "The Sustaining Faith of an Alabama Soldier," *Civil War History* 6 (1960): 425–438.

35. *Lee's Dispatches*, pp. 183–186.

36. Goff, *Supply*, pp. 220–224.

37. Ibid., pp. 212–213; Ramsdell, "Lee's Horse Supply," p. 772.

38. Ramsdell, "Lee's Horse Supply," pp. 769–770.

39. Ibid., p. 774.

40. *OR*, ser. 1, XLVI, pt. 2, 1242; Ramsdell, "Lee's Horse Supply," p. 776.

41. *OR*, ser. 1, XXXVI, pt. 2, 333.

42. Ibid., p. 357.

43. Ibid., pt. 1, 294–302, 307, 310, 317; ibid., pt. 2, 452; ibid., XL, pt. 1, 289–290; Lyman, *Meade's Headquarters*, p. 154.

44. *OR*, ser. 1, XXXVI, pt. 1, 319, 573–590.
45. Ibid., p. 319.
46. Ibid., p. 1070.
47. Ibid., pt. 2, 443; ibid., LI, pt. 2, 890.
48. Freeman, *Lee*, vol. 3, pp. 278–287.
49. Ibid., pp. 288–290.
50. *OR*, ser. 1, XXXVI, pt. 1, 325; Freeman, *Lee*, vol. 3, p. 290.
51. *OR*, ser. 1, XXXVI, pt. 1, 306–307; ibid., pt. 2, 452, 454–455, 459–460.
52. Ibid., pt. 1, 1061, 1063.
53. Ibid., pt. 2, 452.
54. Ibid., pt. 1, 1062; Alexander, *Memoirs*, p. 507; Freeman, *Lee*, vol. 3, p. 205.
55. Freeman, *Lee*, vol. 3, pp. 295–297.
56. *OR*, ser. 1, XXXVI, pt. 1, 133.
57. Livermore, *Numbers and Losses*, pp. 110–111.
58. Freeman, *Lee*, vol. 3, p. 298.
59. *OR*, ser. 1, XXXVI, pt. 1, 1042; ibid., pt. 2, 527, 539–541, 544.
60. Ibid., pt. 2, 565.
61. Ibid., 579–580.
62. *Lee's Dispatches*, pp. 176–177.
63. *OR*, ser. 1, XXXVI, pt. 1, 1071.
64. Ibid., p. 667.
65. Taylor, *Lee*, p. 130; *SHSP* 33 (1895): 23; ibid. 21 (1883): 239.
66. Freeman, *Lee*, vol. 3, p. 310.
67. Henderson, *The Science of War*, p. 332.
68. Freeman, *Lee*, vol. 3, p. 311.
69. *OR*, ser. 1, XXXVI, pt. 1, 667.
70. Ibid., p. 668.
71. Ibid., pt. 2, 614.
72. Ibid., pt. 1, 1046, 1073; ibid., pt. 2, 1019; ibid., LI, pt. 2, 922.
73. Ibid., XXXVI, pt. 1, 1092, 1094.
74. Freeman, *Lee*, vol. 3, p. 325.
75. Ibid., pp. 325–326.
76. Livermore, *Numbers and Losses*, pp. 112–113.
77. *OR*, ser. 1, XXXVI, pt. 1, 5–6.
78. Ibid., pp. 1046, 1073; ibid., pt. 2, 1019.
79. Ibid., pt. 1, 738.
80. For Lee's reasoning in the anticipation of Grant's destination, see Freeman, *Lee*, vol. 3, pp. 341–342.
81. Henderson, *The Science of War*, p. 327.
82. *Lee's Dispatches*, p. 200; Freeman, *Lee*, vol. 3, pp. 341–352.
83. *Lee's Dispatches*, p. 200.
84. Freeman, *Lee*, vol. 3, p. 353.
85. *OR*, ser. 1, XXXVI, pt. 1, 918, 1030–1031.
86. Freeman, *Lee*, vol. 3, p. 356.
87. *OR*, ser. 1, XXXVI, pt. 1, 918, 1030–1031.
88. Ibid., p. 9.
89. For details, see Freeman, *Lee*, vol. 3, pp. 377–384.
90. Ibid., p. 437.
91. *OR*, ser. 1, XXXVI, pt. 3, 863; Freeman, *Lee*, vol. 3, pp. 373–374.

92. *OR*, ser. 1, XXXVI, pt. 1, 11.

93. *B & L*, vol. 4, p. 217.

94. Alexander, *Memoirs*, p. 542; Livermore, *Numbers and Losses*, p. 114.

95. *OR*, ser. 1, XXXVI, pt. 1, 11; Lyman, *Meade's Headquarters*, p. 144.

96. Ibid., pp. 369, 735–736, 747.

97. Ibid., pp. 735, 739–740; Lyman, *Meade's Headquarters*, pp. 144, 147.

98. *OR*, ser. 1, XXXVI, pt. 1, 12.

99. A revealing comment on Grant's untutored pragmatism is found in Sherman's congratulatory letter to Grant on his promotion to command of all Union forces: "My only points of doubt were in your knowledge of grand strategy, and of books of science and history, but I confess your common sense seems to have supplied all these" (ibid., pt. 3, 49).

100. Ibid., pt. 1, 9.

101. Lyman, *Meade's Headquarters*, p. 224; George Gordon Meade, ed., *The Life and Letters of George Gordon Meade* (New York: Charles Scribner's Sons, 1913), pp. 197–198, 201, 207.

102. *OR*, ser. 1, pt. 1, 1033–1034; ibid., LI, pt. 2, 984; Bruce Catton, *A Stillness at Appomattox* (Garden City, N.Y.: Doubleday and Co., 1953), pp. 172–173. Colonel Theodore Lyman is excellent in his battlefield observations on the rituals of fraternization (e.g., Lyman, *Meade's Headquarters*, pp. 181–182).

103. *OR*, ser. 1, XL, pt. 1, 180.

104. Freeman, *Lee*, vol. 3, pp. 420–423; Livermore, *Numbers and Losses*, pp. 115–116.

105. See the detailed itinerary of the Army of the Potomac and of the Army of the James (*OR*, ser. 1, XL, pt. 1, 178–218). See also ibid., pp. 363, 394. For the siege of Petersburg, see Richard Sommers, *Richmond Redeemed: The Siege of Petersburg* (Garden City, N.Y.: Doubleday, 1981).

106. Ibid., pp. 182–183.

107. Ibid., p. 290.

108. Ibid., pp. 17, 286–287.

109. Ibid., p. 397; For Union entrenchments, see *Atlas*, vol. 1, pl. XLIV (1); *OR*, ser. 1, XL, pt. 1, 287; for the Union artillery map, see *Atlas*, vol. 1, pl. XLIV (3); Freeman, *Lee*, vol. 3, p. 463; Alexander, *Memoirs*, p. 560.

110. *Lee's Dispatches*, pp. 254–255.

111. *OR*, ser. 1, XL, pt. 1, 799; for full reports on this controversial incident, see ibid., pp. 796–799.

112. Ibid., XXXVII, pt. 1, 767.

113. Livermore, *Numbers and Losses*, p. 115; *OR*, ser. 1, XL, pt. 2, 156–157, 333–334.

114. Ibid., pp. 268–269.

115. Ibid., pp. 30–31, 36.

116. Ibid., XXXVII.

117. Ibid., XL, pt. 2, 32.

118. This picture is portrayed in the Union correspondence (*OR*, ser. 1, XL, pt. 2).

119. Ibid., p. 468.

120. Ibid., p. 599.

121. Ibid., pp. 333–334.

122. Ibid., p. 399.

123. Ibid., pp. 33–34.

124. Ibid., pt. 1, 34.
125. Ibid., pp. 164, 524.
126. Ibid., p. 285.
127. Ibid., pp. 17, 34, 364.
128. Ibid., pp. 523–524.
129. Ibid., pp. 293, 523.
130. Ibid.
131. Ibid., p. 291.
132. Ibid.
133. Ibid., p. 285.
134. Ibid., p. 17.
135. Ibid., pp. 760, 789; *B & L*, vol. 4, p. 555; *SHSP* 10 (1882): 126–127.
136. *OR*, ser. 1, XL, pt. 1, 42–163. For Union mining and Confederate countermining activity, see also the excellent contemporary report of Colonel Theodore Lyman (Lyman, *Meade's Headquarters*, pp. 195–201).
137. Ibid., p. 918.
138. *Lee's Dispatches*, pp. 288–289.
139. *OR*, ser. 1, XLII, pt. 1, 908ff.
140. L. H. Shaver, *History of the Sixteenth Alabama Regiment, Gracies Alabama Brigade* (Montgomery: Barrett and Brown, 1867), p. 82.
141. *Lee's Dispatches*, p. 342.
142. Ibid., pp. 342–343.
143. *OR*, ser. 1, XLII, pt. 1, 52.
144. Freeman, *Lee*, vol. 4, pp. 42–43.
145. For a breakdown of figures on the density of infantry per mile along the Confederate line on April 1, and comparative figures to show the deterioration from March 27, see ibid., pp. 42–43.
146. Ibid., pp. 58, 60, 66–67, 71, 81–84; *OR*, ser. 1, XLII, pt. 1, 1295.
147. *OR*, ser. 1, XXXVI, pt. 1, 119ff.

11. Organization, Maneuver, and the Strategy of Exhaustion

1. For Johnston's litany of woes, see especially *OR*, ser. 1, XLVII, pt. 1, 1050–1054, 1058–1069.
2. *OR*, ser. 1, XXXI, pt. 3, 502–613, 618, 622–624, 653–654, 736–737, 772–774, 842, 856–857, 860; Goff, *Supply*, pp. 203–209. For Johnston's formal standards for field transportation and baggage, see *NA*, RG 109, chap. 5, vol. 154½. For his reduced ration standard of February, 1864, see ibid., chap. 2, vol. 350, p. 23. For Confederate army regulations, see *Regulations, CSA* (Richmond: West and Johnston, 1861) and *Regulations, CSA* (Richmond: J. W. Randolph, 1862, 1863, and 1864).
3. *OR*, ser. 1, XXXVIII, pt. 3, 615.
4. E.g., see the report of Sherman's chief quartermaster, Brigadier General L. C. Easton, *OR*, ser. 1, pt. 1, 696–703.
5. Ibid., p. 697. Sherman's large supply of horses at a time when they were being phased out of the Army of the Potomac in all but artillery and cavalry service may be a tribute to the close attention he gave to animal care. Sherman indicated that he expected to march with 20,000 additional troops. The army was not reduced for logistical reasons, but from men not returning from furlough and from a failure to recruit (Sherman, *Home Letters*, p. 289).

6. Situations where statistics are not available are not likely to challenge Sherman's standard as the second-highest of the war.

7. Meigs's report for June 30, 1863, to June 30, 1864, *OR*, ser. 3, IV, 888.

8. Moore, "Mobility and Strategy in the Civil War."

9. *OR*, ser. 1, XLIV, 8, 809, 844; ibid., XXXVI, pt. 2, 337.

10. Ibid., XL, pt. 1, 39; ibid., XXXV, pt. 2, 546.

11. For the thinking of Grant and Ingalls as they arrived at a wagon standard of 40 per 1,000 men early in 1864 and stuck with it through 1865, see ibid., XXXVI, pt. 2, 352, 355; ibid., pt. 1, 3, 1113; ibid., ser. 3, IV, 888.

12. *OR*, ser. 3, V, 213–214. For the logistical details of Sherman's movements from Chattanooga to Atlanta, see ibid., ser. 1, LII, pt. 1, 697–698.

13. Ibid., LII, pt. 1, 698–701.

14. *OR*, ser. 3, V, 227. One can only speculate on whether the antagonism to the eastern command elite and their institutional setting, the Corps of Engineers, that Sherman voiced after the war was a factor in his seeming distance from Meigs, who was commissioned in the Corps of Engineers.

15. *OR*, ser. 1, XLIV, 13.

16. Ibid., pp. 8–9.

17. Ibid., LII, pt. 1, 701–702; ibid., LIII, 45; ibid., XLIV, 7; Sherman, *Home Letters*, pp. 313–314.

18. *OR*, ser. 1, XLIV, 8, 809, 844; Sherman, *Home Letters*, p. 321.

19. Meigs noted with interest, upon hearing of Sherman's logistical column, that in walking the route of Lee's march during the Gettysburg campaign, he had discovered that Lee had similarly marched his columns in the fields beside the supply trains, which occupied the roads (*OR*, ser. 1, XLVII, pt. 2, 592; Sherman, *Home Letters*, p. 321).

20. *OR*, ser. 1, XLIV, 13, 76–77, 85; ibid., pt. 2, 512; ibid., XLV, pt. 2, 511–512; ibid., LII, pt. 1, 694–696; ibid., XLVII, pt. 1, 213–219.

21. Ibid., XLIV, 13.

22. Ibid., LII, pt. 1, 702.

23. Ibid.

24. Ibid., p. 703. The movement was eased by each column having its own pontoon trains and each division its pioneer force to cross streams and repair roads. This proved very efficient. Streams were sometimes crossed and roads repaired without slowing the movement of the troops.

25. Ibid., p. 45; ibid., XLIV, 83.

26. Direct distance from Atlanta to Savannah was approximately 250 miles. This estimate on actual distance traveled and average miles per day is speculation from one piece of information from the march. The evidence needs the benefit of some guesswork and comparison with detailed division itineraries that estimate the rate of march for the Carolinas campaign—which has its risks (ibid., XLVII, pt. 1, 76–165; ibid., XLIV, 89.) The itinerary of actual distance traveled during the Carolinas campaign indicates that direct distance was on average about three-quarters to three-fifths the actual distance traveled, varying with the movements of different divisions. The only calculation of mileage for the march to Savannah that this author has been able to uncover is that of Major General Peter Osterhaus in command of the XV Corps, Army of the Tennessee, which includes movements before the Savannah march. Osterhaus reports that during forty-six actual marching days (which, coincidentally, was the approximate marching time during the Carolinas campaign) within the period October

14 to December 21, 1864, his corps covered 684 miles, an average of approximately 15 miles on actual marching days. Allowing that Osterhaus was engaged in near-continuous marching from November 15 when he left Atlanta to December 21, approximately 80 percent of his actual marching time was on the march to the coast. Details of the remaining marching by the corps are vague, but based on the performance of Sherman's army before the march to the sea, it was probably lower. Also allowing for approximately 80 percent of the 684 miles to be on the march from Atlanta to Savannah, the XV Corps traveled approximately 550 miles. This would be the outer limits of the comparative distance traveled during the Carolinas campaign. The 15-mile-a-day average by the XV Corps is considerably above the 9- to 10-mile average per actual marching day during the Carolinas campaign; but the figure is realistic against the itinerary of day-to-day marching. The 15-mile daily march is the most common daily rate. Days of 16 to 18 miles' march occur, but are not common. The march to Savannah did not have the problems of terrain and weather that caused the cluster of 5- to 8- or 9-mile-a-day marches during the Carolinas campaign.

27. *OR*, ser. 3, V, 237.

28. *OR*, ser. 1, XLIV, 716, 455. For statistics on the enormous quantity of forage purchased by Sherman, see ibid., pp. 237–239.

29. Ibid., pp. 807–844. Sherman had wagons that had come through all his campaigns (ibid., ser. 3, V, 243).

30. Ibid., ser. 1, XLIV, 843.

31. Ibid., p. 569. Although only occasionally and incidentally interested in the organization of field transportation and field supply, Barrett, *Sherman's March through the Carolinas*, is a useful study of Sherman's campaign of total warfare from more general perspectives. See also Walters, *Sherman and Total War*; Walters, "General William T. Sherman and Total War."

32. Ibid., LIII, 44–46.

33. Ibid., XLVII, pt. 2, 443.

34. Ibid., LIII, 46.

35. *OR*, ser. 1, XLVII, pt. 2, 512.

36. Ibid., LIII, 45; ibid., ser. 3, V, 227.

37. Ibid., LIII, 46–47.

38. For a sense of Johnston's organizational obsessiveness, see *NA*, RG 109, chap. 2, vol. 350, pp. 1–79.

39. Ibid., pp. 79–81. For Hood's outspoken criticism of Johnston's defensive strategy upon assuming command, see *OR*, ser. 1, XXXVIII, pt. 3, 628–629. Hood's slanted yet valuable account of his experiences is John Bell Hood, *Advance and Retreat: Personal Experiences in the United States and Confederate States Armies*, edited by Richard Current (Bloomington: Indiana University Press, 1959).

40. *NA*, RG 109, chap. 2, vol. 350, p. 23.

41. Ibid., pp. 102, 107–108, 131.

42. Ibid., chap. 5, vol. 154½; ibid., chap. 2, vol. 350, pp. 87–90, 95, 98.

43. Hattaway and Jones, *How the North Won*, p. 632.

44. *OR*, ser. 1, XLVII, pt. 1, 1050–1051, 1053.

45. Ibid., pp. 1050–1054, 1058–1060; ibid., XLV, pt. 2, 704–705.

46. For the itinerary of Union forces during the Carolinas campaign, see *OR*, ser. 1, XLVII, pt. 1, 76–168. See especially pp. 77–78, 80–81, 85–87, 98. For statistics on actual marching days, see especially ibid., p. 85.

47. Ibid., p. 98.

48. Ibid., pt. 2, 795.

49. Special Field Orders, no. 69, ibid., p. 972. Cornelia P. Spencer, *The Last Ninety Days of the War in North Carolina* (New York: Watchman Publishing Co., 1866), has some interesting observations by a contemporary North Carolinian on Sherman's "bummers," the more or less outlaw bands of foraging parties who operated independently of military control. This small minority of foragers who terrorized civilians and contributed greatly to Sherman's reputation in the South grew up during the march to Atlanta (Barrett, *Sherman's March through the Carolinas*, pp. 36–38). The occasional tightening of organizational control over foragers was in part a response to the proliferation of the "bummer" problem. For the bummers—as well as the general character of Sherman's rank and file—see also Joseph T. Glatthaar, *The March to the Sea and Beyond: Sherman's Troops in the Savannah and Carolinas Campaigns* (New York: New York University Press, 1985), pp. 71, 103, 119–133, 141.

50. Ibid., LIII, 47.

51. Sherman's final wagon standard was close to that for the Army of the Potomac during the early history of the flying column in the Chancellorsville campaign. The Army of the Potomac was, however, a much larger army at the time, which made its standard in fact lower. The Army of the Potomac also successfully moved with an animal standard of 4 men per horse, approximately half that of Sherman.

52. Ibid., LIII, 47–48. With the net closing on Lee at Petersburg, and Johnston consolidating what was left of the forces under his command on Sherman's front, Sherman, after resupplying for the first time since he had left Atlanta, changed his strategy to the destruction of the enemy's army in battle. The result was the aborted Battle of Bentonville, March 19–21, where Sherman went directly at Johnston, who, after opening action, withdrew when faced with Sherman's entire army (ibid., XLVII, 30).

53. Ibid., LIII, 48.

54. For animals, wagons, and the Wehrmacht, see Larry H. Addington, *The Blitzkrieg Era and the German General Staff, 1865–1941* (New Brunswick, N.J.: Rutgers University Press, 1971).

55. *OR*, ser. 1, XXXVIII, pt. 1, 68–69.

56. Ibid., pp. 69, 196–197.

57. Ibid., pp. 68, 530.

58. Ibid., p. 134.

59. For the expression of these sentiments before Atlanta's defenses, see ibid., XLIV, 10, 12.

60. Ibid., pp. 72, 88.

61. Ibid., p. 89.

62. Moseley, "Tactics," pp. 361–363.

63. E.g., *OR*, ser. 1, XXXVIII, pt. 1, 537, 541. For the tactical pattern during the Atlanta campaign, the report of Capt. Orlando M. Poe, Sherman's chief engineer, is very good (ibid., pp. 127–139). See also the itinerary of the journal of the 1st Brigade, 1st Division, XIV Corps (ibid., pp. 527–534), and the report of the 88th Indiana Infantry (ibid., pp. 540–544).

64. Sherman, *Memoirs*, vol. 2, pp. 394–395; Jamieson, "Tactics," pp. 116, 118–119.

65. *OR*, ser. 1, XLVII, 236, 1124, 1055–1057.

66. Ibid., XLVII, 1124. There is a good record of entrenching activity for

some divisions in the itinerary of the Union forces for the campaign in the Carolinas (ibid., pp. 76–164).

67. Moseley, "Tactics," p. 376.

68. *OR*, ser. 1, XXXVIII, pt. 1, 84, 133.

69. Ibid., XLVII, pt. 1, 176.

70. Ibid., XXXVIII, pt. 1, 136.

71. For the improvised organization of engineering, see Poe's report, ibid., pp. 127–139. See especially p. 128.

72. Ibid., pp. 120–121.

73. Ibid., XLIV, 363, 365, 369, 381.

74. Ibid., pp. 370, 377, 408; ibid., XLVII, 30, 1120.

75. The best description of Johnston's entrenching is by Poe (ibid., XXXVIII, pt. 1, 129–131).

76. The battlefield at Bentonville, remarkably preserved when this author viewed it in 1961, has up to three lines of Confederate entrenchments. Nowhere is the scope of the entrenching habit more vividly displayed than in the remarkable extent of Confederate fortifications in wilderness so dense that a soldier would have been separated from troops in his line more than a few feet distant.

77. Order of June 1, 1864, *NA*, RG 109, chap. 2, vol. 350, p. 70.

78. Orders of June 3, 1864, ibid., pp. 2–3.

79. July 7, ibid., pp. 74–75.

80. Ibid., pp. 57–68.

81. Ibid., pt. 3, 628–629.

82. Jamieson, "Tactics," pp. 132–133B.

83. *NA*, RG 109, chap. 2, vol. 350, p. 93.

84. *OR*, ser. 1, XLVII, 1130–1132.

Works Cited

The basic documents available for any consecutive narrative analysis of tactical and strategic ideas and organization during the Civil War are the published official records of the Civil War and the unpublished holdings of the National Archives of the United States on the Union and Confederate armies. There are complementary materials in the Library of Congress. Material in the Virginia Historical Society in Richmond pertaining to the Confederate army is occasionally helpful, but in general is more useful for other aspects of Confederate military history than for tactical and strategic ideas and organization in relation to field operations. Personal papers, both published and in manuscript form, contain the occasional insights that almost make the search worthwhile. But they, too, are more valuable for research into other perspectives.

Some of the material necessary for a complete development of what happened, let alone why, is difficult to assemble: material on Confederate signals, for instance. What little I have found assumes organizational shape from the generous sharing of knowledge by David W. Gaddy, who perseveres in his quest to write a history of Confederate signals development. The step-by-step operational detail of Union signals in the official records can be elusive. I have not investigated some archival material not in the official records that might fill in more detail on the later use of the Beardslee field telegraph. Material on Confederate field transportation and supply prior to the spring of 1863 is not available, and presumably disappeared in the fire that destroyed Confederate quartermaster records. Early Union field transportation records also force the historian to speculate from data that are incomplete and difficult to interpret.

Treatises, textbooks, army regulations, field manuals, and official military reports are basic sources for military theory and doctrine for the Civil War and antebellum period. Memoirs and diaries contain some supplementary material. Last, but certainly not least, I have built on the wealth of scholarship in books, articles, and, to acknowledge a special debt, theses and dissertations.

Primary Sources

MANUSCRIPTS AND PUBLIC DOCUMENTS

Barnard, John G. *A Report on the Defenses of Washington.* Washington, D.C.: Government Printing Office, 1871.

Confederate States Congress. *The Statutes at Large of the Provisional Government of the Confederate States of America, from the Institution of the Government, February 8, 1861, to Its Termination, February 18, Inclusive.* Edited by James M. Matthews. Richmond: R. M. Smith, Printer to Congress, 1864.

Confederate States War Department. *General Orders from Adjutant and Inspector-General's Office.* Columbia, S.C.: Evans and Cogswell, 1864.

George B. McClellan, Sr., Papers. Library of Congress.

Papers Relating to the Subsistence Department, Confederate States Army. Virginia Historical Society, Richmond, Virginia.

U.S. Senate. *Military Commission to Europe in 1855 and 1856.* Report of Alfred Mordecai. Senate Executive Document, no. 60. 36th Congress, 1st Session, 1860.

―――. *Report of the Secretary of War Communicating the Report of Captain George B. McClellan,* one of the officers sent to the Seat of War in Europe in 1855–1856. Senate Executive Document, no. 1. 35th Congress, Special Session, 1859.

―――. *Report on the Art of War in Europe in 1854, 1855, and 1856.* Report of Richard Delafield. Senate Executive Document, no. 59. 36th Congress, 1st Session, 1860.

U.S. War Department. *Atlas to the Official Records of the Union and Confederate Armies.* 3 vols. Washington, D.C.: Government Printing Office, 1891–1895.

―――. *The War of The Rebellion: A Compilation of the Official Records of the Union and Confederate Armies.* 128 vols. Washington, D.C.: Government Printing Office, 1880–1901.

U.S. War Department Collection of Confederate Records: Record Group 109. Transportation, Subsistence, Special, General, and Field Orders and Circulars for Geographical and Higher Mobile Commands, Confederate States Armies. National Archives of the United States.

U.S. War Department Collection of Union Records.: Record Group 92. Records of the Office of the Quartermaster General; Record Group 94, Return and Inspection Reports, U.S. Army; Record Group 393. Records of the United States Army Continental Consolidated Commands, 1821–1920; unfiled and uncatalogued tri-monthly Quartermaster returns of the Union Army. National Archives of the United States.

MILITARY TREATISES, MANUALS, REGULATIONS

Beauregard, P. G. T. *Principles and Maxims of the Art of War—Outpost Service; General Instructions for Battles; Reviews.* Charleston, 1863. Reprinted in Beauregard, *A Commentary on the Campaign and Battle of Manassas, July,* 1861.

Board of Artillery Officers. *Instruction for Field Artillery.* Philadelphia: J. B. Lippincott and Co., 1860, 1861, 1863, 1864.

Butterfield, Daniel. *Camp and Outpost Duty for Infantry.* New York: Harper and Brother, 1863.

Casey, Silas. *Infantry Tactics, for the Instruction, Exercise, and Manoeuvers of the Soldier, a Company, Line of Skirmishers, Battalion, Brigade, or Corps D'Armee.* 3 vols. New York: D. Van Nostrand, 1862, 1865.

Charles, Archduke of Austria. *Principes de la stratégie, dévellopes par la relation de la Campagne de 1796 en Allemagne.* Translated from the German by Antoine Henri Jomini. Brussels, 1841. Originally published in 1818.

Cooke, Philip St. George. *Cavalry Tactics or Regulations for the Instruction, Formations, and Movements of the Army and Volunteers of the United States.* 2 pts. Washington, D.C.: Government Printing Office, 1861, 1862. Philadelphia: J. B. Lippincott, 1864.

Dodge, N. S. *Hints on Army Transportation.* Albany: Charles van Benthuysen, 1863.

Dufour, G. H. *Strategy and Tactics.* Translated from the French by William P. Craighill. New York: D. Van Nostrand, 1864.

Gay de Vernon, Francois Simon Marie Jules. *A Treatise on the Science of War and Fortification.* Composed for the use of the Imperial Polytechnic School and military schools; and translated for the War Department, for the use of the Military Academy of the United States. Translated by John Michael O'Connor. 2 vols. New York: J. Seymour, 1817.

Gibbon, John. *The Artillerist's Manual.* New York: D. Van Nostrand, 1860, 1861, 1863.

Halleck, Henry. *Elements of Military Art and Science.* New York: D. Appleton and Company, 1846.

Hardee, William Joseph. *Rifle and Infantry Tactics.* Revised and improved. Mobile: S. H. Goetzel and Co., 1855.

_____. *Rifle and Light Infantry Tactics.* Philadelphia: Lippincott, Grambo and Co., 1855.

Jomini, Antoine Henri. *Summary of the Art of War.* Translated by Captain G. H. Mendell and Captain W. P. Craighill. Philadelphia: J. B. Lippincott and Co., 1863.

_____. *Treatise on Great Military Operations.* Translated from the French by Colonel S. B. Holabird. New York: D. Van Nostrand, 1865.

Lloyd, Henry. *The History of the Late War in Germany: Between the King of Prussia and the Empress of Germany and Her Allies.* 2 vols. London: R. Horafield, 1767.

McClellan, George B. *Regulations and Instructions for the Field Service of the United States Cavalry in Time of War.* Philadelphia: J. B. Lippincott and Co., 1861.

MacDougall, P. L. *The Theory of War.* London: Longman, Brown, Green, Longmans and Roberts, 1858.

Mahan, Dennis Hart. *A Complete Treatise on Field Fortification.* New York: Wiley and Long, 1836.

_____. *An Elementary Treatise on Advanced-Guard, Outpost, and Detachment Service of Troops.* New York: Wiley and Putnam, 1847.

_____. *A Summary of the Course of Permanent Fortification and the Attack and Defense of Permanent Works.* Richmond: West and Johnston, 1863.

Morton, James St. Clair. *Letter to the Hon. John B. Floyd, Secretary of War, presenting for his consideration a new plan for the seacoast of the United States.* Washington, D.C.: William A. Harris, 1858.

_____. *Memoir on the Dangers and Defenses of New York City.* Washington, D.C.: William A. Harris, 1859.

_____. *Memoirs on American Fortification.* Washington, D.C.: William A. Harris, 1859.

The Quartermaster's Guide. Being a Compilation of Army Regulations from the Army Regulations and Other Sources. Richmond: West and Johnston, 1862.

Regulations, CSA. Richmond: West and Johnston, 1861.

Regulations, CSA. Richmond: J. W. Randolph, 1862.

Regulations, CSA. Richmond: J. W. Randolph, 1863.

Regulations for the CSA and for the Quartermaster's and Pay Departments. New Orleans: Bloomfield and Steel, 1861.

Regulations for the CSA for the Quartermaster's Department and Pay Branch Thereof. Richmond: Ritchie and Dunnavent, 1862.

Scott, Winfield. *Infantry Tactics: Or Rules for the Exercise and Manoeuvres of the United States Infantry.* 3 vols. New York: George Dearborn, 1835; Harper and Brothers, 1840, 1842, 1846, 1847, 1848, 1852, 1860, 1861.

U.S. War Department. *Regulations for the Army of the United States, 1857.* New York: Harper and Brothers, 1857.

————. *Regulations for the Army of the United States,* 1861. Philadelphia: George W. Childs, 1862.

————. *Revised Regulations for the Army of the United States,* 1863. Washington, D.C.: Government Printing Office, 1863.

Wheeler, Joseph. *A Revised System of Cavalry Tactics for the Use of the Cavalry and Mounted Infantry, CSA.* 3 pts. Mobile, 1863.

Wilcox, Cadmus M. *Rifles and Rifle Practice.* New York: D. Van Nostrand, 1859.

Willard, George L. *Manual of Target Practice for the United States Army.* Philadelphia: J. B. Lippincott and Co., 1862.

PUBLISHED PERSONAL PAPERS, DIARIES, AND MEMOIRS

Alexander, E. P. *Military Memoirs of a Confederate.* New York: Charles Scribner's Sons, 1903.

Beauregard, P. G. T. *A Commentary on the Campaign and Battle of Manassas of July, 1861.* New York: G. P. Putnam's Sons, 1891.

Brown, J. Willard. *The Signal Corps, U.S.A. in the War of the Rebellion.* Boston: U.S. Veterans Signal Corps Association, 1896.

Buell, C. C. and R. U. Johnson, eds. *Battles and Leaders of the Civil War.* 4 vols. New York: Century Co., 1884–1888.

Chetlain, Augustus Louis. *Recollections of Seventy Years.* Galena: Gazette Publishing Co., 1889.

Dowdey, Clifford, and Louis H. Manarin, eds. *The Wartime Papers of Robert E. Lee.* Boston: Little Brown, 1961.

Early, Jubal A. *Autobiographical Sketch and Narrative of the War between the States.* Philadelphia: J. B. Lippincott, 1912.

Freeman, Douglas S., ed. *Lee's Dispatches.* New edition with additional dispatches and foreword by Grady McWhiney. New York: G. P. Putnam's Sons, 1957.

General Scott and His Staff; comprising memoirs of Generals Scott, Twiggs, Smith, Quitman, Shields, Pillow, Lane, Cadwalader, Patterson, and Pierce; Colonels Childs, Riley, Harney, and Butler, and other distinguished officers attached to General Scott's army. Freeport, N.Y.: Books for Libraries Press, 1970.

Grant, U. S. *Personal Memoirs.* New York: World Publishing Co., 1952.

Higginson, T. W. "Regular and Volunteer Officers." *Atlantic Monthly* 14 (1864): 348–357.

Hill, D. H. *Bethel and Retreat: Personal Experiences in the United States and Confederate States Armies.* Edited by Richard Current. Bloomington: Indiana University Press, 1959.

Howe, M. A. DeWolfe, ed. *Home Letters of General Sherman.* New York: Charles Scribner's Sons, 1909.

Johnston, Joseph E. *Narrative of Military Operations.* Bloomington: Indiana University Press, 1959.

Prince de Joinville, Francois Ferdinand Philippe Louis Marie d'Orleans. *The Army of the Potomac: Its Organization, Its Commander, and Its Campaign.* Translated from the French by William Henry Hurlbert. New York: A. D. F. Randolph, 1862.

Lee, Fitzhugh. *General Lee.* New York: D. Appleton and Co., 1894.

Lenney, John J. *Caste System in the American Army: A Study of the Corps of Engineers and Their West Point System.* New York: Greenberg, 1949.

Long, A. L. *Memoirs of Robert E. Lee.* New York: J. M. Stoddart and Co., 1887.

Longstreet, James. *From Manassas to Appomattox.* Philadelphia: J. B. Lippincott, 1896.

Lowe, Prof. T. S. C., "The Balloons with the Army of the Potomac." In Francis Trevelyan Miller, *The Photographic History of the Civil War*, 10 vols., pp. 370–380. New York and London: Thomas Yuseloff, 1957.

———. "Observation Baloons in the Battle of Fair Oaks." *Review of Reviews* 43 (1911): 186–190.

Lyman, Theodore. *Meade's Headquarters, 1863–1865: Letters of Col. Theodore Lyman from the Wilderness to Appomattox*. Edited by George R. Agassiz. Boston: Atlantic Monthly Press, 1922.

McClellan, George B. *McClellan's Own Story*. New York: Charles L. Webster and Co., 1887.

———. *The Mexican War Diary of George B. McClellan*. Edited by William Starr Myers. New York: Da Capo Press, 1972.

Mahan, Dennis Hart. "The Cadet Life of Grant and Sherman." *Army and Navy Journal* 3 (March 31, 1866): 507.

Mahan, Frederick Augustus. "Professor Dennis Hart Mahan." In *Professional Memoirs of the Corps of Engineers, U.S. Army and Engineer Department-at-Large*. Washington, 1917.

Marshall, Charles. *An Aide-de-Camp of Lee*. Boston: Little, Brown and Co., 1927.

Meade, George Gordon, ed. *The Life and Letters of George Gordon Meade*. New York: Charles Scribner's Sons, 1913.

Papers of the Military Historical Society of Massachusetts. 14 vols. Boston: Houghton Mifflin and Co., 1895–1918.

Plum, William R. *The Military Telegraph during the Civil War in the United States*. 2 vols. Chicago: Jansen, McClury and Co., 1882.

Roman, Alfred. *The Military Operations of General Beauregard in the War between the States, 1861 to 1865, Including a Brief Personal Sketch and a Narrative of His Services in the War with Mexico, 1846–1848*. New York: Harper, 1983.

Sherman, W. T. *Memoirs*. Bloomington: Indiana University Press, 1957.

Simon, John Y., ed. *The Papers of Ulysses S. Grant*. Carbondale: Southern Illinois University Press, 1967.

Sorrel, G. Moxley. *Recollections of a Confederate Staff Officer*. New York: Neal Publishing Co., 1905.

Southern Historical Society Papers. 47 vols. Richmond: Various publishers, 1876–1930.

Spencer, Cornelia P. *The Last Ninety Days of the War in North Carolina*. New York: Watchman Publishing Co., 1866.

Taylor, Richard. *Destruction and Reconstruction*. Edited by Charles P. Roland. Waltham, Mass.: Blaisdell Publishing Co., 1968.

Taylor, W. H. *Four Years with General Lee*. New York: D. Appleton and Co., 1877.

Thorndike, Rachel Sherman, ed. *The Sherman Letters: Correspondence between General and Senator Sherman from 1837 to 1891*. New York: Da Capo Press, 1969.

Comte de Trobriand, Philippe Regis Denis de Keredern. *Four Years with the Army of the Potomac*. Translated from the French by George K. Dauchy. Ticknor and Company, 1889.

Von Borcke, Heros. *Memoirs of the Confederate War for Independence*. 2 vols. New York: Peter Smith, 1938.

Welles, Gideon. *Diary of Gideon Welles*. Boston and New York: Houghton Mifflin Co., 1911.

JOURNALS

The United States Army and Navy Journal and Gazette of the Regular and Volunteer Services. New York: Publication Office, No. 29 Park Row, 1863–1890.

Secondary Sources

BOOKS

Adams, Michael C. C. *Our Masters the Rebels: A Speculation on Union Military Failure in the East, 1861–1865*. Cambridge: Harvard University Press, 1978.

Addington, Larry H. *The Blitzkrieg Era and the German General Staff, 1865–1941*. New Brunswick: Rutgers University Press, 1971.

Alger, John I. *Antoine Henri Jomini: A Bibliographical Survey*. West Point: United States Military Academy, 1975.

Ambrose, Stephen E. *Duty, Honor, Country: A History of West Point*. Baltimore, 1966.

————. *Halleck: Lincoln's Chief of Staff*. Baton Rouge: Louisiana State University Press, 1962.

Barker, A. *The Vainglorious War, 1854–56*. London: Weidenfeld and Nicholson, 1970.

Barrett, John G. *Sherman's March through the Carolinas*. Chapel Hill: University of North Carolina Press, 1956.

Bauer, Karl Jack. *The Mexican War, 1846–1848*. New York: Macmillan, 1974.

Bigelow, John, Jr. *The Campaign of Chancellorsville*. New Haven: Yale University Press, 1918.

Black, Robert C. III. *The Railroads of the Confederacy*. Chapel Hill: University of North Carolina Press, 1952.

Blake, R. L. V. Ffrench. *The Crimean War*. London: L. Cooper, 1971.

Boatner, Mark M. III. *The Civil War Dictionary*. New York: David McKay Co., 1959.

Brodie, Bernard and Fawn. *From Crossbow to H-Bomb*. New York: Dell, 1962.

Calhoun, Daniel H. *The American Civil Engineer: Origins and Conflict*. Cambridge: Technology Press, Massachusetts Institute of Technology; distributed by Harvard University Press, 1960.

Catton, Bruce. *A Stillness at Appomattox*. Garden City, N.Y.: Doubleday and Co., 1953.

Chandler, Alfred D., Jr. *Henry Varnum Poor: Business Editor, Analyst, and Reformer*. Cambridge: Harvard University Press, 1962.

————. *The Invisible Hand: The Managerial Revolution in American Business*. Belknap Press of Harvard University Press, 1977.

Chandler, David G., *The Campaigns of Napoleon*. New York: Macmillan, 1966.

Cleaves, Freeman. *Rock of Chickamauga: The Life of General George H. Thomas*. Westport, Conn.: Greenwood Press, 1974.

Coddington, Edwin B. *The Gettysburg Campaign: A Study in Command*. New York: Charles Scribner's Sons, 1968.

Coggins, Jack. *Arms and Equipment of the Civil War*. Garden City, N.Y.: Doubleday and Co., 1962.

Connelly, Thomas L. *Army of the Heartland: The Army of Tennessee, 1861–1862*. Baton Rouge: Louisiana State University Press, 1967.

————. *The Marble Man: Robert E. Lee and His Image in American Society*. New York: Knopf, 1977.

Connelly, Thomas L., and Archer Jones. *The Politics of Command: Factions and Ideas in Confederate Strategy*. Baton Rouge: Louisiana State University Press, 1973.

Cooling, Benjamin F. *Symbol, Sword, and Shield: Defending Washington during the Civil War*. Hamden, Conn.: Archon Books, 1975.

Curtiss, John Shelton. *Russia's Crimean War*. Durham: Duke University Press, 1979.

Dabney, R. L. *Life and Campaigns of Lieutenant General Thomas J. Jackson*. New York: Blelock and Co., 1880.

Davis, William C. *Battle at Bull Run*. New York: Doubleday, 1977.

Edmonds, Sir James, and W. B. Wood. *A History of the Civil War in the United States*. New York: Putnam's Sons, 1905.

Embleton, G. A. *The Crimean War, 1853–56*. London: Almark Publishing Co., 1975.

Forman, Sidney. *West Point: A History of the United States Military Academy*. New York: Columbia University Press, 1956.

Freeman, Douglas S. *Lee's Lieutenants*. 3 vols. New York: Charles Scribner's Sons, 1942–44.

———. *R. E. Lee: A Biography*. 4 vols. New York: Charles Scribner's Sons, 1934–35.

Fuller, Claud. *The Rifled Musket*. Harrisburg, Pa.: Stackpole Co., 1958.

Glatthaar, Joseph T. *The March to the Sea and Beyond: Sherman's Troops in the Savannah and Carolinas Campaigns*. New York: New York University Press, 1985.

Goff, Richard D. *Confederate Supply*. Durham: Duke University Press, 1969.

Govan, Gilbert E., and James W. Livingood. *A Different Valor: The Story of Joseph E. Johnston, CSA*. New York: Bobbs-Merrill, 1956.

Guillemin, Rene. *La Guerre de Crimee*. Paris: Éditions France-Empire, 1981.

Hartje, Robert. *Van Dorn: The Life and Times of a Confederate General*. Nashville: University of Tennessee Press, 1967.

Hassler, Warren W., Jr. *Commanders of the Army of the Potomac*. Baton Rouge: Louisiana State University Press, 1962.

———. *George B. McClellan, Shield of the Union*. Baton Rouge: Louisiana State University Press, 1957.

Hattaway, Herman, and Archer Jones. *How the North Won*. Urbana: University of Illinois Press, 1983.

Haydon, F. Stanley. *Aeronautics in the Union and Confederate Armies*. Baltimore: Johns Hopkins Press, 1941.

Henderson, G. F. R. *The Civil War: A Soldier's View*. Edited by Jay Luvaas. Chicago: University of Chicago Press, 1958.

———. *The Science of War*. New York: Longmans, Green, 1933.

Hill, Forest G. *Roads, Rails, and Waterways: The Army Engineers and Early Transportation*. Norman: University of Oklahoma Press, 1957.

Huston, James. *The Sinews of War: Army Logistics, 1775–1953*. Washington, D.C.: Office of the Chief of Military History, United States Army, 1966.

Judd, Denis. *The Crimean War, 1853–56*. London: Hart-Davis, MacGibbon, 1975.

Kemble, Charles Robert. *The Image of the Army Officer in America: Background for Current Views*. Westport, Conn.: Greenwood Press, 1973.

King, Charles. *The True U. S. Grant*. Philadelphia: J. B. Lippincott Co., 1932.

Klein, Maury. *Edward Porter Alexander*. Athens: University of Georgia Press, 1971.

Lamers, William M. *Edge of Glory: A Biography of General William S. Rosecrans.* New York: Harcourt, Brace, 1961.

Liddell Hart, B. H. *The Ghost of Napoleon.* New Haven: Yale University Press, 1935.

———. *Sherman.* New York: Dodd, Mead and Co., 1930.

Livermore, Thomas L. *Numbers and Losses in the Civil War.* Bloomington: Indiana University Press, 1957.

Lloyd, E. M. *A Review of the History of Infantry.* New York: Longmans, Green and Co., 1908.

Longacre, Edward G. *The Man behind the Guns: A Biography of Henry J. Hunt, Commander of Artillery, Army of the Potomac.* South Brunswick, N.J. and New York: A. S. Barnes, 1970.

Luvaas, Jay. *The Military Legacy of the Civil War.* Chicago: University of Chicago Press, 1959.

McDonough, James Lee. *Shiloh: In Hell before Night.* Knoxville: University of Tennessee Press, 1977.

———. *Stones River—Bloody Winter in Tennessee.* Knoxville: University of Tennessee Press, 1980.

McMurry, Richard M. *John Bell Hood and the War of Southern Independence.* Lexington, Ky.: University of Kentucky Press, 1982.

McWhiney, Grady. *Braxton Bragg and Confederate Defeat.* New York: Columbia University Press, 1969.

McWhiney, Grady, and Perry D. Jamieson. *Attack and Die: Civil War Military Tactics and the Southern Heritage.* University, Ala.: University of Alabama Press, 1982.

Meltzer, Milton. *Bound for the Rio Grande: The Mexican Struggle, 1845–1850.* New York: Knopf, 1974.

Murfin, James. *The Gleam of Bayonets: The Battle of Antietam and Robert E. Lee's Maryland Campaign, September, 1862.* Baton Rouge: Louisiana State University Press, 1982.

Naisawald, L. Van Loan. *Grape and Cannister: The Story of the Field Artillery of the Army of the Potomac, 1861–1865.* New York: Oxford University Press, 1960.

Nevins, Allan. *The War for the Union.* 2 vols. New York: Charles Scribner's Sons, 1959–60.

Comte de Paris, Louis Philippe Albert d'Orleans. *History of the Civil War in America.* 4 vols. Philadelphia: J. H. Coates and Co., 1875–1888.

Quimby, Robert S. *The Background of Napoleonic Warfare: The Theory of Military Tactics in Eighteenth Century France.* New York: Columbia University Press, 1957.

Redway, G. W. *Fredericksburg: A Study in War.* London: Allen and Unwin, 1906.

Reed, Rowena. *Combined Operations in the Civil War.* Annapolis: Naval Institute Press, 1978.

Ripley, Rowell S. *The War with Mexico.* New York: D. Franklin, 1970.

Risch, Erna. *Quartermaster Support of the Army: A History of the Corps, 1775–1939.* Washington, D.C.: Quartermaster Historian's Office, Office of the Quartermaster General, 1962.

Ross, Steven. *From Flintlock to Rifle: Infantry Tactics, 1740–1866.* Rutherford and London: Fairleigh Dickinson University Press and Associated University Presses, 1979.

Schmidt, James Norman. *The Young Generals.* New York: Putnam, 1968.

Sears, Stephen. *Landscape Turned Red*. New Haven: Ticknor and Fields, 1983.

Shannon, Fred Albert. *The Organization and Administration of the Union Army, 1861–1865*. 2 vols. Cleveland: Arthur H. Clark Co., 1928.

Shaver, L. H. *History of the Sixteenth Alabama Regiment, Gracie's Alabama Brigade*. Montgomery: Barrett and Brown, 1867.

Singletary, Otis. *The Mexican War*. Chicago: University of Chicago Press, 1960.

Sommers, Richard. *Richmond Redeemed: The Siege of Petersburg*. Garden City, N.Y.: Doubleday, 1981.

Starr, Stephen Z. *The Union Cavalry in the Civil War*. Vol. 1. Baton Rouge: Louisiana State University Press, 1979.

Sword, Wiley. *Shiloh: Bloody April*. New York: William Morrow and Co., 1974.

Van Creveld, Martin. *Supplying War: Logistics from Wallenstein to Patton*. Cambridge, London, New York, Melbourne: Cambridge University Press, 1977.

Vandiver, Frank L. *Mighty Stonewall*. New York: McGraw Hill, 1957.

_____. *Ploughshares into Swords: Josiah Gorgas and Confederate Ordnance*. Austin: University of Texas Press, 1952.

_____. *Rebel Brass: The Confederate Command System*. Baton Rouge: Louisiana State University Press, 1956.

Wagner, Arthur L. *Organization and Tactics*. London: W. H. Allan and Co., 1894.

Weems, John Edward. *To Conquer a Peace: The War between the United States and Mexico*. Garden City, N.Y.: Doubleday, 1974.

Weigley, Russell F. *Quartermaster General of the Union Army: A Biography of M. C. Meigs*. New York: Columbia University Press, 1959.

Wheeler, Richard. *The Siege of Vicksburg*. New York: Crowell, 1978.

Williams, Kenneth P. *Lincoln Finds a General*. 5 vols. New York: Macmillan, 1949–1958.

Williams, T. Harry. *Lincoln and His Generals*. New York: Knopf, 1952.

_____. *P. G. T. Beauregard: Napoleon in Gray*. Baton Rouge: Louisiana State University Press, 1954.

Wise, Jennings Cropper. *The Long Arm of Lee: The History of the Artillery of the Army of Northern Virginia*. New York: Oxford University Press, 1959.

THESES

Bright, Samuel R., Jr. "Confederate Coast Defense." Ph.D. dissertation, Duke University, 1961.

English, John Alan. "Confederate Field Communications." Master's thesis, Duke University, 1964.

Gibbs, Shirley M. "Lee's Command Procedures." Master's thesis, Duke University, 1962.

Goff, Richard D. "Logistics and Supply Problems in the Confederacy." Ph.D. dissertation, Duke University, 1963.

Griess, Thomas F. "Dennis Hart Mahan: West Point Professor and Advocate of Professionalism, 1830–1871." Ph.D. dissertation, Duke University, 1969.

Jamieson, Perry David. "The Development of Civil War Tactics." Ph.D. dissertation, Wayne State University, 1979.

Lee, Jen-Hwa. "The Organization and Administration of the Army of the Potomac under George B. McClellan." Ph.D. dissertation, University of Maryland, 1960.

McCoun, Richard Allan. "George Brinton McClellan, from West Point to the Peninsula: The Education of a Soldier and the Conduct of the War." Master's thesis, California State College, Fullerton, 1973.

Manarin, Louis. "Lee in Command: Strategic and Tactical Policies." Ph.D. dissertation, Duke University, 1965.

Morrison, James L., Jr. "Educating the Civil War Generals: West Point, 1833–1861." Ph.D. dissertation, Columbia University, 1970.

Moseley, Thomas Vernon. "Evolution of the American Civil War Infantry Tactics." Ph.D. dissertation, University of North Carolina, 1967.

Nesmith, Vardell E., Jr. "Field Artillery Doctrine, 1861–1905." Ph.D. dissertation, Duke University, 1977.

O'Connell, Charles F. "The United States Army and the Origins of Modern Management, 1818–1860." Ph.D. dissertation, Ohio State University, 1982.

Parkinson, Russell J. "Politics, Patents, and Planes: Military Aeronautics in the United States, 1863–1907." Ph.D. dissertation, Duke University, 1963.

Scheips, Paul Joseph. "Albert James Myer, Founder of the Army Signal Corps: A Biographical Study." Ph.D. dissertation, American University, 1965.

Skelton, William B. "The United States Army, 1821–1837: An Institutional History." Ph.D. dissertation, Northwestern University, 1968.

Thiele, Thomas F. "The Evolution of Cavalry in the American Civil War, 1861–1863." Ph.D. dissertation, University of Michigan, 1951.

Valuska, David Lawrence. "The Staff Organization of the Army of the Potomac under General McClellan." Master's thesis, Louisiana State University, 1966.

Walters, J. B. "Sherman and Total War." Ph.D. dissertation, Vanderbilt University, 1947.

Weinart, Peter Richard, Jr. "The Confederate Regular Army: 1861–1865." Master's thesis, American University, 1964.

Winton, George Peterson, Jr. "Ante-bellum Military Instruction of West Point Officers and Its Influence upon Confederate Military Organization and Operations." Ph.D. dissertation, University of South Carolina, 1972.

ARTICLES

Andrews, J. Cutler. "The Southern Telegraph Company, 1861–1865: A Chapter in the History of Wartime Communications." *Journal of Southern History* 30 (1965): 319–344.

Beers, Henry P. "A History of the U.S. Topographical Engineers, 1813–1863." *Military Engineer* 34 (1942): 287–291, 348–352.

Brinton, Crane; Gordon Craig; and Felix Gilbert. "Jomini." In *Makers of Modern Strategy*, edited by Edward Meade Earle. Princeton: Princeton University Press, 1960.

Buechler, John. "Give 'em the Bayonet—A Note on Civil War Mythology." *Civil War History* 7 (1961): 128–132.

Cain, Marvin. "A 'Face of Battle' Needed: An Assessment of Motives and Men in Civil War Historiography." *Civil War History* 28 (1982): 5–28.

Campbell, E. G. "Railroads in National Defense, 1828–1848." *Mississippi Valley Historical Review* 27 (1940): 361–378.

Chandler, Alfred D., Jr., and Stephen Salsbury. "The Railroads: Innovators in Modern Business Administration." In *The Railroads and the Space Program: An Exercise in Historical Analogy*, edited by Bruce Mazlish. Cambridge: MIT Press, 1965.

East, Sherrad E. "Montgomery C. Meigs and the Quartermaster Department." *Military Affairs* 26 (1962): 183–197.

Elting, John R. "Jomini: Disciple of Napoleon?" *Military Affairs* 28 (1964): 17–26.

Gaddy, David W. "William Norris and the Confederate Signal and Secret Service." *Maryland Historical Magazine* 70 (1975): 167–188.

Gow, June I. "Theory and Practice: Confederate Military Administration." *Military Affairs* 39 (1975): 118–123.

Hagerman, Edward. "From Jomini to Dennis Hart Mahan: The Evolution of Trench Warfare and the American Civil War." *Civil War History* 31 (September, 1967): 197–220.

_____. "Looking for the American Civil War: War, Myth, and Culture." *Armed Forces and Society* 9 IX (1983): 341–347.

_____. "The Professionalization of George B. McClellan and Early Civil War Field Command: An Institutional Perspective." *Civil War History* 21 (1975): 113–135.

Harsh, Joseph. "Battlesword and Rapier: Clausewitz, Jomini, and the American Civil War." *Military Affairs* 38 (1974): 133–138.

_____. "On the McClellan-Go-Round." *Civil War History* 19 (1973): 101–118.

Howard, Michael. "Jomini and the Classical Tradition in Military Thought." In *Theory and Practice of War*, edited by Michael Howard. Bloomington and London: Indiana University Press, 1965.

Johnson, Ludwell. "Civil War Military History: A Few Revisions in Need of Revision." *Civil War History* 17 (1971): 115–130.

Jones, Archer. "Jomini and the Strategy of the American Civil War: A Reinterpretation." *Military Affairs* 34 (December, 1970): 127–131.

Luvaas, Jay. "Looking for the Civil War." Unpublished essay. Ca. 1960.

McMurray, Richard M. "The Atlanta Campaign of 1864: A New Look." *Civil War History* 22 (1976): 5–15.

McWhiney, Grady. "Ulysses S. Grant's Pre-Civil War Military Education." In *Southerners and Other Americans*. New York: Basic Books, 1973.

Mahon, J. K. "Civil War Infantry Assault Tactics." *Military Affairs* 25 (1961): 57–68.

Marshall, David J. "The Confederate Army's Signal Corps." In *The Story of the U.S. Army Signal Corps*, edited by Max L. Marshall. New York: Franklin Watts, 1965.

Minter, Winnifred P. "Confederate Military Supply." *Social Science* 34 (1959): 163–171.

Moore, John G. "Mobility and Strategy in the Civil War." *Military Affairs* 24 (1960): 68–77.

Norton, Herman. "Revivalism in the Confederate Armies." *Civil War History* 6 (1960): 410–424.

Papers of the Military Historical Society of Massachusetts. 14 vols. Boston: Houghton Mifflin and Co., 1895–1918.

Partin, Robert. "The Sustaining Faith of an Alabama Soldier." *Civil War History* 6 (1960): 425–438.

Pohl, James W. "The Influence of Antoine Henri Jomini on Winfield Scott's Campaign in the Mexican War." *Southwestern Historical Quarterly* 77 (1973): 85–110.

Ramsdell, Charles W. "General Robert E. Lee's Horse Supply, 1862–1865." *American Historical Review* 25 (1930): 758–777.

Skelton, William B. "The Commanding General and the Problem of Command in the United States Army, 1821–1841." *Military Affairs* 34 (1970): 117–121.

_____. "Professionalization in the U.S. Army Officer Corps during the Age of Jackson." *Armed Forces and Society* 1 (1975): 443–471.

Southern Historical Society Papers. 47 vols. Richmond: Various publishers, 1860–1930.

Squires, J. David. "Aeronautics in the Civil War." *American Historical Review* 42 (1937): 652–669.

Starr, Stephen Z. "Cold Steel: The Saber and Union Cavalry." *Civil War History* 11 (1965): 142–159.

Stonesifer, Ray P., Jr. "The Union Cavalry Comes of Age." *Civil War History* 11 (1965): 274–283.

Swift, Lester L. "The Recollections of a Signal Officer." *Civil War History* 9 (1963): 36–55.

Thompson, George Raynor. "Civil War Signals." *Military Affairs* 18 (1954): 188–201.

Vandiver, Frank E. "General Hood as Logistician." *Military Affairs* 16 (1952): 1–11.

Wagner, Arthur L. "Hasty Entrenchment in the War of Secession." *Papers of the Military Historical Society of Massachusetts*, 14 vols., vol. 13 (1913). Boston: Houghton Mifflin and Co., 1895–1918.

Walters, J. B. "General William T. Sherman and Total War." *Journal of Southern History* 14 (1948): 447–480.

Williams, T. Harry. "The Attack upon West Point during the Civil War." *Mississippi Valley Historical Review* 25 (1939): 491–504.

———. "The Return of Jomini: Some Thoughts on Recent Civil War Writing." *Military Affairs* 39 (December, 1975): 204–206.

Index

Adams, Michael C.C., 305
Aeronautic Department (later Aeronautic Corps), Union. *See* Balloons
Alabama River, 275
Alexander, E.P., 90–92, 95, and early development of Confederate signals organization, 103; and artillery reorganization, 132, 135; at Chancellorsville, 134, 140–141, 145; criticizes Bragg's army, 214; quoted at Chickamauga, 216; at Chattanooga, 224, 228; uses indirect fire, 321
Anaconda strategy, 67–68
Anderson, Richard, 257
Appomattox River, 268–269, 272
Armies. *See* individual field commanders and organizational headings
Archduke Charles of Austria, 14
Artillery: in the Civil War, xi–xii, xv; theory and doctrine, 20–22; infancy of rifled, 22; prevalence of smoothbore, 22, 146; Parrot, 22, 334; Armstrong and Whitworth, 22; Napoleon, 22, 146, 296, 334; in War with Mexico, 22; in early Army of the Potomac, 39; in Peninsula Campaign, 39, 55, 109–110, 309; at Antietam, 56; McClellan's organization of, 65, 296; at Fredericksburg, 88–89; at Chancellorsville, 90, 94, 134–135; Hunt's organizational reforms of and dispute with Hooker, 92–94, 314; in defensive role with rifled musket, 92; at Gettysburg, 93–98, 140–142, 145; in the East during 1863, 96, 136, 142; Joseph Johnston quoted on, 106; Lee's battalion organization of, 131–133; at Shiloh, 170–171; at Perryville, 182–183; at Vicksburg, 190; at Murfreesboro, 194–196; at Chickamauga, 217–218; at Knoxville, 228; in the West during 1863, 229; at Spotsylvania, 258–260; on the North Anna, 261; at Petersburg, 267, 271; in Atlanta, Savannah, and Carolina campaigns, 284, 286–287, 296–297; McClellan's standard for, 296; Civil War battalion system of adopted by European armies, 320; in advance of, in rear of, in line with infantry, 334; and ordnance problems, 334
Atlanta, 180, 213, 276, 282–287, 291, 294–296, 298, 332, 341
Austro-Prussian War, 17

Balloons, xii, 52–54, 79, 82–83, 85, 134, 309
Baltimore, 115
Barnard, John G., 51, 269
Battles and campaigns: Alma, 17; Antietam, 53, 55–57, 116–117, 297, 310; Atlanta, xiii, 276–283, 296–298, 332; Belmont, 163; Bentonville, 295, 298, 343–344; Brandy Station, 94; Bristoe Station, 78, 95–96, 143–144, 256; Carolinas, xiii, 287, 288, 290–292, 295, 341–342; Cerro Gordo, 15; Chancellorsville, 53, 70–73, 76, 78, 82–86, 133–135, 139, 145, 224, 233, 249, 256–257, 314; Chapultapec, 15; Chattanooga, 211–215, 218–226, 228–229; Chickamauga, 212–213, 215–219, 223; Chickasaw Bayou, 191–192; Churubusco, 16, 304; Cold Harbor, 244, 247, 254, 262–266, 268, 274, 293, 296; Contreras, 15; Corinth, 185–188; Fair Oaks, 48–49, 107; Fort Donelson, 162–165, 204, 323, 325; Fort Henry, 161–162, 325; Franklin, 289; Frazier's Farm, 110, 309–310; Fredericksburg, 53, 70, 79–82, 121–125, 133, 145, 248; Gaines Mill, 55, 57, 109, 297, 309; Gettysburg, 73–76, 78, 86–87, 135–142, 146, 217, 243, 248, 255–256, 297, 322; Inkerman Plateau, 17, 24; Island No. 10, 53; Kennesaw Mountain, 293–294; Knoxville, 226–229; Lovejoy's Station, 291; Magenta, 19; Malvern Hill, 51–52, 55, 57, 109; Maryland, 55–66, 115–125; Manassas, First, 36, 67, 103, 105–107, 235, 318; Manassas, Second, 112–114, 132, 139, 277; Mechanicsville, 52, 55, 109; Meridian, Miss., 275; Mill Springs or Logan Cross Roads, 158–160; Mine Run, 78, 95–96, 143, 256; Molino del Rey, 15; Munfordville, 184–185; Murfreesboro or Stones River, 193–197, 218, 228–229; Nashville, 289; North Anna, 261–262; Peninsula, 46–52, 55, 57, 145, 262, 309; Perryville, 182–183, 194; Petersburg, 244, 247, 254, 265–273, 295, 343; Port Hudson, 207; Post-Gettysburg, 76–78, 141–144; Rappahannock Bridge, 78, 95–96, 143–144, 256; Reseaca de la Palma, 304; Savannah, 283–287, 294–295, 341–342; Sebastopol, 17–18, 23–24; Seven Days', 55, 109, 111–112, 262, 309; Seven Pines, 52; Shiloh, 153, 166–174; Solferino, 19, 53; Spotsylvania, 244, 247, 257–260, 262, 265; Stones River or Murfreesboro, 193–197, 228–229; The Tcherynaya, 17; Vicksburg, 199–207, 222, 224, 228–229, 235, 244–245, 254; Waynesboro, 296–297; Wilderness, 246, 254–257, 262, 274; Yellow Tavern, 322
Bayonet, 16, 56, 106, 218, 259–260, 263, 310, 318
Beardslee telegraph. *See* Signals
Beauregard, P.G.T.: in the Mexican War, 16, 106; at First Manassas, 66, 103, 105–106; innovates with signals organization, 105; *Principles and Maxims of the Art of War*, 106; suc-